CHORAL MUSIC

OF THE

CHURCH

Elwyn A. Wienandt

CHORAL MUSIC

OF THE

CHURCH

THE FREE PRESS, NEW YORK

Collier-Macmillan Limited, London

Collier-Macmillan Canada, Ltd., Toronto, Ontario
Library of Congress Catalog Card Number: 65–10187
Second printing March 1966

Preface

THIS BOOK is an attempt to bring together the principal developments of Christian choral music spanning more than ten centuries. It crosses denominational lines, but it devotes most of its space to an examination of music in the three principal liturgical streams that developed in Europe: the Roman Catholic, the Anglican, and the Lutheran. It is not through my own choice that this is the case, but simply because only liturgical ground has been able to nurture the seeds of great religious music.

My aim has not been to review the principal works of great composers, but, rather, to examine the changes that came about in the organization, forms, functions, and styles of church music, both with and without instrumental accompaniment. Sometimes a line of development has led briefly outside the church precincts, but my intention has been to examine church music rather than religious concert music. A number of relatively unheralded composers and works have been brought into the discussion, some readers may think, at the expense of well-known and appealing ones. If I have judged them important in this overview of choral styles and techniques, I have not hesitated to include them, and I do so without apology. If at some points my enthusiasm for some man or his compositions intrudes, I regret that my mask of impersonal evaluation has slipped. On the other hand, unless there is enthusiasm for the material, no book such as this can be endured by its author, much less by its readers.

The subject undertaken here is too large and too complex to be treated exhaustively in a single volume. Even though this study touches only briefly upon some of its topics, it is more complete than any other English language book of its kind. It is hoped that students will find here the incentive to explore some of the areas in greater detail.

The serious study of church music is now more possible than ever before, largely because of the availability of musical materials. The works of some leading composers (Schütz, Haydn, Bach, Gabrieli, Telemann, Purcell, and many others) are appearing in complete editions, either for the first time or in newly revised versions. Information about the completeness of such editions may be found in Anna Harriet Heyer's *Historical Sets, Collected Editions, and Monuments of Music*, the progress of uncompleted editions and the appearance of new sets may be followed in the reviews of some of the periodicals listed later in this book, and American activity in new areas of scholarly research is quite thoroughly covered by the entries in Helen Hewitt's *Doctoral Dissertations in Musicology* (third edition) and its supplements in the *Journal of the American Musicological Society*. Some studies now in progress will probably cast new light on statements that appear in the following pages. Many completed dissertations are pertinent to this subject, and interested readers are urged to acquaint themselves with those works.

The principal function of this book is to serve as a text in courses concerned with the literature and history of church music. While it cannot serve all the needs of the student of general music history, it can be a valuable supplementary volume, for the position of church music tends to be unduly subordinated in music history classes, partly because the relationship between the various styles and forms has not been clearly stated.

Collections of scores (such as *HAM, GMB, EM, TEM, MM,* and *MSO*) that are mentioned throughout the book must be consulted whenever possible in order to follow the discussion to best advantage. Still, examples of religious music make up only a small part of those volumes, and many important types are illustrated inadequately or not at all. For this reason, an anthology to serve as a companion volume to this book is being planned. In the meantime, repeated reference should be made to Erich Valentin's *Handbuch der Chormusik* which, if inadequate, is still indispensable.

Where my opinions conflict with established ones, I have taken the evidence of musical scores in preference to statements of earlier authors, unless those statements were undisputably supported by reference to musical materials. Whenever possible, the musical references are to generally available collections and editions in most institutional libraries. Readers are strongly urged to consult them, for it is impossible to condense their significance to brief prose passages.

It would be convenient to adopt the Roman Catholic distinction between sacred music and religious music, reserving the former term for music appropriate to liturgical observances, and the latter for music that is intended to rouse pious or religious sentiments without being fully acceptable for worship. Such a distinction, unfortunately, does not apply equally to all faiths or to all historical periods. I have, therefore, generally avoided reference to sacred music, using instead the terms "religious music" and "church music" in most cases.

I wish to express my appreciation to all those who assisted and supported my efforts. My students who searched files, copied materials, carried countless books and scores, and remained ever alert for elusive bits of information must accept my gratitude anonymously. The most potent single force in bringing this book to completion was a grant awarded by the Graduate Research Committee of Baylor University. Among the librarians of that institution who contributed generously of their time and assistance, Bessie Hess Smith deserves special thanks. Professor Fred Dempster of Fresno State College was most helpful in supplying materials from his unpublished study on Lassus. Among my colleagues at Baylor University I am indebted to Dr. Henry L. Robinson for his excellent translation of French poetry. Special thanks are extended to Dean Daniel Sternberg and Dr. Robert H. Young of the School of Music for their generous assistance and counsel. Mr. Frederick Freedman, Mr. Edward McLeroy, and Miss Joan Teitel of The Free Press have been most helpful and patient. My most sincere thanks are reserved for my wife, without whose unfailing good humor, encouragement, and energetic typing and copyreading this entire effort would still be in outline.

December, 1964.

Elwyn A. Wienandt

Contents

Abbreviations of Books and Music Collections Cited

Arnold *CM*   Samuel Arnold (ed.), *Cathedral Music.* 4 vols., London: For the editor, 1790.

BG   *Johann Sebastian Bachs Werke.* Issued by the Bach-Gesellschaft. Leipzig: Breitkopf & Härtel,* 1851–1926. Reprinted Ann Arbor: J. H. Edwards, 1947. 61 volumes in 47 (vol. 47 is not reprinted by Edwards).

BWV   Wolfgang Schmieder. *Thematisch-systematisches Verzeichnis der musikalischer Werke Johann Sebastian Bach.* Leipzig: Breitkopf & Härtel, 1950.

Boyce *CM*   William Boyce (ed.), *Cathedral Music.* 3 vols., London: By the editor, 1760–1778.

CW   *Das Chorwerk*, ed. by F. Blume. Wolfenbüttel: Möseler Verlag, 1929–. 90 volumes to 1964.

DdT   *Denkmäler deutscher Tonkunst,* (1. folge). Leipzig: Breitkopf & Härtel, 1892–1931. 65 volumes. Pagination in the volumes of the "revised" reprint is the same as the original; the difference lies in the presence of corrections that precede the musical material.

DTÖ   *Denkmäler der Tonkunst in Österreich.* Wien: Artaria & Co. and various other publishers (copyright by Akademische Druck- u. Verlagsanstalt, Graz), 1894–. 105 volumes to January, 1964.

EM   Harold Gleason (ed.), *Examples of Music before 1400.* New York: Appleton-Century-Crofts, Inc., 1942.

GMB   Arnold Schering (ed.), *Geschichte der Musik in Beispielen.* Leipzig: Breitkopf & Härtel, 1931; reprint, New York: Broude Brothers, 1950.

GR   *Graduale Romanum.* Tournai: Desclée & Co., 1924.

Grove's   *Grove's Dictionary of Music and Musicians,* ed. Eric Blom (5th ed.). New York: St. Martin's Press, 1955. 9 volumes. Supplement (Vol. x), 1961.

*Breitkopf & Härtel is now located in Wiesbaden.

HAM   Archibald T. Davison and Willi Apel (eds.), *Historical Anthology of Music*. Cambridge: Harvard University Press, 1959. Two volumes with examples numbered consecutively through both volumes. The numbering of this edition varies at times from that of the earlier printings.

HD   Willi Apel, *Harvard Dictionary of Music*. Cambridge: Harvard University Press, 1944.

HMS   Gerald Abraham (ed.), *The History of Music in Sound*. New York: Oxford University Press, 1953–1959. Each of the 10 volumes is planned as a companion volume to the incomplete *New Oxford History of Music*. A volume of records has been issued by RCA Victor for each of these volumes. Musical scores are often printed as incomplete samples of what appears in complete form on the recording.

HWM   Donald J. Grout, *A History of Western Music*. New York: W. W. Norton and Co., 1960.

LU   *The Liber Usualis*. Tournai: Desclée & Co., 1934.

MBE   Manfred F. Bukofzer, *Music in the Baroque Era*. New York: W. W. Norton and Co., 1947.

MET   Johannes Wolf (ed.), *Music of Earlier Times*. New York: Broude Brothers, 194–?, reprinted from *Sing- und Spielmusik aus älterer Zeit*, Leipzig: Quelle & Meyer, 1926.

MGG   *Die Musik in Geschichte und Gegenwart*. Edited by Friedrich Blume. Kassel: Bärenreiter-Verlag, 1949–. 11 vols. to 1964.

MM   Carl Parrish and John F. Ohl (eds.), *Masterpieces of Music Before 1750*. New York: W. W. Norton and Co., 1951. A three-record album of recordings of the pieces contained herein is available from the publisher.

MMA   Gustave Reese, *Music in the Middle Ages*. New York: W. W. Norton and Co., 1940.

MR   Gustave Reese, *Music in the Renaissance*. New York: W. W. Norton and Co., 1954; rev. ed., 1959.

MSO   William J. Starr and George F. Devine, *Music Scores Omnibus*. 2 vols. Englewood Cliffs: Prentice-Hall, 1964.

MWC   Paul Henry Lang, *Music in Western Civilization*. New York: W. W. Norton and Co., 1941.

SMRM   Manfred F. Bukofzer, *Studies in Medieval and Renaissance Music*. New York: W. W. Norton and Co., 1950.

TCM   P. C. Buck *et al.* (eds.), *Tudor Church Music*. London: Oxford University Press, 1922–1929. 10 volumes.

TEM   Carl Parrish (ed.), *A Treasury of Early Music*. New York: W. W. Norton and Co., 1958. Recordings are available from the publisher.

THE CARDINAL NUMERALS that are used in this volume to indicate the number of performing parts in a composition are convenient in print, but often act as deterrents in classroom discussion. For the convenience of those readers who may be unfamiliar with their verbalized forms, I am supplying the common ones. Rules of Italian pronunciation apply, of course.

a 2	a due	a 11	a undici
a 3	a tre	a 12	a dodici
a 4	a quattro	a 13	a tredici
a 5	a cinque	a 14	a quattordici
a 6	a sei	a 15	a quindici
a 7	a sette	a 16	a sedici
a 8	a otto	a 17	a diciassette
a 9	a nove	a 18	a diciotto
a 10	a dieci	a 19	a diciannove
		a 20	a venti

THIS SEEMS *to be the true stile for the church: it calls to memory nothing vulgar, light, or prophane; it disposes the mind to philanthropy, and divests it of its gross and sensual passions.*

CHARLES BURNEY, *The Present State of Music in France and Italy (1771).*

CHORAL MUSIC

OF THE

CHURCH

Chapter I

Introduction: The Development

and Diffusion

of Choirs and Choral Styles

THERE has always been some kind of methodical distribution of musical effort in the Church. At some times this division of duties has been made between the clergy and a body of trained singers, and at others among singers who have achieved various degrees of skill. Even before polyphonic music formed any part of the religious observance, such an apportioning of responsibility was usual in the performance of the plainsong compositions that formed the repertory of church musicians, the greater responsibility falling to those who were specially trained to musical duties and the lesser to those lacking in ability or training. It is probable that solo singing was already changing from the simple intonation of texts to a florid style by the end of the fourth century. "A similar development took place with the responses which, originally sung by the congregation, soon passed over to the trained chorus *(schola)* and grew considerably longer, both in text and in music."[1]

The introduction of polyphonic music into the service by no means eliminated the practices that had been established for the performance of plainsong. It is probable that the total number of singers available, as well as the number of more expert performers who sang polyphony, was determined by the importance of the church or cathedral to which the singers were attached, as was the case in British institutions where "polyphony was used to add distinction to the ritual of festivals and was sung by a small group of expert singers,

1. *HD*, 610.

1

while the regular teaching of polyphonic music to a larger group of vicars and choristers was a development of the later Middle Ages."[2]

In the post-Reformation churches, the distinction was more commonly made between the congregation, which was an untutored element, and the trained choir, although the division within the choir itself continued to broaden because of the demands that were made upon singers of solo parts in cantatas, anthems, and Masses. In each major branch of the Christian tradition, the assignment of these activities differed. Regardless of the century or the theological climate in which this development took place, however, it was nurtured by, or opposed to, attitudes about the purposes of church music and the functions of musicians in fulfilling these purposes.

The purpose of church music has always been simply that of praising God; the function of the church musician, financial considerations notwithstanding, has been nothing more than that of implementing the purpose. The functions represent the precise manner of serving the purpose, the fashion in which praise is to be rendered through the medium of music, and the success with which these functions are accomplished is directly related to the completeness with which they fulfill their only reason for existence.

It is possible to reduce the principal functions of group musical performance in church to three, with their relative importance varying to some extent by reason of the demands of the denominational requirements in which they are found:

1. Statements of basic tenets of the faith, common to all daily or weekly services.

2. The emphasis of special observances, holidays, and texts appropriate to situations that occur periodically or occasionally.

3. The utterance of prayer, and the affirmation of prayer.

The manner in which these functions were performed before the Reformation was necessarily modified by the size of the establishment in which they were undertaken; therefore, any descriptions of the employment of a completely staffed choral group must be taken as the ideal rather than as a pattern of constant achievement. It might be thought that the demands made upon the singers of a church prior to the development of any of the traditions of part singing were far fewer than those that were made upon the equivalent groups, say, in the fifteenth or sixteenth centuries; however, it should not be sup-

2. Frank Ll. Harrison, *Music in Medieval*   Paul, 1958), 12.
Britain (London: Routledge and Kegan

posed that vocal technique in the early centuries of the choral tradition was not demanding, or that a steadily increasing amount of
polished artistry was not required. What choral singing may have
lacked in agility when plainsong was the only permissible means of
expression, it may have made up in matters of control and in fine
distinctions of skilled performance. Musical utterances were confined
to plainsong, in which there was no need to consider the balance of
sound between various segments of the group. The assignment of
voices to specific functions was made on their ability to undertake
varying degrees of difficulty in the music, and the music itself made
demands of several kinds upon the singers, so that

> the style of the Chant was chosen to conform to the ability of the
> performers. Thus the Chants entrusted to the ministers who sur-
> rounded the bishop and to the people were necessarily simple,
> therefore syllabic. The trained singers of the Schola, or choir, were
> given more elaborate Chants, in neumatic style, as, for example,
> the Introit and Communion of the Mass. The leaders of the choir
> however—the first cantor and his assistants—were *virtuosi* and
> they sang melodies in florid style, like those of the Gradual,
> Alleluia, and Offertory.[3]

As is all too often the case, time has removed some of the evidence
of early practices in the establishment of choir schools and of the
procedures followed in training the boys and men who were part of
them. We know, however, that their pattern was created as early as
the fourth century when Popes Celestine I and Sylvester laid the
foundation for the entire movement through the establishment and
development of the first *Schola cantorum*. This choir, after its re-
organization by St. Gregory the Great, whose pontificate was between the years 590 and 604, "came to be the pillar and foundation of
the Roman musical tradition."[4] The diffusion of this tradition is
directly traceable to the members of the first choir school, some of
whom also served in the papal choir. The responsibilities of the
singers extended far beyond Rome as numbers of them carried the
Gregorian ideal throughout Europe, teaching the chant and organizing more schools to insure its perpetuation. "The Roman order was
established at Canterbury, for instance, by the Benedictine Augustine,
sent to England by Gregory in 596 and provided with a Gregorian

3. *MMA*, 165.
4. Higini Anglès, "Gregorian Chant," *Early Medieval Music up to 1300*, Dom

Anselm Hughes (ed.), Vol. II: *The New Oxford History of Music* (London: Oxford University Press, 1954), 96.

antiphoner a little later; and under Augustine, as Bishop of Canterbury, a flourishing song school grew up, followed by others at
Wearmouth and York."[5] Augustine's companions, numbering some
two score, were probably as well-trained in chant as he.

The monasteries that were established throughout the civilized
Western world were thus provided with the musical tradition of
Rome through the presence of trained singers from the most important center of liturgical music. These monasteries held undisputed
sway in the field of education, musical and otherwise, until their influence lessened toward the beginning of the eleventh century. The
musical tradition did not lapse with this deterioration of monastic
importance; rather, it was transferred to new centers of learning,
many of which were situated in the secular cathedrals, where it held
a position of importance alongside the liberal arts.

> Apart from these higher studies, including music, in the cathe-
> dral schools, *scholae cantorum* of both monasteries and cathedrals
> provided instruction in Latin grammar, elementary arithmetic, and
> the elements of music; and along with this went participation in
> the many liturgical activities—Masses, offices, and special services
> —which required young voices and which actually gave the song
> schools their *raison d'être*.[6]

A final link in the chain of musical tradition had yet to be forged,
that connecting the cathedral school to the university. As these centers of higher learning emerged, it became as necessary for them to
develop faculties of learned men in all their fields as it was essential
that they find students prepared to continue work at their level of
instruction. The connection between the activities of the Parisian
musical leaders and the work carried on at the University of Paris is
indicated by the fact that musical studies at that institution were

> under the leadership of distinguished composers and musicians
> who lectured in the university and also under the inspiration of
> such active musical groups as the Notre Dame choir and the king's
> personal chapel. A close connection between both these groups and
> the university was inevitable, for musical officials in the cathe-
> dral were at the same time university officials, and many singers in
> the royal choir or masters of the children of the king's private chapel
> were enrolled in the university either as students or teachers. Notre

---

5. Nan Cooke Carpenter, *Music in the*   (Norman: University of Oklahoma Press,
Medieval and Renaissance Universities   1958), 16.
                              6. *Ibid.*, 21f.

Dame's choir school actually served as a preparatory school for the university, constantly sending students to the Sorbonne for higher studies, many of these choristers on scholarships.[7]

It is possible to draw a more or less continuous line of influence beginning from the Roman *Schola,* through the monasteries and cathedral schools, to the universities, with a strong thread leading off to the various chapels of royalty. In each of these places, one of the common ingredients was the trained singer, schooled in the only style that was dignified by a tradition, that of plainsong, but applying to this basic knowledge the series of experiments that led to the later choral developments of the Christian observances, organum and polyphony.

Returning to the relationship between the fully trained singer and the student of singing, with each assigned a proper place in the responsibilities falling to the choir, it is apparent that the flow of expert musicians, first from the *Schola* in Rome, and later from those singing schools that had been developed by graduates of the Roman organization, increased as each of the tributary sources in turn supplied more and more of the product. Still, there was a constant group of learners for whom the simpler music was ever necessary and desirable. The technical demands of the florid sections of liturgical music made it necessary to insure a supply of adequately trained singers for the service, while the use of relatively simpler chants made it possible to employ less proficient singers at the same time. The choir school, gathering the best of church musicians as its teaching staff, undertook to train both men and boys in the skills of plainsong and, later, of polyphony. Apparently a term of service nine years in duration, in the course of which all the elements of psalmody were to be learned from memory, was the standard of the *Schola* in Rome.[8]

The pre-eminent position of the Roman *Schola* was firmly established not only by the length of its tradition, but by the fact that the finest musicians of Europe sought it out as a place of study, as is evident from the presence of such illustrious names as Guillaume Dufay and Josquin des Prez among those of its sometime members. As is true of any establishment that must simultaneously train people through a period of apprenticeship and provide skilled artists, its two functions became somewhat separated in the course of years. As

7. *Ibid.,* 119.
8. Oscar Thompson (ed.), *The International Cyclopedia of Music and Musicians* (7th rev. ed. by Nicolas Slonimsky; New York: Dodd, Mead & Co., 1956), 1729.

membership in this highly specialized group of experts became the
goal of already skilled musicians from the Low Countries, it developed
more and more into a group whose reason for existence was skilled
performance.[9] Whether it was the increasing demands of polyphonic
music or some other factor that caused the growth in the size of the
performing group, the organization remained small until "in the 16th
Century the number of singers was increased from twelve to 24 and
not long after to 32, which figure is still adhered to except on special
occasions."[10] The international flavor of the group in that century is
evident from documents that have been preserved to this time. A
list of the singers in January, 1535, shows that of twenty-two singers,
seven were probably Italian, three Spanish, and eleven either French
or Flemish. The master of the chapel was one Bartolommeo Croto or
Crotti. The choir did not change in size because of the sudden enroll-
ment or promotion of additional singers; it was probably increased
little by little in the course of the century. It is recorded that thirty
singers were present, for example, for the first Mass celebrated for the
soul of Pope Paul III, on November 19, 1549.[11]

The Roman *Schola*, while it set a standard of procedure and accomplishment, never represented the norm for choral organizations
throughout European Christendom. The situation in the English
cathedrals, of which there were nineteen after the Norman reorganiza-
tion in the last third of the eleventh century, is undoubtedly far closer
to the reality of daily musical procedure for the larger establishments
outside Rome.[12] The necessity for a trained musical performing group
and training organization was immediately evident to the mis-
sionaries who made their way to Britain, and within little more than
a quarter of a century after Augustine's arrival there is evidence of

9. Concerning the history of the *Schola
cantorum*, its functions as a training group
and a papal choir, see the articles "Sistine
Choir," *Grove's*, VII, 822–25, and "Song
School," *ibid.*, VII, 964.
10. Thompson, *op. cit.*, 1429. Cf. *Grove's*,
VII, 823. An erroneous and widely accepted idea that all regularly constituted
choirs of the late Middle Ages and Renaissance sang polyphony is clarified by Frank
A. D'Accone, "The Singers of San Giovanni in Florence during the 15th Century,"
*Journal of the American Musicological So-
ciety*, XIV/3 (Fall, 1961), 307 *et passim*. Cf.
also *MR*, 23f, and *SMRM*, 189. Further
documentary evidence is presented in

Robert Stevenson, *Spanish Cathedral
Music in the Golden Age* (Berkeley and Los
Angeles: University of California Press,
1961), 26ff.
11. Léon Dorez, *La Cour du Pape Paul III
d'après les Registres de la Trèsorerie Secrète*
(Paris: Librairie Ernest Leroux, 1932), I,
221f.
12. While the situation in Italy is not
directly parallel to that in England, it is
interesting to note the smaller size of the
Italian singing groups in the fifteenth
century as described by D'Accone, *op. cit.*,
310ff. The number of singers in some
French choirs at the close of the fourteenth
century is given in *MR*, 7f.

the development of training schools, concurrent with the erection of the church buildings, for the service could not be properly conducted without singers, and they, in turn, required training and leadership. The situation at York was probably typical. Paulinus, who had been at Canterbury with Augustine and his successors, was responsible for the founding of the see of York in 625. Two years later a small church was erected by the King of Northumbria on the site of the present cathedral. This modest building, being the seat of the bishop, served as the cathedral and, consequently, had even greater need for trained musical performers than would such simple missionary efforts as caused its existence. That proper attention was immediately given to musical matters is evident, for, "in 627 a song school, probably associated with a grammar school, was founded at York by Archbishop Paulinus, who appointed 'James the Deacon' as master. The establishment flourished under Archbishop Albert, 735–66, and was subsequently divided into grammar, song, and writing schools."[13]

It cannot be assumed that musical learning continued without interruption during this period for, as early as seven years after the establishment of the see of York, Bishop Paulinus was forced to flee for his life, and much of the area of northern England again reverted to paganism. His missionary efforts were, nevertheless, to bear fruit, and during the following centuries the musical practices in the cathedrals, both secular and monastic, are recorded in rolls of personnel, notices of disciplinary action, and the like.[14] The secular canons, who were often away from the cathedral precincts on matters of personal interest, were required to provide substitutes, since

> whether residentiary or not, each canon had to maintain a priest-vicar or vicar-choral, who would deputize for him in the choir. In 1340 the canons of Wells were paying "stall wages" of two marks each to their vicars-choral. The earliest mention of vicars-choral occurs in the second half of the twelfth century, when the famous Bishop Hugh of Lincoln enjoined his resident canons to provide temporary substitutes for the recitation of the offices in the choir.[15]

13. G. H. Cook, *The English Cathedral Through the Centuries* (London: Phoenix House, 1957), 63.
14. Regarding the status of these choral groups in the years after the Reformation, see the article, "Cathedral Music (Anglican)," in *Grove's*, II, 123f, and x, 65ff.
15. Cook, *op. cit.*, 60. Cf. *Grove's*, x, 457f.

According to Harrison, *op. cit.*, 6, vicars might be priests, deacons, or subdeacons. There were also clerks who assisted, but even they had to hold membership in lower orders. However, *Grove's*, II, 123, states that "in some establishments, but not all, the Vicars Choral were in minor orders."

This avoidance of personal responsibility to clerical and musical duties brought with it a number of evils and made necessary the enactment of such measures as those instituted by Bishop Jocelyn of Wells, in the first half of the thirteenth century, in an effort to maintain the good name of the cathedral and the resident canons. Among other things, the bishop ordered that the vicars-choral were to be "suspended for two months 'if they were slovenly in their office or talkative in choir; if they were hawkers, hunters or indulged in noisy loud singing abroad; if they were tavern-haunters, secular traders or public players with dice or at games of hazard', and a century later the vicars who carried arms or committed robbery in the church or cemetery of Wells, were to be 'deprived'."[16]

The foregoing indicates that, even though the vicars were in holy orders, their behavior was sometimes no better than that which might have been expected of the most worldly of mercenaries in their lack of concern for the proper observance of their musical and religious functions. It implies also that the situation had gotten beyond control of the precentor, who was charged with the proper conduct of the musical and ceremonial observances.

Whether in Rome or Worcester, Paris or Aachen, the problems of choirs were undoubtedly similar in many ways, and their duties were identical, for their only liturgically justifiable reason for existence was fulfilling the functions of worship through music. Their success must have been as variable as that of any assortment of choral groups anywhere, but their means for the performance of these functions were limited to the music that bore either the outright or implied approval of high Church authority in any generation. Even before the time of the Reformation, this repertory was marvelously varied, embracing all the music of liturgical plainsong liberally amplified by a variety of tropes, organum in its several stages of development, and the whole realm of counterpoint, all of these appearing in the Mass and Offices in the form of motets, canticles, responsories, and the like.

It was the daily responsibility of the choir to furnish music for the celebration of Mass and for the eight Canonical Hours. Before the ninth century, probably all the choral music employed in the observance of musical duties was monophonic; after that period, a general, although gradual, encroachment upon the monopoly of monophonic liturgical music began. It appeared first in the music for special

16. Cook, *op. cit.*, 60.

occasions and later, for practical reasons, became more prevalent in music suitable to the daily use, although the performance of polyphony seems to have been the special duty of selected singers until the middle of the fifteenth century.[17] Whether simple or complex, single- or many-voiced, the music of the Roman Catholic observance was held together by its venerable tradition which, although often violated, stood firm against the onslaught of many new and experimental devices in music, in principle if not always in fact. Properly, the choir has always been a group of men and boys, specifically trained in the correct execution of a highly complex and elaborate series of musical settings that appear, with only slight variation, as part of the daily worship. The most elaborate and solemn of these services is that of High Mass, a rite that is divided into the Proper (containing variable texts according to the season or occasion) and the Ordinary (containing the invariable texts that apply to daily usage).[18] Within this framework, as within the various Hours of Office, are found the materials that make up the basis of the tripartite musical functions mentioned earlier. First, the statements that are basic to the Christian belief are most pithily declared in the Credo, and, in a broader sense, in the entire Ordinary, and they are further amplified in various psalm settings. Second, the musical settings of text passages that emphasize special observances—holidays, seasonal texts, the texts of many parts of the Proper—are abundant in both Mass and Offices. There remains the third classification of the utterance and affirmation of prayer, into which fall statements of confession, adoration, and thanksgiving, pleas of supplication, requests for intercession, doxologies, and amens.[19]

The impact of the Reformation was felt in many areas of church life, not the least in that of music for the worship service. In both Germany and England the issue was not one of removing the existing forms of music as undesirable elements in the service, but rather was a matter of adapting what could be found useful from the old tradition to the new practices. True, many of the liturgical settings were either abbreviated or excised as time went on, but this was a gradual process that followed the evolution of the new beliefs.

In Germany there was the problem of incorporating existing procedures and personnel into the new practice. It was not possible, though

17. *HWM,* 167.
18. For a discussion of the Mass and its structure in detail, see Chapter II.

19. The application of these functions in the Mass for Easter Sunday is illustrated in *EM,* 3–6 and *MSO,* 1–8.

it later proved to be in England, to shift easily from one area of belief to another, because of the existence of a national Church. Germany had no such firm central political and governmental control as did England, where Church and Crown stood united; strong middle-class population groups in Germany were felt as an influence in matters of education, religion, and public morality. Conflict was incipient in the very existence of the numerous small principalities, temporal and ecclesiastic, as well as in the strength of the free cities. The petty princes saw that any blow against the Church would serve also as a stroke against the hated Holy Roman Empire, and they took any opportunity to assert their independence in this direction. The increase in middle-class wealth and power as this new capitalism emerged lent strength to the movement against the control of wealth by the Church and its officers. Small wonder, then, that the Reformation took a different shape in Germany from that which it was to assume in England. Everyone, save the representatives of the Church, stood to gain by any change that would remove power and authority from those who already held it over both temporal and spiritual matters. The princes had the opportunity to renounce allegiance to the Emperor and to absorb portions of Church lands; the scholars gained the privilege of expressing themselves more freely than ever before; the rising middle class benefited by freeing itself from the burden of double allegiance and taxation. Although nationalism was a force in the weakening of the Holy Roman Empire, it must be recognized that "the Reformation was not primarily a revolt against economic exploitation, because although some might gain through the expropriation of ecclesiastical wealth, the leading reformers were churchmen who forfeited their livings in exchange for meager and precarious stipends at best, and at worst for exile or death."[20]

Developing from this upheaval of the *status quo* was a system of parochial schools established to continue or replace the function of the earlier Church schools, a system under which large numbers of boys now received educations at the expense of the community, and which insisted upon musical training as one of the principal features of the curriculum, as is evident from the fact that the cantor of the school was second in rank only to the rector and was selected for the position only after much searching for a proper candidate. Not only was the

20. Roland H. Bainton, *The Reformation*   Beacon Press, 1952), 23f.
of the Sixteenth Century (Boston: The

tradition of Catholic chapel choirs lost in this transition, but a large amount of the music itself was endangered during the period of transition. The impact of Puritanism had to be reckoned with, and in many cases it was strong enough to cause the destruction of organs and the abolition of centuries of choral tradition, as it sought to root out all evidences of popery. Lutheranism, on the other hand, developed as a far more moderate form of rebellion, retaining what could be put to use of the Roman rite, even to the continued employment of the Latin Mass. Although Luther refused to accept the Mass as a sacrament, he did not deny the use of the Lord's Supper as a rite. Consequently, the use of the Mass with Latin text continued in many parts of Protestant Germany, especially in the larger urban churches with sophisticated congregations, along with the singing of Gregorian chorales and other remnants of the old order. At times it must have been difficult to distinguish what was characteristically Lutheran in the German service because the musical thought of the early Protestants was conservative and solidly based on tradition, and religious tradition was here represented by the liturgy and customs of Catholicism. "It was this spirit which gave a specifically Protestant character to this music founded on the traditions of the old church, and which made it possible to disregard the virtual stylistic identity of Catholic and Protestant church music: the two sounded the same, though they had different meanings in the two camps."[21] As late as two centuries after the German Reformation the music of northern Germany clung to the Mass, although convenience and custom had abbreviated it to two polyphonic sections of the Ordinary, and to the motet as material for the Eucharist and for ceremonial use.

In England the matter was not even primarily one of religious consideration at the outset; rather, "the Reformation in England under Henry VIII was at first a political and personal matter, and, except in regard to the position of the papacy, not a doctrinal departure; the theology of the Church was largely untouched."[22] The monasteries and monastic cathedrals, as we have noted before, had developed a tradition of choral music based upon the choirs of men and boys who had been trained in the practices of the Roman Church. The same sort of development had probably taken place in many of the parish churches where the daily requirements of liturgical devo-

21. *MWC*, 211.   22. *Ibid.*, 275.

tions made absolutely necessary a resident group of singers.[23] The rather abrupt separation of these singers from the familiar liturgical materials of their training brought about a need for a new repertory.

> The abolition of the daily celebration of the Mass in the English churches was a great blow to the excellent musical establishments maintained by most cathedrals and collegiate churches. A demand arose for some suitable substitution which, while conforming to the new religious doctrines, would continue the great choral traditions cherished by the British. At first, adaptations of Latin Masses were used, but with the appearance of the Book of Common Prayer English composers devoted themselves to its musical settings.[24]

The musical result of this upheaval was the diminution of the great body of choral literature to a comparatively small number of settings; the canticles for Morning Prayer and Evening Prayer, and the music for the Office of Holy Communion, the latter in reality a retention of parts of the Ordinary of the Mass, making a group of settings known as Services.[25] In addition to this, the only music of substantial quality developing in the English Reformation was the anthem, a form that served as a counterpart to the motet, religious but not liturgical. Nevertheless, the musical activity that remained was sufficient to insure the continuation of the choral tradition that had been in existence, in the same way that the change in administration in the cathedrals took on a new outward appearance but proceeded in only slightly modified fashion, to the convenience of all concerned. It is, then, not surprising to note that "with the exception of Canterbury, the out-going prior of every monastic cathedral was made the dean of the new secular chapter, and the Crown was thereby relieved of the expense of providing large pensions for the dispossessed priors."[26] These deans found themselves in charge of establishments that were hardly different in size and activities from those they had known under the old system, except that there was a greater emphasis on education in the new organizations. An example of the composition of one such cathedral-priory is illustrated by the disposition of the personnel at Worcester, which was converted into secular status in early 1541, "to be composed of a dean, ten preben-

23. The term "parish church" is not reserved for small or rural churches, but may mean any church, of any size, that is not the seat of a bishop; hence, not a cathedral.

24. *MWC*, 280.
25. See Chapter VI.
26. Cook, *op. cit.*, 66.

daries, ten petty canons, ten singing men, a master and usher of the grammar school and forty scholars, ten bedesmen, a master of the choristers, two vergers, two porters, two cooks, and a manciple, totalling in all a hundred and three persons."[27]

One final contrast between the Church of England and the church in Germany needs to be noted: England had a national church from the outset of the Reformation; Germany, being made up of separate states and cities, had numerous state churches, some of which happened to be Lutheran as, for example, was that of Saxony.[28]

Each of the changes that took place in the recruiting, training, and maintaining of choirs within these new systems caused a corresponding change in the kind of personnel that constituted the choir. In the *scholae* there was no problem of finding a steady stream of young candidates for the positions as treble singers. Not only was the choir school the only convenient way for a boy to achieve an education for a musical career, and sometimes for the clergy, but it served, as well, as a place to which parents could feel they were contributing a part of themselves to the Church while, incidentally, they were perhaps relieving a crowded situation at the family table. That fatherless children were present in some quantity is reflected in the descriptive term, *orphanotropia*, that was sometimes applied to the schools. For these unfortunates the choir school was a place of refuge, in which they served and studied in return for their education. Adult male voices there must have been in abundance, for the achievements of graduates of the *scholae* reflected the quality of their training, and even those who aspired to the priesthood were expected to participate in the musical activities of the services, as is evident from the fact that canons in English cathedrals had either to sing or provide substitutes. It is not entirely proper to refer to these people as professional musicians, for that term carries overtones of mercenary considerations and the singers, for the larger part, must have been dedicated to a life of religious activity. There was no place for amateurs to engage in any other part of the ceremonial rites of worship. Neither in the Church of England nor in the Lutheran tradition does this completely self-sufficient form of organization exist; from an

27. *Ibid.*, 67.
28. Bainton, *op. cit.*, 141–56, indicates that in England the principle in operation was that of "one faith, one king, and one law." In other areas, among them Germany, the choice lay among the following three: (1) agreement to differ; (2) determination of the regional religion by the civil ruler; or (3) comprehension, in which "doctrinal and liturgical requirements are whittled down to such slenderness that only the ultra-scrupulous will decline conformity."

early period there is evidence in England of the employment of "singing men" and "Gentlemen of the Chapel" who were probably lay-
men serving, without clerical standing, in the functions earlier
supplied by vicars-choral, and the uncertain and unsettled state of
the German church in its early years made a continuation of self-
contained music a virtual impossibility. There was, consequently,
an increasing amount of secular participation in the choirs as the
years passed.

Time also wrought changes in the sources of the texts to which
music was written. Choral music is always associated with some kind
of text, and it is composed and performed on the assumption that the
text will be heard and understood by its audience. Prior to the establishment of regular polyphonic singing in church, there was no real
problem about communicating the text; not only was it generally
known to most of the listeners, but it was also clearly audible because
of the simplicity of the music with which it was associated — in fact,
the very pattern of plainsong is in great part a result of this desire
for clarity. The intrusion of polyphonic music into this placid trans-
mittal of text posed a twofold problem that has not been completely
solved by any subsequent change in the style of musical settings for
church use. The new musical utterance caused, or at least paved the
way for, a situation in which the simple, clear text settings became
confused because different syllables of text — or even different words —
were sounding at one time. Worse yet, at some points in the development of musical styles, there were times when different phrases, or
entire poems, were being sung at one and the same moment. Still,
in pre-Reformation music, there was the unifying feature of familiar
liturgical text. It was not usually possible — nor permissible — for the
composer to find a text suitable for church use that went into the
exploratory area of emotional subjectivity. One of the aesthetic problems, then, concerned the relationship of text to music. The decisions
concerning the appropriateness of text settings were, of course, almost
entirely in the hands of Church officials who handed down opinions
at various times on matters of descriptive writing, the use of dissonance, and the degree of simplicity or complexity that was permitted in some kind of music or in a particular composer's style. In
the Middle Ages much of what was permitted or prohibited stemmed
from the medieval attitude toward inventiveness. The authority of
the past was conceived as superior to any experiment of the present,
and any debatable matter not sanctioned by the authority of the

ancients, either classical or biblical, could not be accepted without long scrutiny and debate. Such an attitude undoubtedly was of considerable help in maintaining a great continuity of style, in restricting music to simple functionalism for a longer time than would otherwise have been the case. Related to the principle of the supremacy of authority is the idea that the concept of beauty, as we now view it, had little or nothing to do with music of this early period. Not only is such a concept absent from scriptural writings, it was probably foreign to musical content as well, the latter being so closely interwoven with mathematical matters rather than aesthetic ones. Any experimentation on the part of the composer, whether it was in the direction of modernism or of expansion of established, commonly recognized means, was closely allied with a study of how the rules for procedure could be accommodated to the new technique; experimentation was not a search for a way in which to avoid the requirements of the rule. Generally, however, the musician of the Middle Ages, and Renaissance and Baroque periods who became involved in conflict with established practice or with ecclesiastical authority found that the conflict was greatest when his musical treatment caused the interest in the music itself to predominate over the purity or clarity of the textual statement.

With the Reformation came the realization of a new principle; that man might arrive at truth, and salvation as well, by studying the Scriptures and commenting upon them. This new freedom led to the creation of a great number of texts, more subjective than those of preceding generations, that were highly adaptable to musical presentation. This, in turn, brought about a new kind of complexity, the seeds of which were already planted, but which did not bear their greatest fruit until fertilized by the new freedom that permitted the clergy, or even the laity, to comment upon matters of religious thought. In some climates of belief, such a free and emotional approach to religious practice could not be tolerated, while in others it was the very life of the practice. Some of the sharp differences between the Lutheran and the Reformed traditions can be found to have a close relationship to these very differences of emotional response to religion, as can the differences between Orthodox and Pietistic forms of Lutheranism itself. In each of the varying approaches to the worship experience, a new, or at least different, need for the choir developed in order to accommodate it to the particular belief (or to remove the choir from its age-old function, in the case of the Reformed tradition).

A number of new or modified musical forms, styles, and treatments thereby arose, in order for the choir to fulfill its function in connection with worship. Likewise, as the function of the choir has changed, not only in this post-Reformation period, but at all times, the organization itself has undergone changes in size, personnel, in its music, its appearance, and its very participation (positional or quantitative) in the service.

If we return briefly to the beginnings of choral participation in church as it was found in the *Schola cantorum*, we see a Church-fostered, Church-nurtured organization whose members are entirely supported by and dependent on the Church. We see singers who are singers primarily, but are not marketing their talents freely. Instead, their abilities are entirely directed to the organization that supports them—they are resident members, students, priests, monks.[29] With the expansion of this practice in the schools established in the farther reaches of Christendom, the growth of the parochial establishment, useful in the educating of choirboys in return for, and in conjunction with, their participation in the choir, becomes evident in the cathedrals, both monastic and secular, as well as in the royal chapels of all countries and the church schools of Germany.

Through these centuries a certain amount of musical participation by women is evident, but it fails to make its way into the church itself. The singing of nuns in their own cloisters was not an intrusion into the traditional totally male choir of the public churches, although the music provided by the women's groups drew enthusiastic crowds of listeners; the few creative efforts by women were also probably not taken seriously. The presence of female instrumental performers was likewise common in cloister and home, but such *virtuose* as those who performed regularly at the court of Pope Paul III were doubtlessly viewed more as highly talented curiosities than as sources of competitive effort with the fabulous and renowned performers who were there at the same time. At any rate, the women were there as entertainers and not as church musicians. It was on the stage that women first appeared as the peers of male singers and then their reputations often suffered to the same degree that they achieved artistic acclaim. The view that was commonly held of the morals of public entertainers

29. As time passed, secular singers found it to their advantage to have a strong connection with a chapel, although there seems to have been a considerable move- ment of personnel among the chapels in search of better positions. See D'Accone, *op. cit.*, 325 *et passim*.

could probably have barred them from singing in church anyway. Even so, had it not been for the theoretical as well as the actual gulf between the music of the stage and the ritual music of the churches, women would presumably have made their way into choirs much earlier than they did, even though the participants would not have been those who were receiving the plaudits of the opera audiences. Whatever the case may actually have been, the evidence of their early appearances in church as co-participants with male singers is scant. It is known, for example, that on November 11, 1706, J. S. Bach was forced to explain "by what right he recently caused the strange maiden [Maria Barbara Bach?] to be invited into the choir loft and let her make music there."[30] It is not clear from this brief notice whether Bach and the young lady were alone in the choir loft or with the choir, whether the alleged violation of normal practice occurred in connection with a church service or in a less public musical performance. Spitta believes that this could not have been in connection with any church function, and implies that it would have been nigh unthinkable for Bach to have been in such a situation with anyone other than his future bride.[31] Speculation is pointless and facts are not available; that the issue was raised at all merely serves to point up the fact that women were not expected to appear as musicians in any capacity. It is not many years, however, until Johann Mattheson expresses a desire for female singers in church, basing his argument on the Italian practice that can be traced to various conservatories.[32] Three years later, in 1716, Mattheson brought this hope to fruition when he presented a Madame Keiser, a well-known operatic soprano in

30. Hans T. David and Arthur Mendel (eds.), *The Bach Reader* (New York: W. W. Norton and Co., 1945), 53.

31. Philipp Spitta, *Johann Sebastian Bach: His Work and Influence on the Music of Germany, 1685–1750*, trans. Clara Bell and J. A. Fuller-Maitland (London: Novello, 1884–1885; reprint, New York: Dover Publications, 1951), I, 326ff. Spitta says that "as long as the form of the old church-cantata was retained—and this was the dominant form at that time at least in Arnstadt—the question of employing female voices in church music would not even be broached."

32. *Das Neu-Eröffnete Orchestra*, 206, cited in Beekman C. Cannon, *Johann Mattheson: Spectator in Music*, Vol. I: *Yale Studies in the History of Music*, ed. Leo Schrade (New Haven: Yale University Press, 1947), 50f. See also Percy A. Scholes (ed.), *An Eighteenth-Century Musical Tour in France and Italy*, Vol. I: *Dr. Burney's Musical Tours in Europe* (London: Oxford University Press, 1959), 112ff, 121f, 124f, 130, and 136ff for descriptions of the conservatories. Scholes' two volumes contain Burney's journals, *The Present State of Music in France and Italy* (1771), and *The Present State of Music in Germany, the Netherlands, and United Provinces* (1773), both of which saw publication in various editions and translations. References here are to Scholes' modern edition because of its general availability, and because it contains, especially in Vol. I, material that Burney left in manuscript at the time of the original publications.

Hamburg musical life, and possibly the wife of the famous opera composer, Reinhard Keiser, as soloist in an oratorio, and he continued to bring in operatic singers, both male and female, in subsequent years without apparent criticism.[33] How widespread the effort actually was to bring women into the church choir cannot be determined easily as such events become matters of record only when associated with important figures in the musical world, or when the action of the person who undertakes such a procedure is criticized or praised sufficiently that his attempt becomes a matter of public record. That the efforts of Bach and Mattheson, and any others that may remain unheralded, represented the exception rather than the rule is all too apparent from Burney's comments made during one of his visits to Brussels in July of 1772.

> On the day after my second arrival, there was a mass, in music, performed in the little, but neat and elegant, church of Mary Magdalen. . . . Some pieces of Italian church music were sung, not indeed so well as they would have been in their own country; but the voices here were far from contemptible. Two boys, in particular, sung a duet very agreeably; but there is generally a want of steadiness in such young musicians, which makes it to be wished that females were permitted in the church, to take the *soprano* part, which is generally the principal, as the voices of the females are more permanent than those of boys, who are almost always deprived of theirs before they know well how to use them.[34]

During this same month, however, Burney expressed great pleasure at hearing women sing in a different church in the same city and, in commenting upon their presence, provided further evidence of the rarity they represented.

> In attending high mass at the collegiate church of St. Gudula, on Sunday 26, I again heard the performance of a considerable band of voices and instruments; and I was glad to find among the former two or three women, who, though they did not sing well, yet their being employed, proved that female voices might have admission in the church, without giving offence or scandal to piety, or even bigotry. If the practice were to become general, of admitting women to sing the *soprano* part in the cathedrals, it would, in Italy, be a service to mankind, and in the rest of Europe render church-music

33. Cannon, *op. cit.*, 51.
34. Percy A. Scholes (ed.), *An Eighteenth-Century Musical Tour in Central Europe* *and the Netherlands*, Vol. II: *Dr. Burney's Musical Tours in Europe* (London: Oxford University Press, 1959), 17.

infinitely more pleasing and perfect; in general, the want of treble voices, at least of such as have had sufficient time to be polished, and rendered steady, destroys the effect of the best compositions, in which, if the principal melody be feeble, nothing but the subordinate parts, meant only as attendants, and to enrich the harmony of the *whole*, can be heard.[35]

While these eighteenth-century efforts at putting women into the church choir may not qualify as the proven first attempts in that direction, they do provide our first direct evidence of women, professional or amateur, singing in the church service *at the same time as men.* Even in the Venetian conservatories it was assumed that the young women who were residents of those establishments, and who achieved international recognition for their unusual musical achievements, would not be solely under the tutelage of men and would not perform liturgical music with men.

Women's inclusion in the choral service has not been accomplished without resistance, and there are naturally many groups that look with grave suspicion upon their presence, even now. One of the reasons it is difficult to trace the growth of female musical activity in the choir is that there are times in the development of musical practice, especially in the United States, when it seems almost impossible to distinguish between the congregational function and the choir function. In the congregational singing there is ample evidence of the use of the female voice, with consideration already being made of the possibility of women singing along with the men on the psalms, in a tract published by John Cotton in 1647.[36] This was followed by a pamphlet of 1723 that specifically authorized women to sing psalms in public worship.[37] These reports, of course, do little more than prove that congregational singing was becoming firmly established in the eastern part of North America, and reflect nothing about the acceptance of women into the choirs. There is, in fact, a dearth of material authenticated by research concerning musical practice in this country until the nineteenth century, when definite evidence becomes available about women who, at the early part of the century, often sang on the tenor part because they were not able to carry the soprano line independently.

Coupled with this slowly developing rise of permissiveness over

35. *Ibid.*, 20f.
36. Leonard Ellinwood, *The History of American Church Music* (New York: Morehouse-Gorham Company, 1953), 15.
37. *Ibid.*, 21.

prohibition, and sharply contrasted to it, is the confusion in Epis-
copalian circles brought about by the apparent conflict between the
need for women's voices to serve "where a sufficient number of boys
and men were not obtainable"[38] and the strict interpretation of the
traditional bias against women engaging in priestly functions. Necessity has, in many cases, overcome a strict interpretation of tradition,
and women appear in choirs of that sect, not only visible in the choir
stalls, but clad in vestments and moving in procession. That the distinction between the use of female voices in liturgical and nonliturgical churches in the United States still exists is obvious, but it is
doubtful that the line is as clearly drawn as is implied in the statement that

> a distinction is still drawn between liturgical singing and other re-
> ligious choruses. Where church music is regarded as a kind of
> sacred concert—a performance by trained singers for an audience
> that listens—women are admitted to choirs. But where music is a
> liturgy and the members of the liturgical choir are thought of as
> attendants of the priest at the altar, women are excluded. Women
> may entertain an audience, even in church, and attract people into
> the service by their voices, but they may not be official representa-
> tives of worship. This prohibition applies wherever there is liturgy,
> in its ancient and traditional sense, in the church service—whether
> the church be Catholic, Greek Orthodox, Jewish, or Protestant.[39]

The appearance of women within the choir, engaging publicly
in the act of worship, coincides to a great extent with the expansion
of what has only been hinted at here, the development of a choir that
has a nucleus of experienced or professional singers, assisted by amateurs who are able to sing on easier sections of the music. Inasmuch as
such a combination has proved practical only in churches with adequate financial resources or in those communities where an ample
supply of experienced singers could be found, the less fortunate
churches have had to learn to make do with groups of volunteers
that are under the leadership of people with varying degrees of skill
and musicianship. In itself, the shift of emphasis in choral groups
from boys and men to women and men has had less to do with changing standards than has the fact that the widely varied levels of ability
that resulted from the different combinations of voices has had a
decided influence on the kind of music that is performed in church,
in matters of appropriateness as well as quality.

38. *Ibid.*, 84.   (New York: Coward-McCann, Inc., 1948),
39. Sophie Drinker, *Music and Women*   249f.

Secularism, although it was not so obviously a problem of long standing among musical performers in the churches, had made its appearance in the music itself long before it clearly entered the choir membership. It is not possible to state when secular music first made itself felt in the church, but its first period of great influence came to fruition in the thirteenth century when the polytextual motet of that time was reaching its apogee. These motets, not to be confused stylistically with those of the fifteenth and sixteenth centuries, were usually complex, three-voiced polyphonic compositions performed at Vespers, with the lowest part often played upon an instrument rather than sung. Each of the parts had a different poem to sing, and sometimes more than one language was being sung at one time, yet the meanings of the texts were often related in that two of them served to comment on the set of words that served as a foundation for the entire composition.[40] By the end of the century the situation had become far more complex—and worldly as well. Dance tunes, vendors' cries, love songs, and even lascivious poetry had made their way into the music that was to have been intended only to praise God. Even after the secular elements had come into the motet, however, one of the voices usually clung firmly to the Gregorian melody (the necessary liturgical basis of sacred music of the period), thereby presenting a union of sacred and secular text and music. It is probable that the combination of sacred and secular ideas was more readily accepted in that century than it would be in ours, although the ecclesiastical authorities of that time denounced the practice. By the fourteenth century the motet had lost most of these worldly devices and was more concerned with structural complexities which were of interest to composers, but apparently disturbed neither the clergy nor the public.

During the fifteenth and sixteenth centuries polyphonic Mass-settings were often based on borrowed materials—tunes taken from sacred or secular compositions that already had a successful, independent existence. The resulting works, known as *cantus-firmus* Masses or Parody Masses, according to their specific borrowing technique, used melodies (or complete sections of compositions) from motets or hymns. Those taken from secular sources were often borrowed from well-known chansons or madrigals. In either case the idea was to base the Mass-setting on a tune or composition that had already achieved wide currency.

40. This is a general description of the thirteenth-century motet. Its develop- ment up to, and beyond, this stage is discussed in Chapter IV.

These settings of the Renaissance differed sharply from the medieval motets in the degree of musical sophistication they displayed. Whereas the earlier motet used song material from secular life in a straightforward manner, the later musical forms were usually based on modifications of the popular tunes. Commonly known melodies, including *L'Homme armé, Fors seulement, Je suis déshéritée* and (in England) *The Western Wynde,* were altered by expansion of note values, subjected to a fragmentation process by the insertion of original music between the quoted sections, or dealt with in such subtle ways that the ear did not readily perceive the use of secular elements. In every instance the original connotations were minimized because the text now was that of the appropriate section of the Mass—the Kyrie, Gloria, and so on—rather than something concerning the mighty man at arms or the lover grown wan and pale through loneliness. Actually, then, the degree of recognition of this secular intrusion depended on the musical background and experience of the listener. The person who had never heard *Je suis déshéritée* would not be able to recognize it when Palestrina employed it as material in one of his Masses, and would consequently have to accept it simply as a part of a complete religious composition. The process of borrowing secular ideas for Parody Masses disappeared partly because of pressure from the clergy who saw it as a threat to the dignity of worship.

The use of popular elements in Protestant music is equally distinguishable—and far more enduring. The chorale, developed by Luther and his followers as a means of encouraging congregational participation, relied on secular tunes just as Parody Masses and motets with borrowed tunes had done. In the case of the chorale, however, there was a broadening of the area from which the material was taken, for it included folk songs and popular tunes of the day, in addition to plainsong borrowed from the Roman tradition and melodies especially composed for the new service. It is perhaps sufficient to point out that the famous Passion chorale, *O Sacred Head Now Wounded,* was in its original form a secular song entitled *My Peace of Mind is Shattered by the Charms of a Tender Maiden* and that its employment represented a normal appropriation of current material consciously brought from secular to sacred environment for the purpose of including familiar music of distinctive quality in the church service. One considerable point of difference between the treatment of the tunes that went into Masses and motets and those that were appropriated for use in chorales was that the Catholic composers made rhythmic alterations at the time of composition, permitting the borrowed material to serve as a basis for another composition of greater dimensions and importance than the original, while the chorales that shared secular melodies usually arrived in church with their identifying features intact. It was only after they had spent some time in their new surroundings that they became the rhythmically inert pieces we often mistakenly believe them to have been. In each case, however, the principal features that identified the composition with its secular ancestry were removed; in the case of the Catholic music, immediately; in that of the chorale, during the course of continued usage over a longer period of time.

Inevitably, the question arises: what is wrong with secularism; is the church not of this world? In great part the answer must come from the theological front rather than from the musical; yet, the musician must face the problem as well as the theologian. It is certainly not enough to defend music on the basis of the composer's intentions; probably more bad music has been created in the name of sincerity than in any other cause. Neither can musicians accuse the clergy of a complete lack of understanding in the problem. One critic who is expert in the areas of both theology and music has put the issue squarely before the musical world.

We must fairly admit that the church is entitled to criticize the musicians; and that church music is subject to a kind of criticism from which music outside the church is exempt. It would be ridiculous to suggest that there is one standard for the sacred and one for the secular. Church music has enjoyed "benefit of clergy" for long enough, and has become ridiculous in the eyes of musicians at large because of it. But while church music is not dispensed from the ordinary requirements which music in general must meet, it stands also under the discipline associated with its being used to further the aim of worship. It is always used in a context in which its performers are not exclusively and its hearers not even primarily concerned with music in itself.[41]

Church music stands at a disadvantage. Not only must it fulfill the requirements of music, qua music; it must also be successful in its function as a tool of worship. While it is true that church music is not "dispensed from the ordinary requirements which music in

41. Erik Routley, *Church Music and The-* *Worship*) (London: SCM Press, Ltd., 1959), *ology* (No. 11 of *Studies in Ministry and* 52f.

general must meet," it is forced to forego many of the techniques, styles, and devices that are granted secular music without any question because their presence in religious music is viewed as a contaminating factor. While church music is expected to induce reflection, stimulate imaginative comprehension, heighten awareness, and nurture objective ideals, secular music needs only to entertain, although it may do other things as well, among them the four that have here been assigned to church music. This entertainment is offered at a great variety of intellectual levels, and so is church music—unfortunately, in the opinion of many of its critics. This is not meant to imply an innate superiority of church music over its secular counterpart. Rather, it is intended only to show that the one is, or should be, closely allied to a moral situation, while the other functions only as art. Somewhere within this strange dichotomy there must be found an aesthetic of church music; somewhere there must be a compromise between the music of the world and the music of the church, or else there must be discovered a justification for the differences that exist between the two styles of communication.

When we carefully examine choral music we are, of necessity, forced to evaluate the music as separate from the text to which it is set, as well as to study the relationship between the music and the text itself as appropriate means of religious expression. Disassociated from the text, music may be considered from the standpoints of structure and style. The structure is the architectural skeleton upon which style is placed. The use of symmetrical or asymmetrical forms, and the choice between repetition and recall passages or through-composed sections belongs, with a number of other such devices, to the area of structure. Style is the process of clothing this skeleton with the means of musical expressiveness; homophonic, polyphonic, modal, ornamental, or textural materials serve as flesh for the skeleton of structure. The composer's choice of a structural basis for his composition within the resources available to him in his generation may be largely controlled by functional as well as aesthetic considerations. The length of the composition is greatly influenced by the variety that may be achieved within the materials employed, although length has no direct relationship to the complexity of the technical procedures or component parts. A movement in a symphonic composition, for example, may run to a considerable length because of its adherence to the outlines of sonata-allegro form, while a shorter composition may be more complex because it is based (or although it is based) on a far more esoteric structure, as is Machaut's *Ma fin est mon commencement*[42] in which the structure is entirely controlled by the length of two statements of the melody, one appearing in normal fashion and the other in retrograde. The structure of a piece can as well be controlled by its text, as may be seen in the repeated phrases and ternary form of some Gregorian Kyries.[43]

There is nothing about any certain kind of musical structure that gives it a claim to existence only, or principally, within either the area of secular or sacred music. Binary and ternary forms exist in popular and folk music as well as in the music of the church service and concert hall; French overtures and fugues are found in both the music intended for entertainment and religious observances. Structurally, music cannot be identified as more or less appropriate for either the glory of God or the entertainment of man.

Musical style, on the other hand, has a greater degree of suitability for one or the other of the functions under consideration, although the style that is readily acceptable to one generation may be anathema to another. That there is an intentional separation between the styles for church and those for nonchurch use may be found in music as early as the works of Machaut, where the music destined for religious use was written in the then traditional *ars antiqua* style, while that for entertainment and pleasure was cast in the style of the modern *ars nova*, displaying a greater freedom of both rhythm and harmony, and producing forms that were different from those found in the church music partly because of the structure of the text that was being set to music. Also from this time can be dated an attitude that has come to be commonly accepted, but remains ill-defined to this day; that music for the church must display greater restraint than that written for secular purposes. Unfortunately, the distinctions are not that simple. The flamboyance of the Venetian school and the conservatism of the Roman school share both the same geographical and temporal spheres; liturgically inspired compositions vie for a place in the present century with choral settings of gospel hymns. Despite all this, there is an aesthetic of church music, or rather, a set of variable aesthetic levels, based on differing uses and interpretations of the musical function.

When musical taste was dictated, either realistically or hopefully, by some central authority, the recognition of quality presented no

42. *EM*, 81–84; *MSO*, 23f; *HMS* III, 15ff.   *Deus potentiae, LU*, 28, and the Kyrie
43. As, for example, in the *Kyrie magnae*   *Orbis factor, ibid.*, 46.

great difficulty. The stipulation handed down by authority was not involved with stylistic or structural complexity and technical difficulty, but rather concerned itself with matters of clarity, simplicity, liturgical observance, and restraint. At any time when the evaluations of musical quality are the sole property of local authorities, or of no authority save the music director, the level of musical taste varies greatly from place to place, and each church reflects the current habits and tastes of the congregation, of the director, or of the region. The quality of music in any situation is mostly determined by the abilities, as well as the ambitions, of the participating musicians. There are other matters, in addition, that are partly artistic and partly commercial in nature. A composer may have to compromise his preferences in musical taste, either willingly or with great reluctance, in order to insure acceptance of his work by a publisher who, while not a partner to some plot to debase musical taste, is by necessity engaged in a business where he must sell his product and cannot afford to be idealistic about matters of taste when he can find no market for his ideals among those who buy church music. The result of this economic pressure is the sale of large amounts of mediocre or outright trashy music to directors who either find a limited quantity of suitable material for sale or, worse yet, believe that the average choral pieces represent the highest in quality. That the problem is not confined to this country is also evident. Earlier in this century one British writer complained that

> Sunday after Sunday all over the land compositions are performed of a character and in a manner that would not be tolerated on a concert platform. Is this right? It means no less than that we are offering in the service of God music which we ourselves would not pay sixpence to listen to elsewhere![44]

It was probably the recognition of this low state of church music that had caused him to remark earlier that "it cannot too often be emphasized that *not a note of music is necessary to the performance of our Church Services;* and it follows that every note that is introduced must have some definite and worthy purpose behind it."[45]

Habits of musical taste are transmitted to audiences by performers, especially in the field of church music where the level of acceptance is closely related to familiarity with the music or its style. The acceptance of an aesthetic depends on more than either the qual-

44. Sydney H. Nicholson, *Church Music:*   Press, [1927]), 104.
A Practical Handbook (London: The Faith   45. *Ibid.*, 13.

ity of the the music or its familiar characteristics; the performance must be good or, in the case of the church, at least appropriate to the situation. It is the propriety of church music, its ability to appear convincingly suited to its environment, that is of paramount importance. Paradoxically, what is fit and suitable in one denomination is not at all acceptable in another; what seems properly devotional in sophisticated, urban surroundings impresses rural audiences and congregations with a regional identity as being "High Church" in concept and execution. That this has been so for centuries is evident in the fact that the Latin Mass continued in Lutheran Germany side by side with the vernacular utterance, and that Pietism and Orthodoxy existed as neighbors, each being more suitable to its adherents than anything else they might have chosen.

There has almost certainly been a deterioration of church choral music in the past two centuries, but it may be that the decline in quality has not been general; it may be one of the results of the existence of greater numbers of churches attempting large choral undertakings, or establishing choral services of some sort, without having the human means with which to execute the ideas. It may be that church music is not worse than it was, but that there are so many more church groups of all kinds that the worsening seems to have grown proportionately while, in reality, it has been a numerical growth only.

It is apparent to almost anyone who follows the course of church choral music that its literature does not keep pace with that of other musical areas. Some critics of church music state that the usual choral piece is made up of post-Mendelssohn harmonies, enlivened by a few wrong notes when a touch of modernism is sought. While this is not completely correct, it comes close enough to the mark to deserve consideration. The adherence to a single style by the majority of late nineteenth- and twentieth-century composers has produced a blandness and lack of individuality in service music that is perhaps unmatched by any other musical period in history. It is partly brought on by the ready acceptance of this sort of music by the congregations and clergy; partly by the inertia of singers and directors as a group; partly because publishers and composers have found it profitable. There has sprung up a belief that the church music of Protestantism must adhere to this pattern if it is to be considered acceptable in the eyes of the Lord and the music committee. While it is true that advanced compositional techniques that developed after the Romantic period do not lend themselves readily to choral com-

positions, and especially not to works destined for amateur performance, there are steps that can be taken to remove music from the
trough of conformity into which it has fallen. The volunteer choir
certainly could not cope with the techniques of twelve-tone music
even if it were desirable as service music, and the world has generally
thought of the full-blown Romantic tradition as being too emotional
for music to be performed inside a church. Yet there are composers
and publishers, directors and singers who have taken the step beyond
the unimaginative style of the recent past and who are developing a
new mode of religious expression that, although not denying the
traditional materials of musical composition, embodies certain
features in keeping with new developments in musical style. How
far the composer should go in this direction, and the extent to which
the church should accept his products will be discussed in the final
chapter of this book.

The development of religious choral music has come a long way
from the point at which it was first specifically guided in the Roman
Schola and, despite certain serious deviations from a steady upward
trend, the course it followed has not been entirely downhill qual-
itatively. Among the great dangers it has faced have been those of
the intrusion of secular styles, of lack of guidance from an established
or a commonly accepted aesthetic standard, and of desultory creativity and performance in its latter years. Despite these variables,
all that has come from the ancient roots has been considered appropriate church music by someone in the course of years, and must have
been accepted as beautiful or, at least good, at some step along the
way. Routley has supported this view in saying that

> there is no hideous conventicle, no ghastly religious daub, no mis-
> erable hymn or demoralizing hymn tune, no mawkish anthem or
> organ voluntary, no spiritually depressing piece of church furni-
> ture, but somebody has thought it beautiful. Beautiful, I insist—
> not merely serviceable. All these things are adornments of worship,
> or they are supposed to be so. Nobody will call a building [or piece
> of music] ugly if somebody did not before call it beautiful.[46]

Church music has come from the aloofness, restraint, and abstract adoration of the Middle Ages, through periods of exuberance
and bombast, to the present age when those who seek beauty in the
worship service are ranged against those who deny its right to exist
in the church. Out of this confusion we seek a model, if not a defini-

46. Routley, *op. cit.*, 31.

tion, for church music and, even here, we are beset by confusion, this time in the area of semantics. Shall we speak of church music, devotional music, religious music, or sacred music? Are we to concern ourselves simply with describing the purpose of the music, or shall we invest it with mystical qualities that must pour from it even when it is removed from its reason for existence? Despite the various names under which the music appears, and in connection with which we commonly refer to it, the use that is implied is that of music for worship, as was specified at the outset of this chapter. There is nothing sacred about music in itself; we use the same basic materials in creating a piece of choral music for church as we do in composing for secular purposes.

The matter of appropriateness must be considered in distinguishing between church music and music with texts on religious subjects performed in the church, especially when the latter is music that was not initially intended for the church, but which nevertheless has found its way into the religious service.[47] Such a distinction is not difficult to make when the line is drawn between liturgical and non-liturgical music. In churches that are firmly established on a liturgical foundation, the permissible music is clearly prescribed; in those that have either limited liturgical content or none at all, arias and choruses from oratorios and occasional pieces appear as service music with some frequency. Since many such works were intended for the concert hall instead of the sanctuary, they may draw upon styles and idioms that make them popular rather than acceptable in religious practice. A piece of music that brings to mind the operatic stage, the barbershop quartet, the hit tune, or any other palpably secular musical entertainment, whether by melodic, harmonic, or rhythmic familiarity, is guilty of a stylistic desecration in forcing these associations upon minds that should be bent only upon worship. That it has been possible in the past five centuries to write large quantities of convincing church music, as well as a considerable number of masterpieces, without borrowing overmuch from the obviously secular devices proves that there are certain qualities that may be sought in music for the church. These qualities are to be found in the music, and not necessarily in the life and actions of the composer. Sincerity

47. A distinction partially based on the size of the work is made by Dr. Oskar Söhngen, "Church Music and Sacred Music: Allies or Competitors," *The Diapason*, LII/12 (November, 1961), 34ff. Church music is there described as that intended for, or suitable to, performance in church; sacred music is other music of religious character, such as Passions and oratorios.

on the part of the composer actually has very little to do with quality, although it is always a desirable adjunct to his musical product. William Byrd wrote some of the best Anglican music while remaining a sincere Catholic; some of the worst hymns and anthems are dreadfully sincere, but utterly lacking in good taste, musical or textual.

It seems that the best of Christian music has achieved its position of distinction because of its universality, not merely because it was not intended for denominational use, but because it is, most importantly, the best music that could have been written in its generation, and is, fortunately for us, by the best composers of an era. The product of second- and third-raters of the same period, while perhaps brimming over with sincerity, usually fails to provide this quality.

The least successful music, on the other hand, has often concerned itself with some phase of regionalism, denominationalism, or topicality, any of which must inevitably weaken the possibility of a so-called universal communication of lasting values. It is clear that the music representing the peaks of religious tonal communication, such as that of the Italians at the end of the sixteenth century, the North Germans in the Baroque period, and the English in the Elizabethan era, was clearly intended for situations that we now view as fraught with denominational implications. Nevertheless, the composers were not restricting themselves entirely to the permissible materials of their religious surroundings, but were borrowing either from the musical advances of their own time in secular areas, or, when possible, were expanding their means of expression by augmenting the denominational desiderata with styles and techniques that they had learned from other religious persuasions. The Lutheran cantata is no less Lutheran for having made use of the aria, recitative, and orchestra that were not the sole property of Lutheranism—or of church music generally; Venetian church music lost little but its other-worldly qualities when it absorbed the new *concertato* style; and Anglican music was not bereft of integrity or vitality because of its adherence to certain characteristics that were common to other religious music. All these derived benefit by their relationship one to another, and the interaction of musical practices in the Christian church is seen as a continuing pattern by the examination of the various styles thus achieved. In the ensuing chapters it will be our purpose to trace the development of styles and traditions in connection with each of these major streams, observing where they cross and dilute, or strengthen, each other.

1

THE

CATHOLIC CONTRIBUTION

Althrough we now refer to the Church of the Middle Ages and early Renaissance as Roman Catholic, there is actually no need to make such a distinction in connection with the pre-Reformation Church, which was catholic in that it embraced a comprehensive Christian belief, but Roman only insofar as it managed to affect the religious thought of most of Europe. It is sufficient here to refer only to The Church, that purveyor of Christian thought under the leadership of a pope and his considerable body of officials.

It is this Church, requiring descriptive adjectives only when it is compared with later offshoots, that was the parent of the musical forms and styles that have pervaded Christian music—whether that music ultimately belongs in fact to the Roman Catholic branch or partakes only of the catholicity that stems from the common root of Christian belief. From the functions of praise that have continually been part of its observance have sprung such enduring forms as the Mass, motet, Passion, and oratorio. Their Protestant counterparts, some of them not entirely the property of Reformation musical activity, number among their types the anthem, Service, and cantata, while still other forms continue with modifications brought about through the need for competing with other sacred or secular types, or the necessity for adapting themselves to changing times.

A number of these forms arose as adjustments to the peculiar requirements of the worship service in the Church prior to the development of Reformation practices, and most of them are heavily indebted, in turn, to the collection of liturgical tunes that we call Gregorian chant or plainsong. Their development, as a body of choral music that demands our attention for reasons of historical importance or musical quality, and which we may wish to reconstitute through performance, is guided by the common bonds of the plainsong tradition and a centrally located and firmly administered authority. That the strength of this authority was considerable is evident from the degree of confusion and lack of discipline that came about when the papacy was removed from Italy to Avignon, and by the amount of attention that has been paid to the proclamations of the Council of Trent, even though those pronouncements have had less effect upon the course of music than was intended for them.

The development of Church music during the pre-Reformation centuries was a deliberate process, unfolding slowly under a sun that saw little of conflict—at least, of conflict that it could not solve and control—making simple adjustments to the development of theological direction and musical progress. This held true until the general outburst of revolution that marked the eruption of Protestant thought. With that new development the Church had to reconsider its position in every respect. Its authority had been broken, and this could not help showing in the music that was composed for the service, whether it was for the Mass or some other observance. The time was now also past, or rapidly passing, when church musicians lived in, for, and by the Church. Preceding generations had already produced significant musical figures who had divided their energies and talents between the Church and the courts of the mighty secular rulers. The Church establishments grew, the competition for talented musicians increased, and music took on more and more of secular characteristics. The contribution that is solely, and then later, principally, that of the Roman Catholic Church may be traced up to the period just following the Reformation. At that point a fresh view must be taken of the entire field of religious music.

Chapter II

The Polyphonic Mass
Before 1600

IN the Roman Catholic tradition, there are two principal liturgical observances, the Mass and the Offices, or Canonical Hours. Both have undergone a long and interesting development and both have contributed in some way to the musical activities of Protestantism. The Mass has had the greater influence upon the development of musical practice because it has offered significantly larger opportunity for the growth of numerous techniques of polyphonic music than have the Offices, even though the indebtedness of the Mass to the motet, which is, in turn, closely related to one of the Canonical Hours, will be evident.

There are some portions of the Mass that present little of interest for the musician, as they are either spoken or intoned. Those sections that have been sung, whether in plainsong or in polyphonic compositions, are of importance not only in connection with their function in the Roman rite, but also because some of them have come down to Protestant use in various degrees of transformation. There are two large divisions within the Mass, separated because of their appropriateness to specific occasions or because of their general usefulness. One is called the Proper of the Mass (*Proprium*) because it is made up of texts that are appropriate only to a single day, season, saint, or observance. The other division, and the more important one from the standpoint of choral music, is called the Ordinary (*Ordinarium*) because its texts may be used on any occasion, with only slight variations and omissions in special circumstances. About one-half of all the sections are sung in a Solemn High Mass, the rest being recited and intoned more or less audibly by the celebrant who "uses three principal tones in the Solemn Mass: the singing tone, the subdued

33

tone, and the low tone. In addition, he says one thing, the Last Blessing, in a loud tone."[1]

Those portions of the Mass that are not the sole responsibility of the celebrant fall to the choir to sing either in plainsong or poly-phony. The distribution of these two styles of singing in the choral sections is not uniform throughout the period during which these musical settings develop, and it has varied according to local practice and general customs. Generally, though, it may be assumed that the sections of the Ordinary received the greater choral emphasis. Most of the discussion which follows, then, is in reference to polyphonic settings of the Ordinary, but some attention will be given to the oc-casional settings of the Proper as they occur.

TABLE I

Proper	Ordinary
Introit	
	Kyrie eleison
	Gloria in excelsis Deo
Gradual	
Alleluia or Tract[2]	
Sequence[3]	
	Credo
Offertory	
	Sanctus-Benedictus
	Agnus Dei
Communion	

Interspersed among the sections shown above, and either sung in plainsong, spoken, or intoned by the celebrant, are the Collect (P), Epistle (P), Gospel (P), Sursum corda (O), Preface (P), Canon (O), Post-Communion prayer (P), Ite missa est (O) or, in Lent and Advent, Benedicamus Domino (O), and the Last Gospel (O). The various parts of the Mass, those sung as well as those spoken or intoned, follow each other in an invariable sequence at each celebration of Mass. Because of its important position in the activities of the Church, where it daily commemorates and mystically repeats or re-enacts the Last Supper and the Crucifixion, its observance has been subject to more control than has been exercised over the lesser rites of the Church. Even

1. Laurence J. O'Connell and Walter J. Schmitz, *The Book of Ceremonies* (rev. ed.; Milwaukee: Bruce Publishing Co., 1956), 178.
2. The Tract replaces the Alleluia at Requiem Mass and during Lent and Em-ber Days.
3. Used only at Easter, Whitsunday, Corpus Christi, Feast of the Seven Do-lours, and at Requiem Mass.

though the evolution of this daily service was spread over a period of centuries, plainsong, which has been the musical foundation for the ritual observances of the Church, has been a constant feature in the development of the choral portions, from its beginnings to the present.

It is impossible to undertake a discussion of the polyphonic Mass without making continued references to the singing of plainsong. It, and not the polyphonic sections, forms the musical framework of the Mass. The polyphonic settings of the Ordinary (or, less often, of the Proper), are inserted as substitutes for plainsong renditions of the same text. In many instances, the polyphonic movements are based on plainsong which is, therefore, still present although not always easily perceptible.

Most settings of the liturgical texts found in the Gregorian repertory of plainsong dating from about the seventh century are part of the body of the Proper. Their performance was the responsibility of the clergy, who were better prepared than untrained singers to perform the numerous texts and their various tunes. The Kyries and other sections of the Ordinary, however, were sung by the congregation who, because of the fixed text and the melodically uncomplicated structures of the musical settings, were able to participate with sufficient skill. A change came about in the ninth century when "the Schola Cantorum adopted and elaborated them and there began a new development that reached its highest point centuries later in the polyphonic Mass."[4] Along with the gradual separation of the congregation from the liturgical functions of the service, a growing complexity came about through the adoption of these portions of chant by the trained musical performers. The chants of the Ordinary were, musically at least, now ready to take a position of equal prominence with those of the Proper. The only other step necessary for musical learning to take in leading up to the polyphonic style that is our interest here, was the discovery and acceptance of a set of principles for simultaneous singing of different musical lines, a step that we recognize under the general name, organum. Before embarking upon an examination of the development of polyphony as it affected the Mass, it may be well to emphasize that with the use of this new musical style, plainsong performance did not cease or even wane. It should be remembered that choirs existed for the performance of liturgical plainsong and that when polyphonic singing was employed, it was

4. *MMA*, 183.

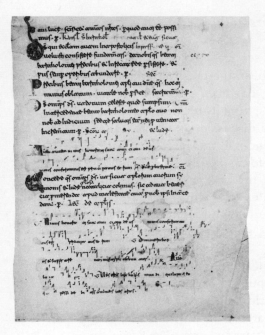

PLATE 1a. *Staffless neumes on a missal leaf, c.* A.D. *1100, Monte Cassino, Italy. Included are an Offertory and an Alleluia for the Feast of Saint Bartholomew, Apostle.* PLATE 1b. *The Gradual for Wednesday in Holy Week. Italian manuscript, c.* A.D. *1390.* (Courtesy of Baylor University Library.)

the best-prepared soloists who took part in its performance, and not the entire choir. If evidence were needed of the continuation of interest and emphasis in plainsong, it would be sufficient to cite the large amount of manuscript and, later, of printed plainsong that continued to flow from the pens and presses to fill the normal functions of liturgical observance in the churches and monasteries throughout Europe and the Americas for centuries thereafter, as well as the printing in our own time of liturgical books, of which *The Liber Usualis* is perhaps the most familiar.

While there is considerable evidence of activity in the writing of organum, both experimental and functional, in connection with music for performance in the Church before the second half of the twelfth century, it is not until that period that the first document showing its employment in connection with Mass settings dates. In the early years of the period that is now termed the *ars antiqua*, two composers of the Notre Dame school were engaged in the writing and revision of a cycle of two-part organa for the church year. This *Magnus Liber*

PLATE 1c.   *Parts of the Tract and Offertory for Passion Sunday,*
c. A.D. *1480, Monastery of Anghiarra, Arezzo, Italy.* (Courtesy of
Baylor University Library.)   PLATE 1d.   *Part of the hymn* Pange
lingua gloriosi *in Gothic neumes. Although it is specified for use on
Passion Sunday, LU, 709 assigns it to Good Friday. The page is from
an antiphonary printed at Mainz in the early sixteenth century.*
(Personal collection of E. A. Wienandt.)

Organi de Gradali et Antiphonario pro servitio divino multiplicando contained more than eighty pieces for use in the Offices (*antiphonario*)
and the Mass (*de gradali*). Most of these organa were intended for use
in connection with Mass, where it should be noted that the texts were
those of the Proper and not of the Ordinary, contrary to what we usually expect such settings to be. Leonin, who wrote the collection, was
the first of four eminent composers of cycles of the Proper. The others
were Heinrich Isaac, Jacobus Gallus, and William Byrd, whose
various efforts date from the sixteenth and early seventeenth centuries
(*cf. pp. 65f.*). The early existence of such cycles may be due to the
practice of the Middle Ages, wherein attention centered more on the
Proper than on the Ordinary, partly because the peak of interest in
the observance of Mass, the climax of the ritual, was the reading of the
Gospel rather than the Elevation during the Canon. This served to
place the greater emphasis on the earlier portion of the ceremony,
during which there is a heavier concentration of sections of the Proper.
When the high point of the rite was shifted to the Elevation and, as

37

a result of the changed emphasis, upon sections of the Ordinary, the need for such cycles was not so great. Two other reasons also developed. First, as the ritual underwent further change, a greater number of chants for the Proper, a larger number of occasional observances, and an increasing body of local ceremonies honoring saints or circumstances of less than international importance expanded the corpus of the Proper to the extent that a setting of a complete cycle represented a major accomplishment rather than a normal compositional activity. Also, the increasing emphasis on the setting of several or all portions of the Ordinary overshadowed the interest that might have been aroused in polyphonic performance of the Proper.

The organa of the *Magnus Liber* were intended to be sung as substitute pieces for the soloist's plainsong in the portions of the Proper which they served and, as such, were probably sung by soloists still, both because of the original function of the setting and because of the complexity that appeared in this new form. The portions that had earlier been sung by the chorus were still retained as plainsong sections and were, therefore, still the property of the choir instead of the soloists. Some of the examples of organa by Leonin are in unmeasured style, in which the rhythmic relationship between the two parts is free, the upper part weaving melismatic patterns above a slow version of the plainsong solo line. Other portions are written in measured, or discant, style. The treatment of *Haec dies (Ex. 1)*, the Gradual of the Easter Mass based on part of Psalm cxvii (118),[5] as shown in *HAM* 29 illustrates the various types of writing that are found in Leonin's organa. As explained in the comments that accompany the example,[6] a great degree of contrast is achieved between the sections that are measured and those that are set in free rhythm. The process of greatly expanding the chant through slowing its motion and the setting of numerous upper notes against a single pitch during the melismatic sections caused the once forthright and simple text to take on a new prominence, because of both its elaborate setting and the time involved for its presentation. This new technique of composition and performance, probably exciting to the twelfth-century listener and also possibly a matter of controversy, still restricted the performance of these modern ideas to the soloists, although several of them may

5. Each psalm will be identified by two sets of numerals; the Roman numerals will show the numbering employed in the Vulgate; the Arabic, that of the English version. Two sets will not, of course, be necessary for the very early and late psalms, as the discrepancy in numbering exists only between numbers 10 and 147.
6. *HAM*, 218.

Ex. 1   Beginning of Easter Gradual, *Haec dies*

This is the day which the Lord hath made;... Psalm CXVII (118), 24

have sung each part, and reserved the total choir for the rendition of the interrupted sections of plainsong. The employment of the whole chorus for polyphonic singing did not become common until the sixteenth century.

One other feature of the Leonin style that was to have a continuing life in compositions for the church, most prominently in the motet, was the application of the rhythmic modes,[7] a set of six rhythmic patterns, one or more of which usually served as a unifying framework for the measured sections of the organa and for entire motets or sections of such compositions. Their continuation is found in the isorhythmic structures of the fourteenth and early fifteenth centuries.

The contribution of Perotin, who was probably Leonin's successor as precentor at Notre Dame from c. 1180 to c. 1230 is principally that of rewriting and expanding the *Magnus Liber* by exclusive employment of the measured style, and the writing of organa in three and four voice parts as well as continuing to produce examples of two-part composition. His style is illustrated, also in an example that uses the *Haec dies* as its basis, in *HAM* 31.

About the beginning of the fourteenth century, interest seems to have turned to polyphonic setting of the separate sections of the Ordinary. The shift of emphasis from the Proper is due to the practical consideration that a text of the Proper is useful only for a single occasion or, at most, a brief season of each year, while a text from the Ordinary may be sung during most, or all, of the year. These settings made their first appearances as tropes,[8] usually as organa, of the Benedicamus and Kyrie sections of the Mass. Until the fifteenth century was well under way, the usual method was that of composing

7. *HD*, 452f.
8. Nonliturgical additions to the author-   ized texts. See *HD*, 768, and *Grove's*, VIII, 559.

single sections that were then probably placed together in some convenient fashion when performance of all or several of them was desired at a celebration of the Eucharist. With only a few exceptions, the
setting of single movements reflected the common practice. The idea
of providing a unified, or at least related, series of movements that
made the Mass similar to a cantata of five large parts was still some
years away. In the fourteenth century, for example, it was convenient
to group all Kyries together in one part of a choirbook, and to place
other chants together in like fashion.

Two notable complete settings of the Ordinary date from the fourteenth century. One of them, the Machaut Mass, was certainly composed as a complete set of movements by one man; the other, the
Mass of Tournai, was apparently not all composed by the same person
or even at the same time. It is to this anonymous, composite effort
that we first direct our attention.

Although it is generally agreed that the Tournai Mass is not the
work of a single composer, there is a point of difference concerning
its complexity. This amounts to disagreement over whether any of
the melodies are from the Gregorian repertory. While there are some
scholars who give credence to the theory that the upper voices of the
Gloria and Credo contain elaborated plainsong melodies, Schrade[9]
claims that none of the tenors is identifiable and he does not point to
any elaboration of known materials in the other voices. The Kyrie,
Sanctus, and Agnus Dei *(TEM 13)* exhibit certain traits that are allied
to practices which, by this time, are relatively old-fashioned. These
sections share a tendency to be cast in conductus style and lean heavily upon the rhythmic modes *(cf. pp. 72–74),* the Kyrie featuring the
second mode, while the Sanctus and Agnus favor the third. The extent
to which this device is employed is illustrated by the rhythmic scheme
of a portion of Kyrie I *(Ex. 2).* The other movements contain patterns that are obviously derived from the rhythmic modes, but that
are treated with considerably more freedom. There are several brief
hocket sections in the Gloria *(Ex. 3),* in which the even flow of the
rhythm is broken by alternating entries in the upper voices.

A close relationship with the motet is apparent in the names given

9. Leo Schrade (ed.), *Polyphonic Music of
the Fourteenth Century: Commentary to
Volume I* (Monaco: Editions de l'Oiseau-
Lyre, 1956), 123ff. The music is given in
Volume I, 110–31. For another edition,
see *Missa Tornacensis,* edited by Charles
Van den Borren (*Corpus Mensurabilis Mus-
icae,* 13) (Rome: American Institute of
Musicology, 1957).

Ex. 2   Use of second rhythmic mode, Kyrie of *Mass of Tournai*

Ex. 3   Hocket in Gloria, *Mass of Tournai*

to each of the voices—*triplum-motetus*-tenor—and the method employed in the composition of the final movement, which is actually a motet, polylingual and polytextual. The *triplum* has a French secular text, the *motetus* a rhymed Latin text, and the tenor carries the liturgical Latin. In the manner used to describe such motets, by listing each text *incipit,* reading from the top to bottom parts, this movement would bear the title, *Se grace—Cum venerint—Ite missa est.*

Guillaume de Machaut's *(c. 1300–1377) Messe de Notre Dame*[10] is considerably more significant in the historical development of this form, for it is not only the earliest known setting of the Ordinary by one composer, but it contains a thematic fragment or motive that binds the movements together in cyclic fashion.[11] The motive is sub-

10. Modern editions include the following: Guillaume de Machaut, *Messe Notre Dame,* ed. Armand Machabey (Liège: Editions Dynamo, 1948); Guillaume de Machaut, *Musikalische Werke (Vierter Band),* ed. Heinrich Besseler (Leipzig: Breitkopf & Härtel, 1943 [reprint, 1954]; Guillaume de Machaut, *La Messe de Nostre Dame,* ed. G. de Van *(Corpus Mensurabilis Musicae,* II), (Rome: American Institute of Musicology in Rome, 1949); Schrade, *op. cit.,* III, 37–64; and *Messe Notre-Dame dite du Sacre de Charles V (1364) à 4 voix égales transcrite par Jacques Chailley* (Paris: Rouart, Lerolle & Cie., 1948). There is also a facsimile of one of the manuscripts:

Guillaume de Machaut, *Messe de Nostre Dame (Summa Musicae Medii Aevi,* I) issued by Friedrich Gennrich (Darmstadt: 1957).
11. Reference in this book to a Mass cycle will mean a setting of the five movements of the Ordinary, or, in the case of many English Masses, of four movements, since the Kyrie is not set polyphonically, and, rarely, to a cycle of the Proper. Reference to cyclic Masses, on the other hand, will imply thematic continuity from one of the movements to the others. The terminology has been known to cause some confusion.

ject to a greater degree of flexibility than that credited to it by some
writers. It is sometimes given as follows: *(Ex. 4).*

Ex. 4 The "basic motive" of Machaut's Mass

A rendition such as this, however, is possible only through the application of *musica ficta,*[12] and even such alteration would not often place
the top note in a position that is a half-step from its neighbor. The
figure does have the following constant features: it consists of a four-
note group appearing at various pitch levels; it is always made up of
four equal note values, usually eighth notes; it is most often found in
descending form; and it may be approached from the same pitch as
its first note, by step, or by skip, and it is usually left by stepwise
motion. This motive appears in every section of the Mass and serves
as its most easily recognizable feature. A number of variants are
found in the accompanying example which illustrates rhythmic variations and the size of the approaching skip in various parts of the
Mass. The staves are without clef signs to indicate that the pattern is
found at several pitch levels *(Ex. 5).* This pattern serves to bind the
work together both motivically and rhythmically.

A feature that is less apparent to the ear, but that certainly was

Ex. 5 Related forms of Machaut's "basic motive"

12. The theory whereby performers, and
nowadays scholars and editors, altered
certain pitches in order to conform to generally established theoretical practice.
The alteration, *prima vista,* of the written
music was apparently common practice;
performers in the Middle Ages and Renaissance were expected to be able to apply
the theory, and the writing out of chromatic alterations was taken as a reflection
on the ability of the singer. Modern practice requires that *musica ficta* alterations
be placed above the staff, leaving the staff
itself free to show those accidentals that
were indicated by a composer. See *HD,*
465ff, and *Grove's,* v, 1014ff.

intended to serve this same unifying purpose, is the use of isorhythmic structure in each section except the Gloria (in which another, simpler type of organization may have been employed in its place).[13] Isorhythm, although more commonly associated with the motet, is found in Masses as well during the fourteenth century, and even into the fifteenth. It is a natural and logical outgrowth of the principle found earlier in the use of rhythmic modes, but is less obvious in its patterns because the statement of a single *talea,* the rhythmic pattern, may be many times as long as a statement of a rhythmic mode or an *ordo,* the repeatable pattern made up of a series of statements of the mode. In one way other than length and variety, the isorhythm represents an advance in complexity, and perhaps in sophistication, over its predecessor—it is susceptible to a melodic repetition *(color)* as well.[14] Machaut's use of these features is apparent only if the student is aware that a composer who employed these devices did not utilize them throughout an entire section of a composition unless he so chose. In many cases, the isorhythmic patterns evade the casual reader of the score because they are preceded by an *introitus,* an introductory section that does not contain the device. In Machaut's Mass, the Kyrie *(MSO,* 20–23) is isorhythmic throughout, although a different pattern is used for each major section; the Gloria is without isorhythmic involvement; only the *Amen* of the Credo is so treated; the process is employed in the Sanctus beginning with the second syllable of *dominus,* the preceding material serving as an *introitus;* and the isorhythmic patterns in the Agnus Dei are set to the text following the words *Agnus Dei, qui*[15] *(MM* 13) for the first and third sections, and following *Agnus Dei* in the middle section. The brief piece in motet style that makes up the Ite missa est is without *introitus.* Whatever audible unification may be brought about by the use of isorhythm is relatively small and becomes even less when the *talea* is preceded by an *introitus* or is interrupted by interludes. That it provides a degree of flexibility not available to composers whose efforts were restricted to the use of rhythmic modes is undoubtedly true, but as a device that supplies

13. Several sections of text are emphasized through being set chordally rather than polyphonically. Long notes of equal value, some as complete triads, and all as root-position chords, are used in connection with *Et in terra pax* and *Jhesu Christe* in the Gloria, and with *ex Maria virgine* in the Credo. The root-position triads were not known as *falsobordone* at that early date.

14. For a more detailed explanation of isorhythm, see *Grove's,* IV, 551–53, and *HD,* 367.

15. The Benedictus is printed in *HMS,* III, 17f.

the listener with some feeling of continuity and unity, it usually lacks the power of communication. It may be partly for this reason that, in the fifteenth century, isorhythmic structure began to give way to a greater interest in movements built upon pre-existent tunes.

The interest in transferring familiar melodic material to polyphonic settings is already evident in four movements of Machaut's Mass. Sections of plainsong were lifted bodily from the monophonic literature and used as the melodic structures upon which he organized his isorhythmic patterns.

TABLE II[16]

Mass section	Plainsong source	Liber Usualis, page
Kyrie	Kyrie Cunctipotens Genitor Deus (Mass IV)	25
Sanctus	Sanctus (Mass XVII)	61
Agnus Dei	Agnus Dei (Mass XVII)	61f.
Ite missa est	Sanctus (Mass VIII)	38

Because of the periodic nature of the Agnus Dei, the resulting isorhythm contains both *talea* and *color,* the melodic statement beginning with *qui tollis* in each instance. Participation in the isorhythmic pattern by the upper voices (*motetus* and *triplum*) may be seen in the *Amen* of the Credo. The second half of each of the three *taleae* brings the upper voices into an isorhythmic pattern different from that of the two lower voices. At the same point in each *talea* the tenor and contratenor employ *stimmtausch* (exchange of parts), with the third *talea* providing a reversed arrangement of the other two as a further refinement that results in a closed form rhythmically *(Ex. 6)*. The participation of the upper voices in isorhythmic activity is easily seen in the Agnus Dei, as well (*MM* 13).

A recapitulation of the contributions of these two Masses shows that they are more widely separated in style and complexity than appears at first glance. While the Tournai Mass is based upon such relatively simple unifying features as the use of rhythmic modes,

16. It should not be supposed that Machaut had any such handy arrangement of the chants of the Ordinary as is implied by the numerical groupings given here. The arrangements of chants into the groups given in *LU* date from after Machaut's time, some of the plainsong sections being dated as late as the fifteenth century, and modifications of some older chants being ascribed to the sixteenth. It might be noted, however, that a composer in the centuries after Machaut could not have taken a plainsong version of Ite missa est from Mass XVII in order to preserve unity as that Mass is intended for the Sundays of Advent and Lent and, therefore, offers only two Benedicamus Domino chants.

Ex. 6 *Taleae* in tenor and contratenor, Credo of Machaut's Mass

Telea I	Telea II	Telea III

an adherence to certain elements of the conductus and motet styles, and the possible use of elaborated plainsong tunes, the Machaut Mass is laden with unifying devices at many points. It employs isorhythm, a far more elaborate technique than the simple rhythmic modes. A motivic pattern in various shapes, and at several pitch levels, is found in each of the sections. An adherence to plainsong sources for most of the tenors, upon which nearly all the isorhythms are constructed, can be traced. In addition, Machaut's work is for four voices, or is at least in four parts, while the Tournai Mass is in only three. Neither Mass has all its movements in the same mode, although the Machaut work is the less diffuse in this respect.

An interesting diagrammatic approach to the isorhythmic structures of Machaut is presented by Gombosi, who stresses "the existence of a well laid out plan of speculative nature behind the apparent surface of isorhythmic constructions,"[17] existing on two levels, the sensuous and the abstract. Gombosi's illustrative diagrams show a perfect balance in the distribution of long and short note values on either side of the center in each isorhythmic structure. The immediate impact upon the ear, however, is that of simultaneous sounding tones, and not their arrangement within an abstract framework. What may be sensuous to one age or listener is often startling or raw to another. The vertical combinations resulting from Machaut's polyphony are, to say the least, far from the smoothly interwoven, placid lines of the sixteenth century. Based upon a theory that required a preponderance of fourths and fifths, the perfect consonances of pre-tertian harmony, the music has a spare and spacious sound that permits the mind—after a period of aural adjustment—to center upon matters of text rather than to become involved with the delights of rich harmonic accidents and contrivances.

Performance of Mass settings of this time could well have been accompanied by some kind of instrumental group. Although our

17. Otto Gombosi, "Machaut's *Messe Notre-Dame*," *The Musical Quarterly*, xxxvi/2 (April, 1950), 223. The startling architectonic principles that are presented here deserve examination by everyone who has more than passing interest in this Mass or in the possibilities of fourteenth-century compositional techniques.

information about such performances is greatly limited, it is certain that some lower voice parts, such as the contratenor, may not have been sung at all, as the text is often lacking. At some points all voices are textless, indicating that instrumental interludes may have been called for, although the sometimes haphazard practices of underlaying the text prohibit our accepting this as definite evidence of non-vocal passages. When some voice parts extend for great distances without providing opportunity for breath, one is tempted to credit this also as evidence in favor of instrumental accompaniment or duplication. Since there are no provable independent instrumental parts, however, it is difficult to base an entire theory of performance practice upon the presence or absence of texts or the length of an uninterrupted phrase. It is generally believed that neither separate accompaniments nor *a cappella* singing were called for, but that *colla parte* instrumental performance was implied[18] as it was in secular music and sacred music performed outside the church service.[19] It has not been proved that instruments were generally used in connection with liturgical observances, but it is known that on the occasions when instruments were used to accompany singers, the ideal was variegated instrumentation rather than homogeneous selection. Each instrument that duplicated a voice part was chosen for its individual tonal characteristics in order to keep the various lines of the polyphonic web clearly separated. That evidence of a more definite nature becomes available in connection with compositions of the Church in the fifteenth century will be seen later in this chapter.

For about half a century after the death of Machaut there was no significant advance in the technique of setting the Mass to polyphonic music. No important development took place in the organization of complete cycles of the Ordinary, and no single composer emerged to demonstrate the presence of new style characteristics.[20] There is,

18. The two terms are used currently with some confusion. *A cappella* (in chapel style), see *HD*, 5; also *Grove's*, i, 1, is the term reserved for an entirely unaccompanied style even though the style prevailing in some chapels may have been that of accompanied music. *Colla parte* accompaniment is that in which the instrumental part represents a literal duplication of the vocal lines. The keyboard part of modern choral octavo pieces that are intended for unaccompanied singing and bear the rubric "for rehearsal only" are examples of *colla parte* writing.

19. *MR*, 57ff; also Thurston Dart, *The Interpretation of Music* (London: Hutchinson's University Library, 1954), 150–162.
20. There do exist, however, the Toulouse and Barcelona Masses, both of which are cycles, the Besançon Mass (more correctly, Sorbonne, according to Leo Schrade) and the Ivrea and Apt manuscripts, both of which reflect the usage at the papal establishment at Avignon. A thorough examination of the period that is usually discussed only in reference to the Tournai and Machaut Masses requires consideration of these sources, among others.

however, evidence of the continuation of the practice of setting single movements, such as the Kyrie or Gloria, and the pairing of certain sections or the organization of them into groups of three, often the Kyrie with a Gloria-Credo or Sanctus-Agnus Dei combination. These pairs were probably coupled with the Kyrie for the same reason that they served as pairs of movements—their texts were structurally similar.[21] It is also possible that the Kyrie-Sanctus-Agnus combinations often came into being because no Gloria or Credo was needed for the performance of a *Missa brevis* on weekdays.[22] Even though it was still common for Mass movements to appear in manuscripts with all the Glorias grouped together, all Credos as another group, and so on, the organization of the movements into related groups of two or three shows a tendency toward establishing musical relationships instead of maintaining the grouping by section—a grouping that bespoke an attitude which considered the pieces principally from the standpoint of liturgical unity.

Certain national characteristics began to appear in these movements, making it possible to decipher the backgrounds of anonymous composers or, at least, their acquaintance with music from other parts of the world. In Italy, some of the settings took on characteristics that may be traced to the madrigal, the ballata, and the caccia. In the French compositions of the Ivrea and Apt manuscripts, an attempt was made to avoid the devices associated with the motet—isorhythm, hocket, and simultaneous setting of different sections of text. In England may be seen the absence of polyphonic settings of the Kyrie, which was always sung in plainsong, although the other four sections appear polyphonically in their four separate groups in such an authoritative source as the Old Hall manuscript,[23] retaining isorhythm as a device in a number of cases. In some settings of the Gloria and Credo, there is a tendency to employ different portions of the same text simultaneously.[24] This is different from motet treatment, in which different texts occurred at the same time. The purpose of this telescoping technique in the English Mass movements was to dispose of the long texts more rapidly. A similar situation prevailed in Russia where "to

21. *SMRM*, 219.
22. Manfred F. Bukofzer, "English Church Music of the Fifteenth Century," *Ars Nova and the Renaissance: 1300–1450*, Dom Anselm Hughes and Gerald Abraham (eds.), Vol. III: *The New Oxford History of Music* (London: Oxford University Press, 1960), 181.

23. The entire manuscript is published under the title *The Old Hall Manuscript*, ed. Alexander Ramsbotham, 3 vols. (Nashdom Abbey: The Plainsong & Mediaeval Music Society, 1933–1938).
24. *MMA*, 421; also Bukofzer, *The New Oxford History of Music*, III, 169.

shorten the service, two or three different prayers were sometimes sung simultaneously."[25] There was, of course, no connection between the practices.

While it is difficult to establish a direct line of influence between the periods of Machaut and Dufay, it appears probable that one of the strongest forces in those years was that of an English school, outstanding among whose members were Leonel Power (fl. 1450?) and John Dunstable *(c. 1370–1453).* The Old Hall manuscript, representing the compositional techniques of roughly the first third of the fifteenth century, contains a number of the compositions of the former, whose conservative early style reflects a knowledge and application of the practices of the previous century — isorhythmic Mass sections, employment of contrasting voice combinations, and harsh dissonances that bear evidence of the "successive" method of composition[26] which, although conforming to established rules, produced some rather strong combinations nonetheless. Bukofzer describes a second period of composition, in which Leonel wrote melodies that were marked by a fluid grace and in which his dissonance treatment became more reserved and tended to lose its earlier harshness. There was also an increased emphasis on the use of imitation and a general neglect of the practice of writing upon a *cantus firmus (Ex. 7).*

While the compositions of Leonel are distributed through Continental and insular manuscripts alike, very few of John Dunstable's are found in English sources. The number of his works that appeared outside England, however, attest to his importance and to his probable influence on later composers as well as on his contemporaries. Despite his considerable fame and apparent importance as a contributor to musical ideas, his product generally may be said to reflect the prevalent English style of his time.

Ex. 7 Fragments typical of Leonel's early style

25. *MMA*, 99.

26. The writing of a single voice at a time, rather than simultaneous, "vertical" composition. The method may have been common until the sixteenth century. See Nanie Bridgman, "The Age of Ockeghem and Josquin," *The New Oxford History of Music*, III, 242.

Our understanding of the importance of the composers of whom Power and Dunstable were the leading figures is recent. This is apparent in the fact that Emil Naumann, one of the most influential and widely read music historians of the late nineteenth century, disposed of Power as one name in a list of thirty-nine given by Thomas Morley. He dealt with Dunstable almost as briefly, devoting only a single paragraph to his life and musical style, the most perceptive sentence of which states that "he shares with Dufay and Binchois the merit of having got rid of the gross successions of fifths and octaves which abounded in the crude harmonies of the thirteenth and fourteenth centuries, as well as of simplifying the movements of the voice-parts, and imparting to the general effect of the music a vigour and a smoothness which did not exist before."[27] The perspective of years and the considered opinions of scholarship have removed the misconception that Dunstable was the only English musician of consequence. Rather, it has come to be understood that Dunstable and Power were two of the best-known and most widely imitated Englishmen, both of whom were skilled in what must have been a commonly practiced English style.[28] This style was one in which was evident a great smoothness of the voice parts, an emphasis upon the upper voice, great dependence upon parallel first inversion chords, either as English discant or as fauxbourdon (the former employing the melody in the tenor, the latter in the top voice) *(Ex. 8* and *MSO, 27),* and full chords that indicate the presence of tertian harmony, in which the combination of a third and fifth above a root is a desideratum.

The fifteenth and sixteenth centuries represent the most vital, inventive, and varied period of Mass composition. Much of the variety is probably due to the fact that composers felt impelled to demonstrate their mastery of musical materials while filling the need for complete sets of sections which we now call Mass cycles. As the performance of polyphonic movements gained acceptance, an increase in settings of the commonly used segments was apparent, as was seen earlier.

Ex. 8 *a)* English discant   *b)* Fauxbourdon

27. Emil Naumann, *The History of Music,* trans. F. Praeger, ed. Rev. Sir F. A. Gore Ouseley (London: Cassell and Company, [1886]), I, 562.

28. Some features of this style may be seen in *MET* 9, 11, and 12. The pieces, however, are not Mass sections.

The establishment of the Mass cycle with five polyphonic movements as a normal musical expression for large churches seemed to loose a flood of ideas among the composers of church music. It was not sufficient to resort to the simple expedient of organizing several unrelated movements into a group. Neither was the fact that the composition of these movements might be undertaken by a single composer a satisfactory solution. Various musical means of unification began to be applied to the compositions, after the fashion that may have been consciously employed by Machaut. These means took on different outward appearances, but their common features were either the employment of pre-existent or current material, from both secular and sacred repertories, or experimentation toward the adoption of a cyclical treatment, in which the same material appeared in each section of the Mass.

One source of borrowed melodies—indeed, the most readily available source—was the Gregorian liturgy itself. It was possible for a composer to borrow the melodic basis for each movement of his Mass from the parallel section of plainsong. The resulting Mass, which exhibited a greater liturgical than musical unity, has been called by a variety of names, but is commonly known as a plainsong Mass. Considerable objection has been raised to the use of this designation, and to the name *cantus-firmus* Mass, as well, since the two types are not always clearly separable. This principle of construction, although it continued to be practiced by Palestrina, was not found in great abundance among others of the later period. Since an exact descriptive term is needed, it might be better to return to the Latin usage, *missa choralis*, which, if not more illuminating, is not misleading, for it simply identifies the Mass as one that uses plainsong material.

The next important stage in the development of unity in Mass movements is usually given as the appearance of the Tenor Mass, which often employs both borrowed melodies and cyclic treatment. An intermediate step, however, has been suggested by Heinrich Besseler, who presents the earlier works of Guillaume Dufay *(c. 1400– 1474)* as illustration of the *cantilena* Mass.[29] Variously called "ballade style" and "treble-dominated style," this technique gives prominence to the upper part through making it the sole carrier of text against a pair of lower parts that are probably instrumental. That voice (or in

29. Guglielmi Dufay, *Opera Omnia,* ed. Heinrich Besseler *(Corpus Mensurabilis Musicae,* 1), Tomus 11. (Rome: American Institute of Musicology in Rome, 1960).

The music mentioned here is in this volume; some of the editorial comments are to be found in Tomus 111 (1951).

some cases, a pair of voices) is also usually more lyrical than the lower lines. These works, bearing the titles *Missa sine nomine, Missa Sancti Jacobi,* and *Missa Sancti Antonii Viennensis,* and representing part of Dufay's production prior to 1450, serve even better to illustrate a feature of performance practice that was touched upon in the previous chapter. The continuing use of the chorus for the singing of plainsong while the soloists were undertaking the more complex polyphony is illustrated by the designation *Duo* in portions of the *Missa Sancti Jacobi* that are scored *a 2,* indicating that soloists are expected to perform, while the *a 3* sections bear the indication *Chorus* at the beginning of the *superius* line, demonstrating that the complete choir was to sing the melodic part while instruments performed the lower lines.[30] Further evidence on the matter of instrumental performance is seen in these Masses. Besseler finds the clue to its existence in the kind of notation used and in the lack of complete texts for the lower voices.

> In manuscripts of the first half of the 15th century the external appearance of the voice or part is equally important. There are some copyists who wrote the text carefully and underlaid it so that it showed some sort of relationship with the individual notes. In good manuscripts of this kind an instrumental part is mostly indicated simply by the first few words of the text. This is true, not only for the beginning of the composition, but also for later sections, as in the Gloria or Sanctus. If only the text incipit is given in a lower voice, this indicates instrumental performance.[31]

The last intermediate step before the establishment of the Tenor Mass as a common and much used category was that of the employment of a motto beginning or head-motif which serves to bind the sections of the Mass together at the beginning of each movement in which it is employed, even though it may later be lost to the ear. Thus, in the *Missa Sancti Antonii Viennensis,* a work once thought to be of doubtful authorship but now unassailably assigned to Dufay,[32] a motto, with slightly varied forms in recurrences, appears in the first four sections *(Ex. 9).* While some related material might be extracted from the Agnus Dei, it would be farfetched. It seems more probable that no unifying attempt was made there.

This unification of the opening fragments of the movements failed to provide the coherence that had been sought in the earlier use of

---

30. For more on this, see *MR,* 62ff.   32. *Ibid.,* II, 1, and III, 1.
31. Dufay, *Opera Omnia,* II, iii.

Ex. 9 Motto from Dufay's *Missa Sancti Antonii Viennensis*

isorhythmic material and in the later integrative attempts that based all movements upon plainsong. "The real unity of the mass cycle depends upon the tenor using the same melody as *cantus firmus* in all five sections."[33] The solution ultimately was to lie in the establishment of the Tenor Mass, which apparently had its beginnings in England and may have become known to Dufay in the form of a Mass on the *Caput* melisma of the Maundy Thursday antiphon *Venit ad Petrum*.[34] Dufay's *Missa Caput* illustrates that he was not entirely ready to forego that felicitous, but insufficient, solution to the search for unity, the motto, in favor of this newer principle. Each movement opens with a motto stated in the superius, while the tenor, carrying the *Caput* theme, enters later *(Ex. 10 a, b)*. The tenor in each movement is allotted two statements of the *cantus firmus*, the first in ternary rhythm, the second in binary. The second statement is also preceded by preliminary material, given out by the upper voices in each case, but that material does not restate the motto or present a new one. Masses based solely on motto beginnings did not drop out of sight

Ex. 10

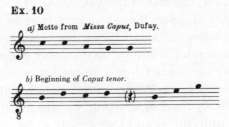

a) Motto from *Missa Caput*, Dufay.

b) Beginning of *Caput* tenor.

---

33. *Ibid.*, III, iv.
34. *SMRM* has as its seventh chapter a study of the *Missa Caput* by Dufay, as well as a discussion of the parallel works by Ockeghem and Obrecht. With it should

be read Bukofzer's "Caput Redivivum: A New Source for Dufay's *Missa Caput*," *Journal of the American Musicological Society*, IV/2 (Summer, 1951), 97–110.

immediately after the acceptance of the practice of using a *cantus firmus* as a unifying device, but continued to be used throughout the Renaissance.

Tenor Masses provided the most successful solution to the search for a means of cyclic unification for the several portions of the Ordinary. During the century and a half commencing about 1450, the date roughly marking the opening of Dufay's mature period of composition, three separate sources of *cantus firmi* came into common use: the tenor could be drawn from liturgical material, as was that of *Caput;* it could be extracted from a secular piece, as in the case of *L'Homme armé* and many others; or it could be based upon the recurrent treatment of a tenor that had been specifically composed for a single Mass. Although none of these methods reigned exclusively as a compositional device, each had a period of prominence during the remainder of the Renaissance. The first two of these types were used with great success by Dufay, his first utilization of the liturgical type being that of *Caput,* and his (according to strong evidence provided by Besseler) *Missa La Mort de Saint Gothard* providing the first use of a secular *cantus firmus* in a Mass. There are two more examples of each type from his pen; the Masses *Se la face ay pale* and *L'Homme armé* borrow secular melodies that act as *cantus prius factus,* and the Masses *Ecce ancilla Domini* and *Ave Regina coelorum,* both of whose tenors are drawn from antiphons, serving as examples of *cantus firmi* drawing upon sacred sources.[35]

Dufay's first excursions in writing Mass sections *a* 4 came after he had experimented fully with writing for three voices. Following his adoption of the principle of the Tenor Mass, he did not return to writing *a 3,* preferring instead to place the *cantus firmus* in the tenor, thereby retaining two treble parts above it, but giving a greater solidity to the composition by providing a part below the *cantus firmus.* Variety of texture was achieved in many works by reducing the number of voices that sang in sections smaller than complete movements. The *Missa Sancti Jacobi,* setting the Ordinary and four parts of the Proper, contains sections that are *a* 4, *a* 3, and *a* 2, providing a great variety of sonorities. The opening sections of the *Missa Caput* movements, bearing the motto beginning and written *a* 2 for

---

35. *Cantus firmus* refers to any pre-existent melody upon which a composer bases a polyphonic work, even one created for a single occasion. *Cantus prius* *factus* is a term more often used in reference to generally known melodies rather than those written for use in only one composition.

fifteen measures or more, serve equally as strong textural contrasts to the basic *a 4* setting which, in that work, does not begin until the entrance of the *cantus firmus*-bearing tenor in each instance.

Another device that was especially adaptable to the Tenor Mass was the employment of riddle canons. In this connection, the proper solution to the performance of a piece lay in the correct reading of the tenor part which had been subjected to some esoteric treatment at the hands of the composer. Canon, in this context, was not simply an imitative device at regulated intervallic and temporal distance; it was rather an inscription that was provided with the musical material, the understanding of which was necessary to the performance of the composition. The word was used in its general sense, rather than in a specifically musical one, and it had reference to law, rule, and authority. The musical result of a correct interpretation of the symbolic or poetic directions produced what the singer recognized as a compositional technique, but it was not achieved through the use of normally written notation. The works that appear in this form belong to the ubiquitous classification, "eye-music," intended for the entertainment or edification of the singer, but unknown to the listener.[36] Such compositions were not less skillfully written nor less seriously conceived than those lacking the enigmatical phrases or symbols. It is dismissing them too lightly to state that "compositions of this nature can only be regarded in the light of ingenious puzzles, bearing the same relation to music that a clever riddle does to poetry."[37] The inventiveness that is displayed in the employment of such devices may have fallen into the category of musicians' amusements, but the result was not necessarily less skilled or less seriously applied when the work was to be performed.

An easily accessible example of such a tenor is found in the Agnus Dei III of Dufay's *Missa L'Homme armé* (*HAM* 66c), the solution of which lies in the correct application of the canon, *cancer eat plenus et redeat medeus.* This phrase instructs the "crab" to proceed full and return half, ostensibly telling the singer of the tenor part to sing his part normally and then to repeat it in retrograde with halved note values. The reference to crab reverses the directional part of the instructions, inasmuch as the normal motion of the crab is backwards. The correct solution, therefore, requires that the part be sung

36. *Grove's*, II, 994ff.
37. *Ibid.*, II, 44. Cf. Willi Apel, *The Notation of Polyphonic Music: 900–1600* (Cambridge: The Mediaeval Academy of America, 1949), 179–88.

retrograde with normal note values, followed by a conventional version at halved values.

Dufay's Burgundian contemporary, Gilles Binchois *(c. 1400 – 1460),* did not avail himself of the new procedure of writing on a *cantus firmus* that was being practiced by Dufay, but apparently preferred to work in the established channels of composition. "His Mass sections either paraphrase Gregorian melodies or reveal treble-dominated style without traceable borrowings from plainsong."[38] Although Dufay and Binchois probably knew each other, there is no great correspondence in their musical styles. It should not be surprising, however, that the newer techniques of one composer of this period did not necessarily appear in the works of another.

The popularity of Tenor Masses is evident from the large number of works based upon identifiable sources. Such a tune as *L'Homme armé,* for instance, goes far toward tracing the entire history of this type of Mass, as there are dozens of known settings. Its position as a favorite melody is demonstrated by the frequency with which it appeared during the next generation of composers. The list of those who based compositions upon the tune extends all the way to Palestrina. It is, however, at the hands of Johannes Ockeghem *(c. 1420 – 1495)* that the next decisive advances in Mass composition are seen.

The fifteenth-century composers who preceded Ockeghem had experimented with changing sonorities, achieved partly by varying the numbers and combinations of voices employed, and examples are easily found of Masses *a 3, a 4,* and *a 5,* with most of the composers tending toward four-part writing. The later Masses of Dufay, as well as the bulk of Ockeghem's, fall into this pattern that has continued as the normal distribution of voices down to the present. As the number of voice parts increased, it became apparent that some adjustment would have to be made in their ranges in order to keep them clearly separated. More space for the voices was needed, so that their movement would not be impeded by the danger of their constantly encountering each other and even having to cross into each other's territory. The solution lay in the addition of a fourth voice and a slight lowering of the range of the tenor, previously the lowest voice *(Ex. 11).* The mere presence of a fourth part did not provide an immediate answer, for, "as writing *a 4* became the norm, the ad-

38. *MR,* 91.

Ex. 11 Voice ranges commonly found in three-and four-part compositions (15th century)

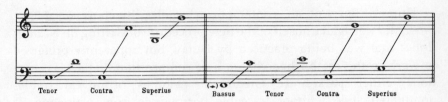

Tenor   Contra   Superius   Bassus   Tenor   Contra   Superius

ditional voice at first caused congestion to reappear, especially within the area of the inner voices."[39] As the voices finally gained working space, a further expansion of compositional technique became practical, that of moving toward a greater degree of equality for the several voices. The treble-dominated (*cantilena*) style of the previous years was destined to become a thing of the past with the new freedom achieved by the lower parts. It was now possible and practical for the *bassus*, tenor, or *altus*[40] to participate as freely in melodically interesting passages as it was previously for only the *superius* or the upper two parts. From this point onward, the type of writing that we call imitative counterpoint was open to development, culminating eventually in the free-flowing, equal interchange that typifies the works of Palestrina and other composers of the Roman school at the end of the Renaissance.

So much stress has been laid upon the technical mastery that is displayed in Ockeghem's *Missa cuiusvis toni*, a work that can be performed in any of several modes by altering the position of the clefs, and upon his *Missa prolationum (MM 17)*,[41] an artistic exercise in the writing of mensuration canons, that it is possible to lose sight of the solid mastery that he had over the normal, less contrived, means of expression that were in use during his time. His adherence to the use of familiar and favorite sources is evident in his employment as *cantus firmi* of *L'Homme armé (MSO*, 28f) and *Caput*, among others; his flexibility in the treatment of a *cantus prius factus* is an indication

39. *Ibid.*, 531.
40. In three-part writing, the designations for the voices had been tenor, contratenor, and *superius* or *discantus*. With the addition of a fourth part, to be placed below the existing tenor, the designations *contratenor altus (altus*=alto) and *contratenor bassus (bassus*=bass) came into being, the tenor and *superius* retaining their former names.
41. The complete Masses are printed in Johannes Ockeghem, *Collected Works*, ed. Dragan Plamenac, 2 vols. (New York: American Musicological Society, 1947–1959), II, 21–36 (*Missa prolationum*); I, 44–56 (*Missa cuiusvis toni*).

of his progressive outlook;[42] and his examples of Masses freely composed without a *cantus firmus* explore the possibility of composition
without resorting to contrived or restrictive patterns. Among this
last group, the *Missa Mi-mi* may serve as an example of his style. This
work belongs to the class of Masses that has no apparent or identified
source for its melodic patterns. Such a composition was often entitled
simply *Missa sine nomine* or, when the composer chose, was called
by a name that identified its mode, as *Missa quarti toni* (*Mass in
Mode* iv), the mode of *Missa Mi-mi*. This designation, which leads
the unsuspecting musician to search for a pattern of pitch repetition,[43]
is derived from the fact that its opening bass notes represent the
syllable "mi" in the natural and soft hexachords which had been
described by Guido of Arezzo in the eleventh century, and still provided the means of solmization in the fifteenth. Serving as a head-
motif in every movement, it imparts a feeling of organization to the
opening notes, even though no attempt is made to recall or imitate
the material within the movement. The rhythmic pattern is consistent
for all movements save the Gloria, and the melodic similarities extend
beyond the opening notes. The second and third settings of the
Agnus, as well, begin with the principal figure which appears also,
in elaborated form, in the Benedictus *(Ex. 12)*. In the entire Mass

Ex. 12 Head motifs from Ockeghem's *Missa Mi-mi*

42. As, for instance, in his *Missa Fors
seulement*, based on a chanson of his own
creation. As *cantus firmus* for the Mass,
Ockeghem relied principally on the
superius of this secular piece, although he
did employ its tenor at times. See *MR*,
126ff. The Kyrie is printed (in part) in
HMS, iii, 47ff.

43. The fact that the opening three notes
of the Kyrie's *superius* and Gloria's *altus*
are repetitions of that syllable may be
fortuitous, or may represent an idea that
Ockeghem found unprofitable to pursue.

(CW 4) there is little use of imitation. In every section, all four voices begin together, although some brief passages using imitation, but restricted to the opening notes, are found at *Et incarnatus* and *Et unam sanctam catholicam* in the Credo, as well as at a few other places in the Mass. Obviously Ockeghem did not feel, as did many later composers, that the absence of a *cantus firmus* required the application of another organizational principle, the use of consistent imitative writing, although he demonstrated his skill in handling canonic imitation in the *Missa prolationum*.

In an expansion of the manner in which Ockeghem created a motto for the opening of each movement, other composers wrote entire tenors that were employed as *cantus firmi*. A well-known example of an artificially contrived tenor by Josquin des Prez (c. 1445–1521) is that of the *Missa Hercules Dux Ferrariae* which, because the pitches of its distinctive theme are literally carved out of the vowels in the Duke's name and title, is called a *soggetto cavato*. The subject, in this case, was not restricted to the simple opening function that was given a motto, but served as the basis for further statements at several pitch levels in normal fashion and in crab-inversion (*cancrizans*). Clinging to statements in long note values, it created for the ear a familiar, though not tedious, pattern of inner melody. The *Missa La sol fa re mi*, apparently deriving its title simply from the constant repetition of the pitches represented by those syllables and their transpositions, but possibly stemming from either or both of two other sources,[44] employs skillful imitation in the voices other than the tenor while that voice reiterates the basic pattern in a seemingly endless variety of rhythms (*GMB*, 59).

Another type of Mass that developed during the Renaissance is the Parody Mass. Here the adoption of a *cantus firmus* from another piece, secular or sacred, was no longer the guiding principle. Instead, whole sections of the parent composition were adapted, modified, or used as they stood in the original. Inasmuch as this practice was far more frequently encountered after Josquin's time, illustration of the technique will be withheld until later in the chapter, when an example will be drawn from the works of Palestrina.

An example of the paraphrase Mass has been left to us by Josquin. In such a work, the composer employed a plainsong tenor as he did in the creation of a *cantus firmus* Mass of any other type, but this

44. *MR*, 238.

borrowed melody was elaborated by the insertion of sections, ranging from a single note to more than a dozen, that gave a melismatic sweep to the melodic contours. Such melodic transformations were not restricted to the tenor part, but permeated the entire melodic structure of the Mass, especially at the hands of Josquin, who subjected them to the technique of imitation that came to such a peak of perfection in his lifetime. His *Missa Pange lingua* (CW 1; MSO, 30–33 [Gloria only]), based on the hymn used at Second Vespers for Corpus Christi,[45] deals with the plainsong one strophe at a time. Each strophe became the basis of a polyphonic cell, the paraphrased plainsong section undergoing imitative treatment after the fashion of the points of imitation[46] that are commonly associated with the motet of this time. Because the imitation pervaded all the parts, the tenor was no longer in the position of predominance that it held when the *cantus firmus* was restricted to that voice. The equality of the voices is further evident in the fact that the tenor lacks even the prominence falling upon the first voice to sound the imitative material, that privilege falling to the other voices in nearly equal proportion, even at the beginning of movements. This free treatment of the chant has caused the work to be called a fantasy, an apt term descriptive of its freedom from the restrictions that were previously found in parts built on a *cantus firmus*. The employment of the basic material is not continuous, as "elements of the chant constantly appear and disappear, the paraphrasing taking on extraordinary variety and being conducted with such freedom that at times only reminders of the plainsong are present, though quotations are quite literal at the beginnings of movements."[47] The degree of elaboration to which the original melody is subjected is apparent in Example 13; the variety that the

Ex. 13   *a)* Hymn, *Pange lingua gloriosi, LU*, 957

Pan - ge   lin - gua   glo - ri - o -   - si

b) Josquin des Prez, *Missa Pange lingua*; Kyrie, Tenor.

Ky - ri   -   e   e - le -   - i - son

45. *LU*, 957. There are several pieces in the plainsong repertory that have the same *incipit*. Cf. the setting in Plate i.
46. The section of a polyphonic piece in which one subject and the text fragment associated with it are treated imitatively. See pp. 88f. where the technique is discussed in greater detail.
47. *MR*, 244.

composer achieves with the rhythm can best be seen from an examination of the printed editions.[48]

By the time that Josquin and Ockeghem were producing their Masses, a new attitude toward performance was beginning to make itself felt. Music for the Church was tending toward an ideal of homogeneous choral sound and, except for festive occasions, was less concerned with instrumental support for the singers. Whereas earlier generations had been accustomed to music that required either the support or equal participation of instruments, this period was establishing a practice that was typified by a cappella singing. Among the evidence supporting this view are the greater attention lavished on the relationship between text and music, the growing equality of the voices that permitted them to act as equal participants in the contrapuntal activity of the music, and the complaints against the lavish use of instruments in certain church observances. This last serves as both a symptom and evidence of change: a symptom of dissatisfaction among those who were concerned with the dignity of worship, and evidence that the practice of unaccompanied singing, or singing supported only by the organ, seemed desirable. It is not to be supposed, however, that instrumental participation disappeared from the services of the Church and that a tradition of a cappella performance was launched to reign supreme as the distinctive feature of mature Renaissance vocal style.[49] The unaccompanied singing that is generally accepted as a trade-mark of the Roman school was not, after all, an equally important element in Venetian style.[50] Neither were the resolutions of the Council of Trent so far-reaching as to suppress instrumental performance. That Council "merely recommended the avoidance of everything that was inconsistent with the dignity of the service"[51] and did not issue specific prohibitions against instrumental music. Concerning vocal style, however, the Council did make itself heard on matters of appropriateness of the music, especially in the areas of polyphony, secularism, and clarity of text. During the numerous meetings that took place between 1545 and 1563, the matter of music was considered several times. Nothing

48. Werken van Josquin des Prez uitgegeven door Prof. Dr. A. Smijers (Vereniging voor Nederlandsche Muziekgeschiedenis) (Amsterdam: G. Alsbach and Co., 1952), Vol. 33.

49. See Bridgman, op. cit., in The New Oxford History of Music, III, 251–54.

50. See Chapter III.

51. MWC, 228. See also K. G. Fellerer, "Church Music and the Council of Trent," The Musical Quarterly, xxxix/4 (October, 1943), 576–94; Hugo Leichtentritt, "The Reform of Trent and its Effect on Music," The Musical Quarterly, xxx/3 (July, 1944), 319-28; and Lewis H. Lockwood, "Vincenzo Ruffo and Musical Reform after the Council of Trent," The Musical Quarterly, xliii/3 (July, 1957), 342–71.

specific came out of the meetings, however, and the general directive that was issued had notably little effect upon those Church establishments that were not directly under the gaze of the officials in Rome. Composers who were at great distances from the Holy See (as, for instance, in Germany and France) were often little affected by the pronouncements, modifying their works only slightly, if at all. Composers who were nearer Rome, or within the city itself, naturally felt that some restraint was called for, but even they did not abandon the hard-won technical achievements of composition. Instead, they exercised a greater degree of control over their means of expression, employing the censured materials with restraint while achieving a command over their material that has been admired ever since.

As was mentioned earlier, the Parody Mass assumed a position of major importance in sacred polyphonic music. Its examples are found in the fifteenth and sixteenth centuries alike, but none are so clearly indicative of the method and variety as those of Giovanni Pierluigi da Palestrina (1525 – 1594), whose total of one hundred and five Masses contains fifty-two of the parody type. A Parody Mass is, in a way, similar to one that is based on a *cantus firmus.* However, instead of a tune from another source serving as the basis for a movement or series of movements, the harmony, texture, melodic lines, cadences, or even complete sections of the original may be employed in the Mass. The music that is chosen for the parody treatment may be drawn from another Mass, a chanson, motet, or even a madrigal — and it may be from the composer's own previous works as well as from some other's. Although we have accustomed ourselves, outside this small area of music, to imply ridicule or weak imitation in our use of the word "parody," the process that is found here reflects neither of these. It is, instead, a subtle, careful modification of the borrowed material. One method employed by Palestrina is illustrated clearly in the Agnus Dei of the *Missa Veni sponsa Christi* (*MM* 24) which may be compared, phrase by phrase, with the antiphon that served as its source. An example by Philippe de Monte (1521 – 1603), *Missa super Cara la vita*, illustrating a parody of a madrigal, is given in *HAM* 146. That the possibility of tracing the composer's methods becomes more difficult without the original material is clear when the examination of another such movement, the Benedictus from Palestrina's *Missa Lauda Sion* (*GMB* 121), reveals nothing beyond a well-constructed three-voice imitative movement. However, when the motet *Lauda Sion* (*MSO*, 52f.) is compared with the Benedictus, and with the rest of the Mass (*MSO*, 54 – 62), the relationship between the original and the parody is at once evident. Fortunately, the sources that are known to have been parodied by Palestrina may be found listed in a table compiled by Oliver Strunk,[52] where, among other clues to identification, each Mass is listed according to its type, and information is given concerning the material upon which it is based.

Because of the opportunities for variety that were available to the composer of a Parody Mass, it is difficult to isolate an example in the hope of finding it typical. Certainly no composer who undertook this genre of composition as often as did Palestrina can be typed. One of his Masses *a 8*, based on his motet *Laudate Dominum omnes gentes*,[53] illustrates one of the methods he employed in creating a parody, but what he did in this case he did not necessarily do in others. The Mass and the motet, alike, are for two SATB groups of almost equal importance, although Chorus I is allotted the responsibility of singing the opening section of every movement. Chorus II, on the other hand, rises to prominence in having the section *Et in Spiritum sanctum . . . per Prophetes* of the Credo assigned to it alone, in contrast to the preceding *a 4* setting for Chorus I of the *Crucifixus*. As may be seen in Example 14, the motet upon which the Mass is based derives its text and the general melodic outline of its opening phrase from the plain-

Ex. 14. Psalm CXVI [117], *LU*, 185

Palestrina, motet, *Laudate Dominum omnes gentes*

52. *MR*, 470ff. While this provides more information about the Masses than other lists, a comparison with the catalogue provided in *Grove's*, VI, 515 *et seq.* is helpful. The latter source, unfortunately, is not so complete as the former.
53. The motet is printed in *Giovanni Pierluigi da Palestrina: Werke*, ed. F.

Espagne, F. X. Haberl, *et al.* 33 vols. (Leipzig: Breitkopf & Härtel, 1862–1907), II, 164–68; *Le Opere Complete di Giovanni Pierluigi da Palestrina*, ed. Raffaele Casimiri (Rome: Edizione Fratelli Scalera, 1939–), VII, 219–25. The Mass appears in *Werke*, XXII, 1–39.

song setting of Psalm cxvi (117). The plainsong material is both too
brief and too unaffected to serve in any other way. The motet, consequently, is merely reminiscent of the plainsong melody. Similarly,
Palestrina borrows sparingly from the motet in his Mass, isolating
the two opening musical ideas of the motet for special attention, and
modifying the rhythm of the original material to suit the text of each
section *(Ex. 15)*. The opening of each movement employs the material
from the beginning of the motet, but its rhythmic placement is altered,

Ex. 15   Palestrina, *Missa Laudate Dominum*

as in the Kyrie, by compression of the second syllable of text, whereas the first phrase extends a greater distance than in the motet. Inasmuch as each movement of the Mass is of greater length than the motet, Palestrina undertook to delay the entrance of the second thematic section until later than it appeared in the original. Whereas in the motet the entrance of Chorus II introduces the second phrase of text and the new musical material that carries it, in the Mass that group of voices restates the music of Chorus I. The voices of the second chorus enter in the order T-B-A-S, contrasting the S-A-T-B order of Chorus I.

An exchange of voice parts and of choirs, as well, is found in the material that was set to the second phrase of text in the motet (Ex. 16). Entrances of the two choirs are in reverse order, the soprano and tenor parts interchanging while some of the florid line of the motet disappears in the setting of the Kyrie text.

Each movement of the Mass opens with the same material in some modification, although the Agnus Dei approaches a literal restatement of the model in the entrance of Chorus I. Except for the beginnings of the major sections of the Mass, and for the three instances (Kyrie, Gloria, Agnus Dei II) where the material shown in Example 16 is used, the Mass is largely made up of free composition similar to, but not identical with, the motet.

One other type of Mass must also be mentioned here, the substitution Mass. "Such works consist entirely or mainly of a series of motets, each intended to replace a liturgical Mass movement (both the Ordinary and the Proper being involved)."[54] This process involved not merely the insertion of a piece in motet style in place of the Mass section, but the deletion of the liturgically correct text and the substitution of another that served as a commentary upon it, somewhat in the manner of a polyphonic trope. Substitution Masses were rare, for they exist only in a few manuscript sources. Still, a considerable amount of interaction between motet and Mass must have been evident during the entire polyphonic period even though it has gone unremarked in some quarters. The general musical usage that restricts the meaning of "Mass" to designate only the Ordinary serves to illustrate the degree of freedom that must have existed in connection with the settings of texts of the Proper. In the prevailing meaning of the term, the cycles of the Proper are actually series of motets. That

54. *MR*, 227.

these cycles are not numerous has been stated before; that they were less necessary than the settings of the Ordinary because of the already available settings of various sections is evident. The first cycle of the Proper after Leonin's effort is that of Heinrich Isaac *(c. 1450–1517)* who, in the *Choralis Constantinus,* provided "a group of motets in the form of polyphonic settings of portions of the proper of the

Ex.16 Palestrina, motet, *Laudate Dominum omnes gentes*

Mass (Roman rite) for all Sundays of the liturgical year, of the commons of the Saints, and of propers for most of the principal feasts and Saints' days."[55] This effort of high quality, amazing when one views its bulk alone, dates from the first quarter of the sixteenth century. In the last two decades of the same century Jacobus Gallus (Jakob Handl) (1550?–1591) produced his *Opus musicum*, (example in *HMS*, IV, 32f), four books of such motets, and in 1605 and 1607 William Byrd's (1543–1623) two books of *Gradualia*, similar in function and scale, appeared.[56] Although none of these works altered the course of motet or Mass composition, they deserve mention if only for the immensity of their concept and for the evidence they present of the intermingling of the motet and the Mass. Their size alone does not make these cycles worthy of attention, but the fact that they were written by leading composers brings them into prominence.

It must not be believed that the few composers discussed here were responsible for all of the changes that appeared in Mass composition during the sixteenth century. Virtually every Renaissance composer wrote for the Church, and Masses and motets were their normal products. While the principal features of compositional technique are represented by the composers with whom we have been concerned, there are dozens of others whose prodigious and often equally excellent output must be considered if a complete picture of that period is to emerge. The need for music was international, the number of composers was legion, and the product varied according to the tastes, talents, and traditions that were concerned with it. It is impossible in a general study of church music to examine the situation in greater detail than has been attempted here. A few additional names, however, will serve as a reminder that Masses were composed in quantity everywhere that the Church had a fully staffed establishment. The internationally recognized figures Isaac and Lassus (over fifty Masses survive from the pen of the latter); the well-traveled Netherlander, Pierre de la Rue, who wrote more than thirty-five; the Venetian Gabrielis, better known for their contributions to motet literature; the Spaniards, Victoria, Morales, and Guerrero; and Taverner, Tye, and Byrd among the English, are but a few of the large number of composers who wrote Masses of the mature types we have examined.

55. Louise Cuyler, *Heinrich Isaac's Choralis Constantinus, Book III* (Ann Arbor: University of Michigan Press, 1950), 15.

56. James L. Jackman, "Liturgical Aspects of Byrd's *Gradualia*," *The Musical Quarterly*, xlix/1 (January, 1963), 17–37.

Chapter III

The Motet in the Middle Ages

and Renaissance

THERE is no single definition that can be used to identify the motet at all stages of its development. It is impossible, therefore, to speak of a motet form or a motet style in general terms; each large period of its historical growth stands apart clearly from the others. From its first appearance on the musical scene, and until the development of polyphonic settings of the Ordinary, the motet was the principal genre of polyphonic music. As interest shifted to the more stable settings of Mass cycles, the motet became less important. It never slipped from a firm position of secondary importance, however, until the emergence of the new multi-movement forms, which arose with the Baroque practices, overshadowed it.

One widely circulated definition for this important form reads: "As a rule, a motet is an unaccompanied choral composition, based on a Latin sacred text, and designed to be performed in the Catholic service, chiefly at Vespers."[1] While this explanation serves well enough for certain stages of the motet's development, it is not sufficient for the entire period during which the term remains viable. The inability to encompass the many changing features of style and structure in a single sentence reflects the breadth of development that took place. There are many instances where the voices are either duplicated by instruments, substituted for by instruments, or accompanied; there are numerous examples that have no sacred text or function; and, in the case of religious motets, the form eventually appeared in nearly every portion of the Catholic service that was not a part of the Ordinary. We have, in fact, already noted its occasional presence there, as well, in the substitution Mass (cf. p. 64). Since it is obviously impractical to expect a single definition to serve here, a discussion of

1. *HD*, 457.

each major period will be undertaken in which the distinctive features of each type of motet can be seen.

The motet emerged as a leading type of organum along with another form called the conductus. While the two were probably of nearly equal importance for a time, the motet became the preferred means of communicating religious ideas through music. As we shall see, however, its structure much of the time caused it to convey text far less clearly than did the less complicated conductus. The comparison of these two forms is best undertaken by viewing their state of development at the beginning of the thirteenth century.

The polyphonic conductus was based on a Latin poetic text which was sung simultaneously by two or three voices, including a tenor which was based on an invented melody and not on a liturgical chant. The conductus had the advantage of clear, simultaneous utterance of its single text by all the singers. Its communicative power was, therefore, potentially forceful. At the same time, the absence of any liturgical connection must have stood in the way of its common application to the formal process of worship. The strength that was already inherent in the simultaneous presentation of the text was further reinforced by a note-against-note style of writing, which often produced parts that were nearly identical in rhythm.[2] The influence of the conductus style has already been mentioned in connection with the Tournai Mass (*cf. p. 45*) and it can be seen as well in the structure of the first class of motet, which will be discussed shortly. While the other polyphonic forms were copied into manuscript books with the parts distributed over one or two pages in the so-called choirbook arrangement—a method that was in use at least until the early seventeenth century[3]—the conductus was written in score form, an arrangement probably deriving from the felicitous combination of rhythm and text. (See Plate II.)

The motet had neither the simplicity of metrical text nor, generally, the communicative qualities of rhythmic forthrightness. It provided, however, a form which was rooted in the established liturgical practices that had already become accepted in other areas of organum. It offered, as well, almost limitless possibilities for experimental composition and, as will be evident, continuous development.

2. Examples of the two- and three-voice conductus may be found in *HAM* 38 and 39; *MM* 11; *EM*, 41–44; and *GMB* 16.
3. As, for example, in J. H. Schein's *Leipziger Kantional* of 1627. Facsimile in Friedrich Blume, *Die Evangelische Kirchen-* *musik*, Vol. X of *Handbuch der Musikwissenschaft*, ed. Ernst Bücken (13 vols. in 10; Potsdam: Akademische Verlagsgesellschaft Athenaion, 1927–1934; reprinted, New York: Musurgia, [1949?]), 82f.

Those sections of the *Magnus Liber* that were set in measured style were known as *clausulae*. They were based upon brief melismatic sections of the chant which, in turn, served as *cantus firmi* of polyphonic compositions. As such a melisma originally carried no text, but expanded the length of a single syllable, the *clausula* lacked words. It served only as a more elaborate musical expression than did its antecessor. The *incipit,* serving to identify the text upon which the musical idea was based, is presently incorporated into titles of motets to specify the source of their materials. The plainsong given in Example 17 was used in a number of compositions based upon such segments during the twelfth and thirteenth centuries.[4]

This chant, along with many others, served as the basis for organa, *clausulae,* and motets, all of which employed some portion of the original material as their tenors. In one of these elaborations (*HAM* 28d), section "A" in Example 17 was retained as plainsong for the chorus, section "B" was given to soloists as a *clausula* (an expansion of *Domino*), and "C" was again assigned to the chorus. *Clausulae* such as this became the first motets. Two notable features at this stage of development are the absence of any text from the upper part of the *clausula* and the distinctly different rhythm given to the two parts, the upper (textless) voice being considerably more active. The only difference between the *clausula* and the early motet lies in the addition of words *(mots)* to the upper part of the parent form, producing not a new form, but a more easily communicated version of the old. It should be noted here that the motet is essentially a trope. The addition of new words to the existing liturgical text, the creation of new musical ideas, and the insertion of these materials as interrup-

Ex. 17 *Benedicamus Domino, LU,* 124

4. *HAM* 28 illustrates the varied uses of this tune. The development of the early motet is shown in the examples, *HAM* 28–35.

PLATE 2a. *The conductus-motet* Laus domino—Eius, *and the upper parts of* Homo qui vigeas—Et gaudebit, *showing the pairing of* duplum *and* triplum *in score form. The pieces, from MS Wolfenbüttel 1206, are printed in Apel's* Notation of Polyphonic Music, *p. 275, and are reprinted here by permission of* The Mediaeval Academy of America.

tions in the worship service are features that appear with the earliest motets. The textual relationship of upper parts to the tenor creates a trope that is vertical, in contrast to the horizontal structure of monophonic tropes. This upper part, previously designated as *duplum,* now took on the name *motetus,* a term that carried over to identify the entire composition. The part or parts above the *motetus* retained the names they had been given in organum, *triplum* and *quadruplum.* When the parts above the tenor bear different texts, the composition is sometimes called "double motet" if two texts are involved, or "triple motet" if there are three. This terminology has not been generally ac-

PLATE 2b. *The motet* Salve, laborancium — Celi luminarium —
Omnes, *and the beginning of* Ut celesti possimus — Cum sit natus
hodie — Hec dies, *in choirbook arrangement. From Aubry,* Cent
Motets du XIIIe siècle, *f. 11vo.* (Printed by permission of Editions
Salabert.)

cepted, and the practice will not be followed here. A number of
clearly definable motet types may be found in thirteenth-century
manuscripts, illustrating several stages of development and some differences of function.

The first of these types clearly points to a relationship with the
conductus; so much so, in fact, that the name conductus-motet has
been adopted to describe it. Its upper two, or more rarely, three,
voices move in the manner of a conductus, carrying the same text and,
with only minor deviations, the same rhythm. The tenor carries a different text which, being incomplete, appears only as an *incipit,* and

71

is slower in rhythm (*HAM* 32c). The upper parts of the conductus-motet are written in score form, as was the conductus itself; the tenor appears separately because of its different rhythmic character and its correspondingly different length.[5] These motets, and much other music of the thirteenth century, employ modal rhythms, an organizational device to be discussed subsequently. In the meantime, it may be noted that in Example 18, which shows the opening measures of a conductus-motet, both the *motetus* and the *triplum* are in the third mode, the tenor is in the fifth. Because the tenors were slow, bore no text, and were not continuous melodic parts, it has been postulated that they were either vocalized on a single vowel or performed instrumentally. Any of the parts, of course, could as easily have been duplicated or replaced by instruments. Because of their presence in the earlier manuscripts of the period, and their absence from those of later date, conductus-motets are believed to be the earliest of the motet types. The later developments of the thirteenth century show a distinct tendency toward independence of the upper voices in both rhythm and text, something the conductus-motet had not been able to achieve.

The application of the rhythmic modes created a rhythmic inflexibility that kept the conductus-motet from having texted parts clearly separable. This group of six basic patterns served as the groundwork of an organizational principle that lasted through the thirteenth century, to be replaced only by a more abstruse principle, isorhythm. Each of these modes has been identified by a Greek name, but this method of association is less common than that of referring to the modes by number. Nevertheless, both systems are shown in Table

Ex. 18

Opening section of *Laus Domino — Eius*, Conductus-motet

5. Apel, *The Notation of Polyphonic Music: 900–1600*, 275, contains an example of this practice in the facsimile of the manuscript that includes the motet *Laus domino — Eius*. See Plate 2 *supra*.

III. It was not until the end of the century — a case of identification after the fact — that the clear relationship of these modes with the poetic feet of classical poetry was made.

TABLE III

The Rhythmic Modes

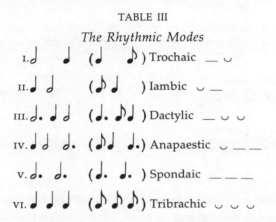

All parts of the motet were affected by these modes, but the first to show their strong influence were the tenors. When a passage from chant was adapted to serve as a motet tenor, it lost much of its identity with plainsong by being forced into a rigid rhythmic pattern that was taken from the modes. These tenors did not flow continuously without interruption, but were periodically broken up by rests. Thus, a tenor written in the first mode was not a regular alternation of long and short notes; nor was one in the fifth mode a succession of long values, but rather an arrangement of these patterns into regular groupings called *ordines*. This was especially true of the motet types that followed the conductus-motet. Such an *ordo*, in any mode, was identified numerically to signify the number of times the modal pattern appeared before it was interrupted by a rest equal to one of the note values of the mode. Finally, these patterns were further identified as perfect or imperfect, as shown in Example 19. This may be compared to what we now call strong and weak beats — although it should be remembered that measure bars were not involved. A perfect mode always finished with a note in "strong" position, and an imperfect mode finished with a "weak" one.

Although these principles have been described in connection with the tenors, they could, in theory, be extended to the upper parts as well. In fact, however, certain modifications were common: the *motetus* and *triplum*, more concerned with melodic qualities and text than were the tenors, were long-breathed, free-flowing tunes and not

Ex. 19 Samples of *ordines*

well suited to the regular interruptions of *ordines;* the modes were not strictly followed throughout a voice part or a composition—a shift might be made from one mode to another, or the employment of a single mode could be varied by dividing or combining the basic values, thus producing other combinations of long and short rhythms. The upper parts did not usually share the same mode, except in the conductus-motet, where two or three parts were composed with nearly identical rhythm, but even there a degree of variety was achieved by placing these concerted rhythms against a highly contrasting, formalized, repetitive pattern in the tenor. In the other motet forms of the thirteenth century, as we shall now see, greater variety resulted from the freeing of the upper parts from each other, rhythmically and textually.

Near the middle of the century there became prominent a type of motet that bore different Latin texts in its upper parts. These texts often kept some relationship to each other, and to the tenor as well. The result was not simply one of conflicting texts being sung at the same moment, but of two or more sets of words approaching a single idea from several directions. The texts of the upper parts were, in effect, tropes of the tenor. One method of identifying this type of motet is to call it "classical." That term is a misnomer. This type of motet is more properly called the Latin motet, since its texts are exclusively in that language, and it represents only one of several stages of development in a short period of time. *Salve virgo—Verbum caro—Veritatem (MET 3)* is such a Latin motet, as is *Ave gloriosa mater—Ave Virgo—*

Domino (TEM, 46–53). *Mariae assumptio—Huius chori,* without a tenor *incipit (GMB* 19), may be considered a variant of this type, both of the upper parts bearing Latin text. The tenor of the middle (vocal) section of the piece employs an exact repetition of its tune, resembling two *taleae* of isorhythm, an uncommon feature of this period. The repetition of extended tenor passages found in French motets soon after this appears to be unrelated.

The sometimes close relationship between the texts is best illustrated in *Alle, psallite cum luya—Alleluya (EM,* 67ff and *HAM* 33a), in which the upper parts are simply troping the tenor *incipit* while engaging in an interplay of *stimmtausch.* This close relationship of texts in Latin would seem to have been short-lived, for the encroachment of French texts, many of which have seemingly little connection with the original tenor source, is apparent from about the middle of the century. It is at this point that one of the periodic cries of secularism in Church is raised, for love songs abound in the French texts and the name of God is as often raised as an exclamation as it is in devotion. Still, it must be remembered that the motet was not the sole property of the Church musician; it had a vital place in the courtly life of the time and was probably sung on numerous occasions outside the Church, many of the pieces in this form being intended only for secular use. The motet was no more the exclusive possession of the Church than the plagal cadence is in our time. While some of these distinctly worldly features must have made their way into religious music, their presence was no more disproportionate than it has been at any other time, if we are to accept the near absence of contemporary complaints as evidence. The importance of secular-religious text conflicts often may have been exaggerated because the secular motets were—for a time, at least—based on the same tenors as were the motets for use in Church. The tenor of the motet *En non Diu—Quant voi—Eius in Oriente (MM* 10 and *MSO,* 18) is taken from an Alleluia, but there is no cause to believe that the melisma that provided the melodic basis for the tenor, or the *incipit* that remained attached to it, indicates that the piece was destined for Church performance. In the Bamberg MS, Ed. IV. 6,[6] the same motet, bearing the variant title *En non Dieu—Quant voi—Nobis,* appears as one of 108 pieces, some entirely with Latin texts, some with French texts to the upper parts, and

6. The entire MS is reproduced in facsimile and transcription in Pierre Aubry, *Cent Motets du* XIII*ᵉ siècle* (Paris: A. Rouart, Lerolle & Co., 1908).

some with combinations of Latin and French. While this indicates a possibility that there may have been no separate group of soloists to perform in the church while another performed outside, it does not prove, or even imply, a common practice of inserting love lyrics into the service.

The motets with texts in both French and Latin[7] *(Ex. 20)*, or two French texts with Latin *incipit* in the tenor, show a separation between the textual and musical relationships of the upper voices that continued to increase until the end of the century. The differences between the texts, and in their poetic rhythms, was probably instrumental in bringing about a standard pattern of characteristics: a slow, formalized tenor; a moderately paced, melodically interesting *motetus;* and a rapid *triplum* of wider range than the other parts (*HAM* 28h2 and 34). The type of composition that first showed the parts disposed in such fashion was known as the Franconian motet, after Franco of Cologne (11th or 12th century) who was associated with the development of the notational practices that made it possible. This difference in the function of the voices lasted, with more or less the same distribution of activity, until the advent of imitative writing, an event that again turned the various parts toward equality of interest, speed, conveyance of text, and involvement in thematic statement that they had attained—at least in the upper parts—with the conductus-motet. The movement of text from Latin toward the vernacular became complete with the fully established French motet (*HAM* 33b; *EM,* 63f; *EM,* 79; *MSO,* 19), although the presence of text in all parts should be recognized as a hallmark of the secular motet in the thirteenth century. The religious motet at this point, while showing

Ex. 20 Beginning of motet *Or voi je bien—Eximium decus virginum—Virgo,*
after Aubry, II, 63

7. A comparatively rare type. *El mois de mai—De se debent—Kyrie* is printed in Aubry, *op. cit.,* ɪɪ, 53f and *GMB* 18. See also Aubry, *op. cit.,* ɪɪ, 63ff, 66f, 71ff, 99–102, 147–50, 151f, and 185f for further examples.

greater freedom in text subjects, remained firmly tied to textless tenors based on liturgical chant.

The freeing of the top part of the motet was the result of Franco's work in connection with musical notation. Modal rhythm, although highly useful as a method of organizing musical material, carried within its very principles a lack of flexibility. Music based on the rhythmic modes was forced to conform to the combinations that resulted from repetitions of these modal patterns. One of the advantages of Franco's system lay in the possibility of dividing the rhythmic patterns of the modes—for his notation was still built on their materials—into predictably measurable fractions. His *Ars Cantus Mensurabilis* codified the notational practices that had been developing in connection with the division of the *longa, brevis,* and *semibrevis.* By using the Franconian system, a musician could be assured that what he had conceived would be performed. To a far greater extent than before, his manuscript could be translated into the exact rhythmic values he had composed. This mensural notation marked the beginning of really measurable music.[8]

It was apparently not long before a weakness was discovered in this important new system. The *brevis* could not be divided into more than three smaller values; the flexibility of the new procedure was limited. It cannot be believed that the solution to this problem lay entirely in the hands of one man, any more than the development of Franconian notation can be credited entirely to Franco. The problem that existed must have been apparent to every composer who tried the new ideas and found them full of promise while still restricting the imagination. The further division of note values served to encompass groups of four to seven smaller notes within the value of a *brevis.* These new note forms eventually appeared under the names of *minima* and *semiminima,* but were first merely identified as regroupings of the *semibrevis* at the hands of Petrus de Cruce (13th century), the man who introduced this new notation and its product, the Petronian motet. His *Aucun—Lonc tans—Annuntiantes (HAM 34)* is discussed by Apel[9] (cf. *HAM* 35).

8. The system is explained in detail in Apel, *op. cit.,* 310–18, and *MMA,* 289ff. Simplified explanations may be found in *HWM,* 101f and 127f, and in Homer Ulrich and Paul A. Pisk, *A History of Music and Musical Style* (New York: Harcourt, Brace & World, 1963), 74ff.

9. Apel, *op. cit.,* 318–24. A facsimile of the work in manuscript is included.

Inasmuch as the thirteenth century was the spawning ground of the motet, and the form had such a strong influence on the development of religious music, it will be well to review its development up to this point schematically.

TABLE IV

Types of Thirteenth-Century Motet

Clausula	Textless, with *incipit* in tenor; the addition of text to *duplum* caused the form to be known as motet.
Motet	At least two texts are used, even if only one is complete. Most thirteenth-century tenors continued to bear only an *incipit* instead of complete text. Usually three-voiced; tenor, *motetus* (formerly *duplum*), and *triplum*. Fourth voice, when present, is called *quadruplum*.
Conductus-motet	Upper parts moving in nearly identical rhythms, bearing a single text. Tenor in slower note values.
Latin motet	Upper parts with different Latin texts and different rhythms as demanded by meter of the poems. Use of rhythmic modes and *ordines*.
	Some motets have Latin *motetus* and French *triplum*, and vice-versa.
French motet (two types):	Both types have French texts in *motetus* and *triplum*, usually Latin *incipit* in tenor. Some secular motets carry a complete French text in the tenor.
a. Franconian	Slow tenor; moderate, lyrical *motetus;* fairly rapid *triplum.* Interest is transferred to the *triplum.*
b. Petronian	Further division of time-values caused the *triplum* to take on extravagant mannerisms.

The intellectual climate of fourteenth-century France was not suitable to the continued growth of the motet. Where it survived at all, it was as an outmoded form, refined rather than experimental. The spirit of the time favored secular art, a fact that is evident in the quantity of polyphonic *rondeaux, virelais, ballades,* and other fixed forms in France, not to mention the *caccie, ballate,* and madrigals that sprang up in Italy where new religious music was even less in evidence than in France.[10] Even Guillaume de Machaut, the poet-musician who stands as the symbol of compositional achievement for this period, was more concerned with the secular music of his time than he was with the sacred—at least, the former has survived in greater quantity. His works, and those of his contemporaries, indicate that the style of religious music was reserved and reactionary, that of secular music adventurous and exploratory. With some few exceptions, this has been true ever since.

There was no avoidance of elaborate structural elements in the religious music of this period, but, if Machaut's practice indicates either the standard procedure or the most adept, it must be granted that there was also no clear distinction between style and function in the motet. His French motets, although bearing Latin *incipits* for their tenors, were set in isorhythmic structure, just as were the Latin motets. At this point it was not only music for the Church that had become reactionary, but the motet form, whatever its function or subject may have been.

During Machaut's youth a work appeared that established firmly the new principle of isorhythm. The *Roman de Fauvel*, a long (3,280 verses), satirical poem, was directed against abuses of power by the clergy and the Templars. In 1316, two years after its completion, Chaillou de Pesstain added a group of 130 pieces of music to the poem. These compositions were not original with the interpolator, who was probably one Raoul Chaillou, but his "contributions, with or without music, are glosses, marginal and interlinear as it were, to the poem of Gervais de Bus,"[11] the man from whose imagination the entire work had sprung. The compositions added by Raoul are varied in style, complexity, and texture. Their ancestry is likewise catholic, for they are taken from the literature of *rondeaux* as well as responds, *ballades* as well as motets. The motets do not contribute directly to the literature of religious music, but they do show a mixture of the styles of the preceding century and of the newer techniques, some of them at the hands of Philippe de Vitry (1291–1361), whose treatise, *Ars nova*, provided the name by which we know that period. The compositions that were gathered there to illustrate and enliven the text of Gervais's poem were not intended—in their function, at any rate—to be sung in connection with religious services. No more, perhaps, were many of the other motets that stem from this period. The

10. *MWC*, 152–55.
11. Leo Schrade (ed.), *Polyphonic Music*   *of the Fourteenth Century: Commentary to Volume* i, 20.

motets of Philippe de Vitry or Machaut do not have a Church connection merely through the presence of Latin text, for this is no longer a sure sign of their function. These works serve as illustrations of the new principle of isorhythm which, similarly, is not restricted to works with Latin texts, but pervades the motet in all its areas of use; Church, court entertainments, ceremonial and laudatory occasions. Machaut's three motets with French tenors are non-isorhythmic, not necessarily indicating that a different attitude accompanied the setting of secular poems, but reflecting the fact that tenors from non-Church sources already possessed a rhythmic organization that required no further adaptation. The isorhythmic principle, and the motet style as well, were temporarily of greater significance as they affected the Ordinary of the Mass which, once established, took over the predominant place in Church music — the place held earlier by the motet. Except for some relatively few English examples in the older style prevalent in the Worcester school (*HAM* 57), the tendency of the fourteenth century was toward secular music and a further separation of the rhythmic and textual relationship of the voice parts.

As these parts achieved increasing degrees of independence, the unity that is necessary to music was retained through more careful organization within the parts rather than between them. The foremost method of establishing this unity was through isorhythmic and isomelic construction, devices that most often served the tenor, but sometimes extended their control into the upper parts as well. The rhythmic features were the more important of the two. Described as a "logical development of the modal rhythm of the 13th century,"[12] the new procedure differs from the old mainly in the variety and length of the basic pattern. While the modal rhythms were made up of numerous repetitions of short, breathless patterns, the isorhythmic sections (*taleae*), while sometimes not much longer than the older rhythmic *ordines*, were not bound to a rule of reiteration of short fragments. They could be modified by such means as diminution, or the variable repetition of the melodic pattern (*color*) which often added interest and complexity by not coinciding with the length of the *talea*.

One such isorhythmic motet, *De bon espoir — Puisque la douce — Speravi*,[13] illustrates Machaut's adoption of this principle not only

12. *HD*, 367.
13. Guillaume de Machaut, *Musikalische Werke*, ed. Friedrich Ludwig (Leipzig: Breitkopf & Härtel, 1926 – [the fourth volume was edited by Heinrich Besseler, the entire printing destroyed in an air raid, and again printed in 1954]), iv. Cf. Chapter ii, n. 10.

for the tenor, but for the *duplum* and *triplum* as well, although some slight modifications were required in the upper voices. The tenor, in which four statements of the *color* are completed in the same time required for six *taleae*, is diagrammed by Grout.[14]

The isorhythmic principle is applied to both the tenor and contratenor of Machaut's *Christe, qui lux — Veni, creator spiritus — Tribulatio proxima est*, a motet *a 4* with *introitus*.[15] The diagram provided here *(Ex. 21)* shows that there are two *colores*, one each for the tenor and contratenor, and differing in length. This difference is compensated for by a corresponding inequality in the two *taleae*. That of the tenor

Ex. 21 Machaut, *Christe, qui lux es — Veni, creator spiritus — Tribulatio proxima est*, after PolMus III, 14-21

14. *HWM*, 111. The example appears to be based on Ludwig's transcription. Schrade's version, while differing in metrical divisions, produces the same relationships.
15. Machaut, *Musikalische Werke*, III, 73–

78; *Polyphonic Music of the Fourteenth Century*, III, 13–21. Still another of Machaut's isorhythmic motets, *Ton corps — De souspirant — Suspiro*, is printed in *MET* 5.

has fewer notes (ten) than that of the contratenor (twelve), but they each complete their statements in the same time, making it possible for four *taleae* to coincide with the completion of one *color*. Their relationship in the complete motet can be expressed in the formula, $8t=2c$. Despite the difference in the number of notes involved in the two parts, each contains the equivalent of thirty breves. One slight modification is present in the *color* of the contratenor: the last two notes are employed only in the first statement, where they complete the fourth *talea* and also serve as a melodic link to the repetition of the melody. Another internal organizational device becomes apparent from Schrade's transcription,[16] in which each *talea* is seen to consist of five groups of six measures each (*Ex. 22a*). When the time values appear in diminution, the *talea* extends over only half as many measures (*Ex. 22b*).

Here, even as in the case of Mass movements that were products of the isorhythmic idea, the question may be raised about the musical value of such esoteric devices. Inasmuch as isorhythm is usually not

Ex. 22 *a)* Six-measure *talea*

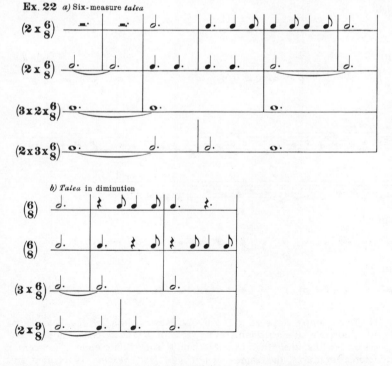

b) Talea in diminution

16. In the contratenor, his ○ should be read as ○ ♩ , and, in the second half, the pattern in diminution should be changed from ♩ to ♩ ♩ , as in Example 22.

audible because of its length and complexity, it serves no immediate need of the listener or composer. Its presence is less closely related to function than it is to attitude. Two attitudes of medieval man involved his penchant for mysticism and his idea of the position of the arts in his world. The mystical concept was already strong in the mind of the thirteenth-century composer who joined together texts that seem ill-assorted to us, but which appeared quite normal to him. The idea of mysticism continued through the Middle Ages. To illustrate some features of this apparent dichotomy we can consider the anonymous thirteenth-century motet, *Cil s' entremet—Nus hons—Victime*.[17] Its tenor is isomelic, made up of five statements of the first two phrases (fifteen notes) of the Easter sequence, *Victimae paschali laudes (MM 3)*,[18] set to the first mode, first *ordo*, perfect *(Ex. 23)*. The rhythmic organization serves to minimize the possibility of easy recognition of the tune and, since it was probably played rather than sung, there was no text to help identify it. The composition is obviously not designed for religious use. The question, then, arises over the choice of the tenor tune. It is not beyond reason to see a relationship between an Easter melody and springtime, between springtime and love. If such relationships are deemed possible, the connection between the tenor and the love poems of the *motetus* and *triplum* becomes clear. The symbolic unity of the parts of a bilingual motet has been discussed by Grout.[19]

The upper voices of our example engage in a quasi-philosophical debate over the merits of love, holding up a mirror to two opposing views. The music to which these poems are set is also organized into *ordines*, each of the parts in a different *ordo* for most of the time, and both sharing the first mode with the tenor. The poems, both of which could not possibly be followed at one hearing, are printed in their entirety.

Ex. 23 Part of Easter sequence

LU, 708

In Mode I, Ordo I, perfect.

17. Aubry, *op. cit.*, ɪɪ, 159f.   19. *HWM*, 93f.
18. *LU*, 780.

Triplum

Cil s'entremet de folie	He undertakes a foolish thing
Qui contre amours vuelt parler,	Who would speak against love,
Car honour et courtoisie	For one learns honor
Aprent on d'amer;	And courtesy from loving;
Et pour ce ne doit on mie	Therefore one must not
Bone amour blasmer,	Find fault with virtuous love
Mais loialment sans boisdie	But faithfully, without guile
La doit cil garder	Must that one cherish it
Qui joie en vuelt recouvrer,	Who would obtain joy from it,
Et garder qu'il n'en mesdie	And [he must] take care not to speak ill
De s'amie	Of his beloved,
Qu'il doit honourer;	Whom he must honor;
Car, s'il en dit vilanie,	For if he says slanderous things about her,
Nul confort n'i doit trouver.	He is unlikely to find solace in it.

Motetus

Nus hons ne pourroit savoir	No one could know
Que c'est, d'amer par amours,	What it is like to love in earnest,
Car tels sent peinne en espoir,	For such a one suffers while hoping
Qu'avoir en puist les douchours,	That he may enjoy the sweetness of it,
Et sert loialment tous jours	And he serves faithfully always
Qui n'en puet avoir	Who cannot derive from it
Soulas ne secours:	Pleasure or advantage:
Fors mals et doulours,	Only pain and suffering,
Ce couvient il recevoir;	This he is bound to undergo;
Dont il me semble pour voir	Hence it seems to me indeed
Que c'est grant folours	That it is a great folly
D'amer ou l'en a pouoir	To love when one is able
D'avenir, car c'est labours	To resist it, for it is labor
Sans preu avoir.	Without profit.

trans. HENRY L. ROBINSON

The place of music among the arts in medieval times was also far different from its place throughout the later periods of history. While it is possible that the untutored considered music only from the standpoint of its joyful sounds, its excitement, and its tunefulness, it is music's place in learned and ecclesiastical circles that concerns us here, for it was at the hands of cultivated people that polyphony was developed. Music, with them, stood as a speculative pursuit, one of the sciences comprising the *quadrivium* — arithmetic, astronomy, geometry, and music. The treatises containing the rules for musical composition concern themselves with matters of measurement, and with the consideration of consonance and dissonance. Attention is centered on discipline, authority, and organization; not on beauty at their expense.

The fifteenth century was not one of the great periods in motet history, any more than was the fourteenth. The earlier century established firmly the growing complexity of structure that was provided by isorhythm, and the longer, unified compositions that were possible through its use. The later century, while continuing to employ isorhythm, was also characterized by the abandonment of polytextuality (and, naturally then, of polylingualism) and the *cantus firmus* upon which isorhythmic tenors had necessarily been built. A new freedom was then possible to composers. They created from their own imaginations the entire composition instead of, as earlier, composing some new parts to set above their variation of a pre-existent tune that served as the basis for the tenor. A return was made to one of the advantageous features of the conductus-motet — the utterance of a single text by all voices. At the same time, this presentation of text was largely limited to nonsynchronous entrances because of the requirements of imitative counterpoint. This preference for single texts and free composition did not make itself felt all at one moment. There are many examples of early fifteenth-century motets that follow the models of the preceding decades; isorhythmic with *cantus firmus* tenors, polylingual or entirely French. These styles continued until the century was well under way. Their disappearance, and the emergence of some new principles will be seen at the hands of Dunstable and Dufay, the same leaders who were of such importance to the development of the Mass.

A strong sphere of motet activity in England is most apparent in the music of Dunstable, whose spiritual relationship to Dufay has so often been remarked. Other English motets, both identified and anonymous, exist in various sources, but those of Dunstable represent what is most probably the entire range of artistic accomplishment by English composers. Seven types of writing have been credited to him by Bukofzer.[20] Interesting as these types are, they do not open new paths for another generation of composers. Instead, they serve to mark the distinctive genius of a single composer who stands as a symbol of English greatness at the end of the Middle Ages. The English style of the period (cf. pp. 48f.) is evident in the works of Dunstable and his contemporaries, but those who had less contact with European activity during these years (as well as in the generation after Dunstable) continued on a reactionary path in composition. Dunstable's motets range from the simple setting of a single text (HAM 62) to the isorhythmic *Veni sancte spiritus—Veni creator.*[21] His interest in isorhythm is evident in a dozen examples of that type, scarcely fewer than the number of other motets he has left. The triadic structure that is a strong feature of his style is apparent in the outlines of his melodies.

There is no composer better suited than Dufay, who was weaned from his early training in the older French style by his acquaintance with the more loosely constructed, melodious Italian style, to illustrate the concurrent mastery of the musical vocabularies of the waning Middle Ages and the rising Renaissance. The mathematical complexities so beloved of the *ars nova* are present in a number of Dufay's motets, involving not only the lower voices, as was the case in those of the preceding century, but restricting the free movement of every voice in the piece, as in the motet in honor of Saint Andrew, apostle; *Apostolo glorioso—Cum tua doctrina—Andreas.*[22] This opens with a textless *introitus* which gives promise of imitative writing between the two upper parts, and between the two contratenors as well, the latter pair presenting a different motive from that of the former. After the *introitus,* the composition is isorhythmic in all voices. The text of the *triplum* is shared by the contratenor and that of the *motetus* by

20. *The New Oxford History of Music,* III, 186–93; *MMA,* 414–18. Some activity before Dunstable's time is appraised in Kenneth Jay Levy, "New Material on the Early Motet in England: A Report on Princeton Ms. Garrett 119," *Journal of the American Musicological Society,* IV/3 (Fall, 1951), 220–39.
21. John Dunstable, *Complete Works,* ed. Manfred F. Bukofzer (*Musica Britannica,*

VIII; London: Stainer and Bell, 1953), 88–91; *The Old Hall Manuscript,* II, 66–76; *DTÖ,* XIV/XV, 203–207; *HMS,* III, 32–35. A modern edition is published by C. F. Peters Corporation.
22. Guglielmi Dufay, *Opera Omnia,* ed. Guillaume de Van (*Corpus Mensurabilis Musicae,* I; Rome: American Institute of Musicology in Rome, 1948), I(2), 11–16.

the second contratenor, and the continuity of the voices is broken several times by the absence of text, indicating that instrumental performance of the interludes was expected. The tenor states twice an antiphon for Vespers and Lauds for the feast of Saint Andrew. Each statement is divided into two *taleae* and the second of these statements is written in note values three times as fast as the first. The piece is apparently *a 6*, but is actually intended to be performed either *a 3* or *a 5*. The sixth voice, a *solus tenor*, is derived from the two contratenors and tenor, and contributes nothing to the rhythmic vitality of the piece.[23] As a composite voice, it also adds no new pitches.

A number of features linking Dufay to the earlier motet tradition are apparent here. The *introitus* generally appears only in the older practice. The involvement of all voices in isorhythm is simply a refinement, albeit a highly skillful one, of the employment of the process in the two lower parts. The optional nature of the performance method and the creation of a sixth voice as a composite of several others, on the other hand, are steps in a new direction.

Another example of Dufay's preoccupation with what appear to be primarily mechanical features of composition may be seen in the motet *Inclita stella maris*.[24] It contains no isorhythm, but depends on the development of a mensuration canon for the performance of three of its four possible solutions.[25] The lower *triplum* (not a *motetus* in this case, inasmuch as it cannot exist without being extracted from the composed uppermost voice) is derived from the upper by the solution of the canon. The lower (derived) part employs perfect values ($\downarrow.$), the upper (composed) employs imperfect ($\downarrow$). Smaller note values are not subject to alteration. The resulting canon at the unison causes the derived voice to fall farther and farther behind the original in the statement of their common melody.

A third type, the treble-dominated, will suffice to show the variety of motet styles employed by Dufay, although this does not exhaust his range of inventiveness. The free-flowing *superius* of *Elos florum*[26] is evidence of the latitude that was gained through Dufay's abstention from the restrictions of isorhythmic structures. Worthy of mention also is the sustained section of *fermata*-marked block-chords that closes the piece. The *fermate* do not indicate prolongation, but serve as a means of calling attention to the block-chords.

The motets of Ockeghem and Obrecht (1450? – 1505) form a bridge

23. *MR*, 78.
24. *Opera Omnia*, ɪ(1), 5–10.
25. *Ibid.*, xv.
26. *Ibid.*, 11–13.

between those of the preceding period and the imitative works that are typical of Josquin des Prez. Generally speaking, the compositions of these transitional composers indicate the presence of a thoroughly assimilated technique that was subject to occasional experimental gestures, especially at the hands of Obrecht. Clinging to the old practice of building on a *cantus firmus* in long notes, Ockeghem surrounded the melodic core with an elaborate web of rapidly moving parts. With Obrecht, the motet began to take on the shape with which it was later identified, that of imitation of a single thematic fragment for each section of text. Avoidance of the florid patterns woven about a *cantus firmus* also made it possible for Obrecht to write sections in chordal style. Such passages are not unique, for they appeared in the works of Burgundian composers, where they were often set off by *fermate*, and in the chordally conscious English products of the fifteenth century. Obrecht's setting of the text, *Ave, regina caelorum, a 4*,[27] based on the same tenor as that of Walter Frye,[28] illustrates his use of imitative passages and the familiar style in connection with a slow-moving tenor. In addition, the *superius* makes a gesture toward paraphrasing the antiphon that is the source of the text.[29]

Although they were more than two full generations apart, the two outstanding composers of Renaissance religious music were Josquin des Prez and Palestrina. At the hands of the latter, the Mass reached its highest point of development, while the former attained greatness principally in connection with the motet. The problems of establishing authenticity make it difficult to state exactly how many motets Josquin wrote, but the numbering in his complete works indicates that there may be ninety. Still, it is impossible to consider the development of the Mass without viewing Josquin's contributions, and it is equally impossible to omit Palestrina from the study of motets. It is with Josquin that the process of writing continuous imitation — often known as "points of imitation" — became a feature of great importance. This type of composition provided each section, or "point," of text with a distinctive musical idea which is imitated in every voice. The procedure is clearly seen in Josquin's *Ave Maria, a 4 (MM 19)*. The phrases of text, however, overlap so that there is no division of the piece into as many sections as there are portions of text. As one section of the piece reaches its conclusion, the next, along with its

27. Jacobus Obrecht, *Opera Omnia*, ed. A.   28. *MR*, 93ff.
Smijers (Amsterdam: G. Alsbach & Co.,   29. *LU*, 1864.
1958), ii(2), 75–81.

distinctive musical figure, is beginning. Also evident here is the division of the motet into contrasting sections, each of which concludes with a cadence that is equally final. The last, brief section returns to a pattern that is reminiscent of one of the earlier figures. Another means of imparting variety was the insertion of chordal passages between the imitative sections. In *Laudate, pueri, Dominum*[30] this combination of features is amplified by still another, the presentation of material by pairs of voices. Phrases begun in this fashion are either repeated by another pair of voices, repeated with single voices entering in the fashion of continuous imitation, or both. Illustrated here also is a feature of many motets of the sixteenth century, dividing a motet into two or three *partes*. Each of these larger sections is a complete musical piece in itself. Josquin's *Tu pauperum refugium*, for example, although apparently complete in textual and musical continuity (*HAM* 90) is *pars* II of his *Magnus es tu, Domine*, and achieves its fullest meaning only when considered as a contrasting section to its *pars* I. The relationship between the *partes* becomes clear from an examination of Josquin's *Levavi oculos meos in montes*, a setting *a* 4 of Psalm cxx (121).[31] The eight verses of the psalm are divided equally between the two *partes* of the motet. The first half of the first verse, *Levavi oculos meos in montes*, also closes the *secunda pars* — although it does not return in the psalm itself — bringing the melodic material that opened the *prima pars* into play once more and binding the two *partes* firmly together. A similar, but not identical, employment of opening text is found in *Laudate, pueri, Dominum*, wherein the words appear at the end of the *secunda pars* in declamatory chordal style with no direct reference to the musical material they bore in the *prima pars*.

A feature that was common to the compositions of most Renaissance composers, and especially associated with the Netherlanders, is the "drive to the cadence." This was not simply a matter of conforming to an established formula of chords, but was, rather, a thickening of the texture by employing all the voices during the concluding measures. Example 24 illustrates a number of these features. Notable are the increased rhythmic activity, repetition of text, and continued movement of one (and often more than one) voice after the other parts have reached a pedal point or the final chord. Not only was considerable variety possible within this pattern, but the device served

30. *Werken van Josquin des Prez*, ed. A.   1955), xlii, 61–69.
Smijers (Amsterdam: G. Alsbach & Co.,   31. *Ibid.*, 83–90.

Ex. 24   *Levavi oculos meos in montes, Werken van Josquin des Prez,* **XLII,** 90

" I will lift up mine eyes unto the hills."
By permission of G. Alsbach & Co., Leidsegracht 11, Amsterdam-Holland.

admirably as a final contrast to the restless motion that was inherent in continuous imitation. The successive upward leaps are the products of text-painting, to the possibilities of which Josquin was ever alert. *Tu pauperum refugium (HAM* 90), referred to earlier, is a readily accessible illustration of Josquin's interest in pictorial writing, with the words *laborantium, errantium,* and *morte* intensified by reason of their being the subjects of text-painting in the midst of an essentially syllabic setting in familiar style.

The imitative motet developed to such a point of stability at the hands of Josquin that it became the favored means of expression for the remainder of the Renaissance. Its acceptance was general throughout Europe, by composers from all the musically active countries. Whereas the earlier motet styles had been popular only with the

French composers and a few Englishmen, this new style was embraced by the musicians of Italy, Spain, Germany, England, and the Low Countries. Little would be gained by isolating the typical works from each of those areas. The existence of an excellent fund of information in a single volume[32] makes it possible to deal in generalizations here. An absence of examples showing wide differences of style in the generation after Josquin does not indicate a loss of interest in motet writing, but it does show that the excitement of creativity that had existed in the development of new musical styles for the Church was transferred to secular works. The formal development of the Netherlands motet had reached a peak with Josquin and was capable of no more than a final polishing at the hands of such giants as Lassus, Palestrina, and Byrd. Their position, along with a few other notable figures of their time, is similar to that held by Bach, Handel, and Vivaldi at the close of the Baroque period. Sheer creativity in the realm of new forms and styles was less a problem than was the highly skilled employment of means already at hand. Matters of form and style under complete control made it possible for them to turn to greater expressiveness. Among the changes that took place after Josquin were 1) a tendency to establish a consistent, uniform texture, 2) the development of subjective, dramatic utterance, and 3) the development of polychoral compositions. This last feature was to become identified with a tradition that is closely connected with St. Mark's in Venice.

One of the changes that came over the Netherlands motet after Josquin's time was a generally more consistent adherence to a thicker texture. While variable density of voice parts had been accomplished by alternating paired voices, piling up the number of active voices with the entrance of new melodic ideas after the few complete cadences, and thinning out, at the cadences, the parts that overlapped each other, the later composers provided more constant activity for all the parts. With all the voices participating equally in thematic material—as they had already done in Josquin's music—the way to a uniform arrangement of the voices was already charted.

The imitative motet shares with the Mass cycles of its time a reputation as the epitome of abstract, restrained communication, yet it has provided examples of dramatically intense utterance, and it served as the basis upon which one of the most dramatic of stories—the

32. Sufficient space is given to each important composer in *MR* that the student may reconstruct the developments for any country.

Passion—was to be set. The path was already prepared when Josquin engaged in the subjective device of recalling initial text at the end of some of his motets. Far more dramatic is the recurrent statement of the middle voice in Cristóbal de Morales's *(c. 1500—1533) Emendemus in melius (HAM* 128) where an ostinato figure, sometimes transposed, intones *Memento homo quia pulvis es . . .* (Remember, man, that thou art dust . . .) against the principal text that conveys a plea for forgiveness of sin. During those moments when the middle voice falls silent, the penitential text of the outer voices continues, and the middle part regularly enters against it in a fashion that is similar to the later use of chorale melodies. Since the middle voice does not participate in the imitative counterpoint, inasmuch as its melody is not directly derived from any of the melodic patterns that are imitated, it expresses its text more forcefully than do the parts that share its polyphonic framework.

Among the composers whose works led to the establishment of the conservative Roman style, as well as among those who paved the way for the flamboyant Venetian practice, the use of expressive and dramatic writing became common. Text-painting, either as the heightening of single words by illustrative writing or as the intensification of words representing anguish, pain, and tragedy by the use of dissonances and suspensions, moved hand in hand with the employment of texts that were readily adapted to greater emotional rendering. The use of emotionally charged texts from the Song of Solomon and the Penitential Psalms is but one symptom of the change.

Conservativism is a relative concept. As it applied to the Roman tradition, it seems to be clear-cut until examples of polychoral writing, not unlike those written by the members of the Venetian school, appear from the pens of the members of the conservative Roman group. As was mentioned in connection with Palestrina's *Laudate Dominum omnes gentes (cf. pp. 62ff.),* two choirs of equal size engage in a brilliant display of antiphonal and concerted sound. This opposition of identical forces is found in all his motets *a 8,* and is even present in modified form in the works *a 6.* The antiphonal treatment in the latter pieces is not so clear, but only because he did not have two complete choirs available. In such cases the upper voices are opposed to the lower.[33] It must be remembered that this was not a new development with Palestrina or his contemporaries, but was a logical continuation of the

33. Examples may be found in *Le Opere Complete,* VII, 219–25; *Werke,* II, 164–68.

variable texture employed by Josquin, wherein paired voices sometimes imitated other pairs, and joined together at other times to provide a full sonority. The conservative style was pregnant with variety, as an examination of the works of its leading representatives will show. The few instances cited here are only a portion of those in accessible sources.[34]

Tomás Luis de Victoria (1548–1611) shared with his fellow Spaniard, Morales, a tendency toward the dramatic utterance. His moving *O vos omnes* (*HAM* 149) employs a restrained text-painting in the falling melodic line that the *superius* sings each time it has the text *si est dolor*. Such a passage as *attendite et videte* is similarly called to the listener's attention through repeated melodic tones. Repeated chords are employed to highlight *viderunt Dominum* in his *O magnum mysterium* (*GMB* 128). Similarly, in *Ego sum panis vivus* (*MM* 25), William Byrd intensified the key words of his text by applying devices that, although obvious, are descriptive without being emotional. In his opening phrase, *vivus* is the only word with melodic elaboration, *coelo* is given the highest pitch in its phrase, and *descendit* is given a predictably downward movement. The clarity of his new thematic material is preserved by his introduction of the new melody only after the rhythmic activity has ceased in the preceding section.

Jacobus Gallus (Jacob Handl), who approached the Venetian style in his works for double chorus, had a command of the Netherlands tradition as well. His *Ecce quomodo moritur* (*GMB* 131) is entirely in familiar style, lacking the contrapuntal involvement of the Netherlands works and the elaborate effects of the Venetian. His use of unorthodox chord relationships and chromatic alteration lead, in this example and others, to cross-relations and a sense of harmonic dislocation in the midst of otherwise strong root relationships. The exact repetition, at the end of each section of *Ecce quomodo moritur*, of the passage *et erit in pace memoria ejus*, invites an echo effect with a single four-part choir.[35]

The tremendous amount of music produced by Roland de Lassus (Orlando di Lasso, 1532–1594) cannot be described adequately in a brief space, nor can a few musical examples do justice to the variety achieved by this unparalleled master of the Netherlands style. The two examples selected here, however, show two facets of his many

34. This variety of styles can be seen in an examination of works by Josquin, Lassus, Obrecht, Isaac, and most other notable composers of the Renaissance.
35. The varied techniques of Gallus are discussed in *MR*, 736ff.

achievements. Both are from his massive *Magnus Opus Musicum.* The reflective *Tristis est anima mea* (*MM* 23) employs a combination of contrapuntal and chordal styles with poignant suspensions marking *tristis,* and further descriptive devices being set to *vigilate, turbam,* and *circumdabit.* The use of madrigalisms in connection with verbs, adjectives, and nouns is common to much of the music of this time. The skill with which it is used varies considerably; its efficacy is sometimes doubtful because of the abstract ideas it is intended to convey. Whether the long notes Byrd used to set *aeternum* in *Ego sum panis vivus* occur because the composer wished to convey a concept of time is not clearly provable. Many felicitous renderings may not have been the intention of the composer, but mere happy circumstance. The interpretation is unassailable in Lassus' *In hora ultima* (*GMB* 127), where his descriptive writing of instrumental sounds, *tuba, tibia,* and *cythara;* and of joyful human expression, *jocus, risus, saltus,* and *cantus,* is laden with rapid figures that are based on chordal figures, scale passages, and irregular rhythms. One is tempted to speculate that the demands made upon the singers are such that the examination of the score must be more edifying than a performance of the music. By contrast, Lassus' setting of the Penitential Psalm, *De Profundis* (*MSO,* 47–51), Psalm cxxix (130), is a model of restraint.

A comparison of Palestrina's setting of *Ego sum panis vivus*[36] with that of Byrd (*MM* 25) shows a similar treatment of the text. Palestrina's melisma on *vivus* is one of soaring vitality that makes Byrd's effort seem a model of restraint by comparison *(Ex. 25).* The melody of *qui de coelo descendi* is given here for further comparison.

It might be expected that the setting of portions of the Song of Solomon in his twenty-nine motets *a 5*[37] would have moved Palestrina to greater efforts of musical picturization. That such is not the case is illustrated in *Adjuro vos, filiae Jerusalem* (*GMB* 122), the nineteenth in the group. Although passages of considerable excitement do occur, as in the rising opening runs of *Surge amica mea* (number 16), there is no indication that the possibilities of the poem caused Palestrina to write more vividly than he would have done with any other text of similar vitality.

As has been observed, there is no typical motet that comes from the so-called conservative composers of the Renaissance. The composers employed restraint as a rule, burst forth into exuberant pic-

36. *Werke,* I, 43–50; *Le Opere Complete,*   37. *Werke,* IV.
v, 54–68.

Ex.25 Motet, *Ego sum panis vivus, a 5*, Palestrina, *Werke*, I, 43-46

torialism when they desired, took advantage of multi-part and double-chorus techniques on occasion, and generally made use of text-painting in sensitive areas of text. Their limits were not imposed by lack of imagination or indifference to the possibilities of their medium. Founded in the strength of a tradition that felt the power of Rome and the influence of the Tridentine Council, the conservatives of Europe brought to its highest expression a kind of vocal religious music that was able to project its message without recourse to instrumental accompaniment, even though it is evident that instruments were both available and used at various times. The situation was entirely different with the Venetian composers.

The Serene Republic did not flaunt a meaningless title. Sheltered from the political and religious storms that swept through Italy and the rest of Europe, Venice had flourished under the steady administrative guidance of the doges, and enjoyed the delights of a strong economy supported by its success in maritime commerce. In strong alliance with the Eastern Empire, the Venetians were influenced by Byzantine culture in a number of ways. The degree of religious influence from Rome was minimal; the doges owed no more than nominal allegiance to the central authority of the Church. Serving at the same time as a temporal administrator and a spiritual leader, the doge stood in a position of authority over the clergy and musicians of Venice and, most of all, over St. Mark's, which took on all the characteristics of a chapel, sacred and secular. Freedom from Roman influence meant also freedom from the restricting influence of the Council of Trent. Celebrations of civic events, as well as observance of the traditional Church feasts and Venetian festivals, produced a musical outpouring that may have been approached in other places, but which reached its most flamboyant limits at St. Mark's, where the doge held sway.

Much has been made of the architectural features of St. Mark's. Its plan, that of a Greek cross, has in the past been credited with giving rise to antiphonal performance in Western Church music. That has been as much discredited as the belief that the choirs were stationed at the most distant points in the building. The galleries containing the principal organs were immediately over the choir, that end of the building containing the high altar, and it was most probably from that area that most, if not all, of the service music was sung.

Some features of what is commonly called the Venetian style, and many of the composers from whose work it developed, were not Venetian at all. It does not diminish the glory of that fabulous musical climate to recognize many of the factors to which its prestige was attached as stemming from earlier composers than Adrian Willaert (c. 1490–1562) who, important though he was to the development of the distinctive style, was a Fleming. In connection with church music, the features that were most closely allied to the characteristic style of St. Mark's were those of brilliant employment of voices with instruments, the use of *cori spezzati* from separate choir lofts, and a solidly consonant utterance that could be tossed about from choir to choir without offending the ear of the listener.

Only recently has sufficient study been completed to permit the clear identification of composers prior to Willaert who were active in developing this distinctive expression. Much of the difficulty has lain in finding examples of writing for *coro spezzato* prior to those of Willaert in 1550. The discovery of compositions, dating from some years earlier, by Fra Ruffino D'Assisi and Francesco Santacroce, and employing two choirs in dialogue with each other, has shown the source of Willaert's procedures without diminishing his own accomplishments.[38]

The true style for *cori spezzati* required the alternation of sections between two full choirs of four parts each. In that sense, the echo treatment of paired voices and the variety achieved by changing tex-

38. Giovanni d'Alessi, "Precursors of Adriano Willaert in the Practice of *Coro Spezzato*," *Journal of the American Musicological Society*, v/3 (Fall, 1952), 187–210.

PLATE 3.   *An interior view of St. Mark's in Venice, showing the
position of one of the organs.* (Foto Böhm — Venezia.)

tures that we have observed in the works of Josquin and others is not closely related to this antiphonal expression. The writing of parts into separate choir books, each *a 4*, implies also some spatial separation between the groups of singers, although it was at St. Mark's that this division was made on a grand scale. The presence of two organs there before Willaert was appointed *maestro di musica de la cappella di San Marco* in 1527 is a generally known fact. Their location had been in two small recesses, one at either side of the high altar. It was probably the idea of their being used in connection with antiphonal singing that caused them to be removed to the two galleries above the choir (apses) and their former places to be filled with smaller instruments. That there were even more organs is possible, but the two that were located in the apses were those at which the two resident organists presided and which were played at the choral performances. It is obvious that two choirbooks were necessary for such performance, and it is equally apparent that such a separation of forces would bring about a more consistently chordal style of performance for the sake of the performers as well as the listeners.

The peak of polychoral development was reached by Giovanni Gabrieli (1557–1612) who spent most of his life in Venice, with much of his musical activity related to his position as an organist at St. Mark's. His religious music achieves a brilliance that is unrivalled. An immediate point of difference from the compositions of his predecessors is his use of performing groups that are unequal either in size or in their constitution. While the works of Fra Ruffino, Santacroce, Willaert, and even Palestrina, depended upon the antiphonal partnership of forces equally matched in size and voice range, the compositions of Giovanni Gabrieli, and of his uncle Andrea *(c. 1520–1586)*,[39] not only called for choirs of different voice ranges, but increased the contrast by employing dissimilar groups of instruments in connection with the choirs. A further contrast, that of setting an unaccompanied choir against other choirs that were supported by instruments, pushed the possibilities to their limit. Giovanni's setting *a 16* of *Omnes gentes plaudite manibus*,[40] Psalm xlvi (47), from the *Sacrae Symphoniae* of 1597, is written for four choirs of four voices each. The

39. See his setting *a 6* of Psalm cxxix (130), *De profundis clamavi (GMB* 130). While the piece makes extensive use of varying texture, only rarely is there a division into two choirs *a 3*.

40. Giovanni Gabrieli, *Opera Omnia*, ed. Denis Arnold (*Corpus Mensurabilis Musicae*, 12; Rome: American Institute of Musicology, 1959), ii, 232–45.

distribution of voices is different in each of the choirs, and the third choir is clearly designated *cappella,* indicating that it is to sing without instrumental accompaniment. Although the instruments that are meant to duplicate the vocal lines are not specified, a clue to their identity may be found in the original clef signs. The absence of instruments in connection with the third choir was not due to a lack of performers, but to Gabrieli's desire for another contrasting group to set against the three varied accompanied choirs. Sixteen to twenty instrumentalists seem to have been available to Gabrieli at all times. He isolated the *a cappella* choir further by setting the portion, *Dominus excelsus, terribilis rex magnus super omnem terram,* for this group alone. On the other hand, the unaccompanied singers are required to participate in the section where the writing has a distinctly instrumental character, set to the words *in voce tubae,* and employing rapid scale fragments and triadic figures. Gabrieli's interest in orchestration is seen in two motets from the *Sacrae Symphoniae* of 1615; the *Jubilate Deo a 10*[41] and *Surrexit Christus a 11,*[42] each with a *basso seguente* for organ in addition to the number of parts specified above. *Jubilate Deo* calls for two *cornetti,* five *tromboni,* and *fagotto.* After an eight-measure *sinfonia,* the instruments are joined by the singers and do not perform independently again. In *Surrexit Christus,* however, the instruments do not duplicate the voice parts, but pursue an independent course throughout the entire composition. Here the two *cornetti* are placed in combination with a pair of violins and a quartet of trombones. Against this combination three voices — alto, tenor, and bass — present the text. After a *sinfonia* of six measures, the voices announce the opening words of the motet several times. This is not a motto beginning inasmuch as the material is not repeated later. The instruments return for an eight-measure interlude based on the opening figure of the *sinfonia,* and the remainder of the piece proceeds in concerted style. These two examples[43] merely hint at the infinite variety that was heard when the choral and instrumental performers of St. Mark's gathered to celebrate one of the major festivals. Most of Gabrieli's motets are identified with one of the principal observances of St. Mark's: St. Mark's Day, the Ascension, Christmas, and Easter.[44] Nat-

41. *Ibid.,* III, 163–92.
42. *Ibid.,* 193–212.
43. Vol. IV of the *Opera Omnia* will contain further works illustrating this variety of instrumentation. Compositions for

twelve to nineteen voices, the remainder of the *Sacrae Symphoniae,* 1615, will make up its contents.
44. *Opera Omnia,* I, i.

urally, each of these called for the employment of the most elaborate music that could be obtained from the performers in residence. That the full performing group was not required at all times, on the other hand, is seen in the presence of simpler works for six, seven, and eight voices. A further example, *In ecclesiis (HAM* 157 and *HMS,* iv, 42ff),[45] also illustrates the distribution of materials between two choirs and instruments.

The Venetian style was carried into Germany, principally through the works of Heinrich Schütz (1585–1672), whose indebtedness to Gabrieli will be discussed in chapter X. For the moment, an example from Hans Leo Hassler (1564–1612), who wrote for both the Catholic and Protestant repertories, may be examined. In his *Laudate Dominum,* Psalm CL *(TEM* 28), the true style of *coro spezzato* is again seen. Two equal choirs engage in antiphonal singing, and join forces for the conclusion of the piece. This somewhat older method of employing two equal choirs without elaborate instrumental support was probably the common style outside the immediate area of Venice, for where else would the situation allow the elaborate compositions of St. Mark's, and how many other courts could boast such a large number of truly skilled performers?

As we saw at the outset of this chapter, the development of the motet was undertaken at the hands of composers from various parts of Europe. Stemming from the early efforts of the French and Netherlands composers, it spread to England, Spain, and Italy, and made its way also into Germany. In England it was destined to become the basis of the anthem, the development of which provides another rich heritage. With the Germans it eventually became elaborated to such an extent that it is often difficult to distinguish between motet and cantata. The two Italian traditions continued to have followers who wrote works often influenced, if not dominated, by the new Baroque practice.

If it was difficult to find a definition to cover the varied types of motet in the thirteenth century, it is virtually impossible to provide one that will describe the entire motet literature of the Middle Ages and Renaissance. In addition to serving as a secular entertainment, it was called upon for sundry church functions of varying degrees of solemnity and grandeur. Its development over four centuries, and the many situations to which composers adapted it, resulted in a large

45. Modern edition, London: Eulenburg, 1962.

number of types of compositions. Because either the title or the style can be found in every kind of religious composition that was not a part of the Ordinary, every piece of that kind has sometimes been considered as a motet. Some of these pieces, however, grew to considerable length. As they developed under separate designations during the same years we have just been concerned with, they have been reserved for examination in the next chapter.

Chapter IV

Requiem Mass, Passion,

and Magnificat

MANY of the motets that were performed during the Middle Ages and Renaissance belonged to the general class of "occasional" music because of their connection with a special observance, either religious or civic. In the same way, some other larger works that had no connection with the Ordinary of the Mass came into existence. Some of these were truly occasional pieces, written to observe or commemorate a unique event, while others belonged to a general category that permitted their performance on recurrent festivals, either daily, seasonal, or annual. The discussion of these widely differentiated forms within a single chapter should not be taken to mean that there was any structural or functional connection between them. They fall together here only as a matter of chronological convenience. If common ground for these forms must be sought, it is best to inquire after their possible relationships in plainsong literature. In most cases, the function for which the music was required was already capably served with plainsong performance. It is not to be expected, then, that the function will be found to change when the polyphonic form comes into existence. Variety will be achieved, and greater complexity, but the function of liturgical music is inseparable from the worship activity to which it is attached.

Liturgical practice did not ignore such important events as burial or commemoration of the dead. Suitable plainsong was in existence, and prior to the development of polyphonic substitutes, as well as after, this simple, but entirely complete and proper form of observance was celebrated.[1] The Requiem Mass (*Missa pro defunctis*) is sung on All Soul's Day (November 2) to commemorate the faithful departed.

---

1. The plainsong forms in use today are given in *LU*, beginning on p. 1806, and the arrangement of sections of the Requiem, with text *incipits*, may be found in *Grove's*, VII, 126.

TABLE V

Changes of Structure in the Renaissance Requiem

	Before Council of Trent					During Council	After Council			Uncertain (See n. 14)
	Ockeghem	Brumel	Prioris	La Rue	Morales	Clemens	Monte *a 4*	Victoria *a 6*	Asola	Palestrina
Introit	×	×	×	×	×	×	×	×	×	
Kyrie	×	×	×	×	×	×	×	×	×	×
Gradual										
Si ambulem	×		×				×			
Requiem aeternam					×			×		
Tract										
Sicut cervus	×			×						
Absolve, Domine						×				
Sequence										
Dies irae		×			×¹					
Offertory	×	×	×	×	×	×	×	×	×	
Sanctus		×	×	×	×	×	×	×	×	×
Agnus		×	×	×	×	×	×	×	×	×
Communion		×	×	×	×	×	×	×	×	×

1. Verse 20 only.

It is also the appropriate observance on the day of burial and anniversaries of that date. Other dates on which it may be celebrated are the third, seventh, and thirtieth day after the death. The designation "Requiem" is taken from the opening text of the Introit. Liturgical requirements are fulfilled by plainsong performance, but along with the development of contrapuntal forms, polyphonic settings of the principal sections of the Requiem came into existence, although later than the settings of the Ordinary. Even those composers who produced many polyphonic Mass cycles were usually content to write a single Requiem.[2] The Masses for the Dead include polyphonic settings of some sections of the Proper, a few of which are viewed as optional by the Renaissance composers. Among the sections of the Ordinary, those that are felt to express joy (the Gloria and Credo) are appropriately absent.

There is no evidence that any polyphonic settings of the Requiem existed before the fifteenth century. It is probable that the first such setting was that of a *Requiem pro defunctis* written by Dufay, who had specified in his will that the Mass be sung on the day after his funeral. Unfortunately, the work has not been found. The first extant Requiem is that of Johannes Ockeghem. It has a number of features commonly found in works of this nature that appeared before the meetings of the Council of Trent. One of these is its incomplete form; apparently the sections after the Offertory were not set polyphonically. (Table v shows the polyphonic movements in each of the eleven Requiems discussed here. The reader should consult it repeatedly.) Another unusual characteristic lies in the use of the Gradual, *Si ambulem in medio umbrae mortis* (Yea, though I walk through the valley of the shadow of death), Psalm xxii (23), and the Tract, *Sicut cervus desiderat ad fontes aquarum* (As the hart panteth after the water brooks), Psalm xli (42), instead of the presently used Gradual, *Requiem aeternam*, and Tract, *Absolve, Domine*.[3] The *Dies irae* (*MSO*, 10f) was slow in coming into use in France, but it was more often used in Italy, the land of its origin, although it does not appear with great frequency in polyphonic settings even there. The polyphonic sections of the Ockeghem *Missa pro defunctis* are the Introit, Kyrie, Gradual, Tract, and Offertory. When Ockeghem employed Gregorian intonations, he placed them in the *superius*, and most of his polyphonic sections can be traced back to

2. Morales, Guerrero, and Victoria each wrote two. There is no evidence that Josquin des Prez wrote even one.

3. Complete text and melody for *Si ambulem, GR* (1945 ed.), 137; *Sicut cervus, GR*, 232f, and *LU*, 753f.

Gregorian origins.[4] Paraphrase of the plainsong by the *superius* is found in abundance, as it is in other Renaissance Requiems. The major parts of Ockeghem's Mass are broken into subsections. These are variously *a 2, a 3*, and *a 4*. Each of the subsections keeps its voice arrangement throughout, and variety is achieved by the changing voice combinations that are introduced with the new sections.

Four other Requiems dating from before the Council of Trent exhibit considerable variety of treatment when compared with each other and that of Ockeghem. The *Missa pro defunctis* (CW 68) of Antoine Brumel (fl. 1483–1520) departs from the normal practice of the time by including a polyphonic setting of the Sequence, *Dies irae.* Brumel avoided monotony in the lengthy section by providing an alternation setting. The odd-numbered strophes are polyphonic, as is the final (twentieth) one, while the even-numbered strophes are not included. It was intended that they be sung in plainsong. Brumel included neither the Gradual nor the Tract, but did make polyphonic settings of all the other sections that were to become standard. The work is *a 4*, with two sections of the *Dies irae* set for two voices, and another for three. Gregorian intonations precede the Introit and Communion. Paraphrase of the plainsong is present also, most noticeably in the *superius* throughout the Sequence.

A Requiem showing a different choice of the optional Gradual-Tract group is by Johannes Prioris (fl. 1490–1510), another Netherlander. He did not set the *Sicut cervus,* but added polyphonic versions of the Sanctus, Agnus Dei, and Communion. The composition is *a 4* throughout, employing paraphrase of the plainsong material in all its sections.[5]

Among the Requiems that appeared before the Council of Trent, that of Pierre de la Rue (fl. 1477–1518) is foremost in musical interest. The style is consistent with that found in the later compositions of the Josquin period, filled with a variety of voice arrangements and employing imitative counterpoint. This is not surprising, for la Rue and Josquin were close contemporaries. While the piece is mostly *a 4* and *a 5*, the use of contrasting pairs of voices in both the Tract and the Offertory produces several sections that are first heard as *a 2*, although the illusion is dispelled when the other pair of voices enters. The Tract employs the upper pair of voices for the first nineteen measures, the lower pair for the next fifteen, and the combined pairs for the

4. Ockeghem, *Collected Works,* ii, 83–97.   5. *MR,* 264.

remaining twenty-four. The contrast between the pairs of voices is heightened by the fact that no sopranos are called for until the opening of the Tract, the highest voices in the Introit (*HMS*, III, 53f) and Kyrie being altos. The importance of a text that expresses hope and confidence is thus emphasized by a sudden brilliance of high voices. The generally low range of the entire Mass is most unusual for its time. Friedrich Blume, editor of the modern edition (*CW* 11) has placed the entire composition a fourth higher than it appeared in its original form. Singers would experience difficulty in performing it at any lower pitch level than that provided by Blume; the original required that the basses frequently sing B-flat below the bass staff. The low *tessiturae*, and the avoidance of high voices in some complete sections — the Benedictus and Agnus Dei, as well as the Introit and Kyrie, are written with the alto as the highest voice — give a dark, somber color to the composition. The close adherence to plainsong sources is apparent in the presence of Gregorian intonations in five of the sections. The Agnus Dei is clearly in *cantus firmus* style, with the plainsong fragment in the middle voice of the *a* 5 section.

The five pre-Tridentine Requiems that have been mentioned here display a trend toward the standardization of some movements that is consistently followed in the compositions of succeeding periods. Only with Palestrina is there any deviation from the practice of providing polyphonic settings of both the Introit and Kyrie, after which the composer inserted the Gradual, Tract, Sequence, or as with Palestrina, none of these optional sections. The Offertory, Sanctus, and Agnus Dei plus Communion also became standard settings.

The *Missa pro Defunctis* by Morales[6] is a work of great restraint. There is no overt display of the composer's mastery of technique. Against basically slow-moving notes, one voice, sometimes two, and rarely, three, engages in a quicker, imitative dialogue. The material is always close to plainsong, especially in the *superius*, which carries the Gregorian material only slightly paraphrased in long notes. What has been called the reappearance of themes from one movement to another[7] may actually be nothing more than the common pattern of the plainsong melodies upon which Morales drew for his subject material, and the common vocabulary of thematic patterns of the

6. Cristòbal de Morales, *Opera omnia*, ed. Higinio Anglès (Barcelona: Consejo Superior de Investigaciones Cientificas, 1954), III, 114–53. Concerning the presence of this figure in another Morales Requiem (unpublished), see Stevenson, *op. cit.*, 44f.
7. *MR*, 590.

sixteenth century. One of these formulas *(Ex. 26)* appears with such
regularity that it takes on the character of a thematic fragment by the
sheer weight of its repetitions. It is perhaps closer to fact if it be compared to the characteristic motive of Machaut's Mass than to a theme.
It is true that this figure, and others of great similarity, can be found
in many other works of this period, of both Morales and other composers. But it is the insistent regularity of its presence in the Requiem
that makes it worthy of comment. The Mass is *a 5*, with part of the
Gradual (from *In memoria*) *a 3*, and a section of the Offertory (from
Hostias et preces) *a 4*. Morales did not set the *Dies irae* polyphonically,
but made a gesture in that direction by providing a contrapuntal
setting of its final verse, *Pie Jesu Domine*, quoting the plainsong in the
superius.

Ex. 26 Thematic formula from Morales' *Requiem*, found at various pitch levels.

The period of the Council of Trent is represented here by the work
of only Jacobus Clemens non Papa (1510–1557?), who avoided setting
the Gradual and Tract that had seen common employment in earlier
years. The absence of the *Dies irae* in all settings after Brumel's with
the exception of Asola's, and in the fragmentary version supplied by
Morales, demonstrates clearly that it was not employed regularly at
this time.

Clemens' *Missa defunctorum*[8] presents nothing of unusual interest
in the organization of its movements, for it employs the Tract, *Absolve,
Domine*, as its only optional section. The manner in which the texts
are put to music, however, is unusual. The Kyrie is the only section
that is not preceded by a Gregorian intonation. There are three types
of treatment present. Chordal writing is found in the part of the Introit
that follows the *Te decet* intonation, in the Kyrie, and in the Agnus
Dei. A second type, combining a subsection of chordal writing with
another in imitative counterpoint, is used in the Offertory, Sanctus,
and Communion. The third type, that of complete sections in imitative
counterpoint, is found in the first half of the Introit and in the entire
Tract. Clemens' setting of the *Absolve, Domine* text is a short motet in
two brief *partes*. The Mass is *a 4* throughout, and uses all the voices

8. Jacobus Clemens non Papa, *Opera
Omnia*, ed. K. Ph. Bernet Kempers *(Corpus
Mensurabilis Musicae* IV) (Rome: American Institute of Musicology, 1959), VIII,
1–15.

constantly. The intonations provide the only relief from a consistently full texture.

The Requiems of the late sixteenth century generally adopted the newer texts for the Gradual and Tract, but an exceptional instance of the continued use of the *Si ambulem* Gradual occurs in the Mass by Philippe de Monte (1521–1603).[9] There is no evidence that indicates a refusal on Monte's part to submit to the will of the Council. He seems to have made an effort to conform in other instances for, among his total of forty-eight Masses, "six are settings of the Ordinary that are based on liturgical melodies and thus probably represent an attempt to meet the Council's requirements."[10]

Victoria wrote two complete funerary compositions, a *Missa pro defunctis, a 4*, published in 1583, and an *Officium defunctorum, a 6*, composed in 1603 for the funeral of the Empress Maria, in whose service he had spent nearly two decades.[11] The latter work was published in 1605, dedicated to the Princess Margaret, to whom he remained chaplain after the death of her mother, the Empress. The Responsory, *Libera me, Domine*, is set polyphonically in both works, paraphrasing the plainsong, and the *Officium* contains also a motet, *Versa est in ductum, a 6*, as well as the Lesson, *Taedet animam meam, a 4*. In several instances, the *Officium* takes material from the earlier Mass, the most obvious instance being the exact quotation of the three-voice *Tremens factus sum* section of the *Libera me, Domine* Responsory.[12] The opening of the section makes what may have been a deliberate alteration in the liturgical melody in order to bring it closer to the outline of the ensuing verse, *Dies illa, dies irae*, which approximates the same melody *(Ex. 27)*. The *Dies irae* Sequence—not the same chant—even though Victoria did not set it polyphonically, was sung in plainsong immediately before the Offertory.

Among these post-Tridentine compositions, only the *Missa pro defunctis* [13] of Giovanni Mattheo Asola *(c. 1550–1609)* is notable for containing a polyphonic setting of the *Dies irae*. As did Brumel, Asola made settings of only alternate verses, but while Brumel had set

9. Philippe de Monte, *Opera*, ed. C. Van den Borren and J. van Nuffel (Düsseldorf: Sumptibus L. Schwann, 1927–1935), XIII.
10. *MR*, 703.
11. Both works are printed in Tomas Luis de Victoria, *Opera omnia*, ed. Felipe Pedrell (Leipzig: Breitkopf & Härtel, 1902–1913), VI.

12. The two sections appear on pp. 118 and 145 of Vol. VI of the complete edition. Cf. the plainsong, *LU*, 1767.
13. *Musica Divina*, ed. Carl Proske *et al.* (Ratisbon: F. Pustet, 1853–1875), I(1), 259–86.

Ex. 27 Section of Responsory, *Libera me, Domini*, Victoria, *Opera*, VI, 118

the uneven verses, Asola left those for plainsong performance and rendered the even-numbered ones polyphonically. Plainsong melodies are not confined to a single voice in Asola's Mass, but move about from one to another.

There remains only Palestrina's *Missa pro defunctis*,[14] *a 5*, from the group shown in Table v, and it is a work about which we have no certain chronological data. The only section that sets it off from the daily Ordinary is the Offertory. Not only are the Introit and Communion absent, but Palestrina set none of the optional sections. The Offertory exhibits no unique characteristics, even though it is the only portion of the Proper to appear. It and much of the rest of the Mass employ the appropriate Gregorian material as the basis of the imitative counterpoint that runs throughout the composition. The absence of several of the necessary sections from Palestrina's polyphonic settings avoided any conflict with the pronouncements of the Council of Trent, for it placed the selection of the debatable items into the hands of the officiating clergy. That imitative counterpoint was acceptable we judge from Palestrina's consistent use of it although Costanzo Porta *(c. 1530–1601)*, in dedicating his book of Masses to a high official of the Church, took the trouble to point out his concern with making the text intelligible. Still, Porta employed some imitative counterpoint in a Requiem.[15]

Several things deserve further comment in connection with the course of action chosen by the composers of Requiems during the Renaissance. One is the restraint of technical display exhibited by all the composers. Certainly the solemn occasions that generated these compositions had much to do with their generally reflective nature. Composers did not concern themselves with experiments in texture,

14. Palestrina, *Werke*, x, 138–52. Stevenson, *op. cit.*, 395, dates it from 1554; *MR* gives its first publication as 1591.

15. *MR*, 494.

rich harmonic sounds, polychoral display, or any of the other tech-niques they employed in connection with the composition of the Ordinary. This commendable restraint was not destined to last, for the composers who followed were to introduce polychoral writing, instrumental doubling of the vocal parts, strongly contrasted sections, the new *basso continuo* idea, and dramatic writing in connection with the *Dies irae*.[16] Completely lacking among the Requiems mentioned here is the use of parody.[17] The borrowing of secular material would have exceeded the bounds of good taste, even at a time when secular melodies appeared regularly in other religious music. The composi-tion of a *Missa pro defunctis* "could not in decency be treated on the parody-system of a motet, a canzona or a madrigal."[18]

The apparently random selection of the optional sections of the Requiem may be due, in part, to the changing practice of the period. Some of these works were written for specific occasions, but it may be that those intended merely to serve as music that could be drawn from the repertory when required reflect local customs in their inclu-sion of certain sections, or avoid setting them entirely in an effort to meet whatever demands the changing times might make. Since the appropriate, and locally acceptable, Gradual, Tract, or Sequence could be inserted in plainsong, there was no pressure upon the composer to provide such a setting. It might be remarked that the change brought about in the approved settings of the Gradual and Tract served to remove from currency the highly personal verses that dealt with individual hopes and fears, and substituted for them the imper-sonal texts that conveyed an application to all mankind. What occurred was the addition of the awe-inspiring *Dies irae* to some comforting texts that had universal application.

Concerning itself with the events leading up to the Crucifixion is that story called the Passion *(Passio Domini nostri Jesu Christi)*. Litur-gical practice allows for the annual presentation, during Holy Week, of the Passion story as it appears in each of the four Gospels: the version according to St. Matthew to be read (or sung) on Palm Sunday; St.

16. Charles Warren Fox, "The Polyphonic Requiem before about 1615," *Bulletin of the American Musicological Society*, No. 7 (October, 1943), 7.

17. Two borrowings of secular material from Josquin are present in a Requiem by by Jean Richafort; the *Circumdederunt me*

canon, and a canon based on a phrase from Josquin's chanson, *Faulte d'argent*. For the symbolic meaning of these bor-rowings, see *MR*, 335f.

18. Charles Van den Borren, in Philippe de Monte, *Opera*, unpaged preface to Vol. XIII.

Mark on Tuesday; St. Luke on Wednesday; and St. John on Good Friday. The story, in any of its four renderings, is laden with drama. In view of its association with the most solemn season of the liturgical year, it is not surprising that it has received the attention of the leading composers since the time it first began to be treated as a choral vehicle. The early presentation of this tragic series of events followed two paths, both of them taking advantage of the intense drama that unfolded in the telling. One of these paths was theatrical; the other, musical. Although the theatrical performances are the less important, their connection with the Church and with music requires that they be mentioned briefly.

That certain of the major feasts were celebrated by the inclusion of dramatic dialogues, sung and acted by the clergy, is commonly known. These little plays, intended to convey forcefully the principal events of early Christianity, are called liturgical dramas. Inasmuch as they often exceeded liturgical bounds in their contents, they are better called religious dramas. Although plays of this kind exist in some quantity, there are no surviving Passion settings from before the thirteenth century. The nearest example in content and dramatic intensity is the *Quem quaeritis* trope, performed at Easter,[19] relating the arrival of the women at the sepulchre. The absence of Passion settings from the surviving examples may be attributed, in part, to the tragic story that is unfolded in these Gospels. The earliest examples of dramatic presentation are more concerned with the joyous aspects of Christian history. A more important cause may be that by the time religious drama began to appear on the scene there was already a firmly established method of presenting the Passion story. It is to this older tradition, dramatic in content but less obviously theatrical in presentation, that we must turn for the history of the Passion.

The musical exposition of the Passion story seems to have developed as early as the fifth century. It was then that the practice of assigning each of the Gospels to a different day in Holy Week was instituted. Apparently until the fifteenth century the dramatic projection of the story was limited to simple presentation of the text itself. It was transmitted by a single singer who used the different ranges of his voice in presenting the text that was assigned to the

19. A description of a tenth-century performance of the *Quem quaeritis* trope is given in *MMA*, 194f. The detailed instructions concerning costume, props, action, and music take on the character of stage directions. See *GMB* 8 and *HMS*, II, 23f for music and text. Another liturgical drama and further discussion may be found in *TEM* 5.

various participants in the story.[20] The words uttered by Christ were sung in a low register, those of the Evangelist, in the middle register, and the text assigned to other characters and the crowd of onlookers, in the high register. One is tempted to speculate on the theatrical impulse that is evident in this connection between the characters and the voice ranges by which they are delineated. Not only do the various pitch levels contribute to the dramatic intensity, but the several speeds indicated in old manuscripts develop the differences between the parts even more. The gravity of Christ's words is magnified by their slow tempo and low range; the objective narration is appropriately in the medium pitch-range combination; and the excitement of the crowd is conveyed through delivery in a high register and fast tempo. The entire range employed in the delivery of the three styles was only an eleventh. The presentation of the three parts by one person does not, then, represent a *tour de force*, but only a normal rendition of a special set of plainsong formulas.

In the fifteenth century, the modern practice of plainsong chanting of the Passions was begun. This new method assigned three singers to the task that had in the past been the duty of one. The narrative sections were now assigned to a tenor, the words of Christ, to a bass, and the words of the crowd (*turba*) and of minor characters to an alto. This composite of crowd and lesser participants was also known by the name *synagoga*.

These plainsong Passions, whether sung by one or three deacons, are also known as choral Passions in the works of British writers, a combination of terms bringing confusion to many. The proper German designation for this type of presentation is *Choralpassion*. In German, of course, *Choral* refers to plainsong[21] as well as to the Protestant hymn. The adoption of the same term by English authors, in a sense that is not entirely the same, has led to misinterpretation. Since the danger of ambiguity is present, it is probably more desirable to refer to these as plainsong Passions in discussions in this country, especially since neither of the other terms has taken firm hold here.

The development of the polyphonic techniques that came into prominence about the fifteenth century left its mark on the Passion, just as it had on various types of motets and Masses. The method by

20. *HD*, 558, says that this practice prevailed until the twelfth century; *Grove's*, vi, 578, written in direct refutation of the view held by Apel and others, indicates that the practice continued until the fifteenth century.

21. However, *MGG*, ii, 1266–1303, avoids any reference to the Reformation hymns in discussing the *Choral*.

which this contrapuntal style was adapted to the Passion story was twofold: either the sections for *synagoga* were written in polyphony and those for the *Evangelista*, and sometimes the *Christus*, presented in plainsong; or the entire story was presented in the style of a motet, with no sharp distinction between the characters. The former, only partly polyphonic, is known as the dramatic Passion (sometimes also called scenic Passion); the latter, polyphonic throughout, is known as the motet Passion. The dramatic type was the first to be widely used, and the motet type waited not upon the complete mastery of the polyphonic medium by composers, but upon the adventurous composers of the Catholic tradition and upon the Protestants, who were not bound by centuries of strong tradition. Once the ability to create lengthy sections of polyphony was common among church musicians, and when the acceptance of such pieces as substitutes for partially or completely chanted renditions was general, the motet Passion blossomed forth for a brief period, losing some of the dramatic intensity of the earlier type, but producing an art form that depended more upon subtle shades of expression than on sharply contrasted dramatic situations. The setting of brief episodes from the Passion story, or of texts related to it, can be found in motet form as well.[22] These are properly not Passions, but motets employing a portion of the Passion story or its sentiment.

What now appear to be the earliest attempts at polyphonic rendition of the Passion date from the middle of the fifteenth century in England. One of these is a setting according to St. Matthew, the other according to St. Luke.[23] The only sections composed for contrapuntal performance are those of the *synagoga*, and the remaining sections are for plainsong rendition. The plainsong does not appear in the manuscripts, but is intended to be inserted at the appropriate points from a plainsong collection. The polyphony is *a 3* and, considering the period from which it stems, is to be viewed as music for three soloists, not for a three-part choir. The voices show no great degree of independence, as may be seen in the conductus-like settings in the St. Luke Passion.[24] Another English Passion, *a 4*, by Richard Davy (fl. 1491–1506)[25] written about 1500, is intended for Palm Sunday and, therefore, is based on the Gospel according to St. Matthew. There are

22. *MR*, 225f (with musical example); *GMB*, 60.
23. *Grove's*, VI, 579.
24. *MR*, 764.

25. *Musica Britannica*, XII, 112–34; example in *The New Oxford History of Music*, III, 317f, and *HMS*, III, 62f.

forty-two polyphonic sections comprising the words of the crowd *(turba)* and various individuals—Pilate, Judas, and Peter, among others—while the plainsong is principally reserved for the narration of the Evangelist and the words of Christ. Davy, then, assigned the parts that in plainsong had been in the high register to polyphony; those that had been in low or medium registers were retained as plainsong. The printed edition is a partial reconstruction, as portions of Davy's material have been lost.

Until the recent discovery of the manuscript containing the two fifteenth-century Passions mentioned above, it was believed that the earliest examples were two anonymous Italian Passions dating from the last part of the fifteenth century. One of these settings is from the Gospel according to St. Matthew; the other, according to St. John. It should be noted that a preference for the former version is already apparent in its appearance in three of the five instances mentioned thus far. Neither of these works presents music for Jesus or the Evangelist, but the other solo parts are set to the appropriate formulas of the Gregorian Passion,[26] ensuring a satisfactory relationship between plainsong and polyphony. The sections for the *turba Judaeorum*, in *fauxbourdon*, are the only choral portions of the St. John Passion; the St. Matthew setting is somewhat more elaborate, with some of the sections actually being *a 6*.[27]

The setting of text from any one of the Passions provided no opportunity for the composer to introduce as a group the Seven Last Words of Christ, which are found distributed among three of the Gospels; three each in Luke and John, and one in Mark. The wide use of the St. Matthew version, even though it contains none of the words on the Cross, may be ascribed to its assigned position on Palm Sunday and to its highly dramatic content. As a Sunday text, it was naturally a source of greater interest to composers, who saw in it a subject that was worthy of their best efforts, as it would reach a large number of listeners. The combination of the four Gospels occurs first in a motet-type Passion by Longaval (Johannes à la Venture, French; Antoine de Longueval, Flemish, fl. 1509–1522), who was active in France during the first quarter of the sixteenth century. His organization of text is clear from the announcement of the subject in the *Exordium* that opens the work, in which the choir names all four sources at one time. The

26. The formulas may be found in the *Officium majoris hebdomadae et octavae Paschae* (Dessain edition, 1932).

27. *MR*, 165. A six-voice *turba* setting is given in *SMRM*, 186.

practice of identifying the text in an *Exordium* derives from liturgical practice, where the source of certain sections is announced before they are read. The usual practice in the Passions, both before and after Longaval, was through the announcement (by the Evangelist in a dramatic Passion, and by the choir in a motet Passion) of the source, as follows: *Passio Domini nostri Jesu Christi secundum Matthaeum* (or *Lucam, Marcum, Johannem,* as the case may be). The German Passions likewise begin with the same formula, *Das Leiden und Sterben unsers Herrn Jesu Christi nach dem heiligen Mattäo.* Longaval's solution to the identification of all four sources lay in his naming them simultaneously.[28]

Passio Domini nostri Jesu Christi secundum $\left\{ \begin{array}{l} \textit{Johannem.} \\ \textit{Lucam.} \\ \textit{Matthaeum.} \\ \textit{Marcum.} \end{array} \right.$

The practice of using portions of all the Gospels, in order to incorporate the Seven Last Words, continued in many settings after this time, culminating in the type of work that in later centuries placed the emphasis on the Seven Words rather than on the entire Passion story.

Throughout the rest of the sixteenth century, the motet Passion continued to appear along with the dramatic type. It was common until the end of the century in both the Latin Passions and those with German text, the latter to be discussed in another chapter.

The St. Matthew Passion of Claudin de Sermisy *(c. 1490–1562),* printed in 1535, is based entirely on the text from which it takes its name; therefore, none of the Seven Last Words is present. It is classified as dramatic, even though the words of individuals appear in polyphonic settings. It must be remembered that in order to qualify as a motet Passion, all the text of a setting must be given to the chorus. The retention of the words of the Evangelist and of some other individuals in plainsong is the hallmark of the dramatic type. The fact that Claudin set some of his forty sections as polyphonic substitutes for plainsong does not qualify his work as a motet Passion.[29]

Adopting the same plan as that used by Claudin, the St. Matthew Passion by Maistre Jhan of Ferrara (fl. 1540–1550) also excludes the Seven Last Words. His method was to assign a small vocal combination to the words of each of the characters of the drama, such as the

28. The music for this section is given in *MR,* 274. The work was formerly mistak- enly attributed to Obrecht.
29. *MR,* 339.

three lowest parts of his SAATBB group which represent Christ,[30] thus providing the equivalent of a motet with variable texture. The part of the Evangelist, however, seems to be exclusively in plainsong. Maistre Jhan was in the service of Hercules II (Ercole II d'Este) at Ferrara. Cipriano de Rore (1516–1565), who was also employed by that illustrious patron, published a St. John Passion in 1557, patterned after Maistre Jhan's work. Its full complement of voices is *a 6,* and the smallest number employed at one time is two; in the case of the *Christus* part these are again the lowest voices.[31] The tradition of giving the part of Christ to a bass seems to have been uninterrupted from the time when the plainsong version gave that text to the lowest register of the deacon who sang all the parts. It continued through the works discussed here, where His words were supplied in polyphonic form, in which cases the text was assigned to a low combination of voices.

All four of the Passion stories were set by Francesco Soriano (1549–1621).[32] Of the four, the setting according to St. Matthew is the most extensive for chorus, including six *si placet* sections. Among these are some of Christ's words at Gethsemane. While the texture of all four Passions is mainly *a 4,* and quite restrained, the accusation of the damsel *(Ex. 28a),* set for three high voices, provides a sharply dramatic touch. A degree of excitement is also evident in the brief *turba* section where the crowd asks for the release of Barrabas *(Ex.*

Ex. 28 *a)* Soriano, St. Matthew Passion, after *Musica Divina,* I (4), 10

30. *Ibid.,* 366.
31. *Ibid.,* 376.

32. *Musica Divina,* I(4), 3–48.

28b), and an obvious bit of word-painting is found at the point where the jeering observers taunt the crucified Christ *(Ex. 28c)*.

Of the four settings, the St. Mark is the simplest, containing only the *turba* passages; the St. John has two *si placet* utterances of Christ; the St. Luke, five—two on the Mount of Olives, one on the way to Calvary, and two Last Words; the St. Matthew is the most elaborate with its six *si placet* sections and its *obbligato* sections *a 2* and *a 3*.

Ex. 28 *b) Ibid.*, p. 13

c) Ibid., p. 15

Multiple settings were also produced by Giovanni Matteo Asola, whose versions according to Matthew, Mark, and Luke are simpler in nature than the contrapuntal examples of Soriano.[33] The choral sections are chordal rather than contrapuntal, in the style called *falsobordone*, conveying text in note-against-note fashion with most chords in root position. This style, Italian in origin, held small possibilities for dramatic delineation. There was also little danger of its wooing the ear of the listener from the text by either the complexities of counterpoint or the delights of dissonance.

There are four Passions, one according to each of the Gospels, dating from 1580, by Francisco Guerrero (1528–1599), a pupil of Morales.[34] Despite his expressive use of dissonance,[35] the writing is generally without distinction. In the two instances where the crowd, in the St. Matthew Passion, demands the crucifixion of Christ *(Ex. 29a)*, no attempt was made to portray the excitement of the moment. The second statement of *crucifigatur* is simply a modified transposition of the first *(Ex. 29b)*.

The two versions by Victoria are drawn from Matthew and John, and both are *a* 4.[36] The Matthew version is the more extensive, although the polyphonic settings are quite brief in total, and it includes

Ex. 29 Guerrero, St. Matthew Passion, after Pedrell, II, 31

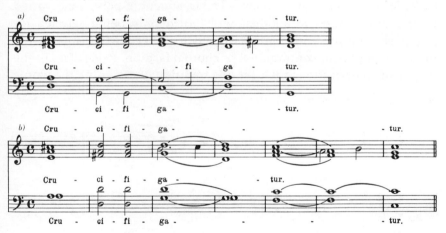

33. *MR*, 493.
34. Stevenson, *op. cit.*, 178. The Passions according to St. Matthew and St. John are printed in *Hispaniae schola musica sacra*, ed. Felipe Pedrell c. Barcelona: Juan Batista

Pujol, 1894–1898), ii, 24–47.
35. *MR*, 596.
36. Victoria, *Opera omnia*, v, 113–18; 170–73.

two sections *a 2* (one of them *si placet*), and one *a 3*. In that section of text where the crowd derisively invites Christ to descend from the Cross to demonstrate His omnipotence, Victoria's restraint is evident in his limiting of *descende* to a falling minor third *(Ex. 30)* as compared to the scalewise ninth employed by Soriano. The tradition of annual performance of Victoria's Passions in the Sistine Chapel for three centuries is doubtless due to their restraint and unobtrusive expressiveness. The music did not stoop to the colorless chordal rendition adopted by some of his contemporaries, nor did it indulge in excesses of emotion.

The only later English effort in the Latin tradition is that of William Byrd, whose *Turbarum voces in Passione Domini Secundum Joannem* was included in his *Gradualia*.[37] It consists of thirteen settings of the *turba* phrases *a 3*, with the other portions to be inserted in plainsong as they existed in the Sarum Use.[38] The rhythmic vitality and melodic contrasts are especially worthy of comment. The opening and closing sections are given uncomplicated chordal treatment, but the setting of *Ave, Rex Judaeorum* successfully conveys a feeling of mocking scorn, and the *Crucifige eum* phrase generates a great sense of excitement.

As most of these settings of the Latin Passions have been of the dramatic type, it can be seen that the expository sections were generally left to be sung in plainsong. The treatment of polyphony varied from one composer to another, with *turbae* only being selected for group singing, or with parts assigned to other participants in the drama being set in contrapuntal or chordal fashion. Regardless of the degree of complication, however, the tradition of assigning the words

Ex. 30 Victoria, St. Matthew Passion, after *Opera omnia*, V, 117

37. *The Collected Works of William Byrd,* ed. Edmund H. Fellowes (London: Stainer & Bell, 1937–1950), v, 198–206. 38. *Sarum* is the Latin for Salisbury. The liturgical practice of that cathedral differed from that of the commonly practiced Roman Rite. The Sarum Use was accepted into many of England's religious establishments until it was outlawed by the *First Book of Common Prayer* (1549).

of Christ to the low voice or a low group of voices had become stand-ard. Some Latin Passions had appeared in Germany by this time, and their presence will be noted when the subject again appears in con-nection with German developments stemming from the Reformation (See p. 190).

The Passion exerted a considerable influence on the early develop-ment of the oratorio. Because the major part of the development of that important form is concerned with the composers who were active during and after the years of the Reformation, the study of its back-grounds and developments will be undertaken in connection with a later chapter. While the oratorio is a church-connected composition, it bears no traditional attachment to religious music as a form that belongs to a religious service, nor has it usually been performed as a substitute for the service.

A number of other texts have been used by the masters of poly-phony after having begun their existence as plainsong settings. Both the Magnificat and Te Deum, for example, have survived in English translation in the Anglican Service as canticles, and have appeared sporadically at the hands of Protestant composers. It is, nevertheless, as Catholic forms that they are considered at this point. Where they appear as part of the Protestant practices, they will be discussed in connection with their surroundings.

In its polyphonic form, the Magnificat usually is a large motet, or group of short, motet-like settings based on the canticle of the Virgin (Luke 1:46–55) to which is added the Lesser Doxology. There are eight Gregorian recitation Tones upon which it is sung[39] and the one that serves as the basis of a polyphonic version may often be recog-nized from the title; e.g., *Magnificat quinti toni*. The Catholic procedure, with which we are concerned here, was to perform the Magnificat as the principal music of Vespers with alternating verses assigned to plainsong and polyphony, the opening word standing alone in plain-song whether the odd- or even-numbered verses were sung poly-phonically. The practice of setting the text to each of the modal recita-tion formulas in alternation persisted well beyond the Renaissance. Some exceptions may be found, however, in which the entire text was rendered polyphonically. Another method of alternation was that of

39. *LU*, 207–13; the Solemn Tones are printed on pp. 213–18. A review of tradi-tional practices in Magnificat composi-tion, and a number of new discoveries as well, may be found in Gustave Reese, "The Polyphonic Magnificat of the Ren-aissance as a Design in Tonal Centers," *Journal of the American Musicological So-ciety*, xiii/1–3 (1960), 68–78.

composing organ versets for the even-numbered verses of the Magnificat, leaving the odd-numbered verses to be rendered in plainsong.[40]
Since no part-singing is involved, these need not concern us here.

It is from England, so often unjustly accused of musical sterility,
that the earliest polyphonic Magnificats come to us. An example survives from the second half of the fourteenth century. The same music
in conductus style is found for each verse, and the plainsong appears
in the middle voice of the three that are composed.[41] The first verse no
longer survives, but the existence of music for all the other verses
shows that no plainsong interpolations were used. Dunstable's *Magnificat secundi toni*[42] distinguishes between the odd- and even-numbered verses, but not by alternating polyphony and plainsong. The
odd-numbered verses, instead, are written *a 3*, and the alternation is
made with duet settings. The first word was left in plainsong, just as
we have seen that the *incipits* of the Credo and Gloria were separated
from the body of the Mass section. In every verse, the plainsong is
freely treated in the upper voice, but the sections *a 2* are more elaborate than the three-voice settings. The rhythmic scheme of the composition divides it into three sections of equal length. The first four
stanzas are in triple meter; five through eight are in duple; and the
remainder are in triple. The polyphonic setting of all verses required
varied treatment of style and texture if it was to avoid falling into a
series of monotonous repetition patterns that were different only as
the text required adjustment.

The two Magnificats by Dufay[43] are set to polyphony throughout,
after the initial word in plainsong, and are divided into four sections
rather than the three that were used by Dunstable. The *Magnificat
octavi toni* has the first verse in each of its sections set in *fauxbourdon;*
the second, as a duo; and the third, *a 3*. Each of the four sections consists of a verse *a 2* framed by verses *a 3*. The entire composition is in
triple meter. His *Magnificat sexti toni* is more complex. Its sections are
not so clearly defined, as the *a 2* settings are only half a verse in length,
the second half being *a 3*. Verses 4–5, 8–9, and 12 are set in duple
meter, each of these changes coinciding with a change of texture from
a 3 to *a 2*. Finally, the plainsong in two instances is removed from the
superius and its opening notes appear in the tenor.

The alternation of meters appears in the *Magnificat secundi toni* by

40. The settings of Girolamo Cavazzoni
give the odd-numbered verses to the
organ, leaving the even-numbered ones
for plainsong rendition. *MR*, 536.

41. Example printed in Harrison, *Music
in Medieval Britain*, 346.
42. *Musica Britannica*, VIII, 95–98.
43. *DTÖ*, XIV/XV, 169–74; 174–78.

Gilles Binchois (*GMB* 43). The scheme found in Dunstable's composition appears here again; the middle group of four verses is in duple meter, the outer groups are triple. Alternation of texture also appears regularly. The even-numbered verses are *a* 2; the odd-numbered, *a* 3. There are only small differences between the various sections of each type; that is, all of the odd-numbered settings are substantially the same, and the even-numbered ones also have a great degree of similarity. Most of the difference can be attributed to the necessity for setting lines of different lengths. The settings for Tones I and IV also treat the entire text polyphonically, but the version in the third Tone alternates between polyphony and plainsong, with only the odd-numbered verses provided.[44]

The Eton choirbook, compiled near the end of the fifteenth century, supplies a group of English Magnificats by six composers from the last half of the century.[45] Two of these, by Nesbett and Robert Fayrfax, are reconstructed from other sources, but the remaining four, by William Horwood, Hugo Kellyk, Walter Lambe, and William Stratford, appear complete in the choirbook. The works have many features in common. Each provides a setting of only the even-numbered verses, and each sets verses six and eight in duple meter, leaving a pair of triple-meter verses at the beginning and end. The plainsong is found in the tenor. The similarity of patterns in the several tenors has been commented on elsewhere by Harrison.[46]

Johannes Martini (fl. 1475–1492), a Fleming who spent his productive life in Italy, is represented by a *Magnificat secundi toni* (*CW* 46) in which the polyphonic settings of the odd-numbered verses are *a* 4 except for verse three which is *a* 3. Since he provided no variety through changes of meter, and little by varying the number of voice parts, Martini turned to other methods of maintaining interest in his verses. Numerous instances of imitation are present, often affecting several figures in a verse or sometimes, as in the seventh verse,[47] continuing two voices in canon until the entrance of the third voice, which appears one-third of the way through the verse. The fourth voice, when not participating in the imitative figure — as the tenor does not in verse seven — appears in longer note-values than the other parts. The elaborated plainsong moves quite freely from one voice to another.

44. *MR*, 91.
45. *Musica Britannica*, XII, 63–111.
46. *The New Oxford History of Music*, III,

324ff.
47. Numbered IV in *CW*, which numbers the polyphonic verses consecutively.

If it seems that attention has been focused on formal characteristics rather than on content, it must be remembered that the close
adherence of the Magnificat to its plainsong Tones made variety in
content difficult to achieve. So long as no repetition of text took place,
the usual procedure called for florid elaboration of the plainsong in
one or more parts, with a longer melismatic flight before the final
syllable. Variety was more accessible in metrical and textural change.
The method employed by Martini, in which imitative segments similar to points of imitation were tossed about among the voices, made
the direct relationship with the Gregorian Tones less clearly evident,
even when the imitation was based on the plainsong material.[48]

While the *cantus firmus* technique was common in Masses and motets by this time—and even on the verge of becoming old-fashioned—
it has been conspicuously absent from the settings of the Magnificat.
It appears, however, in Magnificats by both Nicolas Gombert (after
1480–c.1556) and Costanzo Festa (fl. 1517–1545). The application of
imitative counterpoint, with its resultant repetition of text, opened
the way to longer settings of the verses and to a greater degree of
sophistication in technical matters. While there were no examples of
the esoteric mensuration canon, at least one composer was moved to
attempt mathematical games of the simpler sort. Gombert, whose
Magnificats were actually cycles of short motets, increased the number
of voices in each verse of his Magnificat in Tones III and VIII. In setting the even-numbered verses, he began with three voices in verse
two, increasing by one voice in each of the following verses, until he
was writing *a 8* in verse twelve. This final verse required the resolution of two canons in order to produce the eight voices.[49]

Palestrina's total contribution in Magnificats was exceeded by
that of Lassus, but the Palestrina works loom larger because his total
of thirty-five is available for examination.[50] Every contingency is
provided for in the total of four complete series and three additional
settings, one each for the first, fourth, and sixth Tones. Of the complete series, one sets the odd-numbered verses *a 4;* two provide settings of the even-numbered verses *a 4*—many of these have some
sections for three voices, and some for five, while another, *a 5* and *a 6,*

48. This period is studied further in
Edward R. Lerner, "The Polyphonic Mag-
nificat in 15th-Century Italy," *The Musical
Quarterly,* L/1 (January, 1964), 44–58.
49. Nicolai Gombert, *Opera Omnia,* ed.
Joseph Schmidt-Görg (*Corpus Mensur-*

abilis Musicae, XI) (Rome: American Institute of Musicology, 1951–1963), IV,
34–37.
50. Palestrina, *Le Opere Complete,* XVI;
Werke, XXVII.

provides only the even-numbered verses.[51]

It is reasonable to expect that among thirty-five settings of this text, some means of achieving variety, beyond altering the number of voices in each setting and changing from odd-numbered verses to even, may be found. An examination of the set reveals a sort of loosely conceived, but skillfully executed plan. Among the sixteen Magnificats published in the *Liber primus* of 1591—the only ones to appear in print during his lifetime—none has any change in the number of voice parts until after two of the polyphonic verses have been sung. After that point, usually one verse appears *a 3* instead of *a 4*. The need for variety among these simpler works did not appear to be so pressing to the composer. Each verse is set as a short motet of about twenty-five measures in the style of imitative counterpoint that was used for any other motet form. The points of imitation are taken from the Gregorian Tones, and repetition of text, as may be expected in this style, is common. The freedom with which the Tones were used can be seen in the *Gloria Patri* (verse eleven) of the Magnificat in Tone III. The opening of the plainsong and the beginning of verse eleven are given here *(Ex. 31)*. The tune is familiar to Protestants as the hymn, *The Strife Is O'er, The Battle Done*, which is, of course, an altered version of Palestrina's original. This is one of the rare appearances of triple meter in his Magnificats.

The series that makes up *Liber secundus,* while still basically *a 4*, is considerably more complex than the two preceding sets. Palestrina chose to expand the choral texture instead of thinning it as he had

Ex. 31 Tone 3, *LU*, 208

Palestrina, *Magnificat Tertii Toni* [♮] Verse 11, *Liber primus*, 1591

Glo - ri - a   Pa - tri,   et Fi - li - o,

51. In the *Werke*, each setting of this last-named set opens with *Anima mea Dominum,* the second hemistich of the first verse, in polyphony. These settings from verse one have been removed in the newer *Opere Complete* because they fail to conform to normal practice and, more important, are not to be found in the sources from which the Magnificats come. See *Le Opere Complete,* XVI, xivff.

done in the earlier examples. The two instances in which he limited his parts to three occur in relatively early sections of the setting—the eighth verse in Tone III and the sixth verse in Tone IV—while the number of parts in later verses, especially the last, is increased to five or six. In three instances he adds the complication of a canon that must be resolved in order to produce the fifth or sixth voice, and the length of each section now reaches about thirty-five measures.

It is with *Liber tertius* that the composer began to extend himself. While he found it practical to increase the length of some few verses to forty and fifty measures, most of his alterations appear in the form of changes of texture or canonic intricacies. His greatest degree of complexity is reached in the setting in Tone IV[52] which provides something different in every verse. The second verse—this is one of a series of even-numbered settings—requires that the sixth voice be extracted from the first tenor part by resolution of a canon. The fourth verse employs canon between the same voices, along with the presentation of material by successive pairs of voices. The texture, which had been *a 6*, is reduced to *a 4* in the sixth verse, returning to *a 6* in the eighth verse which again features canon, but in triple meter. Not satisfied with this, Palestrina has so contrived the movement that its performance in duple meter is equally effective. Verse ten is a straightforward motet for five voices, but the concluding verse expands the sonority to seven parts, of which five are written out. The other two (Cantus II and Altus II) result from the resolution of canons at the fifth and the octave. The only other device that Palestrina used in connection with this form was that of the *coro spezzato*, which is employed in the *Magnificat primi toni*,[53] one of the three examples that did not belong to any of the four series. Coupled with the *coro spezzato*, however, is a continuous method of writing that is not available to any composer who sets alternated verses. In this one Magnificat, Palestrina, by choosing to set all the text after the opening word, produced a lengthy motet that is not interrupted by sectional divisions. While each verse, and even a number of hemistichs, can be found to divide the text between choirs and different textures, the variety with which Palestrina accomplished his settings of the verses is impressive. Alternation of hemistichs or lesser portions of a verse is the most common procedure, although variety is present even in such an apparently simple approach, either through differences in the length of the seg-

52. *Le Opere Complete*, XVI, 229–45.   53. *Ibid.*, 328–34.

ments assigned each chorus or the order in which they are presented. Changes of texture are achieved by combining portions of both choirs, as in verse four where *cantus* and *altus* of Choir I are combined with *cantus* and tenor of Choir II; or in verse five, which combines the three lower voices of each choir. The two full choirs sing together in only two places; for four measures at the end of verse three, and for six measures at the end of the composition. Verse eleven, *Gloria Patri, et Filio, et Spiritui Sancto,* is in triple meter.

A Magnificat in Tone I by Giovanni Gabrieli[54] exhibits many characteristics similar to those of the Palestrina work just discussed. It is set as a continuous motet after the chanting of the initial word, it employs alternation of choirs for either hemistichs or shorter sections—often of single words—and it moves into triple meter for a brief four measures at the Gloria Patri. In two respects the Gabrieli setting differs sharply from that of Palestrina: the setting is entirely syllabic, and it alternates harmonic segments rather than contrapuntal textures. The contrast is always between the two full choirs rather than between selected parts of each. It is heightened by the procedure that Gabrieli commonly adopted of using two choirs of different voice combinations: Choir I is SSAT, Choir II is ATTB.

Among the motets of Gabrieli's *Sacrae symphoniae* (1597), is one other Magnificat,[55] also in the first Tone, in which the entire text is given to the polyphonic singers after the opening intonation. The work presents sharply differentiated sonorities in three choirs: Choir I, SSAT; Choir II, SATB *a cappella;* Choir III, ATBB. While the unaccompanied choir alternates freely with the instrumentally supported groups, it also sounds by itself at several points. There is also one instance, in a *Magnificat sexti toni,*[56] where Gabrieli set the opening word polyphonically. Three choirs are employed, in the same voice distribution as in the work discussed above. Choir III sings the opening word with ascending canonic entrances. Following this, the second hemistich is introduced with a pyramid of choirs rather than parts, producing an effect of dazzling pomp.

Returning to the Spanish contrapuntists who flourished in the sixteenth century, we find two sets of Magnificats by Morales, published in 1545. One is a cycle of the eight Tones with settings of the

54. Gabrieli, *Opera Omnia,* II, 44–54; *Music of Gabrieli and His Time* (Ossining, N. Y.: William Salloch, 1960), 18–23. Reprinted from Carl von Winterfeld, *Johan-*

nes Gabrieli und sein Zeitalter (Berlin: 1834). 55. Gabrieli, *Opera Omnia,* II, 177–97. 56. *Music of Gabrieli and His Time,* 124f. Only the first two verses are printed.

odd-numbered verses; the other, of the even-numbered.[57] They are mostly four-voice compositions in imitative counterpoint, their thematic material quoting from the Gregorian formulas. The voices occasionally are only three in number, but expand to six parts in the twelfth verse of the even-numbered settings, with only one exception. Six of these final verses depend on a canonic resolution for their full complement of parts, the canonic voices announcing the plainsong with little alteration in long notes. The end of each of these settings is thereby unified through a presentation of the Chant, while it conforms to the general practice of bringing the most elaborate music into play at the end of the composition. The *Magnificat octavi toni*[58] (*TEM* 23) of the even-numbered set adds a further unifying touch in which the plainsong migrates from one voice to another throughout the entire composition, beginning in the uppermost voice and returning there when all of the others have completed their presentations of it, each of the presentations being confined to a single verse. In verse twelve, the two canonic voices are assigned the plainsong.

Two complete series of Magnificats by Victoria,[59] one setting the odd-numbered verses, the other setting the even-numbered, follow the usual pattern in having mostly four-part writing, but with variable numbers of parts for some verses. To the general description given by Reese[60] may be added the fact that the method of setting the final verse differs in each series. Victoria increased the number of voices in the final verse. Verse eleven, *Gloria Patri, et Filio, et Spiritui Sancto,* always *a 5,* is less elaborate than the setting of verse twelve, *Sicut erat in principio, et nunc, et semper, et in saecula saeculorum. Amen.* The last even-numbered verse usually calls for an increase to six voices by the use of canon.

Victoria's two polychoral Magnificats with organ are of interest not merely because they call for organ in addition to the choirs, but because they set the entire text of the canticle, with the exception of the opening word. His *Magnificat primi toni* is for two equal choirs and organ.[61] The general plan of the work calls for each choir to sing a verse by itself, after which the two join forces for the next verse. However, since both choirs sing the final two verses together, Choir I loses one opportunity to sing by itself at verse eight. Instead, both

57. Morales, *Opera omnia,* iv. Stevenson, *op. cit.,* 80–89, presents strong evidence that these are eight continuous polyphonic settings of the canticle, separated into odd- and even-numbered sets by publishers.

58. *Ibid., 126–32.*
59. Victoria, *Opera omnia,* iii, 1–80.
60. *MR,* 605.
61. Victoria, *Opera omnia,* iii, 81–94.

choirs sing that verse, after which the sequence of appearances, Choir II, Choir I, Tutti, is continued. The contrast between verses is heightened by the further difference that, while both choirs are SATB, the organ part appears only with Choir I. When both choirs are singing, the organ does not provide a composite part, but is performing, *colla parte*, the music of the first choir. Two versions of verse five are provided; the first for Choir I with organ, the second, a *Canon ad unisonum* III *vocum si placet*. This appears to be an additional setting rather than an alternate one.

The *Magnificat sexti toni*[62] calls for three equal choirs. The organ is again played only when Choir I sings. The addition of the organ seems to be less an effort to emulate the Venetian style than to produce more elaborate works than usual without completely violating the principles of restrained polyphony. Victoria was probably able to write for only one organ, as it is not to be expected that several organs were available to him in a single building. While he was probably aware of the possibilities of contrast open to him through the use of an independent instrumental part, his restraint is always evident in the restriction of the organ part to duplication of the voice parts of Choir I. He eschewed the *concertato* effects of the Venetians, but grasped the opportunity to set his choirs apart by modest contrast. The pyramid effect of successive entrances in verse eleven is an example that is perhaps symbolic as well as musically variegated. Choir III sings *Gloria Patri*, Choir II, *et Filio*, and Choir I finishes the verse, *et Spiritui Sancto*, with organ.[63] If his choirs were spatially separated, the effect must have been stunning in contrast to the usual *a cappella* style, even though it may seem pallid in comparison with the Venetian productions.

The polyphonic Magnificat came to Germany at a relatively late date. Its presence in both Catholic and Protestant areas indicates a thriving interest in its production in the old and new beliefs alike. Such compositions, whatever the religious belief of their creators, generally appeared as settings of the Latin text. It is, therefore, difficult, if not impossible, to establish from the composition itself whether the work was intended for the old tradition or the new. Many composers, as well, moved freely between Protestant and Catholic areas, studying and working with the leading figures of Italian music, thus making it impossible to state clearly whether each composition with Latin text was intended for one belief or the other. In the case of

62. *Ibid.*, 95–106.   63. *Ibid.*, 104.

Adam Rener *(c. 1485–1520)*, whose eight Magnificats were published more than two decades after his death in 1520, there is no doubt of adherence to the Catholic tradition. His *Magnificat primi toni*[64] makes no new contribution to composition of the form, although its clear statement of the plainsong material in the setting of even-numbered verses demonstrates that the prevailing Italian style was known in Germany during the first quarter of the sixteenth century.

Nearly three-quarters of a century later, in 1591, there appeared in print two Magnificats by Hans Leo Hassler, who had studied with Andrea Gabrieli in Venice. This association, coupled with Hassler's friendship with Giovanni Gabrieli, left its mark upon his musical style, but not in connection with these two works. That Hassler had absorbed the polychoral spirit is shown by the presence of compositions *a 8* and *a 12* in the same volume, but the two Magnificats are brief, simple settings *a 4* of the even-numbered verses. The one in Tone v[65] is principally chordal in style with two short sections of imitative writing. The polyphonic sections are in the form of insertions between the plainsong verses rather than as alternating musical sections, by reason of their failure to quote or reflect the plainsong material. The Magnificat in Tone VIII,[66] however, bases the material of the second verse on the Gregorian melody, and is a short motet with each of its two points of imitation derived from the melodic formulas of the two hemistichs of the Tone. References are made to the Chant in the following verses, but no clear quotation is heard until verse twelve when the bass proclaims the entire Chant in long notes against the upper three voices which engage in flowing counterpoint.

Although Lassus (1532–1594) wrote exactly one hundred Magnificats,[67] only a small number of these are readily available in print.[68] A group of nine, printed a century ago,[69] should not be considered typical of his style, as they are the simplest of the entire hundred.

64. T. W. Werner, "Die Magnificat-Kompositionen Adam Rener's," *Archiv für Musikwissenschaft*, II, (1919), 195–265.
65. *DdT*, II, 33–35.
66. *Ibid.*, 36–39.
67. References to a total of 101 Magnificats seem to stem from an error in the thematic index of R. Eitner, *Chronologisches Verzeichniss der gedruckten Werke von H. L. von Hassler und O. de Lassus* (Berlin: Bahn, 1874), where one Magnificat is listed twice, once as a *Tonus peregrinus* and

again as a parody.
68. Professor Fred Dempster has kindly provided detailed information about the Lassus Magnificats that are not readily accessible. Most of the material here is a condensation of information supplied by him.
69. *Musica Divina*, I(3), 253–81; 290–97. The second verse of a *Magnificat sexti toni, a 5*, appears in *Music of Gabrieli and His Time*, 53ff. The Chant appears as a *cantus firmus* in the tenor.

If Lassus felt himself to be free of the restrictions of the Council of Trent—such freedom seems to have been generally enjoyed by German composers, and Lassus spent most of his life in Munich—it may be reflected in his liberal adoption of the parody technique in connection with Magnificats as well as with Masses. Forty of these works can now be linked to earlier pieces and three others may yet find their way into the total (see Table VI).

TABLE VI

Sources of Lassus' Magnificats

  9 are based on chansons by Lassus
  3 are based on chansons by other composers
  2 are based on madrigals by Lassus
16 are based on madrigals by other composers
  5 are based on motets by Lassus
  2 are based on Masses by Josquin[70]
  3 are based on paraphrases of hymns
57 are based on Magnificat Tones[71]
  3 are not based on Magnificat Tones, but
      have not been definitely identified as parodies.

A comparison can be made between Lassus' Magnificat *Da le belle contrade (Ex. 32)* and the madrigal by Cipriano de Rore (1516 –1565) upon which it is based (*HAM* 131). In this, and the other thirty-nine parodies, Lassus draws upon the entire complex of the original piece and never restricts his borrowing to quotations of the melodies or tenors.

In the Magnificats that do not borrow from other compositions, but are based on the Magnificat Tones, Lassus apparently had strong preferences. Among the individual versets based upon the Tones, 175 use a *cantus firmus* technique that employs the Tone either in long

70. In as recent a volume as Wolfgang Boetticher, *Orlando di Lasso und seine Zeit, 1532–1594. Repertoire-Untersuchung zur Musik der Spät-renaissance.* Band I. *Monographie.* (Kassel & Basel: Bärenreiter-Verlag, 1958), these two Magnificats are classified as *cantus firmus* settings based on hymns. Professor Dempster has since established their parody relationship.
71. Lassus set all the verses of three Mag-nificats in this group, thus deviating from his usual practice of writing polyphony for only the even-numbered verses. One of the three has continuous music throughout, in motet style, including a polyphonic setting of the initial word; another has the verses set separately and includes a polyphonic setting of the first word; the third has separate units and the opening word is sung in plainsong.

Ex. 32 Parody technique in Lassus' Magnificat No. 48, *Da le belle contrade* (1585), extract from transcription by F. Dempster.

note-values or in free rhythmic treatment; 94 are based on paraphrases of the melodic formulas; 29 use sections of the formulas as motives for imitation; and 28 individual versets are freely composed.

A number of further developments in German Magnificats may be found also, and they will be discussed in connection with music of the Reformation composers, in another chapter.

In some types of musical expression there is confusion over whether a Latin setting in England was intended for Catholic or Anglican use. The matter is far more clear in connection with the Magnificat settings than with the early anthems, for those in English are almost without doubt related to the Anglican Service, while those with Latin text belong to the Catholic practice. The course followed by composers of Latin Magnificats in England during the sixteenth century can be seen in the works left by Robert Fayrfax (1464–1521) (*HMS*, iii, 65–67), John Taverner (*c. 1492–1545*), Robert White (*c. 1530–1574*), and Thomas Tallis (*c. 1505–1585*).

There are three Magnificats by Taverner; one in the sixth Tone, *a 4*; another apparently based on the third Tone, *a 5*; and the third a free elaboration of the first Tone, *a 6*.[72] All of them are settings of only the even-numbered verses, but they differ from Continental models in their clear division of each verse into two parts. The two hemistichs are sometimes separated by a complete cadence in all voices; sometimes by weaker cadences when the new and old sections overlap. References to the plainsong usually appear in an inner voice, often beginning as a declamatory statement in long notes and later participating in the polyphonic texture as does the tenor in the Magnificat *a 6*. Imitative counterpoint prevails throughout.

Robert White's Magnificat[73] is largely *a 6*, with complete sections for three and four voices. Based on the first Tone, it provides clear statements of the plainsong, which appears in the tenor in verse two, bass in verse four, tenor in verse six, the uppermost voice in verse ten, and is shared by the bass and tenor in the final verse. Whenever the plainsong appears, it is surrounded with polyphonic activity. Verse eight, which contains no statement of the Chant, is simply a brief motet without *cantus firmus*.

A Magnificat *a 4* and another *a 5*,[74] the latter linked with a *Nunc dimittis* based on the opening material of the Magnificat, represent the contribution of Thomas Tallis to this form. Both works are completely in imitative style and set only the even-numbered verses, as did those of the other Tudor composers. The four-voice example makes clear divisions of each verse into hemistichs with contrasting material, but the first hemistich of each verse opens with a three-note motive that appears with various rhythmic alterations in one or more of the voices (*Ex. 33*). The Magnificat *a 5* makes no division within

72. *TCM*, iii, 3–8, 9–16, 17–25.   74. *Ibid.*, vi, 64–72, 73–84.
73. *Ibid.*, v, 3–13.

Ex. 33 Motive from Tallis' Magnificat *a 4*

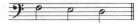

the verses; each verse instead is a short motet built on successive points of imitation.

The wide adoption of the Magnificat in the Catholic service is intimately connected with the veneration of the Virgin, a practice that assumed such large proportions that it is commonly known as the Marian cult. The great number of pieces dedicated to Mary reflects this practice in motets, votive antiphons, Masses, and especially in the use of the Magnificat in the daily Vespers, where it is the principal point of interest. Its close adherence, in most cases, to the Gregorian Tones has served to limit its composition to a less complex form of display than is found in some forms of polyphony, although the poly-choral settings, apparently for special occasions, sometimes border on the dramatic. These large-scale pieces, while elaborate, seldom employed the techniques of word-painting that formed such a large part of the composer's vocabulary. Tradition demanded restraint as a visible evidence of devotion, and the only common exploitation of symbolic writing appeared regularly at, or immediately preceding, the reference to Abraham in verse ten, where a gesture of respect was made to the patriarch by an elaborate musical treatment or, more often, the setting of a brief section in triple meter. Likewise, the opening of the Gloria Patri, with its reference to the Trinity, brought about the common use of triple meter at that point.

The transfer of this Marian devotional music to the Anglican and Lutheran services, both of which were strongly opposed to gestures that reflected worship of the Virgin, clearly demonstrate the strength of tradition that was associated with this canticle when the break with Rome came about. The Anglican Church adopted it as a part of Evening Prayer, and it also appeared in the Lutheran service as a part of the evening worship.

It has not been possible or practical to cite examples from all the composers who contributed to the development of the Magnificat in Latin. Its practice was international, its acceptance general, and its mutation continuous. Among those composers who produced either cycles or significant individual settings, but who have not been mentioned, are Josquin, Soriano, and Clemens. Even in Poland, where outside influences were known through the arrival of the Jesuits and some Italian musicians, a Magnificat for three choirs by Mikolaj Zieleński — but printed in Venice — may be noted.[75] The dissimilarity of the voice arrangement of the three choirs points to a knowledge of the Venetian practice, if not to a direct association with it.

A number of other polyphonic forms that have their origins in plainsong have achieved places of importance in religious music of the Renaissance and later periods. The Lamentations[76] for the last three days in Holy Week were widely set by Renaissance composers. They have not been transmitted into the framework of Protestant practice, as have most of the other notable forms that blossomed in the Renaissance. Best known are the Lamentations of Palestrina, Allegri, Carpentras, and Lassus, but numerous other settings are of interest. They are generally restrained in expression because of the mournful spirit of the text.

By contrast, the Te Deum,[77] employed on occasions of thanksgiving and rejoicing has evolved from a plainsong canticle to a daily part of the Anglican Morning Prayer. Sometimes massive settings have been made to celebrate national victories, more often military than spiritual, and a tradition of polyphonic setting also exists in the Renaissance.[78] Some instances of elaborate settings occur in more recent history, often intended for use outside the church.

75. *Music of the Polish Renaissance*, ed. Jozef M. Chominski and Zofia Lissa ([n.p.]: Polski Wydawnictwo Muzyczne, 1955), 274–305.

76. *LU*, 626–32. A list of the principal Renaissance composers of Lamentations is given in the Index to *MR*, 982f; see also *Grove's*, v, 34f and *HD*, 392f.

77. *LU*, 1832ff.

78. For Renaissance composers, see *MR*, 1014; brief discussion may be found in *Grove's*, viii, 353ff and *HD*, 734.

2

CATHOLIC TRADITION
AND
PROTESTANT INNOVATION –
A MARRIAGE OF CONVENIENCE

I T I S D I F F I C U L T to escape the feeling that vernacular communication is more capable of moving the emotions than rendi-
tions of the same idea in Latin or another foreign tongue. However
intense may have been the expression of faith, supplication, fear, or
hope, conveyed in the text of the Mass or motet, its transmission in
Latin carried a concept of religion in the hands of intermediaries
possessing special power in their command of a secret tongue –
a quasi-thaumaturgical communication with God through the intercession of a select emissary. Although the thought that is conveyed is not altered, nor the intensity of its emotion increased
thereby, the presentation of an idea in one's native tongue – his
daily means of expression – permits the auditor to move a step
nearer to participation. He feels that the expressed idea may be his,
rather than that of a large and impersonal group.

A tremendous advantage was available to the Protestant composer in this new type of communication. His expression was
clothed in the language of the listener, and bore either the familiar
message of Scripture or the earnest yearnings of the individual.
When the text of *Herr, wenn ich nur dich habe*, or *O Lord, bow down
Thine Ear* was set, the emotional fire of the composer using the

vernacular may have been no greater than that which inspired his Catholic counterpart who conveyed the same idea in Latin, but the subjective response of his listener was probably far different from that of the recipient of its Latin equivalent.

Although a basic principle of the reform movements was congregational comprehension of the form and substance of the religious service, it did not bring about an immediate suppression of Latin. The mingling of English and Latin in the English Church continued for years after the break between England and the Roman Church; German and Latin likewise served the Lutheran Church as alternating or equally acceptable languages. Composers who served both causes with their music, and who provided both the Latin and vernacular settings for worship, were numerous. When changes in liturgical practice came about, the music often continued to employ stylistic features that were still clearly related to the old tradition, even though the language of the setting or its particular place in the service underwent a change. The new musical forms closely followed those that had been in use in the Catholic observance, while the styles also changed slowly, both form and style developing in relation to musical function as well as to liturgical requirements.

Chapter V

The Anthem in the

Anglican Church

THE transition from Catholicism to Protestantism in England was neither sudden nor painless. More than a simple change of Latin liturgical music into English equivalents was necessary before the distinctive music of the Anglican belief could stand on its own ground. A common misconception is the one that sees close, continuous musical relationships across the abrupt and severe rupture between the English Crown and the papacy. The action of Henry VIII, severing the connection between his religious establishments and Rome, did not introduce a new set of beliefs into English life. Catholicism continued in England, but the influence of the pope was thereafter gone. Nor was the use of Latin text a thing of the past. English choral music continued with Latin text, but increasingly large amounts of music with English words date from this period, both in compositions borrowed from the Roman tradition with English words instead of Latin, and in those composed specifically for the English Church. The two forms that developed uniquely in England were the anthem and the Service, both remaining vital to the present time in the land of their origin and appearing in America as well. The Service appears in the rites of the Episcopal Church, while the anthem, in addition to serving its time-honored function in that branch of Christian belief, has made its way in greatly simplified form into other areas of Protestantism.

These two bodies of musical material developed with the movement of the English religious practice from Catholicism to Protestantism. The anthem followed a course that provided it with at least two clearly distinguishable types, and the Service likewise underwent certain changes. For the present, it is sufficient to say that the Service comprised three principal groups of musical settings: those for Morning Prayer, those for Evening Prayer, and those for Communion. Of the three, the settings for Morning Prayer became most common, although many composers provided music for the entire series.

While there is a direct connection between the motets that so admirably served the Catholic Church and the anthems that sprang up as their partial substitutes in England, it must be stressed that the anthem served only as a musical, and not as a liturgical substitute for the motet. The relationship between motet and anthem, as well as that between Mass and Service, has been greatly oversimplified; it was a "musico-technical one, and not musico-liturgical."[1] While it was possible to dispense entirely with any musical expression at the point in the religious observance that was served by the anthem, the motet had a fixed liturgical position and function that was undeviatingly observed except when the presentation of text through plainsong was provided at the same point.

> The term "motet" . . . was loosely applied to polyphonic music for the choir office and the Proper of the Mass. The Elizabethan anthem, designed to follow the Third Collect at Morning and Evening Prayer "in Quires and Places where they sing" was, as the Prayer Book tells us, by no means an essential part of the liturgy. It was a pleasant adornment to the ceremony, but one which could easily be dispensed with. The so-called "motet" could not be dispensed with unless plainsong took its place.[2]

The freedom that was exercised in the placement, or even the omission, of the anthem is evident in the absence of early specific directions regulating its presence and position in the order of worship. Even as late a regulatory volume as the Prayer Book of 1559 lacked specific directions concerning the position of the anthem, although it commonly appeared at the end of Morning and Evening Prayer. A century later those churches that could do so performed two anthems at each of those formal observances of public worship. By 1663 those churches that could provide a completely staffed choir were including four anthems as part of the Sunday services. Two anthems were sung at Morning Prayer and two at Evening Prayer, the second coming after the sermon.[3] The anthem was an important part of the Anglican Service even though it did not figure as a liturgical portion of it. While it was impossible to use Latin motets after English became the official language of the Anglican Service, it was desirable, even before the abolition of Latin, to introduce English settings. These were provided not only by the creation of entirely new

1. Denis Stevens, *Tudor Church Music*   2. *Ibid.*, 51f.
(London: Faber and Faber, 1961), 51.   3. *Grove's*, I, 166.

compositions, but also by the simple method of adapting an already available piece to English text. In 1548 a Royal Injunction specified that the music at Lincoln Minster should henceforth be marked by three new principles: the substitution of English for Latin; the abolition of Marian texts and pieces in praise of saints; and the institution of syllabic settings.[4] The observance of these principles had far-reaching effects upon English church music.

The adaptation of a Latin piece to English can be seen in a portion of Taverner's *Missa Gloria tibi Trinitas.* The *in nomine* section of the Benedictus[5] was, in its original setting, a polyphonic elaboration of three words. The English adaptation to the text, *In trouble and adversity*,[6] probably made by Thomas Causton (Caustun) (?–1569), sets an eight-line paraphrase of the first two verses of Psalm 20 (xix) to the same music. The substitution of this comparatively lengthy text required that certain rhythmic alterations and repetitions be made in the music. Syllabic writing, although Causton apparently strove for it, was not always possible, and some awkward combinations of words and music occur. The anthem, while filling the need for music in the new service, was bound to the old tradition by everything except its English text *(Ex. 34)*. It may be assumed that the reason the adaptation did not include the opening of the Benedictus lies in its assignment of the opening three words to a different group of singers from that used in the borrowed portion. The opening section of the Mass movement is assigned to a TBB group, while that bearing the text *in nomine Domini* is SATB. The need for texts based on the Psalms was responsible for a large number of adaptations from motets and Mass movements.[7] While it is not always possible to identify the person who made the English arrangement, it is known that some of the adaptions were made by the original composers.

Among anthems composed expressly for the English services, Christopher Tye's *(c. 1500–1573) I will exalt thee*[8] illustrates a number of features that appear commonly in compositions in and after the Tudor period. As was the case with lengthy motets, it is divided into two *partes,* each of which may be performed independently of the other, but which provide a more completely satisfactory exposition of the text when their relationship is preserved. The texture of *pars* I

4. *MR*, 796.
5. *TCM*, i, 148f; a practical edition of the Mass is published by Stainer & Bell. Benedictus in *HMS*, iii, 68–70.
6. *Ibid.*, iii, 199f.
7. Some of these are listed in Stevens, *op. cit.*, 60f, and *MR*, 795ff.

8. Boyce, *CM* (London: By the editor, 1760–1778), ii, 10–18; practical edition by Oxford University Press. A list of Tudor music in practical editions is given in Stevens, *op. cit.*, 78–86.

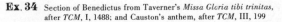

Ex. 34 Section of Benedictus from Taverner's *Missa Gloria tibi trinitas*, after *TCM*, I, 1488; and Causton's anthem, after *TCM*, III, 199

is polyphonic, and calls for considerable alternation between the *decani* and *cantoris* sides of the choir. The measures leading up to the final cadence are completely in chordal style. *Pars* II, while not entirely homophonic, gives more attention to clear divisions into sections, especially at the points where new text is presented and at the cadence where the change from half choirs to full choirs occurs *(Ex. 35)*.

The alternation between the two halves of the choir—*decani* on the south or Dean's side; *cantoris* on the north or Precentor's side—is not directly related to the antiphonal style of Italian church music. The division of the choir was a long-standing tradition, useful in the singing of psalms and other responsive music. While antiphonal singing in the rest of Europe carried with it the contrast between two choirs, often of different composition, that merged into a larger, multi-voiced group, the English pattern at this time simply alternated and joined two equal groups of singers without increasing the number of voice parts. The middle section of *O Lord, the maker of all things*,[9] attributed to King Henry VIII, is a homophonic segment between two contrapuntal sections. It alternates twice between the two equal sides of the choir, and closes with a section for full chorus *(Ex. 36)*. The polyphonic sections that enclose the homophony are intended to be sung by the full complement of voices. The cross relations at many of the cadences are characteristic of English style.

In compositions that required more than four parts, the additional voices were drawn from the choir in such a way that half-choirs and other small groups were not always together as performing units. A five-part piece in which the sopranos were divided would have the altos, tenors, and basses of both sides of the choir singing, but the soprano I would be heard from the *decani* side, and the soprano II from the *cantoris*. Dividing the choir in this fashion actually weakened the divided part while it thickened the texture. Only when all four parts were divided was balance maintained; anything less tended to upset the equality of the parts. Byrd's *Bow thine ear*,[10] a full anthem in five parts, uses the SAB group from both sides of the choir, but divides the tenors; Gibbons' *Hosanna to the son of David*,[11] *a 6*, calls

9. Boyce, *CM*, II, 1–4; practical edition by Oxford University Press. The attribution is open to doubt. Some writers believe that the style of the anthem represents a more sophisticated expression than that which could be expected of Henry. Cf. Henry Leland Clarke, "John Blow, 1649–1708, Last Composer of an Era" (unpublished Ph.D. thesis, Harvard University, 1947), I, 140. However, Thomas Tudway, "A Collection of the Most Celebrated Services and Anthems . . ." British Museum MSS Harley 7337–7342, cred-

its the work to Henry, adding that it was originally his setting of a Latin text and that it was sung in the Royal Chapel. It must also be mentioned that *MR*, 802, favors William Mundy (*c. 1529–1591*) as the probable composer. See also Edmund H. Fellowes, *English Cathedral Music* (London: Methuen & Co., 1948), 41f.

10. Boyce, *CM*, 29–33; practical edition by Novello.

11. *Ibid.*, 41–47; practical editions by Novello and Oxford University Press.

Ex. 35 *I will exalt thee* (Pars II), Tye (Boyce, *CM*, II, 14f)

Ex. 36 *O Lord, the maker of all things*, attributed to Henry VIII (Boyce, *CM*, II, 2-3)

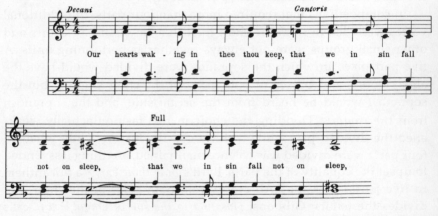

for the trebles and contratenors from each side separately, while all
tenors and basses sing as undivided units; his eight-voice *O clap
your hands*[12] requires the constant efforts of all singers in both the
decani and *cantoris* sides of the choir. In none of these works, and
commonly in no other English music of this type until the time of
Blow and Purcell, was any effort made to set the two sides of the
choir against each other as contrasting groups. While trebles sang
occasionally in opposition to the lower voices, each group was made

12. *Ibid.*, 59–74; practical editions by Novello and Oxford University Press.

PLATE 4. *A Carol Service at Westminster Abbey. The choir of boys and men is divided in the traditional* decani-cantoris *arrangement.* (Photo courtesy of The British Travel and Holidays Association.)

up of singers from both sides of the choir, an arrangement that made spatial antiphony impossible. The lofting of phrases from one side of the building to the other by separate, complete choirs that played such a prominent role at St. Mark's and its musical heirs was not an ingredient in the music of Anglican composers, as a rule.

In the foregoing examples, the relationship of the anthem to its Latin counterpart, the motet, can be seen in the use of imitative counterpoint and in the division into two *partes* of the longer works. Thomas Tallis' *Heare the voyce and prayer of thy servaunts (TEM 27)*, from the Wanley MS in the Bodleian Library at Oxford, illustrates this close relationship while it follows the restrictions imposed on the form by the English church authorities. It is bound together by a thematic unity that pervades all the points of imitation. Each of the points develops from the one preceding it, as was often the case in Latin motets, and the hidden cadences of the motet style are also present. The text, however, is so placed that one syllable falls to a note, for the most part, and the imitative passages are broken up by chordal writing before the cadences are reached.

Had the anthem stopped developing at this point, it would not have stood as a notable form, but merely as an English counterpart to the motet, more syllabic in nature and less closely related to the religious observance than was its progenitor. Toward the end of the sixteenth century, however, a modification appeared in the form of the verse anthem. Its appearance required that the form known up to that time simply as the anthem be given a distinctive title to clearly distinguish it from the new style of composition. From that time onward, an anthem in which the choir sang throughout, or was sometimes interrupted by sections of choral singing in thinner texture, was designated as a full anthem; verse anthem became the type in which solo voices singing separately or together appeared in alternation with the chorus, the whole supported by string instruments or, lacking those, by the organ. During the solo sections the supporting instruments provided an independent polyphonic accompaniment, joining the chorus *colla parte* during its appearances. Orlando Gibbons (1583–1625), who, along with Thomas Morley (1557–1603) and William Byrd (1543–1623), was responsible for the early development of the verse anthem, produced one of the finest examples of the type in *This is the record of John (HAM 172).*[13] Composed for contratenor

13. *TCM*, IV, 297–304; practical editions by Novello and Oxford University Press. See also William Palmer, "Gibbons's Verse Anthems," *Music and Letters*, xxxv/2 (April, 1954), 107–13.

solo and chorus *a* 5, it provides no new text for the chorus, but, in each case, repeats that which the soloist has just sung. Contrast is achieved by the alternation of solo and chorus, by the change from independent accompaniment to duplication of the chorus parts, and by alternation between contrapuntal texture in the solo sections and the chordal opening of each chorus section. A device borrowed from the Italian declamatory style that was to become increasingly more common, the delayed accent that placed the opening strong syllable of text on a weak musical beat, is used by Gibbons with good effect. Text-painting is limited—understandably, for the text presents few opportunities—but the rising melodic line attached to some of the interrogative phrases of text may be viewed as attempts in that direction. William Byrd's *Christ rising again*[14] (*HAM* 151), for two sopranos and chorus, similarly provides a change of texture between the polyphony of the solo sections and the more homophonic choral passages. The sopranos join with the chorus, but only either the *decani* or *cantoris* soprano soloist at any moment, making the piece *a* 5 until the very end, when both join the lower voices in a brief six-part cadential section. The ending on a half-cadence is not merely an old-fashioned close, but is a device to link the piece, which is actually *pars* I of a long two-part composition, with its *pars* II, *Christ is risen again*.[15] There is the same emphasis on five-part writing in the first half of this second division, with only one of the solo voices joining the basic low-voiced chorus in the full sections during the first two-thirds of the piece. The final choral section adds the soloists to the other voices in an extended jubilant close, but the soloists always stand apart from the choral voices by reason of their greater melodic and rhythmic interest. The greater emphasis on text intensification is apparent from the very opening of *pars* I. The phrase "Christ rising," is successively placed against an initial melodic interval of a third, then a fourth, and a fifth.

This first period in the history of the anthem began under Henry VIII and continued through the Elizabethan period into the reigns of the Stuarts. The music borrowed from the Catholic tradition, as well as that composed initially for the Church of England, depended strongly upon the polyphonic tradition. The political strife that accompanied the establishment of the Commonwealth under Oliver Cromwell, and the stifling of elaborate musical activity both in and

---

14. *The Collected Vocal Works of William Byrd*, XIII, 280–90; practical edition by Stainer & Bell.

15. *Ibid.*, 291–301; *pars* II is not given in *HAM*. Byrd's full anthem, *Look down, O Lord*, is printed in *MSO*, 39f.

out of the churches, brought an end to the first period of anthem and Service composition. Although it was not many years until the Restoration produced a society that again welcomed music as a mark of the good life and as an ornament to worship, an entirely new approach to music was evident by that time. Not only had some of the composers from the previous era disappeared, but foreign influences from both Italy and France began to make themselves strongly felt upon English music. While the Italian styles of church and theater had brought England a declamatory style that dwelt upon delayed accents, expressive melodic leaps, recitative-like passages, and "pathetic" diminished intervals that expressed grief and pain, the French court, through the stylistic importations engineered by Charles II, emphasized instrumental background, dance rhythms, and a general air of ornate massiveness in the compositions that were produced in the Royal Chapel.

Anthems, whether full or verse, were built on a grand scale. Their similarity to cantatas has been a matter of frequent comment; their indebtedness to the large motets that were being composed in France, for instance those of Michel-Richard de Lalande (1657–1726), can also be seen. Orchestral accompaniments and interludes, solos, duets, and larger ensembles of soloists in alternation with chorus, as well as extended length, made of the anthem an elaborate piece that was at its best in churches with large forces of musicians. While these factors contrived to provide the Royal Chapel with excellent music, they did little for the smaller parochial churches where musical forces were meager, at best.

A new style had already begun to appear in the generation before Purcell, influenced to a great extent by the Baroque tradition that stressed clarity of text and declamatory singing, but also marked by those foreign styles that came more from the theater than from the church.

Four separate groups of composers can be identified with the development of the Baroque anthem.[16] While it might be profitable to examine works by all the composers of those groups, we are by necessity limited to representative compositions. Typical of the first group is William Lawes (1602–1645), who, together with his brother Henry (1596–1662), William Child (1606–1697), and Walter Porter (c. 1595–1659), brought an early taste of the Italian style into English church

16. *MBE*, 199f.

music. A gentleman of the Chapel Royal, vicar-choral of Salisbury Cathedral, and student of Coperario (John Cooper), Lawes was well grounded in the Italian ideas that his teacher had adopted, and he was given favorable notice as a composer by Charles I. His verse anthem, *The Lord is my light*,[17] opens with a brief passage for organ, followed by a verse *a 3* in which the solo voices first declaim the text successively and later change to imitative counterpoint. The organ part throughout the anthem moves independently of the voices, providing a strong, supporting harmonic foundation. The full section that closes the first half of the anthem repeats the last line of text from the preceding verse, a common procedure in verse anthems. An organ interlude precedes the second verse, which is expanded to four voices, and the closing full section again repeats text from the verse. There is no distinction made between the *decani* and *cantoris* sides of the choir in the assignment of voices. Two notable instances of chromaticism occur, one in a melodic passage in the first verse, the other in the bass line of the closing cadence *(Ex. 37)*.

Belonging to the second group, among whom were numbered also Orlando Gibbons and Benjamin Rogers (1614–1698), is Matthew Locke *(c. 1630–1677)*. In *Lord, let me know mine end*,[18] the text is broken into short phrases with the phrase endings often occurring simultaneously in all voices, and the melodic line is jagged *(Ex. 38a)* in contrast to the smooth contours of polyphonic works. The declamation in the

Ex.37 *The Lord is my light*, W. Lawes (Boyce, *CM*, II, 219-225)

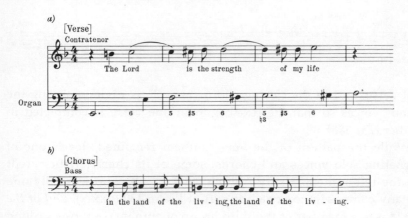

17. Boyce, *CM*, II, 219–25.   18. *Ibid.*, II, 226–34.

Ex. 38 *Lord, let me know mine end*, M. Locke (Boyce, *CM*, II, 226)

final verse, and in the closing chorus as well, is divided among the various voices so that the text begun in one voice is completed in another *(Ex. 38b)*.

While the pattern of the verse anthem remained clearly one of alternating solo voices and chorus, some of its characteristics crept into the full anthem. Henry Aldrich (1647 – 1710), who was only one of many composers to set all or part of Psalm 130 (CXXIX), *Out of the deep*,[19] was a member of the third group of anthem composers, along

19. *Ibid.*, II, 135 – 39.

with Pelham Humfrey (1647?–1674) (*HMS*, v, 38f), Michael Wise (*c. 1648–1687*), William Turner (1651–1740), and John Blow (1649–1708). This full anthem included a section for the full *decani* complement, a section that Aldrich called a verse. It serves, however, merely as a contrasting middle segment between the two parts of the psalm that are given to the full choir, and it contains no other characteristics of the verse anthem. This method of designating the contrasting sections of full anthems as verses is quite common, and it does not indicate that the composer meant that any relationship with the verse anthem existed. An opening theme that rises an octave through the g-minor triad emphasizes the opening words through repeated contrapuntal entrances. The organ part is a *basso seguente* that never deviates from the function of duplicating the lowest sounding voice part.

A consistent weakness in the compositions that had appeared before, and sometimes during, the Restoration was inept rhythmic treatment of text. The improper accentuation that resulted was the subject of considerable comment, but much of the difficulty was overcome by those composers who had been exposed to the Italian declamatory style or who had experience with the careful prosody of the French music for theater and church. While the music of William Lawes and Matthew Locke suffered less from poor text placement than did that of most of their contemporaries, it was Pelham Humfrey who took an even greater step in finding a solution. Attention to the length of syllables in relation to the strong and weak beats in music could have been more diligent, although there are anthems that show the problem was recognized, and even solved. Humfrey apparently devoted constant attention to the correct placement of verbal inflections. Three other procedures which may be fruits of his study in France (and possibly Italy) appear in his anthems, the use of recitatives, changes of meter, and tempo changes. Two verse anthems may be considered as illustrations of his methods. *O Lord, my God*[20] (*HAM* 242 [incomplete]) uses both recitative and change of meter, devices that permit longer anthems approaching the style of the cantata in variety and interest, as well as in length. Whereas the anthems of Humfrey's predecessors, and of many of his contemporaries, confined their efforts to an unrelenting duple or quadruple meter, he inserted contrasting sections of triple meter which contained a further contrast by the relaxation of the usual trochaic rhythms through the use of

20. The entire anthem is printed in Boyce, *CM*, ii, 242–47.

occasional iambic measures and hemiolas. Recitative passages for
one or more voices are not frequent, but their occasional appearances
assist greatly in breaking the anthem into varied sections. Immediately after the closing passage given in *HAM* 242 is such a recitative,
leading to a slower triple meter section in chordal style, *(Ex. 39)*. In
Have mercy upon me, O God,[21] Humfrey adds to the techniques already
described the further contrast of changing tempo indications. A passage in triple meter, setting the phrase, "Thou shalt make me to hear
of joy and gladness," is marked "lively," and is followed by the text,
"that the bones which thou hast broken may rejoyce," in slow quadruple meter.

A direct line of influence may be seen in the works of John Blow,
who not only succeeded Humfrey as master of the children of the
Royal Chapel, but was also Henry Purcell's teacher, as possibly was
Humfrey. Blow was the most prolific composer of full-scale anthems
of his generation, and perhaps of all time. While he wrote full anthems
in the polyphonic motet style, as well as some with antiphonal treat-

Ex. 39 *O Lord, my God*, Pelham Humfrey (Boyce, *CM*, II 245)

21. *Ibid.*, ii, 235–41.

ment, it was in the verse anthem that he exploited the full potential of the vocal and instrumental performers of the Chapel Royal. Some of his verse anthems are principally solo declamations in which the choral writing is incidental commentary to the verse sections; others fall into a number of sections, separated not only by a division of verse and full passages, but employing a variety of meters and textures; a third group approximate the cantata in the employment of the new ideas that came from the theater—recitative, aria, small vocal ensembles, chorus, and orchestra. The cantata-anthems are impressive works, even though some of them lack unity because they are made up of short, contrasting sections. Blow devoted much more attention to the introductory *Symphony* and interludes than had composers of the previous period, possibly because of the fine group of twenty-four stringed instruments that Charles II had established in imitation of the *vingt-quatre violons* that graced the Court of Louis XIV. One cantata-anthem that makes extensive use of the orchestra is *And I heard a great voice*,[22] which appears under the title, *I was in the spirit on the Lord's day*[23] in a Novello edition as well as in the Boyce and Stevens collections. The dual identification was not Blow's, but resulted from an adaptation at the hands of Henry Aldrich. Originally the anthem opened with forty-four measures of *Symphony* in ternary form, the opening and closing sections of which were built on a four-measure ostinato pattern. The instrumental section is given on four staves by Tudway, as are all the interludes, but appears in Boyce in radically shortened form, comprising only the last thirteen measures, and is set for organ. Showing the outer voices only in the instrumental sections, and the bass line along with figures when there were parts for voices, was Boyce's usual practice. At the end of the introduction Aldrich made his alteration of the original, adding nine words of text to his own melody. *(Ex. 40).* Blow had chosen his text from Revelation 19:1–7, omitting unsuitable portions of the second and third verses. Aldrich, apparently concerned with the unsuitability of beginning a composition with "And," prefixed the first half of Revelation 1:10 in what is not the most felicitous emendation.[24] The opening bass pat-

22. Harley 7339, 333–46.

23. *Boyce, CM*, II, 248–57; R. J. S. Stevens (ed.), *Sacred Music for one, two, three & four Voices* . . . (3 vols., London: Charterhouse, c.1798–1802), II, 22–33.

24. Harold Watkins Shaw, "John Blow's Anthems," *Music and Letters*, XIX/4 (October, 1938), 429, brings to light a possibility that the alteration could have been made by W. Hayes. However, Henry Leland Clarke, *op. cit.*, I, 198f, refutes the suggestion with evidence of the revision in a collection assembled by Aldrich himself.

Ex. 40   *I was in the spirit on the Lord's day,* Blow, with opening text
          by Aldrich (Boyce *CM,* II, 248)

tern appears occasionally during the rest of the anthem, and the entire
first section of the introduction is repeated later as an interlude. These
reappearances of an easily apprehended pattern help to bind together
a composition that is made up of many small sections further differentiated by the use of hemiola, change of meter, declamatory solos,
ensembles, and choruses. The anthem closes with a Halleluja section

that appears first for solo voices and later, with alternating iambic and dactylic measures over two different repeated bass patterns, in the chorus. The practice of closing anthems with a short Hallelujah chorus was common in the Restoration, and examples may also be found before that time, even outside England. The several internal sections setting that jubilant word in this anthem, however, grow out of the text itself, for the word occurs in the passage that Blow chose to set, and the closing chorus here had less the appearance of a conventional appendage than it has in many other cases where the Hallelujah section is arbitrarily attached.

It has been mentioned that the English composers did not adopt the Venetian polychoral style, although they had employed antiphonal treatment of the divided single chorus. Blow's generation appeared to be aware of its possibilities, for he and Purcell both approached it in some works. Naturally, they had to progress beyond the simple alternating and combining of equal groups that was seen in *O Lord, the maker of all things* (cf. p. 143) to the process of separating and rejoining groups of different vocal character. Blow's *I beheld, and, lo, a great multitude*,[25] based on selected verses from Revelation 9, sets off opposing forces in a fashion that qualifies it as true polychoral composition *(Ex. 41)*. The verse sections do not include any trebles, but are made up of contratenor, tenor, and basses for verses *a 4*, omitting the second bass in the three-voice phrases. The full choir adds another group of a contrasting timbre — treble, contratenor, tenor — so that the antiphonal singing is between SAT and ATBB or ATB, as in the example shown here. This contrast prevails throughout, except in the closing Hallelujah chorus, which is scored for SATB. The fact that this is a verse anthem precludes any closer parallel to the Venetian style, which employs continuous polychoral treatment throughout an entire composition. Had English composers been able to circumvent the syllabic requirement, the presentation of smaller segments of text with florid treatment and repetition of text might have moved them to cultivate the verse anthem, with its numerous sections for reduced forces, less assiduously, and to develop a form that had greater breadth and continuity.

Blow's importance in English music has often been underestimated, yet he outdid his contemporaries in the production of church

25. Boyce, *CM*, III, 245–56; Harley 7340, 202–11. As is usual, the version given by Boyce omits the full instrumental parts. Lacking there, also, are the *ritornelli* which Tudway gives in full. A modern edition is published by Oxford University Press.

Ex. 41 *I beheld, and, lo, a great multitude*, Blow, (Boyce, *CM*, III, 254)

music; he taught many of the leading musicians of his time, including Purcell, the outstanding figure of the fourth group of Baroque anthem composers, whom he survived. He has suffered unjustly from the barbed pens of eighteenth-century writers who found little of value in his music. Nonetheless, much of his spirit survives in the music of Purcell, who, if he had greater genius than his fellows, also had fewer years than most in which to exercise it.

While the total number of sacred compositions by Henry Purcell (1659–1695) does not loom large among his complete works, there are enough such pieces to establish his position in that field of composition. Not only was much of his time absorbed by the production of secular music, but he was constantly influenced by the dissolute life at the Court of Charles II. Still, his religious music, while greatly affected by secular styles and devices, is not frivolous or superficial, even though it lies far from the reserved expression of his predecessors.

A wide variety of treatments can be found in the anthems of Purcell, along with certain stylistic features that were previously hinted at, but not fully developed. A full anthem, *O God, thou art my God*,[26] for four voices without instruments, but with figured bass given by Boyce, contains sections that use selected groups from *decani* and *cantoris*. After an opening full section, the ATB *cantoris* group provides a brief section marked "verse." This is apparently not intended as a section for soloists, but rather for all the specified voices from that side of the choir. Another full section follows, after which the *decani* sopranos and the *cantoris* SA group combine in another verse segment. The remainder of the anthem is scored *a 4*, first for full choir and then alternating between the complete halves. The closing Hallelujah section is first sung *alternatim* and then by the full choir.

The verse anthems frequently go beyond the limits of similar works by Blow in their technical demands upon the soloists. Not only are the bass solos, many of which were written expressly for John Gostling of the Chapel Royal, unusual in their requirements, but those for other voices are unusual as well. Purcell's understanding of the possibilities and limitations of the voice is evident at all times, and undoubtedly stems from his own experience, for he enjoyed a considerable reputation as a countertenor. Florid runs, which do not yet

26. Boyce, *CM*, II, 148–53; Harley, 7339, 450–54.

make an appearance in chorus sections, call upon the entire solo group for their execution, as in the final verse of *O give thanks unto the Lord*[27] (*Ex. 42a*). The writing for chorus, on the other hand, clings firmly to the tradition of syllabic settings, while the music for soloists displays affective writing that draws upon the pictorial possibilities of vocal range and dotted rhythms, as in the opening solo from *They that go down to the sea in ships*,[28] written for Gostling (*Ex. 42b*). It is not unusual for such solo lines to cover a span of two full octaves. The entire anthem is made up of the opening bass solo, a series of duets for bass and contratenor, and a closing chorus *a 4*.

Purcell brought the cantata-anthem to a point that had never been reached by Blow. Where Blow's efforts had brought about a type of composition made up of numerous short sections that were related more through textual than musical continuity, Purcell achieved a completely integrated result that called upon the repetition of complete vocal sections, as well as the recapitulation of instrumental *ritornelli*. Even though *It is a good thing to give thanks*[29] lacks solo recitatives, it

Ex. 42 *a) O give thanks unto the Lord,* Purcell (Boyce, *CM*, II, 290)

27. Boyce, *CM*, II, 281–91; Harley 7340, 297–308.

28. Boyce, *CM*, II, 269–74; Harley 7338, 451–58.

29. Henry Purcell, *The Works of Henry Purcell* (London: Novello and Co., 1878–), XIV, 1–20.

b) *They that go down to the sea in ships*, Purcell (Boyce, *CM*, II, 269)

They that go   down _____   to _____   the sea _____ in _____   ships

For at   his   word _____   the   storm -   -   -

- - y wind   a - ris -   eth,   for   at   his   word _____   the

storm -   -   -   - y wind   a - ris - eth   which

lift - eth up,   which   lift - eth up   the   waves _____   there - of.   They   are

car - ried up   to   heav'n and down _____   a - gain to   the   deep. _____

is, in other respects, a cantata-anthem with solos, ensembles, chorus, and instrumental accompaniment. The composition is constructed on a modified arch form, having as its keystone the bass solo which, although brief, is the most elaborate musically. The arch form itself is enclosed by sections that are not necessary parts of the anthem (insofar as the function of an anthem is to present text over a series of musical sections), although the fashion of Purcell's time decreed that these extraneous sections be important in church works of any considerable size. The exclusion of the French overture and the alleluias makes the form of the basic vocal sections (and *ritornelli*) clear, as may be seen in Table VII. Here, solid lines connect the balancing sections on either side of the central bass solo and dotted lines connect a new section with the one it replaces when a repetition of the earlier text would have served no useful function. The second section of the French overture merits its repetition in the middle of the anthem because of its suitability as an introductory instrumental piece before the bass solo, the pivotal point for the entire composition. Its placement there is not entirely due to Purcell's probable intention of heightening the significance of the solo, for the second section of the overture often appeared as the middle instrumental section of a cantata-anthem, even when no arch form is apparent. Recognition of the secondary function of the overture, of the repetition of its second part in the

TABLE VII

Modified Arch Form in Purcell's *It is a good thing to give thanks*

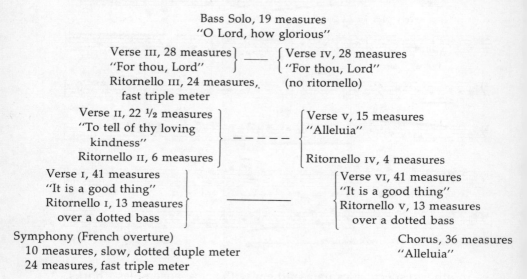

Bass Solo, 19 measures
"O Lord, how glorious"

Verse III, 28 measures ⎱ ___ ⎰ Verse IV, 28 measures
"For thou, Lord" ⎰   ⎱ "For thou, Lord"
Ritornello III, 24 measures,   (no ritornello)
    fast triple meter

Verse II, 22 ½ measures ⎫   ⎧ Verse V, 15 measures
"To tell of thy loving ⎬ _ _ _ _ ⎨ "Alleluia"
    kindness"   ⎪   ⎪
Ritornello II, 6 measures ⎭   ⎩ Ritornello IV, 4 measures

Verse I, 41 measures ⎫   ⎧ Verse VI, 41 measures
"It is a good thing" ⎬   ⎨ "It is a good thing"
Ritornello I, 13 measures ⎪ _____ ⎪ Ritornello V, 13 measures
    over a dotted bass ⎭   ⎩   over a dotted bass

Symphony (French overture)   Chorus, 36 measures
 10 measures, slow, dotted duple meter   "Alleluia"
 24 measures, fast triple meter

middle of the anthem, and of the closing choral "alleluia" that serves
only as a convenient means to involve the chorus, makes the arch
form of the principal parts of the anthem clearly perceptible. The solo
for bass holds a central position around which the remaining sections
of verses and *ritornelli* are hung in perfect balance. While the solo
itself does not have impressive length, it contains the most elaborate
music of the entire anthem, as is appropriate to its text. Verse II is
linked to a *ritornello* of about one-fourth its length; verse V and its
ritornello bear the same relationship to each other. While this architectural feature does not completely satisfy the requirements of an
arch form, violating as it does the unity of musical material, exact
repetition was probably not practical at this point because the text,
"to tell of thy loving kindness early in the morning," lacks the element
of direct praise that is found in the repeated texts used elsewhere. As
a text of secondary importance, it is well replaced by the "Alleluia"
that makes up the fifth verse. The bases of the arch are formed by the
two large sections, verses I and VI and the *ritornello* that concludes
each of them. Naturally the sections that are exact repetitions show
no difference in meter. The probability of Purcell's consciously adopting an arch form is strengthened, however, by the fact that the substi-

tute verse v bears a further relationship to verse II. The latter is in quadruple meter, and the former in duple, both of them framing the only other section not in triple meter—the bass solo—except for the opening of the overture, which is quadruple by custom rather than by mere choice.

Purcell's use of ground basses has often been the subject of comment, and Bukofzer has suggested that their comparative absence in church music is the only thing that differentiates its style from that of chamber music.[30] While the one example mentioned by Bukofzer is rare, it is not unique, for the opening Symphony of *In thee, O Lord, do I put my trust*[31] is based on a five-measure ostinato, and a two-measure ground serves as the foundation for an "alleluia" section.[32] Portions of other anthems, as well, are found to use repeated bass patterns, sometimes transposed and incomplete, as in the closing chorus of the coronation anthem, *My heart is inditing (GMB* 246 [incomplete]).[33] This anthem calls for no solo voices, although there are sections of thinner texture than the prevailing eight-voice choral and orchestral *concertato* passages that are marked as verses. Inasmuch as the absence of ground basses is not nearly so great as implied by Bukofzer, it is probably better to avoid considering their presence as a strong indication of secular usage in Purcell's music. In view of the small number of religious works he composed, it would be surprising if we found that many more of them did contain ground basses.

Recent studies by Franklin Zimmerman have produced evidence that Purcell was aware of parody technique, and that he employed it on at least one occasion.[34] Whether other unsuspected practices remain to be discovered is a moot question, but Zimmerman speculates on the possibility of an Anglican parody tradition, a matter that will require years of study before an answer can be found.

The course of English religious choral music from Purcell to the end of the Baroque is relatively uneventful. George Frederick Handel (1685–1759) has always loomed large but, again, it must be emphasized that little of his music was intended for the church. His lesser known contemporaries who, following Purcell and Blow, worked with greater interest in religious music, must be considered as

30. *MBE*, 207.
31. Purcell, *Works*, xiv, 53–55.
32. *Ibid.*, 73–77.
33. Complete in Purcell, *Works*, xvii, 69–118.

34. Franklin B. Zimmerman, "Purcell's 'Service Anthem' *O God Thou Art My God* and the B-flat Major Service," *The Musical Quarterly*, L/2 (April, 1964), 207–14.

stronger influences upon the English scene of that day, even though
we rank their compositions below those of Handel. It is necessary,
then, to consider their efforts before turning to Handel as a composer
of religious music.

The collections of Tudway, Boyce, and Arnold[35] give evidence of
the continuing production of English church music after it began to
decline from the peak of quality reached during the Restoration. The
anthems gathered in these volumes range from pedestrian to outstanding; the styles from uncomplicated four-part writing to the
concertato style that was found in the works of Purcell and Blow, and
that was destined to reach its English perfection in the oratorio choruses of Handel. Only a few of these composers, however, produced
works of consistent quality and interest. William Croft (1678–1727),
who is represented by a dozen anthems in the collections mentioned
above, and by seven in the Page collection[36] which supplements those
of Boyce and Arnold, was a chorister under Blow and succeeded to the
various positions held by his teacher upon the latter's death. His
verse anthem, *Be merciful unto me, O God*,[37] contains the conventional
"pathetic" figures of the appoggiatura and diminished intervals, a
ground bass accompaniment to a solo, iambic meters in triple rhythms,
a setting *a 4* written first in minor mode and repeated — with some
changes — in relative major, and a concluding chorus *a 7* made up of
heavy polyphony framed by phrases set to ponderous note-against-
note harmony. That his style is not always so heavy is evident in
Put me not to rebuke, O Lord[38] (*HAM* 268 [two sections only]), a full
anthem with a middle verse section. The final section, a fugal chorus
a 4, is not markedly different from the opening chorus.

During this post-Purcellian period a mutation, called the solo
anthem, reached a brief peak of importance, but was soon over-
whelmed by the works that called for concerted forces on a large
scale. Some writers since the eighteenth century have indicated that
the solo anthem was no different from the verse anthem. Surviving
examples, with few exceptions, tell a different story. Purcell's *My
song shall be allways*,[39] called a solo anthem by Tudway, is a verse anthem for one voice and chorus, but most later examples do not fit
comfortably into the mold of the verse anthem. The compositions des-

35. Arnold, *CM* (4 vols., London: For the
editor, 1790).
36. John Page, *Harmonia Sacra* (3 vols.,
London, 1800).

37. Arnold, *CM*, ii, 69–87.
38. Complete in Boyce, *CM*, ii, 193–201.
39. Harley 7338, 459–67.

ignated as solo anthems in Arnold's collection are by Boyce, John Travers *(c. 1703 – 1758),* John Weldon (1676 – 1736), and Maurice Greene (1695? – 1755) *(HMS,* v, 40). Not many cases display the characteristics of the verse anthem in matters of introductory instrumental sections, *ritornelli,* or interspersed choruses. They have, in common with each other, an emphasis upon the solo voice as the conveyor of text; always a closing chorus *a 4;* sometimes a shorter chorus in the course of the anthem; and a high degree of contrast between the several short solo sections. Boyce's *Lord, teach us to number our days*[40] shows the usual treatment given works in this genre, although the order and frequency of the solo sections varies from example to example, and most solo anthems have instrumental introductions. Written for tenor and chorus, it is provided with a figured bass, and there is no indication that instrumentation other than organ was ever used. After a slow recitative and somewhat more lively aria, both in e minor, there follows a recitative, an interlude, and an aria in C major, after which another recitative establishes the key of E major. After another interlude, there follows an aria in this new key. A short chorus in the original key appears next, then an arioso, and the work concludes with another, longer chorus. This arrangement of sections, and the emphasis on projection of text through related recitatives and arias, bears a closer resemblance to the solo cantata with closing chorus than it does to the verse anthem.

It would be convenient if evidence could be produced that no confusion existed in connection with the recognition of the solo anthem, that it was never classed among the types of verse anthem. A single further example, nevertheless, is listed among the verse anthems compiled by Boyce, identified as an "anthem for one voice." The structure of this anthem, *How long wilt thou forget me,* by Jeremiah Clark *(c. 1659 – 1707),*[41] differs in no way from the typical solo anthem as found in Arnold's volumes. It consists of short arias and a recitative for treble voice, the lot preceded and interspersed by brief organ passages and closing with a short "praise" chorus, *a 4.* That Boyce did not call it a solo anthem may well be due to the phraseology he used throughout his collection. The terms "verse anthem" and "full anthem" appear only in the table of contents; identification on the first page of each anthem is by key and number of voices only. A separate heading in the table of contents for only one example may not

40. Arnold, *CM*, iii, 32 – 43.   41. Boyce, *CM*, ii, 285 – 88.

have seemed worth the effort. It is significant, also, that all of the
solo anthems given by Arnold are from composers a generation after
Clark. The cultivation of the form may be linked with the decline in
church music that was evident after Purcell's time, a decline that
made it necessary to create music for fewer skilled voices with less
emphasis on the chorus. As Arnold was moved to comment in his
Preface, "it is not the fashion to study Church, so much as secular
Musick; and if the Cathedrals and Churches in England, Scotland,
Ireland and Wales, where Choir Service is performed (and for whose
use this work was principally intended) do not encourage it, the time
may come, when this sublime, tho' much neglected stile of Composition (so well understood by our forefathers) will be totally lost
in this Kingdom."[42]

Whether the performance of church music was deteriorating or
not, some anthems of Weldon and Greene show that large-scale
compositions were still being written, although some of the festive
qualities of Purcell's greatest works had been cast off, probably because the necessary performers were not available. Most of the
great English composers following Blow and Purcell were children of
the Royal Chapel who, elevated to positions of authority in that
establishment, exercised an almost dynastic control over its musical
practices. The disappearance of the orchestral features of the anthems,
and of the large-scale verse anthem, reflect not a lack of familiarity
with the procedures in high places, but rather a difference in the
fashion and the potential of English church music. While Weldon
seems to have devoted more of his attention to the development of
the full anthem, Maurice Greene was writing some verse anthems
in the older style, but at the same time was adapting the form to what
had been seen in the solo anthem. Anthems "for two voices," such as
I will magnify thee, O Lord,[43] and Like as the hart desires the water
brooks,[44] are again short cantatas (with duets, solos, recitatives, and
closing chorus) with organ, and are not to be classed with the elaborate multisectional verse anthems of the earlier period.

That the English anthem fell on evil days cannot be disputed. The
blame should not be placed so squarely on the students and successors
of Purcell and Blow as it has been. They made great efforts to accommodate their church music to the changing forces and fashions that
were bursting forth in secular life and that were relentlessly making

42. Arnold, CM, I, 5.
43. Ibid., II, 144–52.

44. Ibid., II, 59–68; Stevens, Sacred Music . . ., III, 54–61.

themselves apparent in religious music. Croft, Weldon, and Greene could not have changed the course of the anthem had they desired to do so. The glittering secularism of the Restoration Court was gone, and it had left behind only the concept that there was no great distinction between music within the church and without. When a difference of musical styles again emerged after Handel had left the scene, it was a difference that identified church music with tedium, hackneyed formulas, and endless stretches of predictable and tiresome music of a type that has aptly been termed "choir-fodder."

Handel is important on the English musical scene, although his actual contribution to church music is meager. We must, in all honesty, forego any consideration of his sacred oratorios as actual church music; they were not intended for, nor performed in, church. While they may have grown, in part, out of religious enthusiasm felt by Handel, they were frankly commercial works, a fact that does not diminish any qualities of musical greatness that they possess. His contribution to anthem literature numbers only the Chandos Anthems and a few coronation anthems plus some wedding and funeral works. None of these was performed regularly in an English church. Their importance is seen in retrospect; their value in the eighteenth century was as works for specific occasions in specific places. Together with a few earlier Latin religious works and some English pieces written to celebrate military victories, the Chandos Anthems represent the core of Handel's church music. Viewed by itself, this body of music is unimpressive; yet Handel, who borrowed freely from the works of others and himself, built upon the patterns of these works many times in his later, better-known compositions. The Chandos Anthems stand as monuments to Handel's exploration of choral writing; they are not to be considered as pinnacles of accomplishment. In them he produced, for the first time, some of the ingredients that eventually made up his distinctive choral style as found in the oratorios and occasional works of his later years.

It was Handel's practice to adapt the works of others to his own purposes. While this custom was common, Handel appropriated materials with greater frequency than did most other composers, but he was no less prone to use his own tunes over and over. That this was not merely for speed or convenience is indicated by his alteration of material when he used it for a second or third time. The adaptation, parodying, or expansion of other men's work was even less frequent with Handel than the repeated use of his own material, and the extent to which he indulged in both is perhaps no better demonstrated than in connection with the Chandos Anthems.[45]

These twelve anthems, written before 1720 while Handel was serving as chapel-master and organist to the Duke of Chandos, contain many sections that he had used earlier or was to use later. That the employment of the same materials in a number of situations does not merely represent laziness or lack of interest on Handel's part is seen in the care which he exercised in many of his selections, as well as in the fact that alternative versions of the same material often show his efforts to improve it.

The anthems are neither typical of English church music of their time nor do they predict a future course for anthem literature. They are, actually, not even anthems in the sense that the Restoration compositions of that name were. Rather, they are German cantatas with strong elements of Italian influence, especially in the solo sections. Handel clearly recognized the German influence in his use of chorales in connection with three anthems, among them the sixth Chandos Anthem. The twelve anthems in that group do not represent Handel's ideal for this kind of music, as he found that certain adjustments had to be made to the limited instrumental and vocal forces at Cannons, the palatial country establishment of James Brydges, the first Duke of Chandos, in whose service Handel followed Pepusch as chapel-master.

The first Chandos Anthem, *O be joyful in the Lord*,[46] except for its instrumental introduction, is nearly the same as the Utrecht *Jubilate* that dates from a few years before Handel entered the Duke's service. The limited musical forces at Cannons required Handel to restrict his chorus to three parts, whereas the original *Jubilate* had been written for four- and five-part choruses. The orchestra at Cannons, likewise, did not provide the full instrumentation that was available at larger establishments, and Handel was forced to substitute oboes for trumpets, while omitting the violas entirely. Except for these changes, the anthem is substantially the *Jubilate* with an instrumental prelude.

45. Basil Lam, "The Church Music," *Handel: A Symposium*, ed. Gerald Abraham (London: Oxford University Press, 1954), discusses in great detail the interchange of musical materials between the various Chandos Anthems and their musical relationship to other compositions. See especially pp. 164–76.

46. *Georg Friedrich Händels Werke*, ed. F. Chrysander (96 vols. and 6 supplements, Leipzig: Breitkopf & Härtel, 1858–1894, 1902), xxxiv, 1–36. A new edition of Händel's works is in progress and is being published by Bärenreiter-Verlag, 1955–).

The sixth anthem, *As pants the hart for cooling streams*, not only exists in four different versions,[47] but is also one of the rare examples in which Handel incorporated a chorale tune into a composition. Three of these versions provide fine points of contrast that illustrate Handel's various approaches to the same text, and his adaptation to the changing conditions of performance. Version A was intended for use at Cannons, and is written for three-part chorus, STB, with the same instrumental combination as that found in the first anthem. Version B, apparently prepared for the Royal Chapel, has an opening chorus in six parts, SAATBB, and the rest of the composition is *a 4.* The orchestra is that of Cannons with a viola part added. The voice arrangement of version C is that of B, but the accompaniment is re-written for organ, and version D is based upon that third version. The Chandos version is in e minor; the others, d minor. While the first three versions maintain a close parallel in text, the musical treatment, for the most part, presents a considerable degree of variety. The fugue, *In the voice of praise and thanksgiving*, is much the same in all versions, its compression to three voices in version A notwith-standing. The duo, *Why so full of grief?* however, varies in the three settings: A is written for soprano and tenor; B for alto and tenor; C for soprano and alto. In A and B it appears with the delayed accent and employs a series of pathetic, falling fourths melodically. C pre-sents a straightforward rhythmic setting that avoids the deep pathos of the other versions.

The closing chorus, *Put thy trust in God*, is a fugue in versions A and B, while C is composed in nonfugal luxuriant counterpoint that stresses delayed accents and iambic measures *(Ex. 43)*. The elaborate setting for version B closes with a lengthy "Alleluia" chorus, identical with that used by Handel in *Athalia*. It is also this version that incor-porates the chorale tune, *Christ lag in Todesbanden*, although the words with which it is associated are far from those of its original setting. The melody is sung in its entirety by tenors and basses in unison against rugged counterpoint in the orchestra[48] *(Ex. 44)*. While it has been postulated that the singularly inappropriate use of the chorale may be explained as an English adaptation of an exercise submitted to Friedrich Zachow during his student days,[49] it may equally prob-ably have been a gesture in the direction of George i, to whom the tune must have been well known, and who, even though a thorough reprobate, must have attended the Royal Chapel at times.

47. *Ibid.*, 207–38; 239–76; 277–88. Also xxxvi, 233–47.

48. *Ibid.*, xxxiv, 255f.

49. Lam, *op. cit.*, 169.

Ex. 43 *a*) "Put thy Trust in God", from *As pants the hart for cooling streams*,
    Werke, XXXIV, 232 (Version A)

b)   Version B, *Werke*, XXXIV, 266

Handel's other works that are religious in their function are either the Latin and German works that he completed early in his career or the large works that signalled important state occasions; coronations, funerals, weddings, or victory celebrations. These latter works, aimed at impressive functions that could command the presence of the best instrumental and vocal performers, represent English musical practice in the church no more than did the Chandos Anthems. Handel's compositions were not religious pieces first and musical expressions second. Rather, they were musical compositions designed for situations that were best suited to expression through means connected

c) Version C, *Werke*, XXXIV, 287

with religious text. We cannot find, certainly, a continuation of the tradition of Purcell and Blow in Handel's compositions of this type. The English masters themselves closed an important period that was carried on in simpler form by their countrymen. After Croft and Greene there was a lull in English anthem composition until the time of the Wesleys, of whom more will be said in a later chapter.

Ex. 44 *a)* Chorale, *Christ lag in Todesbanden*, as adapted by Handel,
Werke, XXXIV, 255 f

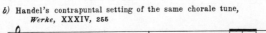

b) Handel's contrapuntal setting of the same chorale tune,
Werke, XXXIV, 255

Chapter VI

Protestant Substitutes

for the Mass

JUST as the motet was replaced by the anthem because it had no place in English musical life after Henry's break with Rome, the Mass was removed from its position as the central musical expression of liturgical text. In England its place was assumed by the Service. In Germany, the attempts to produce a suitable vernacular setting of the Mass went hand in hand with the continuation of the Latin tradition by both the Protestants and the Catholics.

The challenge of creating anthems had stirred English composers to the production of distinctive, although not unique forms; the need for Services failed to attract their best efforts, probably because the great restriction on textual variety proved to be a limiting factor. It will be remembered that the Mass took a secondary position to the motet for similar reasons. Still, because of the peculiar requirements of Anglican procedure and the changing emphasis on certain sections of this body of music, an interesting evolution of the substitute form may be traced until the Restoration, after which the principal interest of composers seems to be upon the anthem as a vehicle for individual expression and stylistic improvement.

The manner in which Services are described seems to be plagued with ambiguous terms, but clear identification requires nothing more than that we recognize the existence of a *trinitas in unitate*. The musical setting of The Office for the Holy Communion is called a Service or, more properly, Communion Service; the musical setting of the canticles for Morning Prayer, with or without the Invitatory Psalm, *Venite*, is likewise known as a Service; the settings of the canticles for Evening Prayer are known by the same name. When all three of these separate groups have been composed as a related, continuous musical group — all in the same key — they are known as a Full Service. Such a Full Service does not, as did a full anthem, require that the writing

171

be entirely for chorus without solos. Since "Full" here describes the number of sections in the setting rather than the disposition of voices, we may expect to encounter Full Services that are at the same time verse Services. There is a further distinction between the Short Service and the Great Service, neither term concerning the number of sections of the liturgical material that are set musically, but only the manner in which they are set. A Short Service is one in which chordal, syllabic style prevails, while a Great Service is constructed along the lines of polyphony, thereby being considerably extended because of the musical means employed.

Services were not the first liturgical settings to appear in English, for vernacular adaptations of Masses were known by the second quarter of the sixteenth century. Evidence of this apparently common practice is found in the Wanley MS of the Bodleian Library (MSS Mus. Sch. E420–422), dating from before the middle of the century, which contains, in addition to ten Communion Services in English, adaptations of Taverner's Masses *Sine Nomine* and *Small Devotion*. In accordance with common practice in England, these Masses contained all the parts of the Ordinary except the Kyrie, which was rendered in plainsong.

The Communion Services, which provide the closest parallel to the Mass, did not simply adopt the choral portions of the Ordinary as English substitutes. Doctrinal matters entered into the selection of only certain of the existing parts, and a setting of the Communion Office usually contained only the Kyrie and the Creed. Omitted entirely were the Gloria, Benedictus, and Agnus Dei; and the Sanctus appeared in choral settings only rarely. Even the Kyrie was different from the Mass, for while the Catholic tradition had embraced the ninefold Greek Kyrie, that of the Communion Service was a choral response to be sung after each of the Ten Commandments. As a response to each of the first nine, the choir sang "Lord, have mercy upon us, and incline our hearts to keep this law." Following the tenth Commandment, the response was "Lord, have mercy upon us, and write all these thy laws in our hearts, we beseech Thee." The Gloria again made its way into the Service, but took up a new position at the very end, and it did not often receive choral treatment there. The composer in the late sixteenth century, and throughout the seventeenth, thought of the Communion Service almost entirely in terms of the Kyrie and Nicene Creed. This is true even of Byrd's Great Service, one of the monuments of the genre. The pattern prevailed until the

Restoration, when the Sanctus again appeared with somewhat greater regularity.

The Morning Service consists of the musical settings of the Invitatory Psalm, *Venite exultemus Domino,* and the canticles, *Te Deum* and *Benedictus Dominus Deus Israel.* In response to the protests of the Puritans, the setting of *Jubilate* as an alternative to the latter was authorized in 1552. The use of *Benedicite* as an alternative to *Te Deum* has received choral treatment less often.

Two canticles constitute the Evening Service, and they also have alternatives which, although they also date from 1552, are not commonly found as choral settings until the Restoration. Magnificat and *Nunc dimittis* are the basic canticles, and their alternatives are the Psalms, *Cantate Domino* and *Deus misereatur.*

A Full Service, whether of the short or great variety, will consist of at least the Kyrie and the Creed from the Communion Office as well as the choral sections of both the Morning and Evening Services, usually all in the same key.[1] The organization of the Full Service is shown in Table VIII. We can now proceed to an examination of some of the musical means employed by the early composers of Services.

An early example of a Full Service is Thomas Tallis' *(c. 1505–1585)* Dorian Service for four voices, with Responses and Litany *a* 5[2]. It opens with the *Preces*[3] and choral Responses. The *Venite* that follows is not a polyphonic setting of the entire text, but a harmonized chant to which the psalm may be sung.[4] That any choral setting of *Venite* is provided at all is somewhat unusual, for the other eight Services printed in Boyce's first volume ignore the Invitatory completely, and most other published Services omit it also. Beginning with the settings of *Te Deum* and *Benedictus,* Tallis' Service unfolds along lines that can be anticipated from our knowledge of the anthem. Its style is syllabic, in accordance with the existing restrictions placed upon elaborate settings, and it makes much of the division of musical materials between the *decani* and *cantoris* sides of the choir. The full choir is called into action principally at the beginning, middle, and

1. In the nineteenth century, the remaining Mass sections were again restored to the Communion Office. The circumstances under which they returned, as well as the period in which their restoration to use came about, fall outside the scope of the present discussion.
2. Boyce, *CM,* i, 1–42; Harley 7337, 1–33. The Morning and Evening Services were published by Bayley & Ferguson, and the Evening Service is published by Oxford University Press.
3. Short intercessory prayers chanted by the priest, to which the choir sings brief responses.
4. See Fellowes, *English Cathedral Music,* 47f.

TABLE VIII

The Anglican Service and its Catholic Counterparts

Anglican	Roman

Morning Service
Venite

Invitatory at Matins (Psalm xciv [95])

Te Deum
Benedicite (alternative)

Matins
Lauds

Benedictus Dominus
Jubilate (alternative)

Lauds
Lauds (Psalm xcix [100])

Communion Office
Kyrie (Response to Commandments or ninefold Greek Kyrie)

Kyrie

Nicene Creed

Credo

Gloria (not regularly used)

Gloria

From Ordinary of the Mass

Evening Service
Magnificat
Cantate Domino (alternative)

Vespers
Matins (Psalm xcvii [98])

Nunc dimittis
Deus misereatur (alternative)

Compline
Psalm lxvi (67)

end of each complete piece; the full sections are separated by numerous subsections in which the half-choirs alternate.

The Communion Office includes settings of the Sanctus and Gloria immediately after the Kyrie and Creed.[5] The presence of the Gloria indicates that the work is an early one, as such settings dropped out of use until a few Restoration composers again began to use them.

5. Settings of only the Kyrie and Creed are also known as an Ante-Communion Service. The term is more commonly found as a theological usage, and not a musical one.

The inclusion of a Sanctus may also be considered as evidence of the age of the setting, probably from the reign of Edward VI rather than that of Elizabeth. It can be noted here that Tallis' *Te Deum*, Creed, and Gloria begin for choir only after the opening phrase has been intoned by the priest. This practice, following the Catholic procedure, prevails in most instances throughout the development of the Service, but is more subject to deviation in *Te Deum* settings than in those of chants based directly upon sections of the Ordinary. The *Te Deum* text, in many instances, is introduced directly by the choir instead of being intoned by the priest.

The usual canticles for Evening Prayer, Magnificat and *Nunc dimittis*, close Tallis' Service. It will be remembered that a choice existed for the Catholic composer of Magnificats; he could set the odd- or even-numbered verses for choir, and leave the others to be rendered in plainsong, or he could set the entire text for choir. No such freedom was available to the composer who wrote for the Anglican Church. His settings had to be continuous as well as syllabic so that, while the performance of the English Magnificat did not take up much time, it also provided little possibility of musical interest. The advantage of setting an even number of verses here becomes apparent. By alternating verses between the two halves of the choir, the English composer was able to impart a small amount of variety to this otherwise self-limiting text. No indication of such alternation is given for the Tallis Magnificat by Boyce, but, if the composer's intention was not to provide for such an alternation, the idea must soon have presented itself to those who performed the Service. Tallis' pupil, Elway Bevin *(c. 1560 – c. 1640)*, achieved even greater variety than the simple alternation of half-choirs suggested above by writing the first three verses of the Magnificat of his D minor Service[6] for full choir *a 4*. Verse four is given to *decani*; verse five, to *cantoris*. The next two are for full chorus *a 5*, verse eight is assigned to *decani a 4*, the next two verses are given to *cantoris*, and the concluding pair is again for full five-part choir. By varying both the texture and the regularity of the periods in which he shifted from textures or sides of the choir, he went far beyond the forthright approach of his teacher.

The A minor Service of Richard Farrant (?–1581),[7] when com-

6. Boyce, *CM*, I, 85–114.

7. Printed in g minor in Boyce, *CM*, I, 53–84. Concerning the original key and some errors in Boyce's version of the text,

see *MR*, 802, and *Grove's*, III, 34. The Morning and Evening Services are in Harley 7337, 322–38; Communion Service, Harley 7339, 139–43.

pared to the Tallis work with its numerous unessential sections, seems to provide only a minimum of choral settings, as it contains only the *Te Deum* and *Benedictus* for Morning Prayer, the Kyrie and Creed for Holy Communion, and the Magnificat and *Nunc dimittis* for Evening Prayer. This, however, is the rule and not the exception, for the remaining Services printed by Boyce are so constituted until his final example, by Purcell, is reached. The most striking feature of Farrant's Service is found in his alternation of verse and chorus sections, after the fashion that prevailed in full anthems, where the designation of verse did not always signify the use of solo voices, but of a portion of the choir instead of all available voices. Farrant, in addition to calling upon the two sides of the choir for antiphonal singing, also creates interesting contrasts in texture by preceding a section for full choir with a verse section using the *decani* sopranos in ensemble with the SAT group from the *cantoris* side. At other points he calls for different combinations, including ATBB, AABB, and SSTT. These effects, it should be noted, are restricted to the settings for Morning Prayer. The Communion Office and Evening Prayer, although they contain a wealth of antiphonal writing for the complete *decani* and *cantoris* sides, are not the subjects of experiments in varying textures. The canticles of Evening Prayer are, nevertheless, the most rewarding musical settings, their lack of experimental techniques notwithstanding.

Four Services by William Byrd (1543–1623) are extant. The first is a Full Service, but of the short variety; that is, it provides music for all of the liturgical observances of the day in syllabic settings.[8] The second is a setting of only the canticles for Evening Prayer, almost entirely in syllabic style.[9] It contains what probably is the earliest application of the true verse technique, with solo voices, to the writing of Services. It opens with a contratenor solo setting, with organ, for the first verse of the Magnificat. Verses seven and ten are also set for solo voice and organ; the rest of the verses are choral. The third Service also sets only the Evening canticles,[10] and is notable principally for being in triple meter and for using five voices. Although it employs alternation of the halves of the choir, it contains no writing

---

8. *TCM*, ii, 51–98; Byrd, *Collected Vocal Works*, x, 52–107; Boyce, *CM*, iii, 1–32. Boyce omits the setting of *Venite* and gives the entire Service in d minor instead of f minor. The four Services are also published by Oxford University Press.

9. *TCM*, ii, 99–110; Byrd, *Works*, x, 108–21.

10. *TCM*, ii, 111–22; Byrd, *Works*, x, 122–35.

for soloists. The fourth, better known as the Great Service,[11] is a veritable masterpiece in Byrd's finest polyphonic style. Except for its contrapuntal complexity, it differs from the Short Service only in the fact that it contains no Sanctus. It is possible, however, that the Sanctus that appears with the Short Service is spurious.[12] If that is the case, no difference was actually involved in Byrd's plan for the two settings. Because of the repetitions of text that naturally occur in polyphonic structure, the Great Service is unusually long. Restriction of all the sections to the same key, in keeping with the usual practice followed in writing Full Services, gives the impression of a lack of variety. It must be kept in mind, though, that a Full Service is not sung as a continuous musical performance, but is spread over three separately constituted orders of worship, the first two of which — Morning Prayer and Holy Communion — proceed as if they form a single, uninterrupted sequence. Still, the Magnificat and *Nunc dimittis* are removed from this continuity by a space of several hours and some of the wearisome lack of variety in key is therefore confined to the visual impact made by the score. Although much of the composition is for five voices, it achieves great variety through a constant shifting of textures within all its sections, except for the brief Kyrie, which is SAATB throughout. By a further division of these five parts into the *decani* and *cantoris* half-choirs, Byrd was able to call upon as many as ten parts at one time, as he did briefly in the closing measures of the *Venite*.

The same impulse that caused composers of cyclic Masses to search for unifying principles may have moved Byrd to make use of a device similar to the head-motif (*cf. p. 51*) that appeared in connection with the composition of polyphonic Masses. The similarity of phrases that either open sections of the Service or appear early in those sections to the plainsong intonation that precedes the *Te Deum*, and, in turn, its relationship to the same intonation in the Gregorian usage, requires our consideration of Byrd's probable intentions of creating such an audible link between sections (*Ex. 45*). That this relationship of thematic material to the intonation is not entirely accidental seems evident in the fact that the greatest similarity exists at the beginning of each musical setting. On the other hand, Byrd often normally ran his musical line to the level of the tonic before beginning a downward

11. *TCM*, ɪɪ, 123–222; Byrd, *Works*, x, 136–252; W. Gillies Whittaker, "Byrd's Great Service," *The Musical Quarterly,* xxvɪɪ/4 (October, 1941), 474–90. 12. *Grove's*, vɪɪ, 720.

Ex. 45 Byrd's use of Te Deum intonation in the Great Service

melodic curve, and the emphasis on that upper tone seems to be less one of associative intention when his normal melodic structure is considered. In only a few instances in the entire Service does the melody rise to the level of the supertonic, usually because Byrd either was attempting an intensification of text or was making directly pictorial attempts at text-painting. On the whole, the evidence seems to point toward flexible use of the head-motif principle as a method for unifying the several sections. Even though the effect of such unification would be lessened by the fact that the Evening Service was not performed without a lapse of time, the same concept that caused the discrete movements to be set in a single key would have influenced the desire for thematic unification. The regular alternation of these similar passages between first and second soprano is too noticeable to ignore, but at the same time it is too tenuous to put forth as definite proof of another type of unification.

The verse technique found in Byrd's Second Service was continued by Thomas Morley (1557–1603) in a Full Service *a 5*, one of four that survive him.[13] His treatment of style was not confined to the use of one solo voice at a time, but extended to passages that called for three and four soloists. This emphasis on solo voices, so popular in the development of anthem literature, continued to make its way into the Services until it threatened to become a toy of the composers. Thomas Tomkins (1572–1656) applied the verse technique to both his Fourth and Fifth Services.[14] His use of the solo voices is more exuberant than his writing for chorus, and is almost flamboyant at times. Each entire composition is supported by an organ part that is constantly busy, often to the point of covering the effects for which Tomkins strove so mightily in the solo voices. Neither of these verse Services is of the full variety. The Fourth sets only *Te Deum*, Magnificat, and *Nunc dimittis*, while the Fifth sets the usual sections of both the Morning and Evening Services. The Magnificat of the Fourth Service illustrates Tomkins' preoccupation with the solo voices. The canticle is divided into three distinct sections. Each involves solo singing and choral passages; the organ provides continuous accompaniment in the solo passages and *colla parte* when the chorus sings; and the organ and voices make a complete break at the end of each section. The first section is made up of the first five verses of text, and changes of musical texture take place with each new verse, in the following order: solo, two soli, choir, two soli in canon, and choir. Section two contains verses six through eight, calling for four soli in canon with highly obvious text-painting, two soli, and choir. The last section begins with four soli, the next verse again has four soli (but not the same voices as in the preceding), verse eleven is set for choir, and the

---

13. *MR*, 805.
14. *TCM*, VIII, 176–212; 213–50. Both the Third and Fifth Services are published by Oxford University Press.

last verse presents the choir with two solo sopranos added in the last hemistich.

Sharply contrasted in style from the verse Service is the Third Service for ten voices. Each side of the choir is a full SAATB chorus. These join in various combinations, one of which employs all ten parts in tossing antiphonal phrases back and forth in true polychoral style. The organ does not intrude upon the vocal texture as it does in the solo sections of the other two Services mentioned here.

The two Services by Orlando Gibbons (1583–1625) bring to a close the contributions of Renaissance composers. His Short Service[15] is a full setting of the seven usual sections comprising the three daily observances. It is written for four voices throughout, and, even though it makes liberal use of the two halves of the choir, it never calls upon them to join forces—all of the full sections are still *a 4*. It is definitely not, as has sometimes been stated, a verse Service. Although all the movements and their subsections begin in simple homophonic style, as one would expect in a short Service, the texture becomes increasingly polyphonic after the first phrase or two, developing a greater complexity than is usual in a short Service. This procedure is reasonable, however, in that it makes an initially clear presentation of a familiar text which tends to become somewhat obliterated as the movement continues. This did not necessarily bring confusion to the congregation who knew the entire text from memory and could easily supply any words that were lost in the complex sections. If this tendency toward polyphony seems out of place in a work that passed as a short Service, a still greater deviation from simplicity was made in the Gloria of the *Nunc dimittis*, where Gibbons wrote the two upper voices in canon.

Gibbons' Second Service,[16] a verse setting of the Morning and Evening canticles, treats the chorus in more direct fashion, varying only slightly from a strictly homophonic setting for five voices. The Magnificat is set more simply than that of Tomkins' Fourth Service, although Gibbons also employs solo voices and text-painting to a considerable degree. The entire canticle is divided into two sections— coming to a complete break after the eighth verse—instead of the more elaborate tripartite division made by Tomkins. The first two verses are set for two soli in canon, and much of the remainder parallels

15. *TCM*, iv, 30–67; Boyce, *CM*, i, 115–44; Harley 7337, 234–60. Modern edition   published by Oxford University Press.
16. *TCM*, iv, 68–124.

Tomkins' selection of vocal combinations quite closely. That much of the selection could have been influenced by the possibilities of text-painting and intensification is apparent in the manner in which the two composers dealt with the second hemistich of the sixth verse (*Ex. 46*). Verse seven, *He hath put down the mighty,* is equally subjected to elaboration by both composers, although Tomkins is far more obvious in his use of large downward leaps than is Gibbons.

The Restoration composers did nothing significant in the further-ance of Service settings. Their interest in writing Services is evident

Ex. 46 *a*) Tomkins, Fourth Service, verse 6b of Magnificat, *TCM*, VIII, 200

Used with permission of The Carnegie United Kingdom Trust.

b) Gibbons, Second Service, verse 6b of Magnificat, *TCM*, IV, 108

Used with permission of The Carnegie United Kingdom Trust.

in the quantity of examples they left, but these must have been products of a sense of duty, and not of pleasure in creation. For the most
part, the works are unimpressive settings of the short variety, setting
the text in the simplest, most direct fashion possible. The perfunctory
treatment accorded the Service by most of the composers of the
Restoration is little short of astonishing when one recalls the attention they gave to variety and inventiveness in their development of
anthems at the same time. Yet, it must be noted that a similar lack of
attention was given the Mass by composers who were more excited
by the expressive possibilities that lay in the motet, where a freedom
of choice existed in the selection of texts. The restricted material of
the Service, along with the ever-present injunctions concerning syllabic settings—probably more stringently observed in connection
with the liturgical materials of the Service than with the freely selected
texts of the anthem—may well have intimidated composers and discouraged them from giving more than a token effort to this facet of
church music. It is sufficient to examine the style of Blow and Purcell
in estimating the level of accomplishment during this period.

John Blow's (1649–1708) G-major Service,[17] setting the canticles
for Morning and Evening Prayer and the Kyrie and Creed from the
Communion Office, is in many ways a perfunctory work. The parts
proceed together in block-chord style with few exceptions, and the
organ part is provided with only a figured *basso seguente*. The work
could easily be sung without any help from the organ, and probably
gains nothing from the addition of the instrument. The alternation of
verse and chorus sections is predictably regular in the *Te Deum*. The
Jubilate (*TEM* 43) is given sectional treatment, opening with a homophonic setting which, at "O go your way into his gates with thanksgiving," shifts briefly to a double canon in which the soprano and
tenor soloists give out one melody canonically while alto and bass
share another. This is followed by the entire *decani* side in block-
chords and, later, in imitative counterpoint. The whole piece closes
with the full chorus singing the Gloria in canon. The rest of the
Service uses these same ingredients, and text-painting in portions of
the Magnificat is again noticeable.

An Evening Service,[18] in which Blow used the substitute texts
for Evening Prayer, is substantially the same as the one in G major,

17. Boyce, *CM*, i, 252–81; alternative
triple-meter settings of Kyrie and Creed,   *ibid.*, 282–88.
18. *Ibid.*, iii, 69–103.

although no canonic settings are included in this case. An examination of the alternative psalms shows that no special treatment was accorded them beyond the composer's taking advantage of some portions of the new text to which he could apply imaginative treatment *(Ex. 47)*.

The Purcell Service in B-flat major[19] is the most extensive setting that can be found anywhere; extensive not from the musical standpoint, for there it is surpassed by Byrd's Great Service, but from the

EX. **47** Blow, E minor Service, text-painting in Cantate Domino (Boyce, *CM*, III, 94)

19. *Ibid.*, III, 104–64; Purcell, *Works*, XXIII, 1–79. Harley 7340, 273–96, prints the six usual sections under the title, *Full Service by Henry Purcell in B♭; ibid.*, III, 403–25, gives the four optional sections as *Morning and Evening Service by Henry Purcell in B♭*.

number of sections of text that are included. It provides music not only
for the usual six sections of the full Service, but adds settings of all
the alternatives; *Benedicite, Jubilate, Cantate Domino,* and *Deus misereatur.* For the most part the chorus is *a 4,* although it expands to six
voices in some brief passages. There are numerous verse sections,
calling upon a variety of combinations from the two sides of the choir
and, in addition, the alternation of the half-choirs as units is common.
Purcell's skill as a contrapuntist is nowhere more evident in his church
music than in this Service, in the course of which he included no less
than ten sections in canon, all of them *a 4.* If ever he displayed his
ability in strict polyphony, it was here, for he set down two separate
canons four-in-two, in which he employed different voice combinations in each, one example each of canons two-in-one and three-in
one, and two canons four-in-one. There are also four instances of
canon by inversion, one each involving two and three voices in the
canonic activity, and two in which all four voices participate in the
resolution of the subject. The employment of canons was not a random
choice by Purcell, nor was it a matter of inserting them at regular
intervals in the composition. Six of them occur in settings of the
Gloria, and the others are in connection with text that has more than
average importance. One of the latter group occurs as a part of the
Jubilate (Ex. 48), in which it is preceded by a section for full choir
and followed by a verse for the *cantoris* ATB group. Only seven of the
canons are set for full choir, the rest being verses that use voices from
the *decani* or call for some from each side.

The composers of the eighteenth century, the best of whom are
liberally represented in the collections of Boyce, Arnold, and Tudway,
contributed little to the writing of Services except a declining standard. It is barely possible that some passages could be isolated from the
numerous works of King, Nares, Boyce, Weldon, Greene, and the rest
of their contemporaries that would stand up under close examination.
Unfortunately, the picture that develops from a survey of these works
is one of generally dull writing for four voices; half-hearted gestures
in support of a musical style not of their own time; lack of enthusiasm
for interesting harmony, skill with counterpoint, and perception concerning the relationship between textual and musical rhythms.
Among these composers William Croft, who had the good fortune
to live early in the century when the level of composition had not yet
reached its lowest point, exhibited skill in counterpoint and the use

Ex. 48 Canon four-in-two by inversion from *Jubilate Deo* of Purcell's Service in Bb(Boyce, *CM*, III, 150)

of variable textures, as in his Morning Service (with Sanctus and Gloria) in B minor,[20] which contains not only a canon four-in-one, but occasionally expands the basic four-voice writing to as many as eight parts. On the whole, this century must be viewed as the nadir of English Service composition. While the musical offspring of some earlier generations may not have maintained a constant high level of beauty, they had at least an amiable variety to support their claim to existence; the consistent drabness of the eighteenth-century product demonstrates only a spiritless fecundity where sterility in production, rather than in imagination, would have been an improvement.

The problem that faced the Lutherans was not simply finding a

20. Arnold, *CM*, I, 151–86.

vernacular substitute for the Latin Mass, for they willingly clung to Latin as a liturgical vehicle long after Luther's time.[21] That Luther was concerned with musical modifications rather than with complete upheaval is seen in his first efforts to provide a slightly different version of the Latin Mass, before he undertook the planning of a *Deutsche Messe*. Even then, the idea was not that the German version should replace the Latin, but that it should be a parallel usage. It was principally intended as insurance for full perception of the text by the congregation, for education of the young, and for providing congregational participation in the simpler musical portions of the service. Much substitution of German verse for Latin, and of congregational hymns for sections formerly assigned to the choir as portions of the Proper or Ordinary, is found in the German effort.[22] While some parts of the Latin version were simply omitted, others were replaced by German hymns, probably sung by the congregation in unison. Had Luther's German Mass been adopted as a basic pattern, it would have had as great an effect upon Lutheran liturgical practice as the formulation of a standard pattern in English had upon the Anglican Service. His ideas merely provided alternatives to the old forms, and the freedom of interchange between old and new was so great that the entire service could be held in either Latin or German, or a comparatively free substitution of German for any Latin part could be permitted. So closely was this new procedure tied to the introduction of German hymns that the chorale became more important to the future of Lutheran music than did any of Luther's attempts to change the structure of the Mass or the religious service.

The changes that took place cannot, then, be sought solely in the Mass, nor even principally there. The freedom that was permitted encouraged neither a continued conformity nor a tendency toward

21. Martin Luther died in 1546. The continuation of Latin and German side by side in the Lutheran Church after his death is seen in a 1573 volume compiled by Johannes Keuchenthal from the best songbooks he knew. His *Kirchen-Gesenge Latinisch und Deudsch, sampt allen Evangelien, Episteln, und Collecten, auff die Sontage und Feste, nach Ordnung der zeit, durchs gantze Jhar,... Witteberg,* M.D.LXXIII, is a volume of 590 folios. Among its Latin plainsong pieces are numerous Introits, Alleluias, and Sequences, as well as pieces with both Latin and German text. The collection reflects the practice of the time in at least some churches. For Luther's views, see Eva Mary Grew, "Martin Luther and Music," *Music and Letters,* XIX/1 (January, 1938), 67–78, and Walter Buszin, "Luther on Music," *The Musical Quarterly,* XXXII/1 (January, 1946), 80–97.
22. Luther D. Reed, *The Lutheran Liturgy* (rev. ed.; Philadelphia: Muhlenberg Press, 1960), 78. Cf. *MR,* 676. The German substitute for the Sanctus, *Jesaia dem Propheten des geschach,* is printed in *GMB* 77. In Keuchenthal's collection it appears on ff. 23^v–24^r.

rebellion. Not only Masses, but psalm settings, Magnificats, and a a number of other continuing choral forms show the intrusion of vernacular texts as well as of typically German musical materials.

Johann Walter (1496–1570), who was associated with Luther from about 1525, provided a strange mingling of the old and new with a salutation to three of his famous contemporaries in his setting of *Beati immaculati in via* (Psalm 119 [cxviii]) in five *partes a 7*.[23] His employment of more than six voices is so rare that only this composition and one other psalm setting use as many as seven. It is not the number of voices that makes this piece worthy of comment, however. Two voices can be removed completely without damage to the musical structure or to the presentation of the psalm text. The four tenor parts are canonic, and the soprano is a discant to them. While the canonic pattern and discant are different in each of the five *partes,* the alto and bass supply a constant melodic and textual feature, unchanging from one section of the piece to the next. The alto, a verbal bouquet flung to Prince Johann Friedrich, never once moves from the reiterated succession of g's that serves as vehicle for the encomium, *Vivat, . . . Iohannes Friderich, vivat, . . . Elector et Dux Saxonia eius. . . .* At the same time, and unvaryingly during each of the *partes,* the bass intones the praises of Luther and Philipp Melanchthon on a trumpet-like repetition of C-C-C-G-G, to the text, *Vive Luthere, Vive Melanthon. . . .* Undeniably, the reiteration of these panegyrics adds nothing to the piece, and Walter was certainly musician enough to recognize the fact. The dedication of a new chapel at Torgau was the reason for the composition. The presence of the Prince and Melanchthon, as well as of Luther, who dedicated this first church to be built by the Lutherans, certainly moved Walter to include the material which added nothing musical, but which must have been accepted in the same spirit it was offered—a salute to the leading figures of church and secular life who were assembled for the occasion.[24] While no vernacular texts are found, the use of personal reference is worthy of comment, for it may be the first such use in the Lutheran practice. It is only right that attention be called to Walter's settings of the Magnificat, one for each of the modes,[25] that present his work in a manner that permits evaluation on purely musical grounds. Employing variable groups of two to

23. Johann Walter, *Sämtliche Werke* (Kassel: Bärenreiter-Verlag, 1961), v, 3–12.
24. *Ibid.,* v–vii, describes both the circumstances and the music more completely than is done here. Psalm 121 (cxx), *ibid.,* 13–30, employs the same device, but without the laudatory texts.
25. *Ibid.,* 33–107.

eight voices, they are excellent contrapuntal settings of the even-
numbered verses, concluding each time with the entire Gloria Patri;
i.e., a polyphonic setting of verse eleven as well as twelve. No deviations from the usual practice are apparent in the settings.

The music that was distinctively Lutheran was the chorale. It made
its way into every musical form that was associated with the activity of
that denomination, as part of both instrumental and vocal expressions.
It can be found in many works of the earliest composers of that church,
along with favorite tunes which, although they do not properly find
classification among the chorales, found a warm place in the hearts of
the Lutherans. Among these were some tunes belonging to the category of *Leisen*, congregational hymns in the vernacular dating back
as far as the ninth century, and invariably ending with a formula-
phrase, "kyrie eleison," often abbreviated as "kyrieleis" or "kirleis."[26]
One of these *Leisen* is *Christ ist erstanden* (Christ is arisen), which is
possibly derived from the Easter Sequence, *Victimae paschali laudes,*
and which was used as a basis for sections of an Easter Mass (CW 44)
by Johannes Hähnel (c. 1490–?). This Mass, providing settings for
the Proper as well as the Ordinary, differs in no respect from other
polyphonic compositions of German composers of this time, but the
inclusion of the familiar *Christ ist erstanden* in two of its sections marks
it as a distinctly Lutheran work while in every other feature it is
equally adaptable to Catholic use. The *Leise* figures most prominently
in the setting of the Sequence, where the thematic similarities of the
opening phrases of these two melodies work together most effectively.
Each statement of the *Leise* tune is clearly recognizable because of the
German text. The Sequence was performed in plainsong until the first
of the paired lines, beginning with *Agnus redemit oves*, was reached.
At that point Hähnel provided a polyphonic setting of the Sequence
in two sections between which plainsong was probably to be inserted,
plus a third section that is not found in the Sequence itself, with the
text *Credendum est magis soli Mariae veraci, quam Judaeorum turbae
fallaci*, beneath which the plainsong of the first paired verse is underlaid in long notes.[27] This last section does not make use of the *Leise*,
but the first two sections do, each in a different fashion. The first
polyphonic section contains an entire stanza of the vernacular hymn
Christ ist erstanden, complete with the kyrie formula, used as a *cantus
firmus* in the tenor. In the second section, the first phrase, in *ostinato*

26. *Grove's*, II, 270; *HD*, 396; *MR*, 633.   be found in *MM* 3; *GMB* 6; and *HAM* 16b.
27. Cf. *LU*, 780. The Sequence may also

fashion but with variable pitches and rhythms, appears four times to make up the entire bass part. In the Agnus Dei only the first portion of liturgical text is used. After *miserere nobis,* the second half of the *Leise,* with the text *Des solln wir alle froh sein, Christus soll unser Trost sein, Kyrie eleison,* is the basis of the polyphonic material, all the parts of which turn to the German text for the remainder of the piece. It is not astonishing that vernacular materials made their way into musical works from the earliest period of Lutheran composition, but it is of more than passing interest that such materials immediately became equal partners to plainsong and were accorded the same dignity and respect as other musical materials. Another employment of the vernacular repertory is found in Hähnel's Christmas Magnificat in the fifth mode (*CW* 85, 9–18), which uses a different familiar melody in each of the even-numbered verses, the only ones set polyphonically. In every verse, all voices begin with one statement, presented imitatively, of the opening words of that verse of the Magnificat, after which one voice continues with the Latin in *cantus firmus* fashion while the other three sing familiar Christmas songs in mostly chordal style. Among the songs used here are *Resonet in laudibus,* better known to many as *Joseph, lieber Joseph mein; In dulci jubilo,* with its usual mixture of Latin and German; *Exsultandi tempus est,* entirely in Latin; *Psallat clerus de virgine,* which later continues with the German, *Geborn ist uns ein Kindelein; Der Spiegel der Dreifaltigkeit;* and, in the final verse, *Joseph, Joseph, wo ist das neugeborne Kindelein.*

The incorporation of these favorite songs into larger works was not simply a device used by the earliest Lutheran composers, for about half a century later Hieronymus Praetorius (1560–1629) again adopted two of these melodies in connection with a Magnificat in the fifth mode.[28] While Praetorius did not insert the melodies into the verses themselves, he made them available by appending them to the twelfth verse, first adding *Joseph, lieber Joseph mein,* and then *In dulci jubilo.* It is true that they do not have the close identity with the Magnificat that was apparent in Hähnel's setting, for not only do they fail to become an essential part of the verses, but they are mere appendages to the entire Magnificat setting, to be omitted at will. However, their appearance in a double-choir setting, like the Magnificat, indicates that they were considered as closely related pieces. Finally, Praetorius' title, *Magnificat quinti toni cum canticis Ecclesiasticis,* can be taken to

28. *DdT,* xxiii, 129–44.

mean that the German songs were intended as part and parcel of his composition, and not to be removed from context even though the choirs indicated by the clefs of the songs, SSAA-ATBB, are not the same as those for the Magnificat itself, SSAT-STTB.

If any evidence were needed of the great interest in, and the wide dissemination of chorales during the middle years of the sixteenth century, it would be amply illustrated by the contents of the collection of 123 such songs for three to six voices, entitled *Newe deudsche geistliche Gesenge für die gemeinen Schulen* and published by Georg Rhaw (1488–1548) in 1544.[29]

German Protestant composers soon followed old ,patterns with a substitution of German text in setting the Passion story. A motet Passion by Balthasar Harzer (Resinarius) *(c. 1480–?),* entirely in Latin and dating from about 1543, bears the title *Summa Passionis Domini nostri Jesu Christi secundum Johannem (CW 47).* Its date, and the presence of Harzer's music in the *Newe deudsche geistliche Gesenge* (he provided thirty of the pieces therein) leave little doubt of his productivity in both the old and the new styles, both Latin and German at the same time, though all his work was apparently for Protestant use. Works of this kind were in the minority, and a large number of Passion settings appeared with German texts. While the motet type seemed to find greatest favor with German composers, efforts were made to establish the dramatic type as well. As early as mid-sixteenth century, a dramatic setting by Walter appeared,[30] and in another decade a Passion by Antonio Scandello (1517–1580) showed a mingling of both types within a single composition.[31] With the St. John Passion *(CW 27)*[32] of Christoph Demantius (1567–?), the first series of efforts toward establishment of a typical German style in Passions comes to a close. Dating from 1631, the work belongs to an earlier stylistic era, for it reflects none of the new elements that are to be found in Baroque music. Demantius was in his sixty-fourth year when the Passion appeared. His thorough training in Renaissance polyphony is evident in the skill with which the work is constructed, and it is not surprising that he, as one of the older composers of this period, fails to use Baroque techniques in a type of composition that

29. *Ibid.,* xxxiv. For a discussion of the contents, see *MR,* 678ff.
30. The Passion setting in Keuchenthal's *Kirchen-Gesenge* (cf. n. 21), also of the dramatic type, draws upon Walter's version for some of its material.

31. *MR,* 688f.
32. Also printed in the same volume *(CW 27)* is Demantius' *Weissagung des Leidens und Sterbens Jesu Christi,* based on part of Isaiah 53, and similar to his Passion in many respects.

has always tended to be more reserved than flamboyant. The Passion is entirely in motet style for six voices, and it is divided into three sections. The composition is quite short, for the text is not presented in its entirety. An astonishing amount of vitality and variety is achieved with what appear to be limited means, especially when the texture is so largely confined to familiar style after the opening imitative measures of each section. The regular alternation of brief passages between high and low voice groups reduces the possibility of tedium. The most striking feature of Demantius' Passion is the careful and consistent use of expressive musical ideas, of which Friedrich Blume defines three groups.[33] One group is concerned with underscoring the meanings of words and phrases that express action. A second group conveys direct symbolism, as in the cases where references to one person are sung (but only for the duration of that word, *einer*) by a single voice, or where reference to the two malefactors is written in two parts. The third group attempts to deal with abstract symbolism and, in some cases, is related to the concept of *Augenmusik,* which demands visual perception of the score for its full apprehension. References to death, suffering, and crucifixion[34] figure strongly in this group of chromatically altered sections. Examples of this third type, not requiring visual knowledge of the score, express attitudes of the participants in the drama, or underscore dogmatic principles. The abrupt change that is apparent to both eye and ear when Pilate says, *Was ist Wahrheit?* ("What is truth?"), first in greatly exaggerated, ponderous, slow note-values and then immediately in a frivolous, syncopated pattern, belongs to this last group *(Ex. 49).*

The affective treatment of text is not new, for we have seen attempts in this direction in the works of many earlier composers, and we shall consider it again in greater detail in another chapter when Demantius' contemporary, Heinrich Schütz, is discussed (pp. 295– 300). Its appearance as a highly refined and stylized expression will also be discussed in connection with the cantatas of Johann Sebastian Bach (pp. 262 *et passim*).

While the German language made its way successfully and consistently into Passion settings, it did not, as we saw earlier, make any headway in the Mass except in Luther's own *Deutsche Messe.* The

---

33. *Ibid.,* 3f.
34. Especially favored by composers adopting this symbolic means of expression because the German term *Kreuz* denotes both cross and sharp. Its felicitous application in matters both theological and musical is obvious.

Ex. 49 Demantius, *Passion, Zweiter Teil,* after *CW,* XXVII, 16

From Blume, *Das Chorwerk,* 27. Used by permission.

high point of the Lutheran service was the sermon, with the Holy Communion celebrated after it as as a separate service. This new focal point, the delivery of the spoken Word in the vernacular, and the separation of the old materials of worship from the new, placed all of the important musical activity before the sermon. The remnants of the Mass available for use there were the Kyrie and Gloria, a pairing of movements that came to be identified as the *Missa brevis*[35] or, by the Lutherans, simply as *Messe.* This uniquely Lutheran contribution appeared in two forms: the freely composed, imitative polyphony of the sixteenth century, and the contrapuntal style employing a familiar chorale as the basis for the polyphony, either as a *cantus firmus* or as the germ of the imitative phrases. These compositions, of either type, were written both with and without figured bass. An early example of the employment of a chorale tune is found in a *Missa brevis a 5* by Christoph Bernhard (1627–1692), based upon the melody of *Christ unser Herr zum Jordan kam* (CW 16, 23–30). This melody is used

---

35. Not to be confused with the Catholic *Missa brevis,* which is a setting of the en- tire Ordinary, but in simple form.

as the basis of the imitative sections of both parts. The Gloria begins with the words *Et in terra pax*, indicating that even here the opening phrase was intoned as in the full Catholic settings. A *Missa brevis* by Dietrich Buxtehude[36] (1637–1707), also *a 5* but with figured bass, is of greater complexity. The Kyrie is broken into three distinct sections, the first two of which have contrasting material in duple meter, while the closing section repeats the thematic material of the opening part in triple meter. The intonation in the Gloria is given to the bass, and the remainder of that section is broken into two parts, new thematic material appearing at *Qui tollis peccata mundi*. The work is marked by some passages that lean strongly toward instrumental idioms. This, apparently the only Mass of this kind among Buxtehude's works, makes no use of either chorales or vernacular text.

Johann Theile (1646–1724), a pupil of Schütz and teacher of Zachow and Buxtehude (it is possible that he composed his *Missa brevis* during his study with Theile) has left a similar work, *a 5* in the old style; i.e., without figured bass (*CW* 16, 4–22). It is a model of the finest in the then archaic Renaissance technique. That the style was becoming obsolete is not a reflection upon the skill of such composers, but a cause for astonishment that such control of its techniques could still be exercised by one who was conversant with the dominant Baroque style. Throughout the composition, Theile chose to adopt the style of strict imitative counterpoint. Each section of the Kyrie is based on a different subject, and the sections end successively in the key centers of i-v-i. The intonation of the Gloria is assigned to the two soprano parts, beginning in canon, but lapsing into free counterpoint after a few measures. A vigorous "Amen" chorus is appended to the composition, reminiscent of the closing Hallelujah sections of anthems, but more skillfully contrived than most of them.

Friedrich Zachow (1663–1712), who is usually remembered only because he was Handel's first teacher, may be the composer of a *Missa brevis a 4* with figured bass, on a familiar chorale. In the *Missa super chorale: Christ lag in Todes Banden*,[37] Zachow divided the chorale tune into three parts (omitting the repetition of the first two phrases)[38] and assigned each part to one of the sections of the Kyrie. Elimination of the repeat reduces the chorale to twelve measures, four of which

36. Dietrich Buxtehude, *Missa Brevis*, in Dessoff Choir Series, No. 23, ed. Paul Boepple (New York: Mercury Music Corporation, 1942).
37. *DdT*, xxi/xxii, 304–310. Even if the Nikolaus Zachow named in the existing copy (cf. *Grove's*, ix, 393), is another person, the comments made here still apply.
38. The chorale is printed in *MM* 46 and numerous other sources.

are used in each section, thereby binding the Kyrie together through the progressive unfolding of the melody rather than by threefold repetition of its entire contents. In the Gloria—the polyphony begins with *Et in terra pax*—the other approach, that of threefold repetition of the melody, becomes the basis of the entire movement.

Although the practice of basing entire compositions upon chorales, or of introducing chorale sections into works that are not so served by the Lutheran hymn, is usually thought of in connection with cantatas or works for organ, the two preceding examples by no means exhaust the instances that apply to the Mass. Among the others who used the chorale in this manner were Johann Kuhnau (1660–1722), Georg Philipp Telemann (1681–1767), Johann Nicolaus Bach (1669–1753), Johann Ernst Bach (1722–1777), and Johann Sebastian Bach (1685–1750).[39] This last, monumental figure in German Lutheran music wrote five *Missae brevis*, four of which are known still in their original form (*BWV* 233–36),[40] while the fifth became the basis for the supradenominational *Mass in B minor* (*BWV* 232). The horns and oboes in the *Missa brevis* in F boldly state a chorale tune, *Christe, du Lamm Gottes,* in long tones against a relatively florid choral setting of the Kyrie (*HMS*, v, 45f). This, one of the last examples of the chorale as a Mass ingredient and Johann Sebastian's only gesture of this type, does not form an exact parallel to his method of including the chorale in cantatas, for there the voices participate in the chorale while in this Kyrie the melody is presented as a commentary by the instruments.

Figuring much more strongly in these Masses is the practice of employing materials borrowed from other works, mostly cantatas that were composed earlier than the Masses, which date from about 1737. These adaptations, or *contrafacta*,[41] figure most prominently in the B minor Mass where more than a third of the numbers are adapted from

---

39. Karl Geiringer, *The Bach Family* (London: George Allen & Unwin, 1954), 94.

40. Since the works of J. S. Bach are available in a variety of editions, as well as in the volumes of the *Bach-Gesellschaft* edition and the *Neue Ausgabe sämtlicher Werke,* reference will be made only to the numbers assigned in *BWV;* i.e., Wolfgang Schmieder, *Thematisch-systematisches Verzeichnis der musikalischen Werke J. S. Bachs* (Leipzig: Breitkopf & Härtel, 1950).

41. The use of choruses from cantatas could as well be called parody, just as the transfer of motets or secular songs to the Renaissance Mass constituted parody. In those cases, however, one pre-existent composition served as the material for an entire Mass, while here the borrowed material is used in connection with only a few words of text or, at most, a section of the Ordinary. While this is no less a parody in the fashion that was described in Chapter II, the practice here is called *contrafactum* in order to keep the two kinds of treatment separate for the present discussion.

other compositions. Not one of these five Masses is made up entirely of new material, and the G minor and G major examples are constructed entirely of *contrafacta*. Even such a two-movement Mass contains a number of borrowed sections, for only the Kyrie is set as a continuous, related musical idea because of its textual simplicity. The text of the Gloria is broken into a number of sections, the divisions falling at the discretion of the composer. Each of these sections may be set in a different fashion and, in the case of the two Masses in G, to different borrowed materials. Choruses, solos, duets, are all present with accompaniments that may involve full orchestra, string orchestra, or obbligato instrumental solos with *continuo*. The treatment of material is similar to that of the cantata, the oratorio, or the verse cantata-anthem.

The *Mass in B minor* was developed from one of these short *Missae*, although the adjective is misleading. Bach's original versions of the Kyrie and Gloria were built on a grander scale than those of the four other Masses, all of which he wrote later than the one in B minor. He had hoped, as a result of the presentation of this B minor *Missa brevis* to the Dresden court of the Elector of Saxony, to be awarded the title, duties, and privileges of *Kapellmeister*. His best and most impressive efforts were, therefore, submitted, and the proffered material was more extensively treated than that of the similar movements that he composed later. Inasmuch as the Elector was also King of Poland, his court was Catholic. Bach was, then, submitting a Lutheran Mass (although it was an extraordinary one) to a Catholic establishment. He received his appointment after a lapse of some years — he submitted his *Messe* in 1733 and his title was conferred in 1736 — and, if the other four Masses were presented to the court as nominal evidences of his position, he was persisting in his practice of writing Lutheran works for a Catholic court. Upon the music that had been conceived as a complete unit by Lutheran standards, in 1733, Bach built a Mass in the Roman Catholic fashion, the denominational implications of which have been debated for decades.[42]

The B minor Mass is a work of unprecedented length and unparalleled variety, for its twenty-four sections include an assortment of settings beyond the imagination of any other composer. There are

42. Appreciations, analyses, and descriptions may be found in the various studies and biographies of Bach. Convenient references are *Grove's*, I, 306; Geiringer, *op. cit.*, 239ff; Percy M. Young, *The Choral Tradition* (New York: W. W. Norton & Company, 1962), 140–49.

choruses with a variety of orchestral treatments, solos with ensembles or with obbligato solo instrument, each of which could stand as a musical unit, but which together make up a related whole composition. Bach did not arrive at these numerous, and sometimes theatrical, combinations without a long line of outside influences. They stemmed from developments in the Catholic Mass (some of which will be examined in the next chapter) and from the forces that were working their way into the sphere of church music from the opera and the secular cantata. To the vocal materials that were thus borrowed were added the orchestral support that was already popular with other Germans, as well as the *concertato* style that had made its way into German music, by way of Italy, a century earlier. Coming to fruition with Bach's effort, these numerous forces were molded into one of the truly great works of all Christian choral literature, overwhelming not only in size, but in the fullness of its scope and concept.

Chapter VII

Catholic Developments

After 1600

UNTIL the end of the Renaissance, the prevailing flow of influence had been from church music to secular music. With few exceptions, it was the style spawned and developed in the church that had made its way into the field of performance outside. In choral music this was especially true because the established vocal groups, whatever their size, were attached to religious establishments. With the coming of the Baroque period, the pattern of earlier years was reversed. Influence flowed from the theater to the church. In the case of opera, the principal vehicle of theatrical music, such stylistic features as instrumental accompaniment, musical forms, and even solo vocal styles were transferred from its repertory to religious compositions. This new point in musical emphasis did not appear all at one moment, but accumulated over a period of years. Even when it seemed strongest, an enclave inhabited by the composers of the *stile antico* persisted, eventually to become quiescent, but never to wither completely away, although new developments removed from it the necessary nourishment of enthusiastic acceptance by both Church and public.

Of all the forces evident in Baroque choral music, the most important one is the *concertato* style, typified by alternating groups of performers dissimilar in size and organization, either vocal or instrumental. The closely related development of the *basso continuo* also invaded the field of religious music, as we have already noted in connection with the anthem. While it did not simply cause harmony to replace counterpoint, it had a great deal to do with centering interest on the harmonic implications of Baroque music. This combination of *concertato* and *continuo* represented the strongest thrust of new ideas in religious music, but the proponents of the *stile antico* were not to be left behind, for they too fused their usual materials with the *continuo* and produced as a result the style known as the "colossal

197

Baroque." These three styles, the old polyphonic *a cappella* style, the *concertato*, and the colossal combination of *continuo* and polyphony, dominated Catholic music until the nineteenth century and, as we have already seen, were found in Protestant choral music as well. These several different styles were present in the early years of the Baroque period as contemporaneous expressions. They did not develop successively as counterfoils to each other.

The *concertato* was already evident in many of the works that emanated from St. Mark's in the declining years of the Renaissance. In order for it to have practical use in less pretentious establishments than the basilica in Venice, the dimensions of the style had to be severely contracted. In less ostentatious surroundings than those of St. Mark's, the full polychoral combinations of voices and instruments underwent modification, not only because limited forces were often the rule, but, more importantly perhaps, because such flagrant violations of the Tridentine pronouncements and intentions could not be condoned in most other parishes where, at the very least, outward acceptance of Roman practice was expected.

In a direct line of influence between Venice and the rest of the Catholic world was Claudio Monteverdi (1567–1643) who, after 1613, was *maestro di capella* at St. Mark's. His religious works do not cling to a single style, or even to a few broad patterns, for they range from motets in the style of the Renaissance to elaborate polychoral works with orchestra that show a mastery of the *concertato* style. His *Messa a 4 da Cappella* (printed 1640)[1] with *basso continuo* uses a single theme to open each section of the Ordinary in motto fashion *(Ex. 50)*. This theme, with rhythmic and melodic alterations, appears clearly at the beginning of each section and binds the movements together in the fashion that was seen frequently in Renaissance Masses. Another *Messa a 4 voci da Cappella* (printed 1650)[2] employs a diatonic

Ex. 50 Monteverdi, *Messa a 4 voci da Cappella. Opere*, XV, 59

1. *Tutte le Opere di Claudio Monteverdi,* ed. G. Francesco Malipiero (Asolo: The Author, 1926–1942; also Vienna: Universal-Edition), xv, 59–116.
   2. *Ibid.,* xvi, 1–53. The publication date of the work is usually given as 1651, but the title page of the volume containing it is reproduced in facsimile by Malipiero. The date thereon is clearly 1650.

passage of four notes *(Ex. 51)* which, in its original form or in its inversion, appears at the opening of several sections of the Mass. The *continuo* is simply a *basso seguente* with very few figures.

Totally different is the technique used in Monteverdi's *Magnificat septem vocibus et sex instrumentis.*[3] The *concertato* style is used throughout the twelve verses, each of which is set in a different fashion, but all of which use Tone I as a framework upon which the elaborate figures of voices and instruments are built. Common to all the verses is the *continuo,* while the verses are varied by the different combinations of voices and instruments that reflect the text through their various settings. Three verses are assigned to three voices and organ; the others range from solos with instruments to full *tutti* passages. For all the variety of instrumentation and rhythm, the plainsong is never omitted, although it appears both at the original level and transposed. The varied use of instruments plays a large part in this setting, but that Monteverdi had a capacity for variety without orchestra is evident in his *Magnificat a 6 voci,*[4] which uses only organ for accompaniment, while the number of voices and the character of the various melodies changes from verse to verse. It also employs Tone I. Among the other Magnificats, another based on Tone I, a *Magnificat secondo a quattro voci in genere da Capella,*[5] sets only the odd-numbered verses after the fashion of earlier composers. Each of the verses is treated as a brief motet *a 4,* except for two that are *a 3.* The entire composition is underlaid with a *basso seguente* organ line. A similar variety of treatments is found among his motets. Compositions for voices alone, for voices with supporting organ bass, for various vocal combinations in conjunction with instrumental groups, and for solo voice with instruments, abound. There is great variety among the motets, and the proof that the several aspects of Venetian style continued to be practiced widely after Gabrieli's death is evident in many examples.

Coexistent with the *stile concertato* and *stile antico* was the colossal

Ex. 51 Monteverdi, *Messa a 4 voci da Cappella. Opere,* XVI

or

3. *Ibid.,* xiv, 285–326. This is the concluding section of the *Vespers* of 1610, and belongs to the period of Monteverdi's employment in Mantua under the sponsorship of Vincenzo Gonzaga. Monteverdi during this time was seeking the recognition of Pope Paul v, and therefore was not actively espousing the Venetian style.

4. *Ibid.,* xiv, 327–53.

5. *Ibid.,* xv, 703–23.

Baroque, which Bukofzer has said represented the concession of Roman traditionalism to the modern trend. He describes the combination of Venetian and Roman styles as follows:

> The colossal baroque attempted to graft the polychoral techniques of the grand *concertato* on the *stile antico*. The resulting hybrid style was typical of the Roman conservatism. The profusion of vocal and instrumental means, the innumerable echos, solos, and tuttis, reflected the pomp of the church ritual in the counter-reformation, but the affective spirit of the Venetian *concertato* was conspicuously lacking.[6]

The work that is usually chosen to exemplify this style is the Mass, composed for the consecration of the Salzburg Cathedral in 1628, by Orazio Benevoli (1605–1672).[7] While it, with its fifty-three parts divided among two choruses *a 8*, two orchestras, solo singers, and various instrumental ensembles, represents the limits to which the style was to be pushed in Italy, it still is not typical of the marriage of Venetian and Roman styles, nor is it typical of Benevoli's works, for the Festival Mass was composed on commission for an event of great significance, the importance of which was not duplicated during Benevoli's life.[8] It is enlightening, then, to look toward works that may well represent his consistent approach to elaborate settings rather than to the single unique opportunity that was offered him in his early years.

Benevoli's *Missa Pastoralis*[9] is written for two SATB choirs and organ. Binding together the various sections, which lack any such cohesive material as a common *cantus firmus*, is a rhythmic pattern, ♩. ♪ ♩ ♩ , that often has melodic identification possibilities as well. While it acts as a unifying element, this pattern appears so often that it loses its point through tedious overemphasis. A full measure long, it occurs no less than twelve times, in four-voice block-chords, during the first twenty-eight measures of the Mass! A fourteen-voice Magnificat in Tone II attributed to Benevoli[10] makes use of the *concertato* principle among voices alone (with the usual figured bass for

6. *MBE*, 68.
7. *DTÖ*, xx.
8. Reference to some other elaborate works of this period may be found in Grove's, i, 621.
9. Orazio Benevoli, *Missa Pastoralis* (*Monumenta liturgiae Polychoralis Sanctae Ecclesiae Romanae, Ordinarium Missae cum* *duobus choris*, No. 1), (Rome: Societas Universalis Sanctae Ceciliae, 1957).
10. [Orazio Benevoli?] *Magnificat secundi toni* (*Monumenta liturgiae Polychoralis Sanctae Ecclesiae Romanae, Psalmodia cum tribus choris concertata*, No. 1), (Rome: Societas Universalis Sanctae Ceciliae, 1955).

organ) by combining three SATB choirs with a "concerto" made up of two soprano parts to be sung both solo and tutti, as are the various chorus parts. In addition to the full tutti combination, the composer had at his command a number of other dispositions of voices including three basses, tenors, or altos, or up to five sopranos and various other heterogeneous assortments of the foregoing. Each of the twelve verses is set to a different combination of voices, *a 2* to *a 14*, the number and arrangement of them being as significant as the melodic and rhythmic material they are given in their representation of the text. Especially telling is the treatment at the end of verse three in the setting of *omnes generationes*, where a full tutti with imitation of a single figure is stated at several speeds simultaneously (to represent several generations?) in both ascending and descending forms. The beginning of the verse is written for five solo sopranos.

The multi-choir practice was carried on by numerous composers into the eighteenth century, among whom one of the leaders was Giuseppe Ottavio Pitoni (1657–1743), teacher of some of the members of the famed Neapolitan school, himself a composer of well over sixty large polychoral works. His compositions probably represent the standard performance practice at some of the Roman churches where he was employed during the end of the seventeenth and beginning of the eighteenth centuries rather than general practice, for his conviction that music composed for one church should not be performed in another[11] must have caused him to write a large amount of the material that was performed under his direction.

One of the most renowned opera composers of the first half of the eighteenth century was Antonio Lotti (1667–1740), who held positions of prominence at St. Mark's for most of his life. In a period when the operatic style was beginning to encroach upon the field of church music, it is surprising that no evidence of such penetration is seen in the Masses of this internationally recognized master of operatic works. One group of eight Masses[12] adheres closely to the Roman ideal of the Renaissance—a single choir, *a cappella*, singing imitative counterpoint—but with strong harmonic writing implied in the contrapuntal sections and present in the remainder. This is seen in the Mass *a 3*[13] (TTB) and in his *Missa pro defunctis*[14] *(Ex. 52)*, both of which are almost entirely syllabic.

11. *Baker's Biographical Dictionary of Musicians*, ed., Nicolas Slonimsky (5th ed.; New York: G. Schirmer, 1958), 1254.

12. *DdT*, LX.
13. *Ibid.*, 1–12.
14. *Ibid.*, 115–33.

Ex. 52   Lotti: *Dies Irae* from *Missa pro defunctis*, after *DdT*, LX, 119

With permission of Breitkopf & Härtel, Wiesbaden.

    The seventeenth century saw Germany emerge as a strong Catholic musical force — not only southern Germany but also German-speaking Austria. It was influenced by the Italian style of opera, but added the dignity of polyphonic treatment to the instrumental style borrowed from those Italian masters who were receiving a warm reception in the imperial and princely courts. Southern Germany — let us hereafter include Austria in this term simply for convenience — had many things in common with Italy, not the least of which were religious practice and a passionate acceptance of opera, at least in high places. The relationship was such that it modified the Italian style, but did not stifle it. That a distinctive German Catholic musical style failed to develop is due in part to the continuing emphasis on the materials borrowed from opera; orchestral accompaniment, preludes and interludes, solo arias and ensembles, and displays of vocal virtuosity that hardly seem to be divorced from their theatrical surroundings. Three composers whose works show certain of these Italianate features, and of whom some representative Masses are collected in a single volume, [15] are Franz Heinrich Biber (1644–1704), Heinrich Schmeltzer

15. *DTÖ*, XLIX.

(1630–1680), and Johann Caspar Kerll (1627–1693). Some of these features are the division of the usual movements of the Ordinary into a greater number of small sections, the successive sections usually differing in both the vocal and instrumental groups that are used; the mixture of homophonic and polyphonic styles among the various sections; the use of *concertato* style with a high degree of contrast through the alternation of solo and *ripieno* passages; and the use of some or all of the voices at one time in polychoral fashion. Many of these reappeared in Bach's B minor Mass, as we have already noticed.

The intense interest in the Italian style was recognized by Johann Joseph Fux (1660–1741) who, as the greatest figure in German Catholic religious music, demonstrated his continuing mastery of the *stile antico* at the same time that he adopted certain Italian ideas in some of the compositions he wrote for church use. In the dedication to his *Missa canonica*,[16] a setting intended to demonstrate his mastery of strict counterpoint, Fux wrote: "This [the perpetuation of the *stile antico*] has always been my purpose, and my poor talent has collected all its major forces to the sole object of conserving that of it which remains to us." It was not entirely the force of Italian encroachments that caused Fux to write a justification of this work in the old style. Rather, it was the great complexity that was exhibited in the Mass, for it consists of fifteen canonic sections, basically *a 4*, with their resolutions at various intervals foreshadowing the more ambitious exposition of these devices by J. S. Bach in his *Art of the Fugue*. Some of Fux's longer sections, such as the *Et resurrexit*, use several subjects which are resolved at a variety of intervals. The *Crucifixus* segment is given here in its entirety *(Ex. 53)*. The archaic character of the *Missa canonica* contrasts sharply with Fux's *Missa SS^{mae} Trinitatis*,[17] *a 8* with instruments, which includes a mixture of polychoral sections in *concertato* style with *a cappella* sections.

Perpetuation of the old style of church music was not solely the interest of Fux, for it was the custom for composers who were under either the spiritual or physical observation of Rome to continue producing some music in this reserved style. Even Alessandro Scarlatti (1660–1725), credited with giving initial impetus to the Neapolitan school, included Masses *alla Palestrina* among his prodigious number of works for the Church. Dent, in mentioning only a few of the numerous Scarlatti Masses, cites four contrapuntal works dating

16. DTÖ, I, 65. The Mass, dedicated to
Charles VI, also bears the title, *Missa S.*

Caroli.
17. *Ibid.,* 5–62.

Ex. 53 Crucifixus from *Missa canonica*, after *DTÖ*, I, 78f

from the years 1703 to 1716.[18] Sandwiched between his operas and chamber cantatas, these probably represent simply an appropriate type of music for Rome rather than any desire of Scarlatti's to perpetuate the contrapuntal style as an ideal kind of religious music. More in the vein of what we would expect of Scarlatti is his Mass for St. Cecilia's Day, 1720. Although it was performed at Rome, it does not employ the *stile antico*, but alternates between a kind of harmonic counterpoint and bits of imitative writing, the whole accompanied by a string orchestra. While Dent says of the *stile antico* Mass written for Cardinal Ottoboni in 1706, that "it has a sense of modern tonality and a certain amount of feeling,"[19] it is difficult to make an assessment of its qualities, since he provides no example of the work. The Mass for St. Cecilia's Day, however, is discussed with numerous examples, and is also available in a performing edition.[20] As was to become increasingly common in Masses with orchestral accompaniment, the longer movements are divided into separate, contrasting sections, each with a musical style and content deemed suitable to the section of text being sung. The use of such contrasts is seen in the opening sections of the Gloria. For the first four words, Scarlatti wrote a vigorous running passage in thirds for paired solos that shifts from one pair of solo voices to another. Between these sections, and overlapping with them, is an energetic statement of the same text by the chorus *(Ex. 54a)*. The extent to which Scarlatti had assimilated "modern tonality" is easily seen in the bass line. The sharp contrast of the next section, *Et in terra pax*, is achieved by limiting the utterance to the chorus in block-chords and by employing *appoggiature* *(Ex. 54b)*, a device that he transferred to the orchestra in pathetic fashion in the *Qui tollis* against a florid solo for bass.[21] The expressive effects that could be wrung from the common patterns in the vocabulary of Scarlatti and his generation are employed to the fullest.

Another eminent figure of the Neapolitan school, Leonardo Leo (1694–1744), is best known in the field of church music for his *Miserere* for two four-part choirs and *basso continuo*.[22] This setting of Psalm L (51) is made up of twenty short sections that alternate between

18. Edward J. Dent, *Alessandro Scarlatti: His Life and Works* (London: Edward Arnold, 1905, reprinted 1960), 93, 135. These are discussed briefly, and a few more are given in the catalogue of works, with *incipits*, 227f.
19. *Ibid.*, 93.

20. Alessandro Scarlatti, *Messa d. S. Cecilia* (Berlin-Wiesbaden: Bote & Bock, 1957).
21. Example in Dent, *op. cit.*, 185ff.
22. Leonardo Leo, *Miserere*, ed. H. Wiley Hitchcock (St. Louis: Concordia Publishing House, 1961).

Ex. 54 *a*) Scarlatti, Gloria from *Messa d. St. Cecilia*, 13

With permission of Bote & Bock, Berlin-Wiesbaden.

Ex.54 *b*) *Ibid.*, 17

With permission of Bote & Bock, Berlin-Wiesbaden.

freely composed material (usually for the two choirs) and a chantlike formula that is inserted between the freely composed sections. The formula, which is similar to a psalm tone in everything except its rhythmic patterns, is given to each section as a recitative and, after each has had its turn, appears again between the nonformula choruses with each voice part singing the pattern as a *cantus firmus* against the rest of the choir, the first and second choirs alternating in this assignment.

In this fashion Leo achieves a quasi-liturgical severity between verses that flow with the freedom of the operatic melodies he so skillfully wrought for other times and places.

The step that carried melodies and orchestration from the opera house into the church service was, by this time, only a short one. Still, such materials in eighteenth-century religious pieces seem more surprisingly out of place than do the secular intrusions of other generations. The church works of Giovanni Battista Pergolesi (1710–1736) provide numerous instances of this close relationship. It is sufficient to note a few of these characteristics in a single work, his *Messa solenne* which was written about 1730,[23] although any number of his religious pieces would serve the same purpose. Opening with a short instrumental section, as fitting a curtain-raiser for an opera as it is for a Mass, the work moves through a series of settings of the Ordinary that give enormous emphasis to elaborate solo settings, the chorus playing a relatively subordinate role. That the opening instrumental material actually was conceived as part of the Kyrie, and not as an opening piece to the entire Mass, is made clear by its reappearance, along with the short choral setting that follows it, at the end of the Mass where it serves as the Agnus Dei. The opening chorus, complete with vocal parts that bear the stamp of the instrumental idiom, is not essential for liturgical reasons, for it is followed by a complete setting containing a choral fugue for the first Kyrie, and by a tenor solo for the Christe. The return of the Kyrie text is not even written out, for Pergolesi simply resorted to the operatic convention of calling for a *da capo* return of the opening Kyrie.

Direct transfer of operatic style may indicate either a lack of consideration to the liturgical demands of the music, or a search for a convenient mode of expression. It does not necessarily indicate that religious principles were forgotten or avoided, but may mean that they were being interpreted according to the time and mode of life the composer knew.[24] From our viewpoint, the dignity of church music suffered more in the eighteenth century than did its vitality. Melodies took on the character of operatic arias complete with runs, *gruppetti*, surging Lombardic rhythms[25] and sweeping phrases designed to dis-

23. Giovanni Battista Pergolesi, *Opera Omnia*, ed. Francesco Caffarelli (Rome: Gli Amici della musica da Camera, 1939–1942), xxiii, 1–63.
24. *MWC*, 702–708, provides an excellent discussion of the inter-relationship be-

tween Catholic church music and secular music of this period.
25. More commonly known as the "Scotch snap." This inverted rhythmic pattern, ♫. , appeared in eighteenth-century operas with great frequency.

play the virtuosity of the singer rather than to glorify God. These devices do not appear only in Pergolesi's works nor even are they restricted to Italy, but they appear with such abandoned profusion at this point in history that their cumulative impact is more than should be borne in silence. Form, as dictated by orchestral and operatic requirements rather than textual ones, became increasingly important and led to the inclusion of such previously unchurchlike forms as the *da capo* return and sonata-allegro form. Such are the features that make up Pergolesi's *Messa solenne* and many of his other works for the Church. In employing musical ideas that came from beyond the borders of normal religious musical practice, Pergolesi and his generation went no farther afield than did the Renaissance composers who borrowed freely in their use of paraphrase and parody. But, while the latter lived in an age that saw all human activity carried on under God's benign gaze, the eighteenth-century man found religious practice and secular life clearly separated. The same people were often involved in both worlds, and they heard the same music—with different words—wherever they went. Some composers still made a distinction between music that had to please secular tastes and that which served real devotional purposes; Pergolesi, and who knows how many others, carried the theater into the church without hesitation and almost without exception. It is no less to Pergolesi's credit as an operatic composer to admit that his religious music was less appropriate to its purpose than it could have been, the musical vocabulary and taste of his time notwithstanding. What has been said about his Masses applies, with only slight reservations, to his overpraised *Stabat Mater*.[26] It is necessary to insert a reminder that this is not a choral work anyway, inasmuch as it was composed for two solo *castrati*.

The rise of Vienna as an important center of Catholic music is to some extent bound up with the Reutters, father and son, although it is their sphere of activity rather than the quality of their contributions that makes them of interest. Johann Adam Karl Georg von Reutter (1708–1772), more commonly known as the younger Georg Reutter, was awarded the post of *Kapellmeister* of St. Stephen's Cathedral at the death of his father (1738), who had held the position and who had, in turn, followed on Fux's heels there in 1712. While there seems to be little criticism of either the application to duty or the musical suffic-

26. *Opera Omnia*, XXVI, 1–46.

iency of the elder Reutter, his son was better known for his sycophantic behavior, which brought him as much favor at court as did his
music. It was during his tenure at St. Stephen's that the two Haydns
came under his authority. His summary dismissal of Joseph Haydn,
when the boy's voice broke[27] especially marks Reutter as a man who
felt small responsibility for the thorough training of his charges. His
habit of providing only that musical training which he found advantageous to the daily production of music and the maintenance of his
prestige must have made it difficult for his charges to prepare themselves for careers in music. In defense of Reutter, however, it may be
remarked that had he not noticed Joseph Haydn and invited him to
Vienna in the first place, the boy might have wasted his years in some
provincial post, or given up his musical work entirely.

Reutter's Masses performed at St. Stephen's do not impress the
twentieth-century musician profoundly. They do, on the other hand,
represent some of the music that helped to bring him into such high
favor with the prominent figures of Viennese musical and court life,
and they must, by the very fact of their having been rehearsed and
performed, have influenced the boys who sang in their performances.
Inasmuch as most of his 677 compositions were written for the
Church,[28] his influence must have been tremendous, even if many of
the pieces had only a single performance.

Reutter's music, while it fulfilled the outward requirements of
day-to-day activity, caused musicians and informed amateurs of that
period to speak critically of his ubiquitous, rushing violins. Many
features of his music render it unsuitable as a vehicle for liturgical
texts, but the almost constant presence of violins playing rapid scales,
arpeggios, and elaborate figurations, reducing text and chorus to
secondary importance, is one of his hallmarks (*Ex. 55*). The *Missa S.
Caroli*,[29] flatteringly dedicated to Emperor Charles vi, as was Fux's
Missa canonica, is divided into nineteen separate musical sections,
each of which stands as an independent musical unit, often to the
disadvantage of textual continuity. Such division, increasingly common by this time, made possible a variety of vocal combinations, instrumental accompaniments, and obbligato solos. One of his six Requiems opens with a singularly inappropriate and theatrical overuse
of shifting dynamic levels that is far removed from the sometimes
unimaginative, but less visceral, terraced volume levels of the Baroque

27. *Grove's*, iv, 147.   29.   *Ibid.*, 1–57.
28. *DTÖ*, lxxxviii, xiii.

Ex. 55 G. Reutter, Kyrie of Missa S. Caroli (1734), *DTÖ*, XXCVII, I (not shown are parts for two clarini, trombone and timpani)

With permission of Akademische Druck-u. Verlagsanstalt, Auersperggasse 12, Graz/Austria.

(Ex. 56a). Fortunately, the section is confined to the first fourteen measures, after which a degree of dignity is again restored *(Ex. 56b)*.

It will be remembered that the term *Missa brevis*, as it was used by the Lutherans, carried a connotation of excision. Only the Kyrie and Gloria were to be found in works so designated. In the South German

Ex. 56 *a)* G. Reutter, *Requiem* (1753), *DTÖ*, XXCVIII, 58 (cornetti with soprano, trombone I with alto, trombone II

with tenor, bassoon with bass)

and Austrian usage, *Missa brevis* denoted a complete setting of the Mass, but without elaborate instrumentation or division of the longer movements (the Gloria and the Credo) into short sections as was the case in such works as Bach's B minor Mass or Reutter's *Missa S. Caroli* with their numerous complete settings of text fragments. The *Missa brevis* avoided, in addition, the extensive and frequent repetitions of text that were necessary in the larger solemn Masses. Naturally, the shorter version was the norm for an ordinary Sunday, while the ela-

Ex.56 b) *Ibid.*, 59

borate Mass, with expanded orchestral and vocal forces making a
spectacular display in the many-sectioned and contrasting composition, was reserved for special occasions. The length and complexity of
these two types can be easily compared by reference to Table IX, which
compares two Masses by Joseph Haydn (1732–1809). Such a table is
not able to show more than the amount of space allotted to each portion of text. It does not indicate, in any way, the degree of text repetition in the more elaborate setting, the alternation between solo and
chorus, nor the attention to instrumental interludes. The *Missa brevis*
represents simplicity as well as brevity; the festive Mass is a display
of pomp, ceremony, technical accomplishment, and theatrical splen-
dor.

How much of the empty and superficial music of Reutter clung to
Haydn? He seems to have avoided the emptiness that was typified by
the rushing violins, yet similar ideas are found in his accompaniments
and interludes. The fashion of the time required such activity, but
where Reutter had conformed without contributing anything of musical value, Haydn made his busy instrumentalists a part of the composition in a way that gave them purpose and point. His violin parts
support and guide the voices rather than compete with them; the instrumental writing is often ornamented unisonal material *(Ex. 57)*,
giving forth the busy activity that was typical of his time, but always

TABLE IX

Comparison of Two Types of Mass Treatment by J. Haydn

Missa brevis Sti Joannis de Deo (*Kleine Orgelmesse*). c.1775[30]
SATB, Violins I and II, Continuo.

Missa Sanctae Caeciliae. c.1769–73[31]
SATB, Oboes I and II, Bassoons I and II, Clarini I and II, Timpani, Violins I and II, Viola, Continuo.

		MEASURES
Kyrie (Allegro) 25 measures	Kyrie (Largo)	1–7
	(Allegro)	8–63
	(Allegretto)	64–236
Gloria (Allegro) 31 measures	Gloria (Allegro molto)	1–128
	Laudamus te (Moderato)	129–188
	Gratias agimus (Alla breve)	189–334
	Domine Deus (Allegro)	335–578
	Qui tollis (Adagio)	579–635
	Quoniam (Allegro molto)	636–726
	Cum Sancto Spiritu (Largo)	727–731
	In gloria (Allegro molto)	732–821

	MEASURES		
Credo (Allegro)	1–10	Credo (Vivace)	1–92
Et incarnatus (Adagio)	11–46	Et incarnatus (Largo)	93–155
Et resurrexit (Allegro)	47–82	Et resurrexit (Allegro)	156–386

Sanctus (Allegro)	30 measures	Sanctus (Adagio) 9 ½ measures	
		Pleni sunt coeli (Allegro) 9 ½–21	
Benedictus (Moderato)	1–56 ½	Benedictus (Andante)	1–123
Osanna (Allegro)	56 ½–71	Osanna (Allegro)	124–129
Agnus Dei (Adagio)	1–73	Agnus Dei (Largo)	1–22
		Dona nobis pacem (Presto)	23–151

with the purpose of moving in patterns that could give increased strength to the choir.

A dozen of Haydn's Masses are extant. With only one exception, they bear specific identifications, some after the fashion of the sym-

---

30. *Joseph Haydns Werke*, ed. H. C. Robbins-Landon, *et al.* (München: G. Henle Verlag, 1958), XXIII (2), 1–16. This most recent attempt to produce a complete edition of Haydn's works will, if carried to completion, be the only one to achieve its goal. Other editions that were undertaken are listed in Anna Harriet Heyer, *Historical Sets, Collected Editions, and Monuments of Music* (Chicago: American Library Association, 1957), 135ff.
31. *Joseph Haydn Kritische Gesamtausgabe*, ed. Jens Peter Larsen (Boston: Haydn Society, 1951), XXIII (1), 105–269.

Ex.57 Kyrie from J. Haydn's *Missa Sanctae Caeciliae*

With permission of Haydn Society, Inc., Wien.

phonies and quartets, that indicate their original attribution to a
saint or official, or to their musical ingredients or structure (*Paukenmesse, Harmoniemesse, Schöpfungsmesse*). Since some of the Masses
bear several such titles, the connection between them and the situation that gave rise to the writing of the Mass must be examined with
care.[32]

32. The information given in the cata-   167f, is helpful, though brief.
logue of Haydn's works in *Grove's*, IV,

The production of church music filled a far greater part of the life of Joseph Haydn's younger brother, Johann Michael Haydn (1737 – 1806), who shared the somewhat doubtful benefits of Reutter's teaching and influence at St. Stephen's. Most, if not all, of his life was spent as a church musician and he composed for the Church until the time of his death, leaving unfinished, as had Mozart, a Requiem Mass. He completed twenty-eight Masses, four of them with German words. Most of his music is still unpublished, not necessarily because of lack of quality, but because of a combination of events, among them the greater popularity of his brother and the limited market for much church music that cannot be performed regularly in our own time. Three Masses, fortunately, are in print.[33] Only the first of these, the *Missa St. Francisci,* is an expanded work with orchestra. Calling for pairs of oboes, horns, and *clarini* (high trumpets), plus strings, timpani, and *continuo,* the Mass is indicative of what these instrumental forces were able to provide at the beginning of the nineteenth century — the Mass is dated August 16, 1803 — whether as an accompanying group or an instrumental organization independent of voices. The oboes, except in the strictly instrumental sections, duplicate the voice parts, usually the soprano and alto; horns, *clarini,* and timpani provide fanfares and rhythmic punctuation; and the principal task of the violins is to make elaborations upon this simple background. The choir is SATB with soloists in each section. The other two Masses, both dated 1794, are for SATB chorus with a figured bass for organ. The Palm Sunday Mass *(Missa in Dominica Palmarum secundum cantum choralem)* has several complete or partial sections (Kyrie, *Et incarnatus est* from the Credo, Sanctus, Benedictus, and Agnus Dei) written in irregularly measured, equal whole-notes and sometimes labelled *chorale* or *choral.* It is apparently these instances and the appearance of another such section, at *Et incarnatus est* and bearing the designation *Corale,* in the other *Missa brevis* printed in the same volume, a *Missa tempore Quadragesimae,* that gave rise to the statement that Michael Haydn "also introduces (from time to time) chorale tunes."[34] For want of further explanation, one could be led to believe that such a dedicated Catholic as Michael would regularly employ hymns of the Protestants

33. *DTÖ,* xlv. See also Reinhard G. Pauly, "Some Recently Discovered Michael Haydn Manuscripts," *Journal of the American Musicological Society,* x/2 (Spring, 1957), 97 – 103, and Karl Geiringer, "The Small Sacred Works by Haydn in the Esterhazy Archives at Eisenstadt," *The Musical Quarterly,* xlv/4 (October, 1959), 460 – 72.

34. Young, *The Choral Tradition,* 162.

in his Masses. This is far from fact. As was mentioned earlier (cf. 113), "choral" meant plainsong to the Catholics. It is only our familiarity with the word in connection with German Protestantism that has given us a restrictive meaning for common use. If proof of the plainsong source is required, it can be found easily by comparing Haydn's soprano parts with the plainsong for similar texts. For example, the opening of the Kyrie to the Palm Sunday Mass is made up of exact quotations from the second Kyrie of Mass XVII[35] with the syllables of the text adjusted to suit Haydn's purposes. Similarly, the Et incarnatus est fragment is taken from Credo III[36] with only slight alteration. A thorough comparison of the rest of Haydn's "choral" sections would undoubtedly produce a number of other examples. German hymns were sometimes used in the Catholic churches during those years, but they were not the chorales of the Lutherans.[37]

In the Haydns, we are faced with two men of immense talent, both of whom wrote significant amounts of church music. In the case of the elder brother, the Masses were for the most part occasional works that were dedicated to the observance of a state occasion or the aggrandizement of an individual. In the list of Johann Michael's church music[38] we find that the greater share of it was intended to serve the daily church observances rather than to celebrate such events as a prince's birthday or an admiral's victory. Life did not pass Michael by, for he kept in touch with the world of music throughout his life. His works, then, do not represent either lack of sophistication or lack of skill; they are, rather, the works that ever made their appearance to furnish appropriate music for saints' days and to mark the passage of the liturgical year, as do the three works that have been examined here. From such a man as Joseph Haydn, whose principal activity was secular music, works of this kind were hardly to be expected; from his younger brother, they were the norm. Michael Haydn, of whose music we still have much to learn, may represent the end of a long line of composers who devoted themselves to the Catholic Church and who produced liberally and with excellent quality. The names that follow him are those of composers who made their reputations in the world of the opera house and the concert salon. Their connection with music for the Church is quantitatively the least that they composed, although some of the works they produced are

35. LU, 61.
36. LU, 69.
37. Reinhard G. Pauly, "The Reforms of

Church Music under Joseph II," The Musical Quarterly, XLIII/3 (July, 1957), 372–82.
38. Grove's, IV, 207.

among their greatest. Sadly we note that some of the very things that made them great also acted to bar them from the Church and confine them to the concert hall, where simple economic requirements prevent their regular hearings.

It is with the Haydns and their generation — a period that includes Mozart, of course — that the impact of secular entertainment is so strongly felt in Catholic church music, especially in the extended Masses for the observance of signal events. The presence of tunes that seem more appropriate to the opera house is not a new thing, but they seem more sharply different from the *contrafacta* that appeared in the works of composers a generation or more earlier. It was not that the sensitivity of the opera audience or the church congregation had changed sharply from earlier years, but that secular music had taken upon itself a character that was now clearly different from that of church music intended for daily use. Opera was geared to the talents of the best professionals who could be brought together at the major courts; church music subsisted on a daily diet of male choirs made up of boys who lost their usefulness at just about the point of musical understanding — when their voices broke — and men who were not known for their musical virtuosity. It was no wonder that, on those occasions when composers wrote and produced works of greater significance than those that were forced to serve as the usual round of Masses, the professionals were called into action either to serve as substitute forces or to augment the existing choir. As a case in point, one can look at the soprano solo in the Kyrie of Joseph Haydn's *Paukenmesse* and find none of the comfortable identification marks of church music. Here is music for music's sake, music to which any text would be equally suitable, whether secular or religious, music that to our ears seems more at home in concert hall or theater than it does in the sanctuary. Yet it lacks nothing in skill, even in dignity. It simply does not fit into the picture of religious music as easily as do many other works. It may have been for that very reason that composers — especially those who were, or hoped to be, connected with a church in a regular capacity — wrote in the simple style of the *Missa brevis* for regular liturgical needs and in the elaborate, worldly style of the theater for occasions of grandiose display. The *Missa brevis*, after all, made few demands upon the singers and it called for no elaborate orchestra or highly skilled soloists and, perhaps the most important, for no prolonged rehearsal.

With the disappearance of the dedicated, professional church musicians—and the end of the eighteenth century marks their disappearance with only a few exceptions—the need for making a living in the world of opera house and concert hall became uppermost in the mind of the composer. The desire to produce church music may not have been greatly diminished, but the need for establishing a position of prestige and stability in the competitive world of secular music, a new world that had been ushered in by the development of solo instrumental performance, opera, orchestra music, and numerous other new musical vistas, made it foolish for a composer to tie himself to the production of religious music unless he did it for personal, religious reasons. It was into this changing world that the two Haydns—one best known for secular music, but producing significant religious pieces; the other, best known for church music, but with many symphonies, concertos, and chamber works to his credit—and Mozart were born.

The life span of Wolfgang Amadeus Mozart (1756–1791) was bracketed by the lives of the two Haydns. The flame of his genius, one of the brightest and most furious of all time, consumed him rapidly. As with all those who had too few years in which to produce their art, he left us to find the point where the child's production ceases and that of the man begins. Shall we bestow upon him the stature of the mature composer at age twelve? He wrote his first Mass in 1768; seven such works were completed by the time he was eighteen. There is certainly no lack of material to examine. If we choose from the early works, do we see this young man as an imitator, an experimenter, a sycophantic slave to the demands of the occasion, or as a composer expressing religious texts as best he can in the idiom of his time? It is no simple task to assign such labels to the young Mozart, who went through many changes of musical attitude before he matured. The works of his middle and later years are better suited to our consideration, and they too show a wide range of styles.

It is regrettable that two works reflecting most clearly Mozart's freedom to write the music of sincere religious expression, the *Mass in C minor* (K. 427) and the *Requiem* (K. 626)[39] were left unfinished, the latter by Mozart's death. His intense and morbid interest in the *Requiem* needs no recounting; his composition of the C minor Mass

39. These works, and others mentioned below, are printed in the complete edition, *W. A. Mozarts sämtliche Werke* (Leipzig: Breitkopf & Härtel, 1876–1905; reprinted, Ann Arbor: J. W. Edwards, 1951–). A new edition is in progress, issued by Bärenreiter-Verlag.

was in fulfillment of a vow that, should his marriage with Constanze Weber ever take place, he would compose a new Mass to be performed at Salzburg. In August of 1783 the work was performed with Constanze singing the soprano part. But, since the work was not ready on schedule, some of the missing sections were served by substitutions from earlier Masses. Even so, Mozart turned this incomplete work — lacking the Agnus Dei and part of the Credo — to further use by adding more music and Italian words at a later date to make of it a cantata, *Davidde penitente* (K. 469).

For a complete work, we can turn to the earlier D major *Missa brevis* (K. 194), one of the few Masses that was written without external pressure from a patron. As an example of the simpler form of Mass intended for the regular church service where no ostentatious display was needed, this work, in common with some of his other *Missae brevis,* calls for a four-part choir and the convenient trio-sonata combination of two violins and *basso continuo,* although it may be presumed that several violins play each part here. The vocal solo parts, although they are more demanding than those for the choir, make no obviously theatrical demands upon the singers. The various sections of the Mass change tempo, but retain a single key center except for the Benedictus, which moves to the subdominant key (as it does in most of Mozart's Masses of this type) until the *Osanna,* where it again returns to the original key.

Mozart's use of the accompanying instruments is similar to that seen in Joseph Haydn's *Missae brevis (cf. Example 57),* wherein the violins supported the voices by frequent references to the vocal line even while elaborating upon it rhythmically and ornamentally.

There is an extremely economical employment of thematic material. Within a single movement, the same material is used a number of times, sometimes with surprising facility as the basis of both homophonic and polyphonic sections. The Kyrie evolves from a descending triadic motive that is often recalled by the large number of melodic skips of a third or fifth in the later portions of the movement. Enclosing the Kyrie is a five-measure phrase *(Ex. 58)* that is extended by repetition after a deceptive cadence to seven measures at the end of the movement. The central portion of the movement is a series of short fugal expositions, each based on the three-note motive but with various countersubjects, and each of the expositions closing with a strong cadence in block-chords. The result is a closely integrated movement that unfolds with a simple, driving force. Other movements

Ex. 58 Kyrie, *Missa brevis*, Mozart (K. 194)

Ex. 59 *a)* Agnus Dei, *Ibid.*

have a similarly tight organization, especially the Agnus Dei, which alternates between solo and tutti passages three times before a new theme appears at *dona nobis pacem*. The Agnus motive, clearly recognizable because of its large upward leap, is combined with two other themes in the choral sections *(Ex. 59a)*, the three appearing in a different arrangement in the subsequent appearances by the use of in-vertible counterpoint *(Ex. 59b,c)*. The *hemiola*, seen in measures six and seven of the example, is uncommon in Mozart's time.

Textual and liturgical considerations are secondary to musical considerations in this kind of composition; the regularity of form and the strength of cadential patterns play a larger part in the inner divi-sion of material than the sense of the words. The Mass considered here is surely not open to criticism in the same way that the Pergolesi works are, but much superficially religious music of the eighteenth century lacks the ingredient of suitability: "The style, in so far as it is anything besides purely individualistic, is governed by the conditions of patronage in which composers worked. The resources of the private

Ex. 59 *b) Ibid.*

c) Ibid.

chapels and the wishes of patrons determined the form of the works produced, in many cases entirely unfitting them for transference to the conditions of public worship."[40] Far from being the kind of unified, closely knit composition that developed in the Renaissance, many Masses of the eighteenth century were simply *potpourris* of concert and theatrical forms set to liturgical words. Many of the works discussed in this chapter were above this sort of convenient, ready-made production, even though they borrowed the characteristics of the century in matters of phrase and form. It was Beethoven, who with his eighteenth-century training and his unparalleled aptitude for personal communication, applied the freedom of his new expression to the production of works that would stir the imagination of the world.

Ludwig van Beethoven (1770–1827) sits astride the old and the new in church music just as he does in most other forms of musical expression. Although he did not concern himself greatly over the production of music for church use, his two Masses stand as monuments: the *Mass in C* (Op. 86) represents a Beethoven who follows, although not closely, the prevailing style for large-scale Masses; the *Missa solemnis* (Op. 123),[41] on the other hand, is a unique work based on no precedents save those required by liturgical organization and musical continuity. Much has been written about the latter work elsewhere, and little can be gained from repetition. A comparison of the two Masses as they represent Beethoven's changing approach to a single problem may, nevertheless, provide a new view of their respective positions in the entire field of church music.

The vocal forces employed in the two works are identical, for each calls for a quartet of soloists and a chorus *a 4*. The use to which Beethoven puts the voices in each Mass differs considerably. The orchestra of the earlier composition is that of the classical symphony, made up of pairs of flutes, oboes, clarinets, bassoons, horns, and trumpets, plus timpani, strings, and, of course, as required by a church work, organ—or more exactly—a *basso continuo* part with figures that is shared by the organ and the lower strings. Except for the *basso continuo* and its requirement of an organ, this is the instrumentation of a typical late symphony of Mozart or Haydn. By 1807, when Bee-

40. *Grove's*, v, 620.
41. *Ludwig van Beethovens Werke* (Leipzig: Breitkopf & Härtel, 1864–1890; reprinted, Ann Arbor: J. W. Edwards, 1949). See also

W. G. Whittaker, "The Choral Writing in the Missa Solennis," *Music and Letters*, viii/3 (July, 1927), 295–305.

thoven composed the C major Mass, he had exceeded these limitations in his larger works so, in a sense, the restriction to classical proportions may be considered an attempt to write in a style more reserved than that of the Fifth and Sixth Symphonies, both of which date from the same period. No such limitation is evident in the *Missa solemnis*. While most of the instruments are still used in pairs, the horns have been increased to four, and three trombones and a contrabassoon have been added. The organ, also, has been freed of the Baroque-Classical duty of simply supporting the harmony with chords and figures that result from the realization of a figured bass. Beethoven has provided a carefully written part for the organ as an equal instrument in his orchestra. In most other respects, the instrumentation is similar to that of the Ninth Symphony, which dates from the same late years of Beethoven's life.

Again, in the matter of dividing text into smaller divisions than movements, a distinct difference of treatment is evident in the way Beethoven links materials together or sets them apart. The earlier Mass contains few introductory or linking passages for orchestra; the voices, and their presentation of the text, are clearly predominant while the orchestra supports and intensifies them. That relationship is clear in the first measure where the basses sing the opening syllable of the Kyrie without any other voices or instruments for support. Only after the word has clearly begun do other voices and instruments enter to complicate the texture. The orchestra in the *Missa solemnis* provides lengthy introductory passages, links that connect subsections of movements, and passages that communicate, through their emotional intensity, the spirit of the movement better than the text itself. Between the Sanctus and the Benedictus is not a separate link, but an orchestral meditation which the composer calls a *Praeludium*. It leads, in turn, to the violin solo that vies with, and often outshines, the vocal parts for the rest of the movement *(Ex. 60a)*. The section is one of mild contrasts between extreme lyricism in the solo voices and a quasi-plainsong pattern in the chorus *(Ex. 60b)* against both of which Beethoven placed the elaborately soaring lines of the violin solo.

The large scale upon which the *Missa solemnis* was constructed necessitated its division into many smaller sections, just as Bach's B minor Mass was divided into many parts. Neither of the works approached the problem of division arbitrarily, and the result of such division is different in each case. Each of the Bach sections is a set

Ex. 60 *a*) Benedictus from *Missa solemnis*, Beethoven (horn part omitted)

number, as if it were a separate unit of an opera of the period, but the
Beethoven sections are rarely set off from the whole by complete
cadences or pauses, although they may be at points where a modulation has occurred. For the most part, complete breaks are the result of
textual completion, and occur only at the ends of movements or sec-

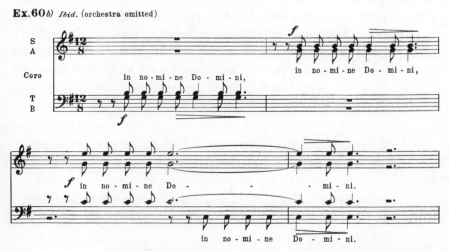

Ex.60*b*) *Ibid.* (orchestra omitted)

tions of movements where they are dictated by the requirements of musical form. The structure of the movements themselves is dictated now by instrumental considerations, now by vocal.

The difference in length between the two Masses is considerable. While the one in C major is a long work, the *Missa solemnis* is on an extravagantly large scale, entirely impossible as a liturgical piece. The voices have infinitely better opportunity to be heard clearly in relation to the orchestra in the *Mass in C*, but this is not due to poorer writing in the larger work; rather, the former clings to traditionalism quite firmly when it is considered in the light of the highly imaginative *Missa solemnis,* in which both voices and instruments soar to expressive heights that Beethoven attempted nowhere in his earlier, simpler, but no less deserving, Mass. Some of the differences in length and expressive qualities can be traced to Beethoven's treatment of individual words or short phrases, for it is not simply text repetition and orchestral interludes that make the one work so much larger in scope. Any number of parallel sections of text could be chosen to illustrate the different treatments in the two works. Let us consider here only the approach to three different words that composers for several centuries had found especially appropriate for musical intensification. In the Gloria, beginning at *qui sedes ad dexteram patris,* Beethoven confined the setting of the passage through *miserere nobis* to thirty-four measures for the chorus, with instrumental accompaniment that simply supports the voices. All is within the boundaries of liturgical propriety; the text is stated first in homophonic style, is intensified by polyphonic repetition, and it subsides into the homophonic pattern at the close *(Ex. 61)*. The same setting in the *Missa solemnis* extends only slightly longer in terms of total measures, but a great difference exists between the two settings, the latter being an expansion in terms of musical complexity and emotional intensity

Ex. 61 *Mass in C* (Op. 86), Beethoven, section of Gloria (voices only)

rather than in length. Here Beethoven was not content with a single statement of the introductory words followed by repetitions of the supplication, for after the homophonic first statement, during which the soloists enter with a more elaborate phrase, a polyphonic re-statement is undertaken by the chorus. The soloists continue in the plea for mercy, the whole terminating in a passage that includes an additional nonliturgical vowel, *O, miserere nobis.* The intensity of the section is further heightened by the transitory character of the key centers and the use of enharmonic modulations *(Ex. 62),* all of which is underlaid by a syncopated and rhythmically active orchestral back-ground. A similar situation may be seen in the Credo, among other places at such words as *crucifixus* and *ascendit,* which are treated with restraint in the earlier Mass and with elaborate pictorial strength in the later. The *Mass in C* makes the traditional gesture at *ascendit* with a rising passage that appears in the chorus and is simply doubled in the orchestra. In the *Missa solemnis* the entire chorus and orchestra surge victoriously to the end of the phrase where the brass and tim-pani join in the joyous announcement of Christ's arrival *in coelum.* The greatest difference between the two works—or better, between the *Missa solemnis* and every Mass other than Bach's B minor Mass—lies in the concentrated emotional content of Beethoven's expression.

While the *Missa solemnis* demands great ability and endurance of the performers, it is not a work designed to display the musical abilities of the human race. The abstract approach of polyphony along with flamboyant operatic showmanship had long been present in Mass composition by Beethoven's time, as had almost every degree of imaginative writing that fell between those two poles. But no one had

Ex. 62 *Missa solemnis*, Beethoven, section of Gloria (voices only)

transmitted the fears and hopes of mankind so successfully as did this musical giant who went beyond both traditional and liturgical boundaries. Certainly the recitatives for alto, tenor, and soprano in the Agnus Dei *(Ex. 63)* are theatrical, but who can doubt that here Beethoven summed up the anxieties and aspirations of the human race?

Ex. 63 *Ibid., Recits* from Agnus Dei (winds omitted)

The conclusion of the *Mass in C,* repeating material from the opening Kyrie, brings the listener back to formal reality and to the liturgy;
the *Missa solemnis* ends not only with a prayer for peace, but implies
Beethoven's faith that such peace was possible, in both a personal and
a universal sense. The *Missa solemnis* is Beethoven's towering achievement, not in spite of the fact that it transcends liturgical limitations
and denominational identification, but because it does so.

Chapter VIII

The German Church Cantata

THE combination of musical pieces that we now call the German church cantata enjoyed only a relatively short season of maturity. Early stages of this important form, with or without the chorales that play such a significant part in their eventual development, are often not recognizable as closely related, because they seem little different from forms that were already firmly established. Some confusion is not to be wondered at, for the predecessors of the cantata retained their earlier names even after they began to take on the shape and function of the cantata as we now know it. By the eighteenth century, the cantata was to embody characteristics of the madrigal, the motet, the Passion, the opera (in both its vocal and instrumental components), the *concertato,* and the chorale. If the genesis of the German cantata is vague, the names that are applied to it during its years of development are downright confusing. The compositions occupying the position, and serving the purpose, of principal music for the service were identified by a variety of terms. Through an examination of some of the pieces that bore these varied titles we may come to some understanding of the composite form we now recognize as a typical German church cantata.

It is again Italy that produces the prototype, a kind of work usually for solo voice and simple accompaniment, and most often secular in nature. Cantata was a general term, designating the performance as vocal, and used in opposition to sonata, which merely identified the piece as instrumental. At the peak of its popularity, the solo cantata was a composite form made up of arias and recitatives of contrasting character with its sections often separated by instrumental *sinfonie.* This conventional structure is found among the cantatas of Alessandro Scarlatti, who is credited with having produced above 600 such works (example in *GMB* 260) — a feat that does not, in any way, compare with

231

the composition of the numerous examples produced by some eighteenth-century German composers who had to create sections of far greater size and who, if sometimes seeming to follow conventional forms, were not so obviously doing so. The principal contributions of the Italian cantata form, which took well over a century to develop, were its name and its sectional structure. However, the development of German cantatas was well under way by the time of Scarlatti's maturity. Care should be exercised, therefore, in assigning credit to Italy or Scarlatti for more than a limited amount of influence. Especially in the case of works that contain extensive choral sections—and our study is necessarily limited to such works—too much stress could wrongly be placed on the importance of the solo cantata in Italy as a precursor of the German choral cantata.

From the standpoint of function, the German church cantata held a position similar to that assigned to the English anthem: it was desirable, but not essential; religious, but not liturgical. The German *Hauptgottesdienst* retained most of the segments of the Catholic Mass, omitting the Offertory for which the sermon was substituted, and adding or substituting German hymns for sections of the Ordinary when local practice decreed (see Table x). The service was still a liturgical unit, regardless of the language employed. The cantata took a normal position before the sermon, between the reading of the Gospel and the singing of the chorale, *Wir glauben all' an einen Gott (We all believe in one God),* by the congregation. There it served as a sermon-motet or, more accurately, as an interpolated sacred concert based upon the Gospel for the day, the text upon which the sermon itself was based.[1] The relationship of such compositions to specific days of the liturgical year was often noted by the composers themselves, and convenient designations that indicated the day to which the compositions belonged often appeared as the only means of knowing the occasion for which a piece was used. Thus an abbreviation such as "Dom. xviii: p: Trin." (Eighteenth Sunday after Trinity) was a simple, but sufficient, identification. Such a reference to a specific Sunday was common but, since several works might be designated for a single occasion (but not for use within the same year) it is easier to identify pieces by titles which, if not supplied by the composer, are derived from the opening phrase of text. The principal music for the

1. A convenient "Table of Lessons for the Sundays, Feasts, and Chief Festivals of the Church Year" is given in *The Lutheran* *Hymnal* (St. Louis: Concordia Publishing House, 1941), 159ff.

TABLE X

Principal Musical Sections of the Lutheran Morning Service
(Hauptgottesdienst) *in Relation to Principal Spoken
and Chanted Portions (Leipzig, 18th century)*

Organ Prelude
Motet
Introit
Kyrie ⎰as a hymn, *Kyrie Gott Vater in Ewigkeit*
      ⎰ or
      ⎰in Latin
Gloria ⎰*et in terra pax* by the choir
       ⎰ or
       ⎰chorale *Allein Gott in der Höh sei Ehr*
Epistle
Hymn by the congregation
Gospel
Credo
*Cantata (preceded by an organ prelude, during which the orchestra tuned)
Hymn *Wir glauben all' an einen Gott*
Sermon
Prayer and Blessing
Hymn
Communion Service with more hymns

*Some cantatas were composed of two distinct parts. These were intended to be sung with one part
before the sermon, and the other after, or, if local practice decreed, the second part was sung after
the Blessing or during Communion. In some churches the two-part cantatas may also have been
divided between morning and afternoon services.

choir was not designated as a cantata, for even as late as Bach's time
the word was still reserved to describe the solo cantata. Common
identification lay in neutral terms, such as *Kirchenmusik* and *Stück*.
Among numerous specific terms in use,[2] *Concerto, Motetto, Ode,
Aria, Dialogo,* and *Psalm* are commonly used when, in fact, any designation is given at all. It is obvious that works that have the size
and characteristics of the oratorio are not suitable for the music that
was to precede the sermon. The range of possibilities for the pre-
sermon music was still wide, for it encompassed *concertato* pieces for
a few voices, compositions in motet style, cantatas that were largely
for solo voice with only one or two sections for chorus, and full-
scale works that used orchestra, solo voices and chorus, with or with-

2. Additional ones may be found in *MGG,* VII, 582.

out the chorale as either a unifying or closing piece. We can now turn
to an examination of some pieces of various types that led eventually
to the cantata of the late Baroque period. Works composed before
about 1700 will not be referred to as cantatas. The general term
Kirchenmusik will be employed until the point at which the more
common designation becomes suitable (see p. 251, n. 25).

Italian characteristics in the hands of a German composer are
copious in the works of Heinrich Schütz (1585–1672), a student of
Giovanni Gabrieli and later an associate of Monteverdi. While there is
no clear-cut group of works that falls in a direct line of development
to the cantata, he left a series of pieces that show the use of the
concertato style in connection with the German service, and his preference for the style of the Italian cantata may be seen in the pieces for
one voice and trio sonata that appeared in his *Symphoniae sacrae*
(1629). The fact that these works have Latin text did not, as we know,
stand in the way of their performance in the Lutheran service. A *concerto* for three voices and trio sonata, and with German text, *O Herr,
hilf (MM 33)*, is typical of such works. After a brief *sinfonia*, the voices
enter with a rhythmic pattern similar to that of the opening instrumental passage, a duple meter section that is supported by *continuo*
only. At the contrasting triple meter section, voices and instruments
engage in *concertato* alternation, a treatment that continues through
the closing duple meter section which, it should be noted, takes the
shape of an additional section and not a return to the opening material. This kind of treatment spread among Schütz's contemporaries,
perhaps even in imitation of his own efforts, and with other composers was added the use of that unique German contribution, the chorale, as exemplified in the chorale concerto, *Erschienen ist der herrliche
Tag, (The glorious day has dawned)* by Johann Hermann Schein (1586–
1630) *(TEM 38)*. In this example the voices, employing the chorale
tune as a basis for the composition, serve as vocal counterparts of the
treble elements in the trio sonata, and only the *continuo* (keyboard
and wind) is required as instrumental support.

There is wide variety in the names applied to pieces of music, in
the styles that are used, and in the combinations of voices and instruments that remain from the corpus of church compositions by Andreas
Hammerschmidt (1612–1675). He produced pieces ranging from solo
songs to choral music "in the madrigal manner," from simple dialogues "between God and a believing soul" to a triple chorus setting

of Psalm 133 that uses a double echo effect. The fifty-nine pieces[3] that make up the two volumes of his *Musicalische Gespräche über die Evangelia (Musical Conversations on the Gospels)*, published in 1655–1656, also contain a variety of styles and arrangements of the vocal-instrumental groups. It is from that wealth of material that we can find a piece of *Kirchenmusik*—not a cantata, concerto, motet, or spiritual madrigal, for Hammerschmidt eschewed specific identifications in these volumes—in the form of a dialogue with chorus, employing a chorale both as part of the dialogue itself and as the concluding chorus. *Woher nehmen wir Brot? (How then shall we find bread?)*[4] is intended for use on two specific occasions, as it is built on fragments of the Gospels for two rather widely separated Sundays, and coupled with a chorale verse that is chosen for its appropriateness to both of the Gospel texts. The Gospel for the Seventh Sunday after Trinity is taken from Mark 8:1–9, the story of the multitude fed by seven loaves and a few fishes. From these verses Hammerschmidt selected a portion of only one (Mark 8:4) which reads: *Seine Jünger antworteten ihm: Woher nehmen wir Brot hie in der Wüste, dass wir sie sättigen?"* ("And his disciples answered him, From whence can a man satisfy these men with bread here in the wilderness?"). The only words from this passage that appear in the piece are *Woher nehmen wir Brot.* The Gospel for the Fifteenth Sunday after Trinity (Matt. 6:24–34) is that part of the Sermon on the Mount that speaks of placing the kingdom of God before earthly needs. Parts of only two of these verses serve Hammerschmidt's purpose. From Matt. 6:25 he uses the words *Sorget nicht für euer Leben, was ihr essen und trinken werdet; . . . Ist nicht das Leben mehr denn die Speise?* ("Take no thought for your life, what ye shall eat, or what ye shall drink; . . . Is not the life more than meat?"). From the following verse he adds the words *Sehet die Vögel*

3. *Grove's*, IV, 35, credits the two volumes of the *Musicalische Gespräche* with sixty-one pieces; however, the tables of contents given in *DdT*, XL, xviif, show that of the sixty-one Sundays and festivals for which music is provided, two have duplications of music. Not only is the same music meant to be performed on the Seventh and Fifteenth Sundays after Trinity, but the Thirteenth and Eighteenth Sundays after Trinity also share a piece entitled *Meister, was muss ich thun (Master, what must I do)*. The Gospels for these last two Sundays are Luke 10:23–37 and Matt. 22:34–46, and both deal with the same general theme, the means of personal salvation. Hammerschmidt actually supplied music for two more occasions than necessary for a cycle of the church year, which requires special musical settings for fifty-nine different Sundays and festivals.

4. Andreas Hammerschmidt, *How Then Shall We Find Bread?*, ed. Harold Mueller (St. Louis: Concordia Publishing House, 1960).

unter dem Himmel an: sie säen nicht, sie ernten nicht, sie sammeln nicht in die Scheunen; und euer himmlischer Vater nähret sie doch. Seid ihr denn nicht viel mehr denn sie?[5] ("Behold the fowls of the air: for they sow not, neither do they reap, nor gather into barns; yet our heavenly Father feedeth them. Are ye not much better than they?").

The remainder of the text is taken from a verse of the chorale *O Vater aller Frommen (O Father of the godly)* set to the melody of *Herr Christ, der ein'ge Gott'ssohn (Lord Christ, the only Son of God)*. Even though the chorale verse concerns bread only in passing,[6] its selection for even that casual reference demonstrates both the adaptability of that immense body of hymn texts and the considerable attention that German composers paid to consistency and appropriateness in their texts.

Hammerschmidt introduced this piece with a *Symphonia* for trio sonata—a normal instrumental group for this type of composition, although only one of several combinations he utilized in the *Musicalische Gespräche*—after which he wrote a dialogue section between the upper voices of the choir, representing the disciples, and the solo bass, representing Christ. The identification of the person of Christ with the bass voice was, of course, already firmly established in the dramatic Passions. This opening dialogue, in which the two soprano parts first engage in *concertato* alternation with the bass, followed by the alto-tenor combination with the bass solo, presents portions of both Gospels *alternatim*. The paired voices (disciples) ask *Herr, woher nehmen wir Brot,* and are admonished by the solo bass (Christ) in the following: *Sorget nicht für euer Leben (Ex. 64)*. The treble instruments are absent from this section of the piece, possibly to insure clear projection of the text. The solo bass then completes the text chosen from the Sermon on the Mount, the entire instrumental group accompanying.

A new section follows in which only the upper voices continue their questioning, and the solo bass remains silent while the paired choral voices present a portion of the chorale in alternation and then together. A brief *concertato* section follows, the bass solo is repeated

5. Slight changes in the text appear in Hammerschmidt's pieces, apparently in order to fit the rhythmic pattern of text to that of the music.
6. The verse freely paraphrases part of the Lord's Prayer:

O Vater aller Frommen,
geheiliget werde dein Nam'.
Lass dein Reich zu uns kommen,
dein Wille, der mache uns zahm.
Gib Brot, vergib die Sünde,
kein Arges das Herz entzünde.
Lös' uns aus aller Not.

Ex. 64 A. Hammerschmidt, *Woher nehmen wir Brot?*

in modified form, and the entire chorale is finally stated by the chorus. At this point the bass part is no longer for solo voice; inasmuch as no text from the Sermon on the Mount is included here, a choral bass part is written because the identification with Christ is no longer required.

Within this short composition are embodied numerous features that appear repeatedly in many later examples of *Kirchenmusik;* free madrigalian texts as found in the unmetrical Bible verses, *concertato* sections interspersed by solo passages and brief imitative fragments that are derived from the older motet style, and strophic chorale verses set to balanced musical phrases. The care with which these texts were selected and interwoven speaks well of the relative position of text and music at mid-seventeenth century, for nothing was permitted to obscure the text, and any specialized arrangement of voices or accompaniment was chosen to support rather than displace interest in the words.

Not only were the Gospels of paramount importance as the principal source of German Protestant text, but the musical treatment given to each type of text also assumed an importance that sometimes moved both musicians and theologians to express themselves forcefully on the relative merits of the various kinds of poetic and prose material. Two distinct types of text are to be found in connection with the *Kir-*

chenmusik of the entire Baroque period; strophic and madrigalian. The former is that of the chorale; the latter, that of biblical passages and free rhymed prose.[7] Chorale verses, because of their need to assume strophic regularity through adherence to a strict pattern in verse after verse, inherently lacked flexibility, not only because the poetry was strophic but also because of the popularity of the convenient, if inflexible, *Barform* that was adopted for the music. Johann Mattheson (1681 – 1764), as Schweitzer tells us, "wears his pen to the stump in proving again and again that the true church music must get rid of the chorale in particular and the strophic song in general, since the strophe interrupts the musical development."[8] Yet, by Mattheson's time, composers had consistently taken steps to prevent tedium and to insure forceful presentation of both text and music. In many instances, among them a number of the works that will be mentioned shortly, the chorales were enlivened by *concertato* sections that were set between their phrases; in other cases, the interruption was made by the injection of instrumental interludes at the same points after the manner of the organ preludes. Sometimes elaborate orchestral writing was added to the straightforward singing of the chorale; and, almost without exception, the close association of the verse to the central idea of the entire composition made the chorale more an integrative than a disintegrative device. In lengthy compositions, the chorale might appear both in the course of the piece and as a *Schlusschoral*.

We have already seen that neither Schütz nor Hammerschmidt chose, nor did they find it practical, to convey the idea of an entire composition through strophic texts. Instead—in their works and those of most other composers as well—passages from the Gospels or freely composed rhymed prosody were found to be preferable, at least, for the greater part of the music that was written. Such passages, which we may term madrigalian because they reflect the madrigal idea in the irregular number and length of their lines, were adaptable to use as *recitativo* or arioso sections, as *concertato* passages, and as full-scale arias.

It was usually a mixture of these strophic and madrigalian verses that appeared in Baroque church music in Protestant Germany, and the common concept of the mature cantata sees these two types of text appearing with a fairly regular alternation as a succession of recitatives, arias, choruses, and chorales set off by varied orchestral sections. One other method of dealing with the restrictions of strophic

7. Albert Schweitzer, *J. S. Bach*, tr. Ernest   1950), i, 60 – 65.
Newman (2 vols., New York: Macmillan,   8. *Ibid.*, i, 64.

text was practiced by composers when they chose not to employ any madrigalian verse in the course of a composition. That was the chorale variation, which also achieved great popularity as an organ composition devoid of text. It is not by sheer coincidence that the chorale variation employing both voices and instruments was favored by Franz Tunder (1614–1667), for his position at St. Mary's Church in Lübeck provided him with the opportunity to surround himself with a capable group of instrumental performers. For them he wrote instrumental pieces, and in recognizing the exciting possibilities that lay in combining these same performers with his singers, he produced elaborate pieces with both Latin and German text, and in a variety of styles. Among these were a number of chorale variations in which the verses are set in different textures and style, and which are sometimes preceded by an instrumental *sinfonia* that is built on one or more passages deriving from the melodic content of the chorale tune. His variation treatment in *Ein' feste Burg ist unser Gott*[9] is to some extent an indication of his control of such methods of sustaining interest in a set of strophic verses. His entire musical forces number two violins, three violas, and an organ and double-bass *continuo* group with an SSTB choir; however, at no point do all of these instruments and voices participate simultaneously. The entire instrumental group plays throughout the *sinfonia,* which is divided into two nearly equal sections; the first in quadruple meter, the other in triple. The first verse is given to soprano alone, accompanied by the violins, one viola, and *continuo.* There is no special emphasis on the voice in this verse, for it does not stand apart from the instrumental writing except between the two *Stollen,* where it is moved to a subordinate position as the last of five canonic entries. All three of the verses aim at variety in tempo, meter, and texture. Tempo indications are carefully marked in all verses, meter changes likewise occur in all three and, while the texture of verses two and three remains unchanged in the use of only trio sonata against the full choir,[10] alternation of homophonic and polyphonic style coupled with repetition of text fragments makes for further variety. Example 65 shows brief samples of some of the varied phrases found in verse two.

It seems that Mattias Weckmann (1621–1674) had little interest in undertaking extended settings of the chorales. His texts, while they were chosen for their appropriateness, are not invariably taken

9. *DdT,* iii, 142–57.
10. It is also possible that Tunder meant for the violas and bass to double the voice parts and did not write separate parts for them.

Ex. 65 Tunder, sections of verse 2, *Ein' feste Burg ist unser Gott*, after *DdT*, III, 145–150

Ex. 65 cont.

from the Gospel or Epistle for the day on which the music was to be performed. A *motetto concertato* for ATB and six instruments,[11] entitled *Weine nicht (Weep not)*, comes from Revelation 5:5, 12–14, a text that is related to the Easter season in the Roman Catholic usage.[12] The madrigalian text makes possible an arrangement of sections comfortably similar to compositions we usually call cantatas. There is an opening *sinfonia*, an aria for alto, another *sinfonia* that contrasts thematically with the first and uses echo effects as well, an arioso for bass, a third *sinfonia*, and an extended chorus in *concertato* style. The composer found no need to bring a chorale tune or verse into the work either for contrast or to serve as a stabilizing element.

On the other hand, Johann Rudolph Ahle (1625–1673) utilized the chorale often in his settings for the Sunday service. Among the most interesting examples is a setting, *a 8*, of the German hymn version of the Nicene Creed, *Wir glauben all' an einen Gott (We all believe in one God)*.[13] This hymn was usually sung by the congregation between the Credo and the sermon, or if the Credo was not rendered in Latin, in its place. Since this setting of the first verse employs complex imitative counterpoint and polychoral effects that would prevent any congregational participation, no matter how familiar the tune must have been, it must be assumed that in this instance the congregation sang the second and third verses only. The *basso continuo*, although plentifully figured, actually contributes nothing to the piece, as it merely follows the lowest sounding voice in *basso seguente* fashion. Compositional practice here reverts to an older style than that of the chorale-tradition composers. Imitative counterpoint for two equal choirs, as in the Catholic motets of the Roman school, is elaborated by the use of the chorale tune as a familiar and flexible *cantus firmus*. The simultaneous use of the melodic sections of the chorale in normal speed and in augmented values, following immediately after a section in short notes, is especially effective *(Ex. 66)*.

The dialogue technique that had found such a receptive advocate in Hammerschmidt is utilized by Ahle in an entirely new fashion; the dialogue is not between individual voices or between one voice and a group, but between two separate choruses, rendering the text

11. *DdT*, vi, 58–78. The instrumentation is three violins, three *viole da gamba*, and organ. The third *viola da gamba* doubles the organ, and is obviously the instrument that is involved in the *continuo* where only organ is specified.
12. *Ibid.*, viii. The Roman Breviary gives this text as a Responsory for *feria* iv *post pascha*.
13. *DdT*, v, 121–31.

Ex. 66   Ahle, *Wir glauben all' an einen Gott*, after *DdT*, V, 125

as impersonally as it was in the motet Passion or, to use a secular example, a madrigal comedy. The text, after Isaiah 63:1–3, is not associated with any particular date in the liturgical calendar, and the chorale verse that brings it to a close, *Dank, Preis sei dir, Herr Jesu Christ (Thanks and praise be to Thee, Lord Jesus Christ)*,[14] does not ap-

14. *Ibid.*, 76–82.

pear closely connected with the rest of the text. The idea of closing a piece with a more or less appropriate chorale verse seems to have been firmly established in Ahle's practice, at least. A setting of part of the Christmas Gospel, Luke 2:10–12, 14–15, is considerably more dramatic. If it were more than a momentary scene from the Christmas story, it would probably have to be considered in the line of the oratorio's genealogy. Except for its dramatic qualities, however, it stands clearly in place with other pieces that served the function of the cantata. Its name is derived from the opening phrase of text, *Fürchtet euch nicht (Fear ye not)*,[15] and the materials of composition are carefully selected to project the scene that follows. The orchestra is made up largely of wind instruments, as is suitable to a pastoral subject, the bassoons holding a special position of importance; there is a soprano solo in the form of an aria for the angel and *continuo;* a chorus of angels follows, utilizing only the upper voices of the chorus, SSST; the chorus of shepherds, ATTB, stands in immediate and sharp contrast; and the *sinfonia* for four bassoons leads directly into the closing chorus *a 8,* i.e., SSSATTTB, a *concertato* movement for voices and bassoons on the chorale, *Gelobet seist du, Jesu Christ (Praised be Thou, Jesus Christ).*

We often hopefully assign relationships to composers and pieces of music when we cannot truthfully document them. In the cases of Ahle and Hammerschmidt, for instance, it is not to be assumed that the use of a device or technique by both of them implies knowledge of each other's work, or that the employment of entirely different means, such as we saw with Weckmann and Ahle, means that each was not equipped to pursue the course that was followed by the other. What they could or would have done remains a moot question. Even when an opportunity comes to trace a line of tradition through successive generations of composers, as we can with Tunder, Buxtehude, and Bach, it is both difficult and dangerous to assign exact influence, for any ideas may well have become part of the common vocabulary of composers by the time we find them reaching the second or third generation. It will, then, have to remain as a matter of possibility rather than probability or established fact that matters of technique first seen in Lübeck came to fruition at Arnstadt, Weimar, and Leipzig. We know without question that Dietrich Buxtehude (1637–1707) developed certain of Tunder's ideas in his celebrated

15. *Ibid.,* 92–99.

Abendmusiken when he became Tunder's successor at the Marienkirche in Lübeck. Tunder had already increased the number of instrumental performers for special occasions at the church; Buxtehude
expanded the orchestral body even more.

A tendency to stress the return of familiar material, if not an actual
preference for closed forms, appears in the pages of one of Buxtehude's *Abendmusiken*, a work for SSATB chorus and orchestra, entitled
Eins bitte ich vom Herrn (I ask one thing of the Lord).[16] Buxtehude
called for an orchestra of flutes, violins, violas, and a bass-organ *continuo* and used the entire group in his opening *sonatina*, a piece in
three distinct sections. It begins with a slow homophonic section that
stresses repetitions in echo fashion, progresses to a lively fugato for
two violins, and then returns to a slow section that is built on new
material, but closes with a quotation of the first four measures of the
piece. The opening chorus, based on Psalm 27:4, is in *concertato* style.
It begins in contrapuntal fashion, but dissolves into block-chords
that prevail for most of the movement *(Ex. 67)*. An aria holds the central position of the whole composition. It is not a continuous piece,
but is comprised of seven verses of strophic text separated by instrumental *ritornelli*. The need for variety is obvious when so many repetitions are involved, and Buxtehude met the need in a number of
ways that are best illustrated in tabular form:

TABLE XI

The Structure of Buxtehude's *Abendmusik*,
Eins bitte ich vom Herrn

Verse

1. Soprano I
   Ritornello A (tutti)
2. Chorus and *continuo*
   Ritornello B (without violas)
3. Alto
   Ritornello B (without violas)
4. Chorus and orchestra
   Ritornello B (tutti)
5. Soprano II
   Ritornello A (tutti)
6. Chorus and *continuo*
   Ritornello B (without violas)
7. Chorus and orchestra
   Ritornello B (without flutes)

16. *DdT*, xiv, 15–38.

Ex. 67 Buxtehude, opening chorus from *Eins bitte ich vom Herrn, DdT*, XIV, 17

The first and fifth verses are given to soprano voices with only *continuo* accompaniment and followed by identical *ritornelli*. The music for this *ritornello* (identified here as A) appears only with the soprano solos. The third verse, for alto solo with *continuo*, stands at the midpoint of the three solo sections or, if we may remove those parts from the entire piece for a moment, as the mid-section of an ABA form. All of the choruses, on the other hand, belong to a different family, differing in whether they are fully accompanied or supported by the *continuo*, and in whether the *ritornello* they hold in common is given

full or selective orchestration. The only identical link between solo and chorus material is in *ritornello* B which serves the alto solo and all of the choral sections. It seems preposterous to suggest that Buxtehude was attempting to interlace a *da capo* form, divided among the soloists, with a group of varied strophic choruses; yet, the arrangement of voices and the selection of musical materials leads us to believe that such was the case. A final and unassailable point of regularity is seen in Buxtehude's instruction for an optional, but highly desirable return of the opening chorus to bring the entire composition to a close with full forces and with fresh, but familiar material.

The foregoing composition depended not at all upon the chorale either as a familiar melodic-textual pattern or as a unifying feature. That Buxtehude used chorales both as conveyors of appropriate text and as sources of motivic material can be discovered in *Alles, was ihr tut*,[17] for the Fifth Sunday after Epiphany, and in *Ihr lieben Christen, freut euch nun*,[18] for the Second Sunday in Advent. The latter was probably one of the works heard at the famous *Abendmusiken*. In the former work, a chorale verse appears first as a soprano solo and immediately after in chorus form; in the latter, the opening chorale is again given to soprano solo and its melody is the source of material for two choruses in which the sturdy tune is enlivened by a shift to triple meter.

Occasionally there appears a composer who excites wonder at how he could have been so productive and still have lived what passed for a normal life. When such productivity is coupled with consistent quality, as in the case of Roland de Lassus, Johann Sebastian Bach, Franz Joseph Haydn, or some other pivotal figure in musical history, the results reach the limits of credibility. When the composer follows a few patterns of convenience, as we feel is the case with such men as Alessandro Scarlatti, Georg Philipp Telemann, and other composers who found convenient molds that they could employ again and again, we still feel astonishment at the sheer amount of ink that has been put to paper. It is possible that if our information were matched by surviving manuscripts, we should unhesitatingly place Johann Philipp Krieger (1649–1725) with those who have been both productive and creative. He composed more than 2,000 church works of the cantata type alone—as compared to a probable total of slightly over 300 for Bach and of about 400 for Buxtehude—of which less than a hundred have so far come to light. These prove that Krieger was a thorough master of composition, for there is no paucity of styles and treatments. The list of his church works[19] whets the appetite for what seems to be

17. *Ibid.*, 39–56; Dietrich Buxtehude, *Every Word and Thought*, ed. Paul Bunjes (St. Louis: Concordia Publishing House, 1957).
18. *Ibid.*, 107–138; Dietrich Buxtehude,

Rejoice, Beloved Christians, ed. Clarence Dickinson (New York: H. W. Gray Co., 1937).
19. *DdT*, LIII/LIV, xxiv–lii.

irretrievably lost. Even among the surviving works there are dialogues, chorale variations, *concertato* pieces, compositions with double chorus and double orchestra, a limitless variety of pieces for the Protestant service.

We cannot attribute Krieger's constant flow of new works to a narrow view that saw all music in religious surroundings, for he carried on a normal activity in secular composition at the same time. He distinguished himself as an opera composer, producing about twenty works that found favor in German cities; he wrote a few keyboard works; and his chamber music includes compositions for wind instruments as well as the usual combinations. His training prepared him well for the work he was to do. After the usual thorough schooling in music that was given to young Germans at this time, he spent a two-year period in Italy, studying composition in both Venice and Rome, where he made the acquaintance of many outstanding Italian musicians. His principal appointment was as *Kapellmeister* to the ducal court of Halle—later, at Weissenfels where it was removed by Duke Johann Adolph—where, in addition to providing chamber music for the entertainment of the court, he was responsible for the production of the music for regular church services. The order of service that was followed is known through a surviving copy of the *Ordnungen wie der Gottesdienst in der NeuAugustusburgischen Schloss Kirchen zu Weissenfelss anzustellen und zu halten sey.*[20] The second part of this document, dated 1688, classifies the various types of services. The order of worship for a morning service with a sermon is shown in Table XII, which should be compared with Table X. The ordinary service apparently made considerable demands upon Krieger and his musicians, but he was apparently also fortunate in having musicians who were capable of producing much demanding music. The unusual effort that was made for the dedication of the *Schlosskirche*, a ceremony that covered two days and a half in November, 1682, makes the Mass that Orazio Benevoli wrote for the dedication of the Salzburg Cathedral seem an insignificant piece, if we are to believe the printed record of what was sung at Weissenfels.[21] Twenty-two choral pieces were sung during the five services that marked the celebration. Each morning featured a Mass for double chorus; one in fifty-six parts, another in sixty, and a third in fifty. Each afternoon a Magnificat was produced; one for double chorus *a 60*, the other for triple chorus *a 63*.

20. *Ibid.*, lxi–lxviii.   21. *Ibid.*, xx–xxi.

TABLE XII

Order of Worship for a Morning Service with Sermon
Schlosskirche, Weissenfels, 1688*

A Psalm (from Dr. Becker's Psalter) to be sung
Kyrie
Gloria, by the minister before the altar
The *Missa brevis* sung
Allein Gott in der Höh sey Ehr
A Collect and the Epistle
An appropriate German hymn
Gospel
Cantata *(wird ein Stück musiciret)*
The Credo sung—*Wir glauben all' an einen Gott*
Sermon
Hr. Jesu Christ dich zu unss wend
Lord's Prayer
Cantata *(Nach der predigt wird wieder ein stück musiciret)*
A German hymn
Collect and Blessing
A German closing hymn, or an additional verse from a previous piece

*Compare with Table x.

Other Latin and German pieces, ranging from five parts to sixty-six, were part of the observance, most of them clearly indicated as Krieger's own efforts.

The texts that Krieger set during his career were from many sources: there are nearly forty settings of the Magnificat, ninety-six Masses (probably *Missae brevis*), four German Masses, and myriad Latin and German texts from the Psalms and other biblical verses.

A fortunate association with Erdmann Neumeister (1671–1756), whose name was later to be associated with a number of better known cantata composers but who spent the years 1704–1706 as court minister at Weissenfels, resulted in Krieger's setting nearly 250 of Neumeister's cantata texts. Neumeister had already been at Weissenfels for several years before his appointment to duties at the court, and a number of Krieger's settings of his texts, including the first complete cycle of cantatas for the Sundays, Festivals, and Feasts dedicated to Apostles, saw completion before 1702. Neumeister's cycles were not published until years after the first works were set by Krieger. His setting of Neumeister's cantata text for the Second Sunday after

Trinity, as found in the second annual cycle, *Rufet nicht die Weisheit?* *(Doth wisdom not call?)*[22] was first performed in 1699 and was used again on the same day in 1713. In discussing the first three of Neumeister's cycles, Schweitzer wrote as follows:

> Neumeister's "madrigal cantatas" have nothing in common with the earlier attempts at the madrigal in German religious poetry, but are imitations of the Italian opera texts, the author himself declaring, in his preface, that for him a cantata is only a fragment of an opera. He makes each of them consist of four arias and four recitatives. He discards altogether Biblical passages and verses from the hymn-books, nor are there any choruses.
>
> In the succeeding cycles he makes some concessions. The second (1708) again gives the chorus its due; in the third (1711) a modest place is again granted to Biblical passages and hymn verses by the side of arias and recitatives.[23]

Since the setting of *Rufet nicht* is from the second cycle, it has both an opening and closing chorus. In other ways it deviates from Schweitzer's description of Neumeister's pattern: for one, it does not present a set of four recitatives and arias; for another, all of the text, except for two stanzas of Neumeister's own poetry, is made up of six direct quotations of biblical passages.[24] The Gospel for that Sunday (Luke 14:16–24) does not appear among them.

Although there is an orchestra of string instruments (violins and gamba), the cantata[25] has no opening instrumental section, but begins with a choral statement of the first of the two biblical quotations that make up the opening chorus. There follows a *da capo* aria for soprano, on the first of Neumeister's two original verses,[26] a bass recitative on another biblical section, and another *da capo* aria for tenor to the same music as the preceding aria, but to the other verse of the poem. The bass line for the aria makes much of a pattern of a quarter note and four sixteenths with repeated bass melodies of two-

---

22. *Ibid.*, 275–90.
23. Schweitzer, *op. cit.*, ɪ, 91f.
24. Prov. 8:1–3; Isa. 55:1–3; Ps. 81:12–14, 17; Ps. 119:174; Isa. 26:9; Ps. 119:76.
25. From this point, reference will be made to cantatas rather than to *Kirchenmusik*. The decision to do so beginning with the works of Krieger rather than with those of another composer is admittedly an arbitrary one. In view of the consistent pattern of works after this time, in the combination of aria, recitative, and chorus, and the beginning of the use of standard text versions, such as those of Neumeister and his successors, it seems that this is the most suitable place for the change.
26. Three such verses appear in the published versions of Neumeister's texts. Either Krieger chose not to set the third one, or Neumeister wrote it after this period, but prior to publication.

252

PLATE 5. *A German church orchestra of the eighteenth century. An engraving used as the frontispiece of J. G. Walther's* Musikalisches Lexikon, *1732.*

measure length that fall short of becoming an *ostinato* bass. The remaining text is given to the chorus in a final *concertato* that closes with a fugue. An "Amen" chorus that stands squarely between similar closing sections of English anthems and the final chorus of Handel's *Messiah* brings the work to an exultant close.

What Krieger composed when he used no previously organized texts, such as those of Neumeister and other religious poets, presents a varied picture too broad to examine in detail here. Settings of entire psalms appear, as do settings of biblical verses joined to appropriate chorale verses. There is also a cantata in the form of a set of chorale variations, *Ein feste Burg ist unser Gott (A mighty fortress is our God),*[27] composed for a minor festival of the church, St. Bartholomew's Day, August 24, 1688. Between that time and 1717 the work was brought into use another seven times, probably because of the strong appeal that it held through association with the important chorale upon which it was built. As the sole surviving example of Krieger's solution to the problem of enlivening a piece made up wholly of strophic text, the work is an interesting combination of variety and unity. It contains neither recitatives nor solos; each of the four verses is written in the same style for SATB choir with an orchestra of two violins, three violas, bassoon, and *continuo*. Each verse is preceded by an instrumental *ritornello,* and each verse is likewise accompanied throughout by the full orchestra. The chorale tune appears in a different voice in each of the verses, in *cantus firmus* fashion, first in the soprano, then in the alto, bass, and tenor. The voice parts throughout are doubled by the violas and bassoon, while the two violins play parts that seem more typical of *clarini* than of string instruments *(Ex. 68)*. The *ritornelli* are different for each of the first three verses, as are the verses themselves. The fourth is a duplication of the first, although the movement of the *cantus firmus* to the tenor part of the last verse requires that soprano and tenor exchange the parts they sang in the first verse while the other two remain unchanged. The use of a closed form and of *cantus firmus* technique in all of the vocal sections greatly enhances the sturdiness that was already inherent in the chorale that stood then, as it does now, as the musical affirmation of Lutheranism.

For all his activity and varied productivity, Krieger seems to have established no tradition that was carried on by his contemporaries or students. The exciting combination of Italian and German musical

27. *DdT,* LIII/LIV, 111–28.

Ex. 68 Krieger, *Ein feste Burg ist unser Gott, DdT,* LIII/LIV, 120 (after two measures, violas and bassoon double voices)

styles heard at Weissenfels was probably overshadowed by the interest that was generated in the more commonly visited centers of musical activity—Leipzig, Hamburg, and Braunschweig, among others—where, if Krieger's name excited any great interest, it was in his operas rather than his church music.

gar ver - schlin - gen, ver - schlin - gen,

und wolltn uns gar ver - schlin - gen, ver - schlin - gen,

schlin - - - gen, ver - schlin - gen,

schlin - - - gen,

7   6   7   6   7   5   6
                                  3   4

During the years that Krieger held his position as *Kapellmeister*, Johann Kuhnau (1660–1722) was organist and, later, cantor at the famous Thomaskirche in Leipzig. Of his total contribution to church music we have no clear picture, for publication was not common and the cry was ever for more new music. The necessity for a continuing flow of composition created also a casual attitude toward what had been composed and once used. When a piece had served its purpose, it was likely often put aside where the ravages of time and carelessness removed it from this world. We possess only a fraction of what was written, and we must hope that what we have is actually representative of the bulk of music that was produced.

We may safely assume that a cantata produced for one of the principal observances of the church year should stand as a fair example of Kuhnau's best work. Such a composition is *Wenn ihr fröhlich seid an euren Festen (When ye are joyful on your Festivals)*,[28] written for Easter and probably performed in Leipzig in 1716, and again in 1720 and 1724.[29] The festive character of the cantata is immediately apparent from the appearance of the opening *Sonata*. The orchestra, consisting of four trumpets and timpani, paired violins and violas, bassoon and *continuo*, begins with a longer than usual piece in modified *da capo* form. The basic material is made up of two contrasting figures;

28. *DdT*, LVIII/LIX, 244–91.   29. *Ibid.*, liv.

a stately homophonic section for strings that gives evidence of Kuhnau's acquaintance with the French overture, followed by a fanfare pattern that cascades through the trumpets and dissolves into a running passage in thirds that is traded back and forth by winds and strings. A similar pair of ideas is repeated in the dominant key, and the original string passage returns, followed by an altered version of the fanfare and running passages. The opening text, *Wenn ihr fröhlich seid an euren Festen und in euren Neumonden, sollt ihr mit den Drommeten blasen*,[30] alternates between solo voices and SSATB chorus. The voices are called upon to imitate trumpets, first in solo and immediately after in full chorus *(Ex. 69)*. There are solos for alto and bass, and an aria for two sopranos, each separated from the others by short choruses. The closing number is an impressive chorus in two sections. It opens with a slow, homophonic *concertato* in which the chorus lists the laudatory attributes of God in one-measure patterns that are echoed by the instruments. The concluding allegro follows without a break, a vigorous fugue that repeats many times, *von Ewigkeit zu Ewigkeit, Amen* ("from everlasting to everlasting, Amen") The first complete fugal exposition is preceded by a statement of both the subject and answer in motto fashion *(Ex. 70)*. No strophic texts are used in the course of the composition, and Kuhnau was free to employ the modern Italian idioms.

Ex. 69 Kuhnau, *Wenn ihr fröhlich seid an euren Festen*, DdT, LVIII/LIX, 254

30. The passage is related to Ps. 81:3, "Blow up the trumpet in the new moon, in the time appointed, on our solemn feast day."

Ex. 70   *Ibid.*, 284f, Final chorus, false entry of subject and countersubject

As an example of the chorale cantata, we may briefly examine Kuhnau's use of Philipp Nicolai's chorale text, *Wie schön leuchtet der Morgenstern (How brightly shines the morning star)*.[31] The chorale text and tune appear only in the opening and closing sections, the former using the first stanza; the latter, the sixth. What appears to be a subtle attempt to keep the memory of an outstanding feature of the melody before the listener appears at intervals throughout the cantata. A number of the sections begin with the characteristic upward leap of the melody, always with the equally characteristic movement from weak to strong beat *(Ex. 71)*. Were the tune less commonly used, this might seem an attempt to imagine something that could not have entered the composer's mind. However, the pattern is present at the opening of the instrumental introduction, it appears strongly in voices other than the soprano during the first stanza, and it reappears as the opening pattern of recitatives, fugue subjects, arias, and the closing chorus. Its almost constant presence as a head-motif in new sections cannot be denied. One feature that appears indisputably is the motto beginning[32] that presents, before the piece actually gets underway, the title, the melodic-rhythmic pattern, and the *Affekt* of the aria or chorus to which the motto belongs. We found this in the closing chorus of Kuhnau's *Wenn ihr fröhlich seid an euren Festen,* and we can find it again in this work, in the tenor aria *Kommt, ihr Völker,*

31. *DdT*, LVIII/LIX, 292–320.
32. *MBE*, 132f, describes the first appearances of this device in the operas and cantatas of the preceding generation of Italian composers.

Ex. 71 Kuhnau's use of characteristic leaps in *Wie schön leuchtet der Morgenstern, DdT*, LVIII/LIX

kommt mit Haufen (Come, ye people, come with throngs), and in the pre-statement of the text to the first *Stollen* of the chorale's sixth stanza. Naturally, it is not implied that the pre-statement of text alone by two sopranos represents a true motto beginning, but it would not have been necessary for a composer to state the melody of this familiar chorale. The gesture may, therefore, be taken as a sufficient substitute for the usual practice of presenting both text and melody.

Up to this point there has been considerable variety in the ways that composers have dealt with the chorale as part of a cantata. Not all the methods that were tried found enough favor to continue in practice — the setting of variations on a *cantus firmus*, for instance, is not to be found again. But a number of new ideas, each a logical continuation of earlier practices, appear until the end of the Baroque period puts an almost complete stop to the use of the chorale as a unifying feature of larger choral compositions. Friedrich Wilhelm Zachow, to whom attention has already been directed as the probable composer of a *Missa brevis* based on a familiar chorale (see p. 193), used chorales in one form or another for seven of the twelve cantatas that are accessible for study.[33] Three distinct uses of the chorale are found in Zachow's works: (1) the *Schlusschoral*, as a summary of the cantata's dogmatic message; (2) the chorale used during the course of the composition as a commentary on the message (the *Schlusschoral* always appears at the end of this type as well); and (3) chorale verses framing the entire cantata, and sometimes making up the entire substance of the composition, in text if not in melody. It may be true that the first class represents more artificiality than do the second and third, as the insertion of an unadorned chorale does, as Mattheson complained, bring the musical development of the composition to an abrupt halt. Such interruption is lessened in those cases in which a chorale text and melody are presented in simple fashion, but with the phrases interspersed with elaborate orchestral passages in *concertato* style or accompanied by an instrumental group that provides a highly imaginative and rhythmically active background. Again, it must be recognized that more than the musical development is at stake, for the cantata's close affiliation with the mandatory *de tempore* texts has not been a random one. Anything that could be drawn upon to emphasize and reiterate the message of the Gospel was an effective means of recalling the attention of the congregation to the religious purpose of the music; the use of chorale texts, forthright and uncomplicated, suited this effort admirably, and when these texts were presented by means of familiar melodies, the effect was increased even more. Complaints that chorales destroy musical continuity are, then, valid only when the composition is looked upon entirely as a concert. We must accept the fact that no matter how much the cantata adopted the characteristics of concert music, it was performed according to the established practice in a service that was liturgically derived, and continued so to be practiced. A composer of Zachow's skill could go far in making the chorale seem a part of the normal format of a composition principally in the Italian style. In his Easter cantata, *Dies ist der Tag*,[34] the opening tenor solo, *Dies ist der Tag, den der Herr macht; lasset uns freuen und fröhlich sein (This is the day which the Lord hath made; let us rejoice and be glad)*,[35] is linked without pause to a choral setting of the opening verse of the chorale, *Erschienen ist der herrliche Tag*. The appropriateness of the chorale verse to the

33. *DdT*, xxi/xxii.
34. *Ibid.*, 236–59.

35. Ps. 118:24. The text used in the cantata varies slightly from the original.

text preceding it cannot be ignored, and the vigorous accompaniment figure that moves swiftly through the violins is an admirable counterbalance to the square and sturdy phrases of the hymn. The treatment of the closing chorale is also unusual. Zachow employs the fourth verse of *Wenn mein Stündlein vorhanden ist (When my last hour is at hand)*, the opening text of which, *Weil du vom Tod erstanden bist, werd' ich im Grab nicht bleiben (Since thou art risen from the dead, I shall not perish in the grave)*, closes the cantata on the reassuring note of Christ's victory over death. The musical treatment is quite elaborate. Instead of a motto beginning, after the manner we have seen in other works, the opening text is presented in motto fashion as a fugal exposition. The subject *(Ex. 72)* then serves as the basis for the orchestral material that accompanies the chorale proper, which does not continue fugally, but proceeds in simple homophonic style. Even in connection with the solo cantata *Ich bin sicher und erfreut (I am safe and filled with joy)*[36] there is a chorale, not for chorus as we might anticipate, but for the solo voice to sing as a closing formula after the last aria.

The regular appearance of the chorale as a summation device within and at the end of the cantata makes it necessary to examine the purpose of the cantata that drew upon sources other than hymn literature. An increasing popularity of long choruses, preferably fugal, is seen in the works that favor nonstrophic text. While some cantatas have interior choruses of considerable length, often in the same position as that held by the interior chorale verse in other cantatas, the more common pattern is that which places a fugal chorus at both the beginning and the end of the composition, and a general rule of minimum use seems to call for a closing fugue if the situation permits. Zachow's cantata for the Visitation, *Meine Seel erhebt den Herren (My soul doth magnify the Lord)*[37] is a setting of the Magnificat with exegetical arias between presentations of the biblical text. Except for the

Ex. 72 Zachow, subject of motto-fugue, closing chorale of cantata, *Dies ist der Tag, DdT*, XXI/XXII, 257

Tenor

Weil du vom Tod er - stan - den bist,

36. *Ibid.*, 260–68.   37. *Ibid.*, 104–28.

setting of the first two verses in fugal form for full chorus and the last two — the Gloria Patri — as successive homophonic and fugal choruses, the words of Mary are symbolically given to a soprano. The explanatory arias are divided among all the soloists including the soprano. The cantata is divided into two parts, the second intended for performance at the afternoon service, and chorales play no part in the work. They have no place as explanatory text, for this function is taken over by the solos, and summary is out of place after a choral framework has been completed around the piece by the performance of the Gloria Patri.

There is another use of chorale tunes that must be noted here, different from those normally employed. The cantata for the Sixteenth Sunday after Trinity, *Ach wie nichtig, ach wie flüchtig (Ah, how empty; ah, how fleeting)*[38] by Christoph Graupner (1683–1760) uses identical music with the three chorale verses that serve as opening, middle, and closing choral sections. Each phrase of the melody is presented separately, first in free writing (imitation, fugal expositions, and so on), and then in block-chords. There is, as a result, no continuous presentation of either text or music; rather, the chorale words and tune are broken into sections that would be more common in madrigalian settings.

We come next to the foremost figure in the history of the German church cantata, Johann Sebastian Bach, whose nearly 300 cantatas, of which about two-thirds are extant, represent the culmination of what we have seen as developmental practices. His cantatas brought to fruition the seeds cast abroad by many of his predecessors, for Bach scorned no techniques or devices of which he was aware; if they did not serve as material for numerous compositions, they appeared at least as experiments, rejected only after they had been put to the test of practical music. Where the works available from earlier composers were limited in number and perhaps not even truly representative of all that the composer produced, we are faced with the opposite problem in the Bach cantatas, an almost limitless wealth of compositions that can be inspected. From such a number of possibilities there is no ideal selection; what is chosen must reflect, to a degree, a combination of personal preference and representative works. We have here chosen an early work, a cantata from the Weimar period, one from Leipzig and, finally, two different types of chorale cantatas to be examined

38. *DdT*, LI/LII, 108–22.

briefly. It should not be assumed that because Bach employed materials, styles, and devices similar to those of the other composers
we have discussed, he was writing in direct imitation of what they
had done. While he was familiar with the music of a number of them,
there is no evidence that he ever took note of the existence of others.
His appetite for music seems to have been without end, and his studying and copying of numerous scores doubtless led him to materials
that provided a common source to him and some of his predecessors.

Whether it was in direct continuation of the long tradition of word-
painting and intensification of text that Bach came to his involved
usage of musical symbolism,[39] or whether he deliberately set out to
move beyond the doctrine of affections, his employment of these
means remains unparalleled. The symbols may be melodic, rhythmic,
diagrammatic, or reiterative. The range of ideas that Bach conveys by
their use is sufficient to serve most of the subjects presented in his
cantatas: grief, joy, foreboding, excitement, tranquility, dignity, exhaustion, Satan, angels, the motion of waves, and the pealing of bells
are only a few. Were these simply common repetitions of the same
motive each time they appeared in the cantatas, the result would be
an unimaginative mechanical representation leading to tedium. The
motives are subject to such a range of alterations and combinations
that no such result is found. Strangely, however, many well-informed
musicians who willingly accept the pictorial representation of a Schubert song accompaniment or, at the other extreme, the word-painting
of a Renaissance motet, will insist that nothing of this sort could have
been intended by Bach. To deny the existence of such a complex series
of patterns, however naïve and obvious some of them may be, is to
deny oneself the complete understanding of Bach's methods of pro-
jecting the text to its fullest and, in many cases, of providing meaning-
ful association of ideas when no text is present.

Early in 1708, Bach was called upon to provide a suitable composition for the Inauguration of the Town Council, which took place in
the Marienkirche at Mühlhausen, the city in which he was then serving as organist at the Church of St. Blasius. That the opportunity

39. Schweitzer, op. cit., II, 74–122, deals
specifically with the use of symbolic
ideas in the cantatas. An extension of this
practice, in which the use of certain instruments or compositional devices is
seen as bearing allegorical meaning, was
described by Manfred F. Bukofzer, "Allegory in Baroque Music," Journal of the
Warburg and Courtauld Institutes, III, (1939
–1940), 1–21. See also Roger Bullivant,
"Word-Painting and Chromaticism in the
Music of J. S. Bach," The Music Review,
xx/3–4 (August–November, 1959), 185–
216.

this presented to the young man, barely into the third decade of his life, was recognized by him as a providential turn in his affairs is evident from the careful complexity with which he organized the composition. The occasion was not of such momentous importance as the dedication of the Salzburg Cathedral had been for Benevoli, or the dedication of the Weissenfels Schlosskirche for Krieger, but it was the best that offered, and its significance in the eyes of the town fathers is seen in the fact that the parts for the work were printed, the composition being identified on the title page as a "Congratulatory Church Motet" (Glückwünschende Kirchen-Motetto). The composition is the one we know as Gott ist mein König (God is my King) (BWV 71).[40] Bach apparently set out to produce as brilliant a concertato piece as he was able to write for whatever forces could be assembled for the performance. Four soloists and a double choir were supported by an orchestra that was itself divided into four distinct choirs, each capable of playing either independently of the others or in concert with them. A "fanfare" group, consisting of trumpets and timpani (used only in the large choruses), a second group consisting of two flutes and violoncello, a third made up of a pair of oboes and bassoon, and a basic group of strings with bass and without violoncello, provide a variety that Bach found too elaborate for use in later years. On this occasion he was bent on displaying his prowess and, even though the result is more a rough, experimental work than a smooth, artistic one, the young composer evidently learned much.

One of the distinctive characteristics of this cantata that appears in those of Bach's later years, although with less fussily detailed directions to the performers, is that of two differentiated ways of using the choir. He gives directions for certain sections to be sung by a coro pleno (full chorus), and others by a lesser number, senza ripieni. This alternation, which finds the full orchestra playing when the coro pleno sings, and usually only one instrumental choir sounding with the smaller vocal group, gives not only a variety of textures but an automatic series of dynamic levels as well. The Venetian practice is not far removed from what Bach undertook in the choruses of this work.

A single, and somewhat unusual use of a chorale is found in the

40. Much has been written about Bach's cantatas. The most exhaustive study is that of W. Gillies Whittaker, The Cantatas of Johann Sebastian Bach (2 vols.; London: Oxford University Press, 1959). Also of interest, but less exhaustive in treatment are Schweitzer, op. cit.; André Pirro, J. S. Bach, trans. Mervyn Savill (New York: The Orion Press, 1957); Russell H. Miles, Johann Sebastian Bach: An Introduction to His Life and Works (Englewood Cliffs: Prentice-Hall, 1962).

duo for soprano and tenor. The tenor is the principal voice of the
pair, singing a text that expresses the longing of an old man for his
native city (II Sam. 19:35, 37) and obviously implying a reference to
one or both of the town councillors, while the soprano enters at intervals with an ornamented version of the lesser known of the two chorales titled *O Gott, du frommer Gott (O God, thou helpful God) (Ex. 73).*
Verse six of the chorale is used, probably because of its appropriate
references to old age and grey hairs. The relationship of the two parts
is such that the same person indicated by the tenor part seems to be
reflecting on his position in life in the text sung by the soprano. The
combination of two such related ideas could well be an extension of
the dialogue idea that we have seen in earlier instances. The cantata
has no closing chorale, providing instead a large chorus that frames a
central fugal section between two homophonic sections. These larger
sections are further subdivided into shorter ones as demanded by the
changing character of the final text sections, and the orchestration is
varied from section to section. Of special interest is the central fugue,
the first exposition of which is for the small chorus with *continuo,* and
the second exposition, an exact repetition for full chorus with the entire orchestra.

A cantata which, in its final form, is intended for performance on
the Third Sunday after Trinity is *Ich hatte viel Bekümmernis (My spirit
was in heaviness) (BWV 21).* The original manuscript, which bears the
date 1714, describes it as a *Concerto a 13* — we must remember that
Bach did not use the term cantata to describe the principal music for
the service — and also notes that it is appropriate *Per ogni Tempo.*
Stemming from the period of Bach's residence at Weimar, the piece

Ex. 73 Stollen of chorale melody, *O Gott, du frommer Gott*

Bach's ornamented use of the same chorale in
Gott ist mein König (BWV 71)

presents many questions concerning its origins and purpose. The theory has been advanced and rejected that the opening chorus borrows from Handel,[41] but the presence of a concerto theme of Vivaldi, which Bach had previously arranged for organ, is now established. It is a cantata of unprecedented length, divided into two parts that were to be presented, we may presume, before and after the sermon. Except in the two closing choruses, the instrumentation is for oboe, bassoon, strings, and *continuo*. The final chorus calls for three trumpets and timpani, and the penultimate chorus for four trombones that double the violins, viola, and bassoon. The trombones were added for a later Leipzig performance, but the question still arises, why were they not kept for the closing chorus as well? Usually a two-part cantata exposed its idea completely in the first half and solved it in the second or, we may say, presented a balance between doubt and assurance after the manner of the two-sectional motets and anthems of the Catholics and Anglicans. In general, this plan is pursued in the structure of the cantata involved here, although the closing chorus of the first part sounds the general tone of hope, resolving the tension of theological conflict before the sermon instead of waiting until the second half. The Epistle for the Third Sunday after Trinity is i Peter 5:6–11, which begins "Humble yourselves therefore under the mighty hand of God, that he may exalt you in due time: Casting all your care upon him, for he careth for you." The general tone of fear and distress is established in the first half, to be replaced by confidence and reassurance in the second. The first half has, in itself, enough substance to pass as a complete cantata, and its closing chorus, which prematurely releases the dramatic tension of the text, may indicate that it was first intended to stand as a complete composition to that point. The organization of parts, sinfonia, chorus, aria, recitative, aria, and closing chorus, the last with the kind of double exposition we saw in *Gott ist mein König*—a first one for soloists with *continuo*, and a second for full chorus with orchestra—points to the pattern that was common for the complete cantata. The most effective chorus of the entire work comes in the second half, a two-section setting of the text beginning *Sei nun wieder zufrieden, meine Seele* ("Come now, and be at peace, O my soul"), sung by soloists from the soprano, alto, and bass sections while the entire tenor group sings the second stanza of the chorale *Wer nur den lieben Gott lässt walten (He who lets only the good God rule)*

41. Whittaker, *op. cit.*, i, 110f.

in long equal notes, accompanied only by *continuo*. This is followed by
a tutti version with the fifth verse of the chorale transferred to the soprano, the whole this time accompanied by the orchestra, including
the trombones, which appear only for this chorus. This repetition of
material is comparable to the double exposition idea used in the
fugues. It is not the use of the chorale that is unusual here, but the del-
icate weaving of the other parts around the sustained melody, as if
Bach were enveloping the singers with a protective web of flowing
counterpoint (*Ex. 74*). Much of the second half of the cantata is based
on the old dialogue idea, perpetuated here first in a recitative and then
in a duet between the soprano, who represents the soul, and the bass,
who represents Jesus. The recitatives generally used by Bach should
be mentioned as differing from those of many other cantata composers
in one respect, they are accompanied by the full string group instead
of the *continuo* only. Both types, the orchestrally accompanied and
the *continuo*-supported, provide a solid flow of sound through the
use of sustained chords rather than the punctuating choppiness of *recitativo secco*, which has little place in such music. The recitative that

Ex. 74   Bach, chorus from cantata 21, *Ich hatte viel Bekümerniss* (SAB soli, with all tenors on chorale melody)

opens the second half of this work flows naturally from its sustained long tones into the more elaborate accompaniment that supports the concluding arioso measures. Both of the tenor arias in the composition, one in each half, use the motto beginning to announce the subject of the solo piece.

Standing as Bach's unique example of a cantata in the form of chorale variations, and harking back to the style seen in Tunder's treatment of the chorale tune in his *Ein feste Burg ist unser Gott* and to Krieger's work on the same tune, is Bach's Easter cantata, *Christ lag in Todesbanden (Christ lay in the bonds of death) (BWV* 4). In a number of ways, his mastery of materials far above that of his predecessors is evident in his solution to the problem of setting seven chorale verses in a manner that was both unified and varied. All seven of Luther's stanzas are set, each in a distinctively individual style. The text and the hymn tune serve to bind the composition together—the text through its easily perceivable relationship of verses, and the tune through its consistent, but sometimes heavily masked presence— while Bach's choice of settings for each of the sections epitomizes seven ways of varying basic material. One notable feature of the work is the arch form that is evident not in thematic materials, forms, or text repetitions, but in the selection of voices for the successive sections of the piece. Thus, the setting of the first, fourth, and last verses for chorus *a 4*, the choice of duo for the second and sixth verses, and of solo for the third and fifth, produces the following arch:

                    chorus
                      IV
                  III solo V
              II   duo   VI
          I   chorus   VII

The choruses stand as the supporting elements and as the keystone of the arch, and the other smaller forms become the pillars. Not so apparent, however, is the highly integrated musical structure that is provided by the continued use of the hymn tune in an imaginative, but sometimes nearly esoteric fashion. The tune is presented in its entirety in each of the seven verse settings, and it is strongly foreshadowed in the opening *sinfonia*. There the theme is not only presaged by the repeated bass pattern that opens the piece, but may also be found hidden within the upper notes, as shown in Example 75. The same melody, exposed in the first violin and ornamented, appears in the next phrase, and the closing notes of the hymn tune may be extracted from the remainder of the *sinfonia*. The melody itself appears in a fairly straightforward fashion in each of the seven verses, and it is the combination of voice and instrumental parts that gives strength, complexity, and variety to the settings. The statement at the beginning of each verse is always offered without much complication *(Ex. 76)*. Contrapuntal involvement or interesting accompaniment later

Ex. 75 Bach, *Sinfonia* of *Christ lag in Todesbanden* (notes in parentheses show a possible thematic statement)

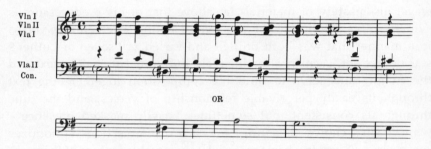

Ex. 76 Opening statements of verses from Bach's *Christ lag in Todesbanden*

causes some loss of the thread, but not until the theme has been firmly reestablished at the start of each new section. If the seven verses bear a close relationship through the discernible use of the chorale tune, they also show great variety in the assortment of styles that Bach chose as their vehicles. The opening chorus is a large chorale fantasia during the first half of which the string orchestra plays a highly contrasting accompaniment to the voices—doubled here and at some other points by a *cornetto* and three trombones— but doubling the chorale tune on all entrances except those given in augmented values. The second half of the opening verse is a hallelujah chorus in fugal style that makes interesting use of hocket at several points. The soprano-alto duo that follows emphasizes the descending semitone that opens the chorale melody and that was evident in the opening *sinfonia*. Bach's expressions of grief are often set apart by such short descending patterns; his intention here is heightened by the insistent repetition of such pairs in the *continuo,* some few of which deviate for obviously harmonic reasons *(Ex. 77),* but which intensify, in their full-octave descent, the vision of death. Verse three is reminiscent of the chorale prelude in its insistent reiteration of two simultaneous rhythmic patterns; one in the violins, the other in the *continuo,* against which the tenor vocal line inserts phrases of the chorale, each separated from the next by the dogged rhythmic patterns of the instruments. Verse four adopts the motet style. The altos present the melody in a simple manner, and the remaining voices move about them with figures and themes that derive from the chorale. Verse five opens with an extension of the descending semitone, now a group of six chromatic notes that obviously are a continuation of the motivic pair. The descending group is typical of passacaglia patterns which, in turn, are the favored patterns upon which to compose music representing grief and death, not only with Bach but with many other Baroque composers. Whittaker notes that in setting the word *Kreuz* (Cross), Bach uses a longer than usual phrase to show Christ's hanging on the Cross,[42] but he fails to mention the use of the standard device

Ex.77 Bass of Verse II, Bach's *Christ lag in Todesbanden*

42. *Ibid.,* ı, 212.

of "crossing" the principal tone with sharped pitches *(Ex. 78).* Verse six has two voices in free imitative writing against a vigorous dotted rhythm in the bass. This rhythm must, however, accommodate itself to the basic rhythm of the upper parts and, therefore, be performed as a long-short triplet combination. The final verse gives us, for the first time, the chorale qua chorale. Accompanied by the full orchestra, this is a sturdy summation of the entire work, emphasizing once again the basic simplicity of the Lutheran expression, untouched by outside influences.

Let us again recall that both Tunder and Krieger wrote works based on *Ein' feste Burg ist unser Gott,* and that both of them felt that the writing of variations best served their needs. Bach used the text of Salomo Franck (1659–1725) which is based on the Luther verses. His first version, from 1716, does not include all the stanzas of the hymn; the revision, dating from 1730, adds the missing first and third stanzas. It is this later version that contains the impressive choruses that are among the cantata's most interesting features *(MSO,* i, 152–82). The instrumentation is that most suitable to a festive piece, the bright and penetrating sounds of trumpets and timpani, and oboes sometimes replaced by *oboi d'amore* or an *oboe da caccia (taille).* In the opening chorus only the brass-percussion group, the oboes, and strings make up the orchestra. There is no instrumental piece preceding the chorus, and the text of the Reformation's *mot de passe* sounds firmly from the beginning. This chorus divides into nine unequal sections, one for each musical phrase, including the repetition of the *Stollen.* Each of these sections features a fugal exposition of a figured version of the chorale phrase, terminating in a statement, without ornamentation, that appears in canon between the first trumpet and the organ pedal. The sounding of the Lutheran rallying cry in stentorian tones, and from the extremes of the orchestral palette, must have given a special satisfaction to Bach who, as one of the most dedicated musicians of that faith, served up this special treat for a major festival.[43] The chorale tune, often elongated and figurated at the cadence points, appears again in the duo for soprano and bass which follows. The phrases of the chorale, sung by the soprano, enter at intervals against the constantly flowing and extremely florid bass

43. The revised version appears to have been made for the 200th Anniversary of the Augsburg Confession in 1730 or, less probably, nine years later for another, lesser festival. See Philipp Spitta, *Johann Sebastian Bach,* trans. Clara Bell and J. A. Fuller-Maitland (3 vols., London: Novello, 1884–1885; reprint, New York: Dover Publications, 1951), ii, 470.

Ex. 78 *Ibid.*, Verse V, suspension and crossing as pictorial-aural text intensifications

des   Kreu - - zes,   des Kreu - zes Stamm

solo that so thoroughly dominates the movement that Bach saw fit to reinforce the soprano line with an oboe playing a further figuration on the chorale phrases. The following aria and arioso for bass are different from those we have seen in Bach's examples heretofore, for he reverts to the style of the sustained accompaniment recitative[44] for *continuo* alone. The same kind of accompaniment supports the aria for soprano as well, thus preparing the way by its simplicity for the massive chorus that follows. Dealing with the conflict between the forces of Satan and simple Christian faith, the third verse of the hymn is strongly projected by the entire choir in unison—a treatment to be found nowhere else in the Bach works—against an active orchestral setting that makes prominent use of long runs and leaping passages for reeds and strings, punctuated by militant soundings of the trumpets and timpani. Whittaker appropriately refers to the chorus as a battle scene. If the unceasing orchestral movement really was meant to portray the forces of evil, and the direct, unanimous utterance of the text to represent good, the fact that the orchestra has the last word must be laid to Bach's recognition of the necessity to produce a balanced musical setting, even at the loss of some part of his symbolism. After such a powerful chorus, there is little left for the composer to do but exhort the faithful to stand fast, as he does in the recitative and arioso for tenor, to promise the peace and blessedness that may be the prize for those who do so, in a duet for tenor and alto, and to summarize the work in the concluding chorale. A final chorale verse often seems, when it lacks parts for all the instruments, to be a weak anticlimax following a most forceful statement of faith or commentary on the Gospel or Epistle *de tempore*. There was inevitably more to the per-

44. To some late Baroque composers, recitative did not fall into the simple classifications of the past; *secco* and *accompagnato (stromentato)*. Their use of descriptive instructions indicates that our terms of reference should be broadened to include the following: *recitativo secco*, skeletal harmonic punctuation assigned to the *continuo: recitativo secco stromentato*, skeletal harmonic punctuation assigned to strings and *continuo; recitativo accompagnato*, sustained chordal accompaniment by the *continuo* group or *recitativo accompagnato stromentato*. See Example 79 for samples of the two *stromentato* types.

formance than appeared on paper, for the entire orchestra was expected to join in with the most appropriate vocal part, adding both color and strength to the final choral section, and the verse that closed a cantata was always chosen carefully for its qualities of summation. Some of the chorale tunes themselves had a strong seasonal association and their verses were able to intensify that association in the minds of the congregation. Rather than coming to the listener as a redundancy, the closing chorale served as an aphorism: inevitable, pithy, and satisfying. In a cantata that was not based upon a chorale, the *Schlusschoral* was a brief homily; in one that derived from a chorale, the concluding verse drove home the final point in the argument that had been developed throughout the course of the composition.

It is often asserted that after Bach's death the cantata deteriorated into a work of less importance. This is true, but it was not the lack of ability of the other composers that caused the cantata to become insignificant. The fact is simply that such music lost its important position in the church service. The combined forces of the Pietists, to whom figural music was an unwelcome intrusion, and of the logical supporters of rationalism, to whom both the elaborate music and the interpretation of the text through flights of poetic fancy was anathema, turned Lutheran music to a new musical path. They sounded the death knell of the exegetical *Kirchenmusik* and caused the choirs, orchestras, and dedicated (or at least skilled) composers to be replaced by congregational singing supported by uninspired organists. The style that Bach perpetuated was an old one in his own time, and all that he produced was a refinement of what had gone before. It is an oversimplification to say that he created nothing new, but to suggest that everything he produced was an improvement upon its earlier counterpart is certainly no great exaggeration. The interest in church music, by the time Bach went to Leipzig, was strongly inclined toward the Italian "modern" style, one that Bach knew but could not force himself to adopt to the exclusion of what he thought was fitting and proper.

It would be interesting to see what the typical church works of these contemporaries of Bach were like. The lack of time and space, and of large amounts of such music in modern editions makes this an impossibility. A look at one such eminent figure may serve to expose a small amount of such music that has passed without much notice.

As musical director for Frederick the Great, Karl Heinrich Graun (1704–1759) was expected to produce a constant stream of operas and chamber music. These things he apparently did with much success, earning the esteem of the Berlin public and the King. For his *Te Deum* and his widely acclaimed Passion oratorio, *Der Tod Jesu (The death of Jesus)*, he has earned recognition even in our own time, and we may assume that these works are typical of what he thought most suitable for special occasions, inasmuch as they date from the last decade of his life and are the largest church works we know from his pen. Passing largely unnoticed, however, are his compositions for the regular activities of the church—his motets and cantatas, his Magnificats and Masses. Perhaps one reason these lesser works have been ignored is the belief that his more widely known festival works represented his style for church music—a rash presumption, for it has not been true of other composers—and that examination of the lesser compositions would bring to light nothing new. This is not the case. Four of his motets, intended for school and amateur use, were published in several volumes. We may assume that they saw wide distribution since they were printed in several volumes that appeared in different years.[45] The works are all SATB and were printed without *continuo*, so they represented a continuation of the practice of unaccompanied singing, certainly not the modern Italian ideal. Two of them are made up of a pair of fugal sections, the second of which is, in each case, simply a modified restatement of the first, beginning in a related key and returning to the original key by the end of the piece.[46] Another begins with a fugue and has a slow homophonic second part. The fourth reverses this procedure by placing the chordal chorus first and the fugue last. Whether the pieces were ever used in connection with a religious service is unknown; they are simple enough for the purposes of their publication, but they could well have seen church use during Graun's lifetime.

We will never know how many cantatas Graun wrote, for, like other composers who produced for the church during that time, his works survive only in manuscript form, and many of them are not extant. A set of five cantatas ascribed to him, although a number of different hands are evident in the copying of the manuscripts, is found in the Öffentliche Wissenschaftliche Bibliothek, (formerly Deutsche Staatsbibliothek), Berlin, the whole set identified as MS 8182.[47] Four of the cantatas are for the Christmas season and the fifth is for

45. *Vierstimmige Motetten und Arien in Partitur* . . . ed. J. A. Hiller (Leipzig: Dyckischen Buchhandlung, 1776, 1779, 1780).
46. See p. 331 and note 17, Chapter X, for further description of one of these motets.

47. The contents are described in greater detail in Elwyn A. Wienandt, "*Das Licht scheinet* . . . , Two settings by K. H. Graun," *The Music Review*, xxi/2 (May, 1960), 85 – 93.

the Eighteenth Sunday after Trinity. The Christmas works are of the dimensions that would be expected for a major festival of the church, employing orchestra, chorus, and soloists in a combination of fugal settings, solo recitatives and arias, and chorales. Except in his largest works, such as *Der Tod Jesu* and a Christmas oratorio, *Mache dich auf, werde Licht (Open thyself, let there be light)*,[48] he used the chorus no more than twice, usually in an opening fugal chorus and customary *Schlusschoral*. Even there his mastery of a variety of choral styles may be seen. A nonimitative chorus featuring paired voices, high against low, as the middle section of a *da capo* chorus in homophonic style, is used in his second setting of the Christmas text *Das Licht scheinet in der Finsterniss (The light shines in the darkness)*. At the other extreme, double fugues for SATB choir are fairly common for the major festivals. For services of no unusual significance, Graun reduced his forces from full orchestra to strings and his singers to a few selected soloists, except for the simple chorale setting which called upon the choir to close the composition. Such a piece is the cantata *O Gott du Brunquell aller Liebe (O God, thou wellspring of all kindness)*, the work from MS 8182 that he wrote for the Eighteenth Sunday after Trinity. The text is only vaguely related to that of an appropriate Epistle (I John 3:1–8) which begins: *Sehet, welch eine Liebe hat uns der Vater erzeiget, dass wir Gottes Kinder sollen heissen! Darum kennet euch die Welt nicht; denn sie kennet ihn nicht.* ("Behold, what manner of love the Father hath bestowed upon us, that we should be called the sons of God: therefore the world knoweth us not, because it knew him not.") The cantata calls for two soloists, tenor and bass, who share an opening duet accompanied by string orchestra. A recitative for tenor precedes a *da capo* aria for bass with obbligato solo violin and *continuo*. A bass recitative and arioso lead into the closing chorale, where the choir makes its only appearance. The variety of styles available to accompany recitative[49] is found in this short cantata. The opening tenor recitative is in the style of *recitativo secco* for *continuo* alone, but the later section for bass begins with *recitativo secco stromentato*, becomes *recitativo accompagnato* after six measures, and concludes as fully accompanied arioso *(Ex. 79)*.

If any single accusation could be made against church composers of the second quarter of the eighteenth century, it might be that they

48. Manuscript in Library of Congress. A portion of the work, with English text, is published with the title *To Us A Child* *is Given*, ed. Elwyn A. Wienandt (New York: Carl Fischer, 1965).
49. See n. 44 *supra*.

wrote in a perfunctory manner, adopting more and more the facile and convenient methods of popular style, excluding the chorus from general participation or, when using it, letting the formulas of technical writing overcome the thoughtful text settings that had been developed by workers before this time. The changing times had taken the composer out of the church, and had put the second-rate musician into his place. The very attitude that caused the Leipzig officials to favor Bach's modern contemporaries, among them Telemann, for the position at the Thomaskirche, and to employ Bach only after the others were not available, tended to lessen the interest in serious church music on the part of the musician and the church member alike. The world was becoming secularized to a point where the musical concerts that were provided as part of the morning service could now be found elsewhere, often by better musicians than the church could boast. No wonder, then, that church composition deteriorated. Fame, prestige, wealth, and position awaited the successful composer of operas and chamber works; hardship, recalcitrant choirboys, critical church officials, and professional oblivion were the lot of the old-fashioned church musician. It was the end of a truly great era.

There is still one question to be discussed, if not answered, con-

Ex. 79 Styles of recitative in Graun, *O Gott, du Brunquell aller Liebe*

grös - ter Un - ruh Kreuz und un - ge - mach   muss un - ser Ru - he und Ver-gnü-gen

blü - hen   auch ob das al - ler grös - ter   Lei - den   soll uns durch dein-er Geis-tes

Kraft von die-ser Lie-be jeh-mahle scheid-en.   Ja   auch der Tod der al - les Trennt findt

cerning the performance of chorales in the cantata. Some writers have implied that the reason chorales were inserted into cantatas and oratorios, and used at their conclusions as well, was to permit the congregation to join the choir in singing familiar and appropriate material. There is no evidence that such was the case; unfortunately, evidence to the contrary is also lacking. In the face of such an impasse, many have felt impelled to deliver themselves of opinions based on "reason." Let us examine the problem one more time with the hope that, if the correct answer is not reached here, a rebuttal will be forthcoming.

The solution must lie partly with some evidence of the ability of the congregation to participate in the singing of even a simple chorale setting in a piece of concerted music. Schweitzer, in studying the number of chorales that could have fallen to the congregation in a normal service, produced some answers that offend our preconceived notions. In the sixteenth century, he says, the Wittenberg congregation left the chorales to be sung by the choir and, as a rule, sang not at all. In Erfurt, and other places, the choir and congregation sang *alternatim* between the Epistle and Gospel—the choir singing liturgical music and the congregation singing chorales that were suitable *de tempore*—but we see that "five or six chorales in the year sufficed for this, since the same chorale was used on each Sunday during that particular period."[50] He goes on to say that in churches that had no choir more attention was given to what the congregation sang, "since in that case the *Kyrie,* the *Gloria* and the *Agnus Dei* were sung in the corresponding German chorales. But here again, as a rule, fifteen or at most twenty chorales, which had been laid down, once for all, for their particular Sundays, sufficed for the whole year."[51]

If there was truly such a small number of chorales to serve as congregational song, how did the chorale find such consistent favor as a structural feature of the cantata? If its inclusion in the pre-sermon *Kirchenmusik* was to mean anything to the congregation, it had to meet them on one of two grounds: either the tune had to rouse some deep-seated emotional response without reference to words, or the simple setting of a verse of text had to convey a thought appropriate to the entire composition or to the segment to which it was attached. The former possibility presupposes the knowledge of a group of tunes that would rouse the congregation with their affective relationship; the latter simply requires clear presentation of text by the choir. Now it is true that the number of tunes intended for use by the congregation, both at home and in church, increased considerably in the sixteenth and seventeenth centuries as a large number of songbooks appeared on the market. The availability of the songs was no guarantee that they would be sung well, or in great variety. There was no place other than the church where an adult could learn the tunes and, outside the few *cantica de tempore* that were commonly sung there, the chorales were rendered in polyphonic form or, at the very least, with the melody at first hidden in the tenor, by the choir. The regular use of a limited number of chorale tunes in cantata literature seems to point to the possibility that certain melodies carried emotional messages in them, easily perceived by the congregation and commonly employed

50. Schweitzer, *op. cit.,* i, 31.   51. *Ibid.*

by the composer. Still, if the chorale melody carried a message in it-self, the words might be judged superfluous, and instrumental rendi-tions could have served almost as well as intermediate chorales, closing chorales, or *cantus firmi*. The careful selection of texts, often verses that were chosen to strengthen the theme of the entire cantata,[52] proves that text and melody went hand in hand, the melody calling up a general mood and the text giving a specific illumination to the cantata text and, through it, to the Gospel or Epistle of the day.

Not all of the chorale tunes used in cantatas were of the most fa-miliar group, not even those set in simple four-part harmony with the melody in the top voice. It exceeds our credibility to imagine a com-poser making allowance for or, worse yet, planning his composition so that the congregation, made up of untrained, undisciplined, and unrehearsed nonmusicians should join in the singing of a chorale in the midst of a complex, artistic creation such as a cantata or oratorio, and to one of the less used verses at that. Why then, one may ask, did composers resort to simple four-part settings in their chorale verses? First, let it be remembered that this was not always the case. Many of the earlier examples of the cantata that we considered, when they closed with a chorale at all, used it in *concertato* style or as the founda-tion tune in an imitative texture, both of which would be beyond the reach of a congregation from the standpoint of when to sing, without even considering what they would find to sing in such a piece. When we remember that the inclination of the Baroque composer was to give only those directions that would be understood by the musicians, leaving unwritten any practice of the time in instrumentation, dynam-ics, and tempo,[53] it is not surprising that economy of effort and ma-terials was practiced by composers and copyists whenever possible. If instruments were to play the same notes as were being sung throughout an entire piece, there was no reason for the composer to take the extra effort required to write out parts for music. There was no reason why the congregation should have sung along with the trained choir on a closing or intermediate chorale. If they were not prevented from interrupting what amounted to a religious concert by simple good manners, they should have been restrained by the very purpose

52. The case of the chorale verse selected by Hammerschmidt to conclude his *Woher nehmen wir Brot?* (cf. p. 236) illustrates the close relationship, one that may be found in many other instances.
53. Readers not familiar with these tradi-tions can find them summarized in Thur-ston Dart, *The Interpretation of Music*, 67–71, and Elwyn A. Wienandt, "Baroque Arrangements," *The Instrumentalist*, xiv/5 (January, 1960), 36ff.

of the chorale verse, for it was there to synthesize the subject at a climax of the composition or to summarize it at the conclusion.[54]

The publication of the cantata text, and with it the chorale verse that was involved, seems not to have been sufficiently widespread to bear on this matter. Still, it might be mentioned that the purpose of such publication was not to permit the congregation to participate, but to occupy themselves by examining it. Certainly the general publication and distribution of such texts was not a common practice.

Finally, it has been theorized that, because of the presence of the *fermata* at the ends of some phrases, one may deduce the participation of the congregation. This is apparently related to the belief that the *fermata* applied to the congregation more than to anyone else; however, there is confusion over what that function was. The folklore of the *fermata* is considerable, and quite unsupported by anything beyond word-of-mouth perpetuation of the unproven. The most popular idea assigns to the *fermata* the function of prolongation, leading to the idea that final tones of chorale phrases are held, and leading again to a painful kind of rendition of those noble tunes. The propensity of congregations for retarding the flow of music is well enough known to render ridiculous such a claim, but the fable persists still, and some performances of chorale tunes suffer accordingly. The prolongation of a note or rest is not the only function of the *fermata*, and its use was more varied in earlier centuries than it is now; it is not beyond the limit of sensible conjecture to give this symbol yet another function. We have already noted *fermate* in the block-chord passages of Renaissance music where the mark was used to set apart either the unusual character of the music or some distinctive reference, personal or dogmatic. At other times, the following additional uses have been prevalent: (1) to indicate the end of a piece, but not to carry any meaning of the extension of time; (2) to indicate the lengthening of a note or rest; and (3) to indicate the point of ending in a piece that contains repeats, or that has either a *dal segno* or *da capo* return. With such a variety of meanings, one other should not be difficult to accept. A clear reference to it, nearly a century ago, has done little to stem the tide of phrase mutilation. As only one of a number of comments on *fermata* functions, one article states: *Auch im Choral hat die Fermate nur*

54. It must be mentioned, on the other hand, that an opposite opinion of congregational participation is presented in Charles Sanford Terry, *Bach: The Cantatas* *and Oratorios* (Musical Pilgrim Series) 2 vols. (London: Oxford University Press, 1926), II, 8.

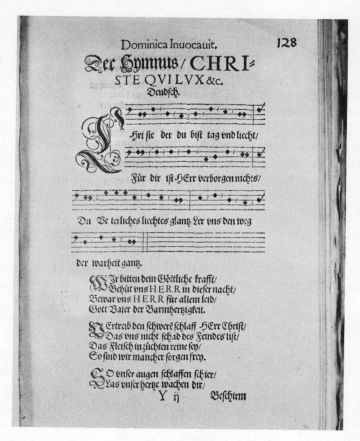

PLATE 6a. *Chorale melody from Keuchenthal's* Kirchen-Gesenge Latinisch und Deudsch . . ., 1573, f. 128, *using vertical strokes to mark phrase endings.*

die Bedeutung eines Schlusszeichens; sie deutet hier nichts weiter an, als eine Endigung der Verszeilen.[55] (Also in the chorale the *fermata* means only a mark of conclusion; it means here nothing other than the end of a line of verse.) Nothing could be more explicit, but why should the end of a line be so marked? The manner in which a chorale tune was printed in relation to its text made necessary a mark that would distinguish the point at which text and music were to end in the verses after the first (see Plate VI) since the music was underlaid with only the words to the first verse. Following verses appeared below, their phrase endings marked by a slanting line that corresponded to the position of the *fermata* in the music. The singer, no matter which verse of text he was following, had a signal that corresponded to an-

55. *Musikalisches Conversations-Lexicon,* ed. Hermann Mendel (Berlin: R. Oppen- heim, 1873), III, 492.

PLATE 6b. Exordium *and opening dialogue of Keuchenthal's St. Matthew Passion. No vertical strokes are used in the music since the pieces have all the necessary text underlaid.*

other signal in the music itself. The fact that the same signal was not used in both text and music does not indicate poor organization, but, rather, a refinement of earlier practice when the line was used to separate both the musical phrases and their text equivalents. Early examples, even those in Schein's *Leipziger Cantional* of 1627, inserted a vertical line to mark the end of the musical phrase *(Ex. 80a)*, but when the use of regular measure-barring entered the picture, the line that had served could be confused with the barline and another device had to take its place *(Ex. 80b)*. What was more natural than to adopt an already convenient symbol, the *fermata*, which had served a number of situations already? There was no reason to change the mark of equivalence in the text, and the line, slightly slanted, was retained. The combination may be seen as a happy compromise, confusing only the unprepared readers of later centuries. Some of the confusion had been

281

Ex. 80 *a)* Chorale melody, unbarred, with phrase endings indicated by vertical strokes.

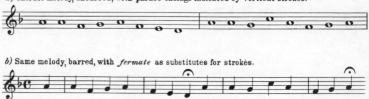

b) Same melody, barred, with *fermate* as substitutes for strokes.

compounded by the retention of the *fermata* in some choral settings, and even in the melodic line of chorale preludes for organ. Those practices, however, were not by any means consistent. Many examples may be found in which no mark of phrase ending is included in the choral version of the chorale.

A practice has developed of performing Baroque church works, in concert halls and on phonograph records, with both organ and harpsichord, sometimes with the former as a tutti instrument and the latter realizing the bass in recitative passages. A comment is in order here, even at the risk of simply stating personal preference. The general practice of the Baroque period sets the organ aside as an instrument for the church and, rarely, for the wealthy private establishment; the harpsichord stands at the other extreme as an instrument of secular use. The employment of an instrument that was at home in the salon and the opera house to support solo singing in compositions intended solely for church use is a distortion of instrumental function that should be strongly discouraged. That there may be a place for harpsichord in the performances of eighteenth-century oratorio is not a point at issue, for those works were performed in secular surroundings and absorbed many features of the opera house in their presentation. But that the opera house should, by some reverse logic, be brought regularly into the church is insupportable.

Chapter IX

The Oratorio Before Haydn

IN one sense the discussion of oratorio should have only a subordinate place in a book devoted to the development of music for the church. Only at certain stages of its development did oratorio have any direct connection with the church service. Many times, even though the subjects were religious in nature, the performances were not planned or produced as part of regular church observances, although they were sometimes held in church buildings. If our consideration of oratorio were to be limited to works that had a liturgical function or even to works that were performed in places of worship, our attention would be confined to only a fraction of those works that are commonly known. The roots of oratorio reach far back into a comparatively unknown period, and we must pause to examine it before going on to the standard repertory.

It is possible to trace the history of oratorio back to the liturgical dramas of the Middle Ages, works in which dramatic situations were presented musically. Neither these early beginnings nor the more familiar dialogue-*laude* that were sung in the Oratorio della Vallicella — St. Philip Neri's church of Santa Maria containing one of the halls *(oratorii)* from which this form may have taken its name — added much to the development of choral participation.[1] Nor is much to be learned from the reappraisal of the epochal *Rappresentazione di Anima e di Corpo (Dialogues between the soul and body)* by Emilio de' Cavalieri (1550–1602) which, for all its elaborate display of new techniques, is more an opera than it is an oratorio. The entire period before, roughly, the middle of the seventeenth century may be summed up as follows: the experiments that led toward oratorio sampled the same ingredients that went into opera — monodic solo singing, dialogue, choruses,

---

1. These early types are described briefly   in *HD*, 516, and in greater detail in *Grove's*, VI, 248.

and, in some cases, staged scenic works that included dancing—
although oratorio divided into two distinct branches itself. One of
these, the Latin oratorio, was a projection of liturgical ideas, usually
in prose, inoffensive to the Church at least in language and content;
the other, the *oratorio volgare,* was usually a poetic rendition in the
vernacular, more interesting to the general public but less appropriate
for presentation in the church itself. The latter type appears to have
been the more popular, inasmuch as the lay public, without knowledge of Latin, could not enjoy the former or be instructed by it. It
may seem strange then, that the Latin oratorios of Giacomo Carissimi
(1605–1674) mark the first important step toward oratorio as we have
come to recognize it, but musical developments do not necessarily
reflect public taste. Rather, acceptance by a composer's peers and the
use of his ideas by his students play an important part. Coupled with
the undeniable qualities that set Carissimi's oratorios apart from other
works of their generation is the fortuitous circumstance of performance in the German College *(Collegium Germanicum-Hungaricum)* in
Rome. Carissimi was *maestro di cappella* at the Church of San Apol-
linare, which belonged to the College, from 1628 until his death.

The oratorios of Carissimi make a convenient starting point for
comparison because it is with them that the external similarities to
later examples are first clearly apparent. They are dramatic works,
shorter than those of a century later, based on a biblical subject that
is often, but not exclusively, taken from the Old Testament. The story
is presented as a series of expository, reflective, or descriptive segments. The exposition of the dramatic idea is given to a character
(or sometimes several voices representing a single character) called
the *historicus,* who relates the story as it appears in the Bible. In some
works of this century the narrator was called the *testo.* Dialogues,
commentaries, and explanations are assigned to other solo voices and
the chorus. The orchestra has the instrumentation of that most convenient of all Baroque groups, the trio sonata, and it is more a supporting factor than one of competing interest. The instruments are heard
independently, however, in introductory and interior *sinfonie.*

There is no one work by Carissimi that can be singled out as typical of the entire surviving group of compositions that we find under
the names *historia* and oratorio. Two examples should suffice, though,
to illustrate their principal features. *Baltazar,*[2] the story of Belshazzar's great feast, his judgment by the moving finger, and his death,

2. Giacomo Carissimi, *Historia di Baltazar,*   per la Storia della Musica, 1955).
ed. Lino Bianchi (Rome: Istituto Italiano

as related in Daniel 5:1–30, divides the biblical and poetic materials in the following manner: An instrumental *sinfonia*, made up of stereotyped figures that bear no relationship to the rest of the composition, precedes the opening scriptural exposition by the *historicus*. This recitative is supported only by *continuo*, as are all others whether they are sung by the narrator, Baltazar, Daniel, or two voices that share the duties of the *historicus* in a quasi-canonic section. The distinction between the *continuo*-accompanied recitative and trio sonata-accompanied solo is made according to the source of the text; that taken from Scripture is sung without treble instruments; that interpolated as description or commentary is accompanied by the entire instrumental group. The chorus, SSATB, acts in the capacity of a crowd, never presenting expository material, but singing Belshazzar's praises and supplying the moral at the conclusion of the work.

Carissimi's setting of the story of Dives and Lazarus (Luke 16: 19–31) is built on a more elaborate scale. The *Historia divitis*[3] calls for two choruses, SSTB and SATB. There are no instances in which the two groups are heard separately as choruses *a 4*. They perform together regardless of whether they sing a separate closing chorus, or whether they comment on the action either as impersonal observers or as the mocking demons that comprise the *turba*. A few lines of one dialogue will illustrate the manner in which Carissimi brought the chorus into the story without destroying the continuity, and a brief section of music will show the relative complexity of the parts. The dialogue opens with Dives, facing certain death, asking how he shall fare in the hereafter:

DIVES:	Where, where shall I live?
SOLO:	In fiery furnaces.
CHORUS:	In fiery furnaces.
DIVES:	What feasts shall I eat?
SOLO:	Snakes and vipers.
CHORUS:	Snakes and vipers.
DIVES:	What wine shall I drink?
SOLO:	Pitch and sulphur.
CHORUS:	Pitch and sulphur.
DIVES:	On what couch shall I lie?
SOLO:	On red-hot iron.
CHORUS:	On red-hot iron.

3. Giacomo Carissimi, *Historia divitis (Dives malus)*, ed. Lino Bianchi (Rome: Istituto Italiano per la Storia della Musica, 1958).

DIVES: What purple shall I wear?
SOLO: Flames, flames.
CHORUS: Flames, flames.

And so on. Dives exhausts all hope of earthly comforts and pleasures
and resigns himself to his inevitable end. The demons, solo and choral, mock him again, and the thread of the story is given back to the
historicus. No effort is made to describe every sensitive fragment of
text with a musical counterpart. Except for such passages as an obvious diatonic descent of a twelfth in the phrase *descende nobiscum in
infernum,* and the florid description of the dreadful demons *(Ex. 81),*
text-painting is rarely employed. There are no set numbers in the
entire oratorio except for the final chorus. Each of the text sections
flows smoothly into the next. The music also connects smoothly,
although each of the sections closes with a firm cadence. In a few cases
there are instrumental passages that connect the vocal sections. During the opening exposition, the lengthy recitative for the *historicus* is
broken by an instrumental interlude. In a number of other cases an
instrumental link, made up of repeated cadence formulas, relieves the
ear momentarily. Despite these interruptions the composition is a
continuous piece of music that moves back and forth among narrator,
principal characters, and *turba.* The sections of dialogue that fall between the narrations are, except for the few biblical conversations,
set in highly dramatic poetic form, thereby serving as exceptions to
the generally accepted idea that the Latin oratorio was usually cast
in prose. Repetition of a solo passage at a new pitch level is a common
device, one that is paralleled by the choral repetition of solo statements
in the chorus of demons. A similar use of melody is often found in
the restatement of passages that seem alike, but that are not exact
repetitions. The story is advanced in two ways: the narrator provides
the broad outline by singing the biblical version in recitative, sometimes assisted by other characters who are named in the biblical
source. Other solo voices, even when they are not identified with a
known character, are given some prominence, and the chorus, in its
role as commentator, conscience, or *turba,* reflects on the action,
heckles the protagonist, and pronounces the moralistic ending, the
last partly in polyphonic style. The orchestra has no function other
than to support the voices and, only occasionally, to provide slight
relief from them. Generally, the solo voices are set with *continuo* only
but, where intensification is sought or repetition is used, the strings

Ex. 81. G Carissimi, *Historia Divitis*, 72-73

"What spectacles shall I enjoy? Terrible demons."

Used with permission of Istituto Italiano per la Storia della Musica, Roma.

may also close phrases with the voice or even accompany it with something other than literal doublings. The solo style varies freely between
recitativo accompagnato and arioso, both types being underlaid with a
bass that seems to be repetitious, even approximating ground bass
patterns on occasion. This is more illusion than fact, for the common
appearance of bass notes moving a third, fourth, or fifth within a
single key inevitably takes on the appearance of deliberate repetition
while it may be simply the regular movement toward cadences within

clearly defined key areas. The variety that is found in these works should make it evident that not all of Carissimi's music was cut from the same pattern as his more widely known *Jephtha* (*MSO*, 85– 90).

Two illustrious students of Carissimi must be mentioned briefly before we pass on to an examination of the more fruitful German oratorio. Alessandro Scarlatti and Marc-Antoine Charpentier (1634?– 1704) developed the pattern of their teacher: the former worked principally in the vernacular style in Italy, the latter produced both Latin and French works. The fact that Carissimi died before Scarlatti's fourteenth birthday indicates that their relationship must have been brief, at best. While Scarlatti's subjects were no less religious than Carissimi's, his titles reveal less dependence upon biblical subjects, for he is concerned with conversions, martyrdoms, and the lives of saints in a number of the twenty titles in Dent's catalogue.[4] Dent says of the texts:

> As a rule the libretti of the oratorios are not very inspiring. They read like inferior opera-books, and indeed, except that the operas are in three acts and the oratorios in two, the only difference is in the absence of professedly comic characters, and of the formal statement in which the author protests that the words *Fato, Dio, Deità &c.*, are only *scherzi poetici* and imply nothing contrary to the Catholic Faith.[5]

Whether Scarlatti can be credited with vast improvements in the oratorio style is not so important as the fact that in his works we can see musical ideas that are far advanced over those of Carissimi. For one thing, instrumental music was a matter of greater interest with Scarlatti, and he provided a more elaborate orchestra, which achieved considerable independence from the voices in overtures, interludes, and accompaniments. He even wrote an air in the oratorio *La SS^ma Vergine del Rosario* to be accompanied "by two violas and a nightingale, the latter being treated in the toy-symphony style, at the player's discretion."[6] While Carissimi's solo voices moved freely between recitative and arioso, the Scarlatti pattern included the fully developed *aria da capo* that was common to his operas and cantatas, as well as his oratorios. This line of development, closely paralleling the Neapolitan opera, proved popular with composers who produced for both the theater and the church until the end of the Baroque period.

Carissimi's influence spread also to France through the works of

4. Dent, *op. cit.*, 210f.   6. *Ibid.*, 98.
5. *Ibid.*, 97.

his pupil, Marc-Antoine Charpentier, who produced at least thirty-four works that have been classified as oratorios.[7] Fourteen of these are *historiae*, nine are *cantica*, six are *dialogi* and five are *méditations*. The last are too brief to concern us here, and the *dialogi* are not typical of most oratorios in their small cast of characters and absence of a *historicus*. Among the *historiae* are some of Charpentier's larger works that call for as much as double ·string orchestra plus flutes, oboes, bassoons, and, at times, trumpets. None of these is available in a complete, yet practical modern edition, but a portion of one, *La Reniement de St. Pierre (The denial of St. Peter)* is printed in *TEM* 42. Convenient to our purposes, however, is his *In Nativitatem D[omini] N[ostri] C[hristi] Canticum*,[8] an excellent example of Charpentier's combination of French and Italian styles. As befits a relatively simple setting of the portion of the Christmas story given in Luke 2:8–16, it avoids elaborate display. The instrumental sections use only the trio sonata as do the choruses, an aria, and an arioso. The remaining sections, two recitatives and an aria, are accompanied by the *continuo* only. Harking back to the practice of Carissimi is the assignment of two voices to the part of the *historicus*, as Charpentier does in the first recitative for two sopranos. Other Italianate features are found in an imitative chorus in motet style and in the *bel canto* style of some of his solos. Hitchcock has indicated that, "on the other hand, the gay minuets of the prelude and the postlude, the *rondeau* structures of the march and the first shepherd's chorus, the binary forms, dance rhythms, and solo-chorus repetitions of the shepherds' air . . . are drawn from French sources, as is the general atmosphere of childlike sweetness and simplicity that pervades the whole work."[9]

The orderly arrangement of sections within the work shows the same kind of attention to inaudible organization that was present in the arch forms we have examined. The composition is in two sections (or scenes) that are separated by a march. Each of these sections is made up of a recitative, an aria, and a chorus, and the entire composition is enclosed by a *praeludium* and *ritornelle*. The first chorus is SSAATB; the second, SSATB. Two sopranos and a baritone are required as solo voices, and the work is within the grasp of an average

7. H. Wiley Hitchcock, "The Latin Oratorios of Marc-Antoine Charpentier," *The Musical Quarterly*, XLI/1 (January, 1955), 41–65.

8. Marc-Antoine Charpentier, *Song of the* *Birth of Our Lord Jesus Christ*, ed. H. Wiley Hitchcock (St. Louis: Concordia Publishing House, 1959).

9. *Ibid.*, [3].

school or church group. What Charpentier had introduced into France could have been the first example of an interesting line of development. Unfortunately, the idea of oratorio seemed to excite little interest there, and no significant works appeared for a long time after Charpentier's death. Instead, the efforts of the next generation of composers were directed toward the development of the grand motet, a form that will be examined in the next chapter.

The introduction of Italian style into Germany, and with it the establishment of an interest in setting biblical stories to continuous music in oratorio fashion, coincided with the return of Heinrich Schütz from his Italian studies and with his production, during succeeding years, of large works in this genre. By the time Schütz reached old age, the period from which most of his important works date, the German Passion had firmly established itself. Its transformation from the dramatic and motet styles that had been common in its early period to one approximating the Italian style—or at least borrowing freely from elements of that style—was completed with Schütz, not in his Passion settings, but in his oratorios. It is necessary, then, that we examine a few other German Passions before passing on to the large compositions of that significant figure in German church music in order to see the extent to which their styles were incorporated into the oratorio or followed another direction.

A setting of the Passion by Ambrosius Beber (fl. 1610–1620), *Das Leiden Unsers Herren Jesu Christi nach dem Heiligen Evangelisten Marco (The Passion of our Lord Jesus Christ according to the Evangelist St. Mark) (CW 66)*, belongs to the family of dramatic Passions. The characters in the drama are not portrayed by solo voices, however, as the only voice to be set apart is that of the Evangelist. The *Exordium* is set for chorus SATB in note-against-note style, a direct and simple approach to the choral singing that prevails throughout the entire composition. For the rest of the Passion, the *turba* always appears in five parts, SSATB, and the SATB combination is reserved for expressing the words of Jesus, with only two exceptions. Insofar as possible, Beber assigned separate voice combinations to each of the identifiable characters within the drama, as follows:

Disciples	ATT
Peter	AT
Judas	ATB and AT
High priest	ATB

Maid	SSA
Pilate	ATB and SATB
Sponge-bearer	AT
Centurion	SATB

A few generalizations may be made about Beber's assignment of parts. There are actually two choral groups in the work: one, the five-part *turba;* the other, various combinations of solo voices as they are assembled to represent the various characters. A common musical identity is given to three such characters who do harm to Christ by their words: Peter, who lies about his association with Him; Judas, in the moment of verbal betrayal of Christ; and the sponge-bearer, who accompanies his proffered draft of vinegar with mocking words. Those who harm Christ through more direct action share a different vocal identity, ATB: the High priest; Judas in the moment of plotting the betrayal; and Pilate, except for his final utterance. The maid who identifies Peter as a disciple is represented by an SSA group. There are two instances when Beber set characters other than Jesus for the SATB group, the combination that is generally reserved for Him alone. These are short expressions by Pilate and the centurion, both of which show at least a trace of recognition of Christ's unique position in the drama. Pilate gives serious consideration to Him as "King of the Jews" and the centurion recognizes that He must truly be the Son of God. The musical identification is conveyed by giving these utterances to the same combination of voices that sings the words of Christ throughout the work.

The part of the Evangelist is written in the plainsong style that was common to some dramatic Passions, such as that of Keuchenthal, a style to be adopted later by Heinrich Schütz in his Passion settings. These expository sections, as short as four notes and as long as nearly three hundred, add not only an abstract clarity to the story, but a necessary style contrast to the choral sections, as well.

From the next generation there comes a setting of the Passion drama that exceeds all others in its flexibility of available performance styles. Thomas Selle (1599–1663), who held important positions in church music in Hamburg during the last two decades of his life, wrote his *Passion nach dem Evangelisten Johannes* (CW 26) of 1643 in such a manner that it could be presented with or without soloists, orchestra, *intermedii* (large motet-like sections), or by any combination of these with chorus as the situation warranted. Assuming that the work was to be performed with the fullest forces possible, it would have three principal parts, each made up of solos for the Evangelist and principal characters, and of short *turba* passages SAATTB. The first part is preceded by an *Exordium* in which the phrase segments are stated by six soloists and answered by the full choir, also *a 6*, the choir supported by an orchestra of three violins, two bassoons, and *continuo*, and the soloists, by *continuo* only. Beber had identified each character in his drama by associating it with a combination of voices; Selle characterized each of his soloists by giving him a unique accompanying group in addition to the ubiquitous *continuo*. The Evangelist always appears in company with two bassoons; Jesus with two violins; the maid, three violins; Peter, two flutes and bassoon; Pilate, two *cornetti* and trombone; and so on. This principle is violated only twice; once when Peter's characteristic accompaniment—if it can be dignified with the adjective, for he sings only three notes in the entire work—is given to the soldier who slapped Jesus and reprimanded Him for His answer to the High priest. Jesus' response to the soldier is made in terms of great gravity, and for this passage only a bassoon is added to the violins that accompany Him.

The three main parts described above are sufficient to relate the Passion story, almost entirely through the medium of solo voices. The *intermedii* serve as choral reflections upon the action of the three main parts; they are not necessary to the continuous exposition itself. Each *intermedium* follows one of the main parts of the Passion; each is, therefore, more of a concluding comment than a link. Each of them is an elaborate motet calling for soloists STB, an SAATB choir, an orchestra of three violins, two bassoons, solo violin, and double *continuo*; harpsichord and violoncello for the soloists; organ and bass for the choir. The solo violin provides a fourth part above the three solo voices, and the forces are sharply set off against each other in a manner that speaks clearly of Selle's almost certain familiarity with the Venetian style. The first *intermedium* (Isaiah 53:4–5), *Fürwahr er trug unsre Krankheit (Surely he hath borne our griefs)*, and the second (Psalm 22: 1–21),[10] *Mein Gott, mein Gott, warum hast du mich verlassen? (My God, my God, why hast thou forsaken me?)*, are both directly connected with the Good Friday liturgy, the former as part of the Epistle and the latter as one of the psalms for Matins. It should also be remembered, in this connection, that the appropriate day for the presentation of the St.

10. In the German, Ps. 22:2–22.

John Passion story was Good Friday. The third *intermedium* is the closing chorus of the entire work, and Selle grasped the opportunity to make a double-chorus setting (between the solo choir *a 3* and the full choir *a 5*, the same combination he had used in the other two motets) of the Passion chorale *O Lamm Gottes, unschuldig (O Lamb of God, how blameless)*. The setting is especially effective. Each phrase of the chorale is introduced by the solo choir, and the last word is echoed by the full choir which then repeats the phrase and is, in turn, echoed in like manner by the solo group. The two then combine for a concerted restatement of the phrase before the next one is taken up in the same fashion. Selle's *Conclusio*,[11] using the text that was common among composers of German Passions at least as far back as Joachim von Burck's (d. 1616) St. John setting of 1568, *Wir glauben, lieber Herr, mehre unsern Glauben (We believe, dear Lord; increase our belief)*, appears at the end of the third section. The final chorus is thereby all the more a supplementary comment and less an integral part of the compositon.

We now return to the works of Heinrich Schütz, both his Passions and oratorios. His period of productivity in works of this type covers more than four decades. It is difficult, then, to place him in exact chronological sequence with his fellows, for some of his compositions fall into early periods and others into later. Schütz typifies the meeting of two relatively new, but equally vital traditions; the liturgical German practice and the exuberant Venetian. His Resurrection oratorio (1623), *Historia der Auferstehung Jesu Christi*,[12] represents the mixture as it existed after he returned from his Italian studies with Gabrieli, but before his association with Monteverdi. The close relationship between the practices common to dramatic Passions and oratorio is generally quite evident. Also, Schütz's use of musical symbolism can be found throughout the composition.

From the earlier Resurrection setting of Antonio Scandello (1517–1580), Schütz borrowed the text, the plainsong formula, and the Psalm Tone, as well as his ideas for the opening and closing choruses.[13] The unique contribution of Schütz was the expansion of the idea and the addition of the instrumental setting, for Scandello's earlier work

---

11. The *Conclusio* was either an expression of thanks or a moralistic tag. It was sometimes also known as a *Gratiarum actio*.

12. Heinrich Schütz, *Neue Ausgabe sämt-licher Werke* (Kassel: Bärenreiter-Verlag, 1955–), III; *Sämtliche Werke* (Leipzig: Breitkopf & Härtel, 1885–1927), I, 5–46.

13. *Ibid.*, III, 69; see also *Grove's*, VII, 645.

(accessible to Schütz because Scandello had been one of his predecessors at Dresden) was completely vocal. Schütz's opening and closing choruses call for different combinations of the voices. The *Exordium* is SSATTB with string orchestra. But in the course of thirty-five
measures Schütz calls for four different distributions of these voices:
SSAT, SSATTB, ATTB, and again SSATTB. Each shift of the vocal
texture is associated with a different phrase or segment of the text.
The final chorus calls for two differentiated choirs; the first, SATB; the
second, SATB plus the Evangelist. Although the Evangelist's part
usually enters with the second of these choirs that alternate in true
polychoral style, he does not belong entirely to either choir. While
they are singing the text of a typical *Conclusio, Gott aber sei Dank, der
uns den Sieg gegeben hat durch unsern Herrn Jesus Christus!* ("But thanks
be to God, which giveth us the victory through our Lord Jesus Christ")
(I Cor. 15:57), the Evangelist sings repeatedly the single word *Victoria*
to this rhythm: ♩ ♩. ♪ | o
                 Vic - to - ri - a,

Ex. 82 Schütz, *Historia der Auferstehung Jesu Christi* (Resurrection oratorio)

At the conclusion of the biblical verse, the two choirs take up the
same word in a vigorous closing section, but with a contrasting
rhythm that embraces the Evangelist's rhythmic identity *(Ex. 82)*.
There is also a brief chorus (15 measures) in the course of the work in
which the eleven disciples are represented *a 6*.

That portion of the piece that falls between the opening and closing
choruses is divided into three separate parts or scenes, on texts chosen
from appropriate sections of all four Gospels. Between scenes one and
two, and again between secenes two and three, there are vocal *intermedii* consisting of short choral passages prefaced and followed by
sections for the Evangelist. The first choral section is for TBB, the
text from Matthew 28:13–14, in which the chief priests conspire with
the guard from the tomb; *Saget: Seine Jünger kamen des Nachts . . .*
("Say ye, His disciples came by night, and stole him away while we

slept.") The second is a setting *a 6* of the message delivered to the disciples gathered in Jerusalem (Luke 23:24): *Der Herr ist wahrhaftig auferstanden und Simon erschienen* ("The Lord is risen indeed, and hath appeared to Simon"). The remainder of the oratorio consists of the narrative sections assigned to the Evangelist and the speeches of Jesus, Mary Magdalene, Cleopas (Cleophas in the German Bible — the King James version distinguishes between two people by varying the spelling), and other characters who figure in the story. Schütz allowed for a wide latitude in performance practice in this composition. Not only did convenience and local custom play a large part in such matters, but the specific desires of the composer are clearly set forth in the introduction to the original 1623 edition.[14] Among Schütz's instructions may be found the following advice: The Evangelist may be accompanied, as one wishes, by a large organ, a positive, or another instrument such as the lute. It is suggested that when the organ is used, the organist should always provide "elegant and appropriate runs and passages" against the "falsobordon" sections; i.e., those sustained passages that consist entirely of root-position chords *(cf. p. 119)*.[15] Finally, he stated his preference: If it can be so arranged, the organ and others are to remain silent, and in their places four *viole da gamba* are to accompany the Evangelist. Schütz also provided the quartet of viols with music for the closing chorus in case they wished to play. A similar variety of methods of performance is permissible in connection with the sections he wrote for vocal duo, but which represent a single person. In such places, Schütz directed, either both voices may sing, or the second voice may be replaced by an instrument or omitted completely.

Many examples of musical symbolism can be noted in connection with this oratorio; some of them appear in the voices and others in the instrumental part. The symbolism is conveyed both in melodic and rhythmic patterns, or it is sometimes expressed in such a simple device as pedal-point. A few such patterns are illustrated in Example 83, and further reference to this type of expression will be made in connection with another of his oratorios to be discussed below.

Schütz's understanding of the power of local custom or simply of

14. *Ibid.*, III, [4f].
15. Hans Joachim Moser, *Heinrich Schütz: His Life and Work,* trans. Carl F. Pfatteicher (St. Louis: Concordia Publishing House, 1959), 367, interprets *falsobordon* to mean fauxbourdon. That interpretation is also held by his translator, Pfatteicher. However, the passages in question fit only the concept of *falsobordone* as it was developed by the Italians and, most probably, as it became known to Schütz during his Italian studies. Cf. *MR*, 91.

Ex. 83 Symbolic figures from Schütz's Resurrection oratorio (after *Werke*, I, 5-46)

the availability of local manpower is again brought out in his diffident notice that was published with the recitatives of his *Historia der Geburt Jesu Christi*,[16] where he noted two significant things: first, that anyone who preferred the plainsong rendition of the Evangelist's text to the new style of recitative—new only for German church music, for this was the year 1664—could perform the part without *continuo* and; second, that the discretion of the performers should prevail in the concerted numbers *(intermedii)* which could be adapted to "their pleasure and the musical forces at their disposal, or even to have them composed by someone else."[17] The sections of the composition alter-

16. Schütz, *Neue Ausgabe,* I; Heinrich Schütz, *The Christmas Story,* ed. Arthur Mendel (New York: G. Schirmer, 1949), v-vi. The English language edition con- tains an excellent discussion of perform- ance practice.
17. Schütz, *The Christmas Story,* vi.

nate between the Evangelist, who is always accompanied by a *continuo* group, and the other solo characters and the choruses. This kind of organization places the *continuo* accompaniment as a constant foil to the various distinctive accompanying groups in other parts of the composition. The soprano solos are accompanied by two violas and *continuo*, the shepherds by recorders and bassoon, Herod by trumpets, and the other groups by appropriate musical combinations. The alternation of voices in these various sections produces another kind of arch form, one that is entirely structural rather than musical (Table XIII).

TABLE XIII

Arch Form in Schütz's Christmas Story

```
                              x
                            tenor

                       IX    XI
             (Wise Men) chorus  chorus (High Priests and Scribes)

                      VIII     XII
                      tenor    tenor

                  VII                    XIII
        chorus (Shepherds)          bass (Herod)

                  VI                      XIV
                tenor                    tenor

                  V                       XV
        chorus (Angels)           soprano (Angel)

                  IV                      XVI
                tenor                    tenor

              III                        XVII
      soprano (Angel)              soprano (Angel)

              II                          XVIII
            tenor                        tenor

            I                                XIX
        Exordium                          Conclusio
```

Whether the apparent parallelism between the solo and choral segments of each side of the arch exists simply because of the regular alternation of tenor recitatives and solos or choruses, or because some plan of balance was part of Schütz's conscious approach to the composition is less important than the resulting balance between the abstract presentation of text by the Evangelist and the more colorful Italianate *concertato* sections that make up the *intermedii* and framing choruses.

For, despite Schütz's apparently offhand dismissal, the concerted sections are essential to the continuity of the work and, even if adaptations were not against his musical judgment, their omission would have destroyed the composition entirely.

Any music director who clung to the plainsong form of the Evangelist's part would have been employing a combination of the German and Italian idioms. The oratorio is, however, an almost completely Italian work if no such adjustment is made. The new style in recitative, and the employment of *concertato* choruses — the most brilliant are the chorus of angels, *Ehre sei Gott (Glory to God)* and the closing chorus, *Dank sagen wir alle (Now do we all thank Thee)* — carry the work firmly back to Venetian roots. It was not that Schütz had permitted his interest in the Italian style to lie dormant during the years after his return from the visits to Italy. His compositions outside the oratorio group fell sometimes into the German tradition of polyphonic writing — even though he hardly ever pursued the convenient devices that were available through the use of chorales — and sometimes into the Italian. His periodic efforts in the German style implied no loss of faith in the Italian. It is probable that interest in the imported style was considerable among other directors and composers, for Schütz thought it advisable at least one time to issue a word of caution, in the preface to his *Geistliche Chormusik* (1648), that the Italian style could not be handled successfully unless the composer first had a thorough training in traditional composition.[18]

The use of musical symbolism is even more extensive in the Christmas oratorio than it was in the earlier Resurrection oratorio. While it may be possible to attribute this in part to Schütz's greater skill in handling his materials after a period of nearly forty years, it is probably more evident here because the story breaks into a number of sharply contrasted scenes of dramatic power, while the Resurrection story maintained a single idea projected through only a few scenes of similar mood. So many examples may be extracted from this composition alone that it would be a pointless exercise simply to display one after the other. Two types only will be illustrated here, both of which illustrate Schütz's practice of creating a symbolic musical pattern that is appropriate for the moment, rather than of employing existing symbols, as Bach was to do half a century later. Some of Schütz's pictorial groups are attached to recurrent ideas and occur

18. Schütz, *Neue Ausgabe*, v, vi.

more than once in the piece; others belong simply to a word that requires momentary intensification or elaboration (in the manner of Renaissance text-painting) and, therefore, appear only one time. From the first group, there are two that give sufficient illustration of the process: the passage that describes the child "wrapped in swaddling," and the rising figure that is associated with the angel's calling to Joseph to get up *(Ex. 84a,b)*. A similar treatment can be seen in the handling of *Stern* (star), where a moving figure is written while the star leads the Wise Men, but a single note suffices at the point where the star simply shines down on the place where they are to go. Schütz's clear reference to the rocking of the cradle in the accompaniment to each of the Angel's solos, *worunter bisweilen des Christkindleins Wiege mit eingeführet wird,* points up his interest in the use of direct pictorial applications in music. In the second group of patterns, active verbs, such as "go," "journey," and "fly" are especially prominent. The last is given an especially florid treatment inasmuch as it must convey not only the idea of motion (which is done successfully in other sections of the piece by patterns of four or a few more notes), but also of great distance *(Ex. 84c)*. There can be little doubt that such an idea was consciously executed by the composer. That passage is

Ex. 84 Schütz *Christmas Story*

unique in being both so elaborate and so long. Another deliberate effect that appears only one time in the composition is the employment of a chromatic movement in both voice and *continuo*, descriptive of Rachel's weeping for her children *(Ex. 84d)*. The effect is a startling, albeit tellingly appropriate one.

Schütz's music for Holy Week is, by contrast, a model of restraint. Only one composition for that season, *Die Sieben Worte Jesu Christi am Kreuz* (HMS, v, 42ff)[19] makes use of instruments. The instrumentation is unspecified, but probably Schütz intended string instruments. The practice of omitting exact designations for instruments stems from the past, and appears to be a deliberate return to the style that existed before the Venetian influence made itself felt in his style. Another remnant of the past is found in the treatment given the Evangelist part; it is sometimes written for one solo voice, sometimes another, and occasionally for a quartet of voices. The characters in the drama are assigned to solo voices. Jesus is sung by a tenor, and his words are accompanied by a trio sonata, in contrast to all of the other solos, which are supported by *continuo* only. Choruses *a 5* appear at the beginning and end, where they serve as the almost inevitable *Exordium* (Schütz calls it an *Introitus*) and *Conclusio*. These choruses provide a frame for the composition, and inside it is still another frame provided by the two *Symphoniae*, which are identical in every respect. The framework stems from the same aesthetic idea that generated such widespread interest in the arch form as a model of symmetry and regularity so beloved by Baroque artists.

Three settings of the Passion story can be attributed to Schütz

19. *Ibid.*, ii, 3–31; English version, Hein-   the Cross, ed. Richard T. Gore (St. Louis: rich Schütz, *The Seven Words of Christ on*   Concordia Publishing House, 1951).

Heinrich Schütz, *Historia der Geburt Jesu Christi* (Band I, *Neue Ausgabe sämtlicher Werke*).
Printed with permission of Bärenreiter-Verlag, Kassel, Basel, London, New York.

without any doubt; the St. Matthew, St. John, and St. Luke.[20] A St.
Mark Passion that was thought to be his work is now generally accepted as spurious. Since our interest in German music of the Baroque
period first focused on the works of Bach, and only recently moved to
earlier composers, the Schütz settings have often been regarded as
interesting predecessors of the Bach Passions. Such a view is unfortunately centered entirely on Bach; it represents an attitude that

20. *Ibid.*, II. The St. Luke setting is found on pp. 35–71; St. John, pp. 74–104;
St. Matthew, pp. 107–44.

places Bach in a superior position merely because he arrived on the scene later; and it ignores the organization and style of the Schütz works entirely. Rather than forecasting the way of later Passion music, the Schütz examples mark the end of a long tradition of choral Passions. They are not concert works in any way, but they are simply musical projections of the tragic story, unfolded in the simplest possible fashion. They are completely shorn of the sophisticated devices that Schütz had learned to use. Their simplicity is conscious, and is not merely an exhibition of naïvete. Coming near the close of his musical career, they show that Schütz deliberately returned to an austere musical style as the one best suited to his subject.

The common characteristics of his Passions are: (1) absence of any instrumental music; (2) undeviating adherence to the biblical text except for the *Exordium* and *Conclusio*; (3) restriction of all individual roles, e.g., Evangelist, Jesus, Judas, etc., to unaccompanied solo singing—that of the Evangelist, in a kind of plainsong style, the others in hardly more lyrical fashion; and (4) all of the *turba* sections and opening and closing choral pieces set for SATB. Most of the choral writing is imitative, and some of it reaches a high peak of intensity through the use of overlapping rhythms. Schütz here avoided convenient devices, optional performance practices, and elaborate settings, choosing instead to write in a style that projects a deeply religious mood untinged by secular associations. The result is no less dramatic than that achieved by Selle in his Passion and Schütz in his oratorios.

Even during those years when Schütz was relatively inactive, just before the appearance of his three Passions in the 1660s, there appeared in performance (although it was not printed until a decade later, in 1672) a St. Matthew Passion by Johann Sebastiani (1622–1683).[21] Among its interesting features are the assignment of a few differentiated instrumental accompaniments to the leading characters and the inclusion of reflective chorale stanzas for solo voice with accompaniment "for the awakening of greater devotion" on the part of the congregation, but definitely not for their vocal participation. While on some few occasions the Evangelist sings with *continuo* only, the part is usually accompanied by two *viole da gamba* (or *da braccio*) and *viola bassa*. A third *viola* is added for the chorales and the SATTB choruses. The words of Jesus are usually crowned by two violins and supported by *continuo*; i.e., accompanied by trio sonata, foreshadow-

---

21. *DdT*, XVII, [1]–103.

ing the treatment applied to the same text by Bach.[22] The *turba* sections are supported by the full instrumental group. The composition cannot be considered a true Passion oratorio, for certain oratorio features do not appear, viz., arias and choruses that expand upon the biblical story are conspicuously absent. Only in the use of chorale verses does it go beyond the usual version.

Three other Passions show a continued search for new methods of expression during the ensuing years. Friedrich Funcke (1642 – 1699) wrote a St. Matthew Passion (*CW* 78/79) probably sometime between 1667 and 1683. It is a step closer to the oratorio style in that it contains reflective solos and choruses as some of its many short sections. A number of the sections are introduced by brief *sinfonie* for strings. The solo chorale with string orchestra accompaniment is also present here. A remnant of the old style, perhaps indicative of the strength of tradition, is seen in the recitatives, which are in plainsong style but supported by figured bass. Somewhere around the year 1670 Augustin Pfleger, concerning whom little is known, wrote a short Passion setting using the Seven Last Words (*CW* 52). It combines features of the German cantata with those we have observed in Passion settings, including dialogue, rhymed sections between biblical texts, and a closing chorale that alternates between solo soprano and ATB choir, the final phrase for the entire SATB chorus. Such treatment of the familiar chorale *O Lamm Gottes unschuldig* (*O Lamb of God, how blameless*), precludes the possibility of any congregational participation, removing another link from the chain of fable that has been projected as tradition in connection with the singing of chorales. The Evangelist is supported by *continuo* only, and the principal solos and ensembles by a trio sonata of two violas and *continuo*. St. Matthew Passions by Johann Theile[23] (1646 – 1724) and Johannes Georg Kühnhausen (*CW* 50) (*c. 1700*) are increasingly dramatic in their presentation of recitative, solos, and chorales for chorus.

It is evident that much of the German emphasis was upon works for Holy Week, and that there seems to have been little interest in the oratorio except for these special seasonal works. There may be no other works because there was no need for their creation. The place

---

22. *Grove's,* vi, 584, says mistakenly, "the *continuo* accompanies the Evangelist and Christ's utterances are supported by the strings, as in Bach's St. Matthew Passion." For most of the work the Evangelist's part is literally surrounded by the sound of the *viole,* some playing above his voice and others below; the words of Jesus are usually sung under the halo-like sound of two violins and supported by the bass.

23. *DdT,* xvii, [105] – 199.

they could have filled in the Lutheran service was suitably filled by
the cantata, as was the same place in England by the cantata-anthem.
Outside the German church there were no established choirs that
could perform large works. Since there was no need for the pieces in
the church, it is obvious that the composers found no cause to create
anything beyond the cantatas and Passions, the latter far less progressive in style because of the solemn occasions for which they were
composed. Until the eighteenth century when the encroachment of
operatic style upon German church music became common and the
development of secular singing societies made it possible, the oratorio
impulse lay dormant. Between Schütz and Bach there were many
compositions, but the bulk of the work that concerns the present
discussion fell into the class of Passions which, once they began to
break free from traditional patterns, became involved with highly
charged emotional projections of the texts that had earlier been given
out with dignified restraint. The courses of opera and oratorio came
as close to complete fusion as they probably ever would.

> In 1704 the Passion succumbed to the popular inclination to drama-
> tize Biblical stories, in a setting by Reinhard Keiser (1674–1739)
> of Christian Friedrich Hunold-Menantes's "Der blutige und ster-
> bende Jesus," an "Oratorio musicalisch gesetz." The libretto,
> rhymed throughout, contained no chorales and dispensed with the
> biblical narrative. The author cast the work in the form of three
> cantatas or "Soliloquia": the Lamentations of Mary Magadalene;
> the Tears of Peter; the Love-song of Zion's Daughter, a character
> later adopted by Brockes, Picander and Bach. Its theatrical music
> and the elimination of the Bible narrative invited grave displeasure,
> and even public condemnation by one of the Hamburg clergy.[24]

Despite the unfavorable reactions to theatrical elements that Keiser
introduced, other composers took up this pattern. It might seem that
between Schütz and Bach there was a great gulf filled only with oppor-
tunists and commercially minded composers. In extenuation, it must
be remembered that this was the period in which Erdmann Neumeister admitted that his cantatas were to be viewed as fragments of
opera, although he perhaps did not imagine that the similarity would
be carried to these lengths. Some brief examples from *Der gekreuzigte
Jesus (The crucified Jesus)*, another of Keiser's oratorios,[25] show considerable variety of style, expressive melodic ideas, and great facility.
No less should be expected of a man who ranked high in the competitive world of Italian and German opera.

24. *Grove's*, VI, 585.   25. *Ibid.*, 252f.

The satisfactory way in which cantatas served the requirements of the German church is again evident in the few examples of oratorio music composed by Johann Sebastian Bach. The tremendous enthusiasm for his music in our own time has provided us with more than the usual amount of information about his efforts, and we may safely assume that we have an accurate estimate of the amount of music that has been lost, in addition to the quantity that is extant. The total number of Passions, even by the most extravagant estimate, does not exceed five. Only two of those, St. John (*BWV* 245) (excerpts in *HMS*, v, 47–50) and St. Matthew (*BWV* 244), survive in complete form. There is no true oratorio included among his works. The Easter and Ascension oratorios do not differ in most respects from the other church cantatas; however, the latter contains some narrative sections, a fact that gives it an affinity to the oratorio. The presence of an Evangelist is also significant.[26] His justly famous *Christmas Oratorio* (*BWV* 248) is made up of six separate cantatas, intended to be performed at six festivals for Christmas and New Year's. Still, it is not proper to dismiss them simply as six random works that are brought together because of seasonal texts. They bear a distinct relationship to oratorio in two ways: first, in the size of the total work and the close relationship of the parts to each other; and, second, in the presence of an Evangelist who presents the biblical story in recitative. It is most significant that the narrative is continuous through all six cantatas. Despite this, it is true that the six cantatas, either separately or cumulatively, lack the dramatic element that is quite essential to oratorio. Whittaker gives a credible reason why Bach should have become interested in the oratorio at all, or at least why he should have taken note of its existence by applying the term to some of his cantatas. As it comes from the same years as the opening sections of the B minor Mass,[27] Whittaker sees it as a work that Bach may have hoped would have performance at the Catholic Court in Dresden, the place to which he sent the *Missa brevis*.

Oratorio was in vogue in Dresden at that time, and Hasse's appointment as Kapellmeister, in 1731, stimulated the demand. Hasse, who was a friend of Bach's, had written fourteen oratorios; it was probably this stimulus and the possibilities of performance at the seat of the Court that caused him to begin the Weihnachts-Oratorium after the great *Kyrie* and *Gloria* were written, and to

26. Whittaker, *The Cantatas of Johann Sebastian Bach*, ii, 40f.
27. The Kyrie and Gloria were completed in 1733; the *Christmas Oratorio* was presented first during the season 1734–1735.

follow it by the "Ascension" Oratorio in 1735 and the "Easter" Oratorio in 1736.[28]

The two Passions are different in their degrees of musical complexity and in the manner in which their texts approach the drama of the Crucifixion. The earlier St. John work (1722–1723) is relatively simple in its musical material. The narration of the Evangelist, as well as the parts of all characters, is supported only by *continuo*; the *turba* sections are entirely restricted to four-part chorus; the numerous chorales vitalize the story for the congregation who were not expected to participate in the singing, but were to apply the drama to their own theological milieu. Not only does congregational participation lack any precedent in the music before Bach's time, but the deviations from the simplest settings of the chorale tunes and the frequent appearance of four-part settings indicate that the attention was centered on the choir and not the congregation.

The text of the *St. John Passion* is harsh; it deals with suffering rather than redemption, violence rather than tenderness. Bach reinforced its strong emotions with a severe and esoteric arch form[29] that is hidden away in the second part of the work, the longer part that was to be sung after the sermon (Table xiv). An examination of the arch immediately dispels any suspicion that it stems from the·imagination of Bach enthusiasts. The only material Bach composed that does not figure in the construction of the diagram is the recitative material. Since it is narrative circumscribed by biblical inviolability it is less likely to be exposed to subjective maneuvering. The first two choruses (38 and 42) have common musical material and both deal with law and its interpretation by Pilate. Bach set both of these choruses as fugues, for in his mind canon was synonymous with law, musical or judicial. The next pair of choruses (36 and 44) share musical material and deal with crucifixion. The third pair (34 and 46) deal with the appellation, "King of the Jews," both in derision and denial. The arias are less clearly related. The pair on the left leg of the arch are addressed to the Soul; that on the right, simply to the "poor souls" among the onlookers. Choruses 29 and 50 seem, at first glance, to have little in common except their concern with negative ideas (rejection).

28. Whittaker, *op. cit.*, ii, 621.

29. Karl Geiringer, *The Bach Family* (London: George Allen & Unwin Ltd., 1954), 234, prefers to call this a chiastic arrangement because it is cruciform in at least one respect. Reference to arch form is used here because it has been employed elsewhere in this book and seems more appropriate to the several examples, even though it is not a superior term in this instance.

TABLE XIV

Arch Form In Bach's *St. John Passion**

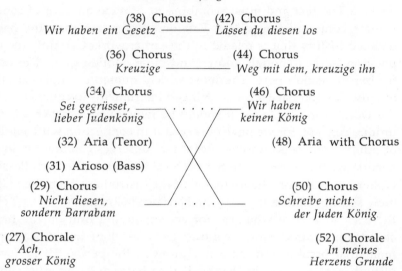

(40) Chorale
Durch dein Gefängnis

(38) Chorus   (42) Chorus
Wir haben ein Gesetz ——— *Lässet du diesen los*

(36) Chorus   (44) Chorus
Kreuzige ——————— *Weg mit dem, kreuzige ihn*

(34) Chorus   (46) Chorus
Sei gegrüsset,   *Wir haben*
lieber Judenkönig   *keinen König*

(32) Aria (Tenor)   (48) Aria with Chorus

(31) Arioso (Bass)

(29) Chorus   (50) Chorus
Nicht diesen,   *Schreibe nicht:*
sondern Barrabam   *der Juden König*

(27) Chorale   (52) Chorale
Ach,   *In meines*
grosser König   *Herzens Grunde*

*Dotted lines indicate textual similarity. Connecting solid lines indicate same musical material. Numbers in parentheses show their order in *BG* xii (1).

However, as the connecting lines show, their relationship—both musical and textual—is not simply to each other, but also to choruses higher on the arch. Numbers 34 and 50 recall the derisive "King of the Jews" material; 29 and 46 deal with the rejection of Jesus by the crowd, first in favor of Barrabas and then in favor of Caesar. The connection between these choruses, even from the musical standpoint alone, brings into prominence the symbol chi (X) within the arch form. The chorales at the extreme points of the arch are not symbolic, but serve as a frame for the entire series of pieces.[30]

30. This group of pieces, including the recitatives, has been called the "heart-piece" of the composition by Friedrich Smend, "Die Johannes-Passion von Bach," *Bach-Jahrbuch*, 1926, 105–28. Several diagrams appear in connection with Smend's article. If it appears that emphasis has been on structural features rather than on those that are entirely and obviously musical, it must be remembered that composers have concerned themselves with arcane ideas since at least Machaut's time (*cf. p. 45*). Those who have so indulged themselves, for whatever reason, had achieved complete mastery of the musical material in their generation. Many more examples than have been dealt with in these pages could be introduced, but I will refrain from burdening the reader with them.

The *St. Matthew Passion* is complex in its performing force — two orchestras and two choruses (*MSO*, 117–25) in addition to the soloists — but it is simple and unaffected in its expression. The usual division into two parts, that sung before the sermon being considerably shorter than that following it, is present as it was in the *St. John Passion*. The text and music combine to provide an aura of compassionate contemplation of the Passion story rather than the harshly detailed history that is related in the earlier work. Certainly the composition is well enough known and often enough quoted to escape further dissection here. The most widely quoted examples are those that dwell upon Bach's use of stringed instruments in connection with the words sung by Jesus. It should be remembered that this is not a unique concept, for we have observed it in connection with a number of other composers. Another point that deserves comment is in connection with the use of the harpsichord in both of the Bach Passions. Walter Emery favors the exclusion of the instrument from the St. Matthew setting, stating that "as the Narrator belonged to the first choir, there is no excuse whatever for accompanying him on the harpsichord, thus introducing a contrast of tone-colour in the accompaniment that breaks with the conventions of the period."[31] Performers of both past and present have failed to be swayed by musicological opinion that is in conflict with their personal taste or convenience. Still, it is interesting to see how Bach approached the matter of the harpsichord in the two Passions, especially as we know that the instrument was very rarely called for as a *continuo* instrument by other composers of church music. Bach's attitude toward the use of the harpsichord seems to have been one of progressive acceptance. Three sets of parts exist for the *St. John Passion:* the first contains simply the indication, "continuo"; the second, "organo ò cembalo"; the third, "cembalo." Whether the apparently progressive favoring of the harpsichord finds fruition in the specific demand for that instrument in the *St. Matthew Passion* is not clear. A century ago, it was considered of some importance that Bach liked to have a harpsichord at hand when he was performing such a work.[32] Such evidence is not conclusive. Spitta's extensive discussion of Bach's use of the instrument[33] is not concerned with the accompaniment of recitatives or arias, but

31. Walter Emery, "Bach and his Time," *Choral Music,* ed. Arthur Jacobs (Harmondsworth, Middlesex: Penguin Books, 1963), 145.

32. *BG*, IV, xxii.

33. Spitta, *Johann Sebastian Bach,* II, 326–32.

is related to the problem of conducting the entire ensemble and of maintaining order among the instrumentalists. From that evidence and the few other references that exist it would be futile to defend the harpsichord as an accompanying instrument for soloists. It is still advisable to consider the consistent style of the entire Baroque period rather than the practice in isolated instances, when we consider matters of performance practice in our time.

Even though the Bach Passions stand out above similar works of the period, there is no line of succession in their style. The course of musical production in Germany was not changed by their appearance. The deterioration of texts and the incorporation of operatic style, bringing into vogue religious entertainments rather than musical intensifications of a religious story, continued. Where the Italian influence remained as the dominant force, the music was no more than suitable for religious purposes; where a degree of German style prevailed, at least the chorale and the fugue contributed a degree of unity and restraint. Unfortunately there was no way of holding back the secular elements that had captivated the taste of Europe.

In adopting the term "oratorio" Bach probably followed a precedent set by Johann Adolph Hasse (1699–1783). The most Italianate of all Germans, Hasse was a product of the Roman tradition that can be traced back to Carissimi and the Neapolitan ideal that stems from Scarlatti and the operatic stage. His *La Conversione di Sant' Agostino*,[34] first produced in Dresden on Holy Saturday, 1750, is a typical product of the marriage of Roman and Neapolitan ideas. The instrumental introduction, a spirited piece for strings and woodwinds, moves without pause into the opening recitative-dialogue, a section that is sharply different in character from the opening music. Each of the two sections of the oratorio is made up of extended recitative and arioso passages, broken by *da capo* arias—five in the first part and four in the second—for each of the principal characters of each section. Each half of the work concludes with a chorus; the one for the first half is interrupted for a brief duet, the one for the second half is in fugal style. If anything in the entire oratorio could be considered discernibly different from operatic pieces, it is the closing fugue, and even that comprises only the last half of the final chorus. The arias are replete with coloratura passages, trills, runs, and stereotyped figures of vocal virtuosity which have little to do with the text. Still, that there was con-

34. *DdT*, xx.

siderable interest in the subject is shown by the fact that the text was printed in both German and Italian—in separate booklets—in the year of the first performance, and that a printed Polish version and a handwritten French translation exist as well. An overwhelming proportion of operatic treatment does not indicate that a less religious climate was inhabited by the Catholics[35] than by the Protestants. Once the liturgical bond of plainsong had been severed, Catholicism had no musical material that bore religious marks save the outdated polyphonic style. Lutheranism, on the other hand, possessed the chorale and a lingering tolerance of, if not affection for, contrapuntal texture. The Catholic interest lay in the meaning of the text, whether it belonged to biblical narrative or religious story as did *La Conversione*, or to the Passion setting or mystical allegory, as other oratorios of Hasse and his fellows did. It is, then, not incongruous for the musical vocabulary of the theater to appear as the vehicle for religious ideas. It was a familiar form of musical utterance and suffered from no comparison with a vocabulary that was associated with religious practice. Apparently female soloists were part of the performance of this and other Hasse oratorios whether they were given in the Court Chapel, a church in the city, or in a theater, for the names of female singers are given in connection with a number of such works.[36] It is not clear, however, whether any women were in the choruses.

The secularization of oratorio became complete with Hasse and Johann Ernst Eberlin (1702–1762), who is credited with the composition of seventy-five oratorios. Of these, *Der blutschwitzende Jesus* (literally, *The blood-sweating Jesus*)[37] exemplifies his style, as do the fragments of other works printed in the same volume of the modern edition. Emphasis lies as much upon the singing and the orchestra as upon the text; this is evident not only in the avoidance of biblical quotation, but also in the preponderant use of solo sections, both accompanied recitative and aria. The chorus figures only in the closing moments, a brief piece that makes no demands upon either the composer or the singers. In place of biblical text there is a libretto that emphasizes Christ's human character by dwelling on His forebodings over the inevitability of suffering and death. Recitatives appear in regular procession, preceding *da capo* arias accompanied usually by

35. Hasse's religious affiliation is not important in this respect, but it should be noted that all of his religious service music was intended for the Catholic tradition.

36. Lucian Kamienski, *Die Oratorien von Johann Adolf Hasse* (Leipzig: Breitkopf & Härtel, 1912), pp. 111, 192, *et passim*.
37. *DTÖ*, LV, 1–70.

strings alone, along with various wind instruments at different times. Contrasts of dynamics are prominent and an unusual interest in Lombard rhythms is seen throughout the work, in voices and instruments alike. Eberlin was a Catholic composer, so no chorales were used.

The distinction between oratorio and cantata became less and less clear in the eighteenth century. Just as earlier we could not expect the cantata to be distinct from other kinds of music for the church, now there was no consistent identification mark for either the cantata or oratorio; in the minds of many people the distinction seemed to be merely one of dimension. We find the terms used interchangeably, not only as they were with Bach, but also in connection with such works as *Der Tod Jesu,* by Karl Heinrich Graun, which is often classified as an oratorio. It is in reality a Passion oratorio, but only in its length does it bear resemblance to the oratorios of other years. There is no narrator, either of biblical or poetical exposition; the recitatives are divided among the various soloists. The earliest printed edition, coming from the presses of J. G. I. Breitkopf in 1760, the year after Graun's death, referred to the work as *eine Cantate.* On the other hand, another of his works that is designated as an oratorio[38] also lacks the distinctive marks of the form, and seems to be simply a long cantata.

The same lack of clear differentiation between cantata and oratorio is found in the compositions of another renowned figure of the same generation, Georg Philipp Telemann (1681–1767). A recent study of his oratorios[39] has shown that fewer than a third of them are now extant. The seven that were known to Rhea are from the period 1730 to 1762. They are not all cut to the same pattern—some of them are indeed the size of cantatas—and it is evident that they, in common with many similar works of that period, have left the prototype far behind, if ever it had been within view. The Evangelist no longer appears in the oratorio; recitatives are divided among the solo voices mostly as preliminary sections to arias; choruses are relatively infrequent; and generally the material makes little or no use of biblical text. The most elaborate of these works, *Der Tag des Gerichts (The last judgment),* appears in printed form,[40] and displays the typical elements on a larger than average scale. It is clearly evident that the

38. *Oratorium in Festum Nativitatis Chr. Mache dich auf, werde Licht, in Musik gebracht vom Herrn Cappelmeister Graun.* MS in Library of Congress
39. Claude H. Rhea, Jr., "The Sacred Oratorios of Georg Philipp Telemann (1681–1767)" (unpublished Ph.D. dissertation, Florida State University, 1958). An edition of Telemann's *St. Nicholai Kirchen Oratorio* (1739) is included in the dissertation.
40. *DdT,* xxviii, 1–119.

influence of opera and the relaxation of orthodox religious principles played large parts in the shape and content of church works in the latter half of the eighteenth century. This does not mean, however, that compositions of this kind were intended to be performed in the theaters rather than the churches as a usual practice. Graun's highly regarded *Der Tod Jesu,* to the text of the popular Berlin poet, Karl Wilhelm Ramler, was not first produced in a theater, as some sources inform us, but had its initial presentation in the Berlin Cathedral on March 26, 1755. Two years later Telemann set the same text,[41] but his version did not achieve the wide acceptance that was accorded to Graun's. His version is straightforward, almost perfunctory, in comparison with Graun's. Where Graun made much use of repeated text sections, indulged his taste for fugues, and wrote highly emotional recitatives, Telemann exercised considerable restraint, avoiding not only excessive *da capo* returns — an unusual practice indeed — but also many of the stock expressive devices of all composers of that day *(Ex. 85).* In the recitatives Graun emphasized text through repetition and enharmonic modulation, another of his favorite devices, while Telemann confined himself to a modest, if unimaginative, traditional utterance *(Ex. 86).* Despite these differences it would be totally inaccurate to state that Telemann represented a stable and reactionary trend and that Graun was among the progressives. In this very work that has suffered most from Graun's detractors — many of whom seem to have been satisfied to criticize without examining his music — he employed a chorale in a fashion that points back directly to the dialogues of earlier *Kirchenmusik.* (The dialogue idea is inherent in Ramler's text; the way each composer deals with it is clearly a matter of personal choice.) Graun sets the three verses of the chorale with orchestral accompaniment. Each verse gathers strength toward a towering climax in the closing statement: the first is for soprano and alto solos with pizzicato strings and oboes; the second is for SAT solos with flutes added to the orchestra; the third, for full chorus with bassoons added to the orchestra and the strings bowed rather than plucked. Each verse begins with the text *Ihr Augen weint!* ("Weep, ye eyes!"), and each verse is answered by a solo bass, accompanied by two bassoons and organ, singing the text, *Weinet nicht! Es hat ueber-*

41. Mus. Ms. 21722, Westdeutsches Bibliothek in Marburg, bears a reference to the year 1757. Oratorio and cantata texts were used over and over, after the fashion of opera libretti. Ramler's *Der Tod Jesu* was also set by J. C. F. Bach in 1769. His version is described in Geiringer, *op. cit.,* 399f.

Ex. 85 *a*) Chorus from Telemann's *Tod Jesu.*

wunden der Loewe vom Stamm Juda. ("Weep not: behold, the Lion of the tribe of Juda, the Root of David, hath prevailed . . . ") (Rev. 5:5).

Telemann's setting of this text is similar insofar as similarity is required by the structure of the text, but different in reference to musical materials. Only the first verse of the chorale is set for chorus; the other two are given as alto solos, one accompanied by *continuo* and oboe; the other, by *continuo* and flute. The solos are not simply statements of the chorale melody, but represent short variations

Ex. 85   *b)* Graun's setting of the same text

thereon. Following each verse, as with Graun, there is a bass solo to the reassuring text, *Weinet nicht.* In each case, the dialogue element was employed, not because Telemann was imitating Graun, but because the organization of the text left no alternative.

Two sons of J. S. Bach deserve notice in connection with oratorio composition. They have suffered at the hands of many observers from comparison with their more illustrious parent. We have observed, throughout this study, that heredity either by blood relationship or

Ex.86 *a)* Recitative from Telemann's *Tod Jesu.*

Fl. trav.

Strings

Bass

Wer ist der pein-lich lang-sam ster-ben-de?   Ist das mein

Cont.

Je - sus?

b) Graun's setting of the same text.

Strings

p

Soprano

Wer ist der pein-lich lang-sam ster-ben-de?

Cont.

p   *mf*

[*p*]

mf

Ist das mein Je-sus?   Ist das mein Je-sus?

[*p*]   *mf*

of teacher and pupil is not clearly predictable. It would be better if the works of these two men were permitted to stand on their own merits as examples of music in their generation rather than as pale images of a more austere period in composition.

Carl Philipp Emanuel Bach (1714–1788) left three works in the oratorio vein: a *Passions-Cantata* and *Die Israeliten in der Wüste (The Israelites in the desert)*, both from 1769, and *Die Auferstehung und Himmelfahrt Jesu (The Resurrection and Ascension of Jesus)*, 1777.[42] *Die Israeliten in der Wüste* is the most widely discussed of the three, probably because it possesses a number of unusual features. It is completely homophonic, not in rejection of old-fashioned principles, but in recognition of changing tastes. The tension lost by the avoidance of polyphony is replaced by another kind of interest, resulting from skillful toying with chromatic harmony. There are four soloists: Moses, a bass; Aaron, a tenor; and two Israelite women, both sopranos. The chorus of Israelites is SATB throughout. The libretto, by Daniel Schiebler of Hamburg, exhausts its action in the first half of the oratorio; the second half is made up almost entirely of a homily upon the events of the first half. The closing section of the first part reaches a peak of dramatic interest when Moses' plea to God is interrupted by the anguished cries of the Israelites: "We perish, we die!" After a prayer in the form of an aria, Moses smites the rock thrice, the waters flow, and the Israelites join in a chorus of joy.

A younger brother, Johann Christoph Friedrich Bach (1732–1795), has been the subject of less attention even though two of his oratorios, *Die Kindheit Jesu (The childhood of Jesus)* and *Die Auferweckung Lazarus (The raising of Lazarus from the dead)*, both dating from 1773, have long been available in a modern study edition.[43] All of Friedrich's religious choral works that can be definitely dated, with the single exception of his setting of Ramler's *Der Tod Jesu*, are from 1773 or later. The two works mentioned here can be considered representative of his period of regular activity in the large choral forms, for no fewer than three such compositions stem from that year, the third being a cantata for Pentecost. The reason for Friedrich's sudden interest in large religious compositions may have been his friendship with the celebrated writer-philosopher, Johann Gottfried von Herder (1744–1803), who

42. Modern edition of *Die Israeliten in der Wüste*, ed. Fritz Steffin (Berlin: Bote & Bock, 1955). A general discussion of C. P. E. Bach is found in *Grove's*, VI, 256f, and a complete study in Geiringer, *op. cit.*, 336–77.
43. *DdT*, LVI.

provided the texts for the three works in 1773 as well as for some others. *Die Kindheit Jesu* was not planned in the usual oratorio format, but was rather *ein biblisches Gemälde* (a musical picture) in which a few scenes are described in relatively uncomplicated music.[44] Dramatic singing plays no part in the arias or choruses, for only the recitatives carry any degree of excitement. The choruses and solo melodies are ingenuous, almost folklike in their simplicity. The principal parts — an angel, Mary, two shepherds, and Simon (who is assigned two verses of a chorale as solos, and a recitative that divides them) — are given to the usual solo quartet. None of the texture is polyphonic, and the simple homophony makes the text clearly understandable. For all their apparent simplicity, these are not the products of a weak musical talent. The need for direct expression was strongly felt by many composers of those years, and Friedrich accomplished his aim with great success.

The place of Handel in relation to the religious oratorio is somewhat anomalous, not because of what he wrote but rather because of the attitudes that have developed about his music. It is felt, especially in the United States, that his oratorios — to many people this means *Messiah* since they know of no others — represent the peak of church music composition in the English language. That these works had no connection with church functions seems to have no bearing upon the case. It is conceded that Handel wrote great choral music in the oratorios, greater than that of the Chandos Anthems, but its reappraisal at length would serve no purpose here.[45] Many of the oratorio texts to which Handel wrote his music were second-rate in concept or execution, and sometimes in both. The poor quality of this vital ingredient weakened the pieces that resulted, and the problem of inferior texts continued to plague composers — especially the English — for several generations. *Messiah* escapes this spate of mere words because its text is biblical, and its wide acceptance is, in great part, due to the strength and familiarity of the scriptural material. Without doubt, many other of his pieces would be competitors for its pop-

44. Both of Friedrich's oratorios are described in Geiringer, *op. cit.*, 402f.

45. For critical analyses and appreciations of Handel's oratorios, the following present a variety of information: Winton Dean, *Handel's Dramatic Oratorios and Masques* (New York: Oxford University Press, 1959); Jens Peter Larsen, *Handel's Messiah: Origins, Composition, Sources* (New York: W. W. Norton & Co., 1957); Rollo M. Myers, *Handel's Messiah: A Touchstone of Taste* (New York: The Macmillan Co., 1948); Bukofzer, *Music in the Baroque Era;* Jacobs, *Choral Music;* Young, *The Choral Tradition.* The principal biographies of Handel should also be consulted.

ularity if they were not saddled with what seem to us to be inane libretti.

The instrumentation of the Handelian orchestra was the same in his oratorios as in his operas. One concession he did make, however, perhaps because he was trying to intensify the difference between the two modes of expression even though both took place in the theater, was the substitution of the organ for the harpsichord. The selection of styles for the vocal solos and choruses comes from church and theater alike. Among the church-generated types may be found choruses fashioned after the pattern of the motet, the fugue, the double chorus, and the *concertato* for chorus and orchestra. Those that show a greater debt to secular prototypes include *da capo* forms, pieces in madrigal style, and choruses based on dance rhythms and ground basses. Handel accepted freely everything that came his way, adapting it to his own uses. Since he used ideas from so many sources, it is difficult to know whether his successors are indebted directly to him or to the same sources from which he derived his material.

Whether we continue to venerate Handel's theatrical oratorios as church music or not, there is no denying that English composers who followed him broke out in a veritable rash of oratorio composition. Their works have been viewed with disdain, tolerance, and even embarrassment by English writers who have apparently examined many examples in an effort to find some unquestionably outstanding works. The oratorio had become a true favorite among English entertainments, and several generations of composers beginning with Greene, Boyce, and Arne, set themselves the task of satisfying the immense appetites of the public. By the last quarter of the century a blight had set in, from which there was to be no relief for nearly another hundred years. The considered opinions of English historians of the period hold out small hope for the unearthing of hidden masterpieces.

The composers of these tons of oratorios were "all honourable men"; their visions of things outside the organ-loft were usually fitful and reluctant, but they worked hard and conscientiously, and their music is nothing worse than intolerably dull. They set, with apparently absolute indiscrimination wellnigh every word of the Bible; and when they were not writing oratorios of their own, they were still making them out of the mangled remains of other men's music.[46]

46. *Grove's*, VI, 260f.

Hardly even faint praise lurks among these damning comments, but at least one good end was achieved along with this mountain of music. The English public had learned to sing and to enjoy listening to choral music. The appetite had been enormously whetted, even though taste may have suffered from the prodigal flow of mediocre works. A tradition, strange though it may seem amidst so much indifferent music, was developing—a tradition that would eventually call forth talented men to produce works of quality, permitting British choral music to take a position of importance when finally it emerged.

Chapter X

The Later Development
of the Motet and Anthem

THE development of monody at the beginning of the seventeenth century influenced motet writing considerably. Since monodic style is so strongly linked to solo singing, however, it remains outside our sphere of interest except as we have already considered it in connection with the development of the cantata and the English anthem. Few-voiced and many-voiced *concertato* practices were found in those forms and need little further examination here, although a number of the composers involved in such activity could not be adequately considered in earlier chapters without placing too much emphasis on this one of many developments in choral music. It will now be necessary to view the motet in three further ways: as it was influenced by the colossal Baroque style, as it came to be a piece supported by the classical orchestra, and as it continued in traditional *a cappella* form. These limitations necessarily preclude consideration of the anthem as a kind of motet. Some writers have found it convenient to place motets and anthems together during the entire span of their common existence, but our view has been that the anthem differed sufficiently from the motet to be studied as a separate, viable form. In function and text sources it may be of the same family, but its development as a musical form kept it separate until the end of the nineteenth century. If the anthem bore a relationship to another existing musical type, it was to the cantata rather than to the motet, especially after it developed into a multisectional piece.

Were we to accept unconditionally as motets all pieces that fall specifically among those called Antiphon, Responsorium, Offertory, Psalm, and so on, we would find an active practice through the nineteenth century at least. As we move forward from the Baroque, however, we limit the use of our term more and more by allowing the specialized terms of function to replace our more general one of style.

We may believe that few motets were written by Mozart or Haydn, for instance, but the total number of their works relating to the Propers and the generally less ambitious musical portions of the religious service is considerable. It will be convenient to deal with all of these various types under the general term "motet" even though there is often a great difference in the external appearance of such pieces. Let us return to the beginning of the Baroque period to observe the course of this kind of music.

We have noted in an earlier chapter how instrumental music was added to choral singing and how it changed the character of what it touched so greatly that we speak of sharply differentiated Venetian and Roman styles in choral music generally, and of motets particularly. Added to this difference in choral writing was the addition of solo parts, probably stemming from the practice first seen in the works of Lodovico Viadana (1564–1645) of writing motets for solo voices. The next step, to motets that used both solos and chorus, was a short and natural one. Claudio Monteverdi was fortunately situated in this respect, for he drew upon his knowledge of Venetian practice at the same time that he called upon soloists to vary the interplay of choruses and instruments. The *Vespers* of 1610 are a case in point.[1] A more modest use of the motet style, adopting the *basso continuo* without incorporating solo sections, is seen in Giacomo Carissimi's *Cum reverteretur*, a canonic piece for three high voices.[2] The motets of Alessandro Scarlatti represent a mixture of styles—perhaps it would be more appropriate to say, a catholicity of taste—for there are some for voices *a cappella*, some for single and double choruses, others for voices and organ, and still others for voices and orchestra. Motets for instruments and voices may be dated from as early as 1714, and some are positively identified as belonging to the year 1720.[3] Scarlatti certainly belongs to the earliest group of Italian composers to use instruments in addition to the organ in motets, a practice abandoned in

1. Claudio Monteverdi, *Vespers,* ed. Denis Stevens (London: Novello, 1961). The editor differentiates between motets (which do not appear as part of the composition) and the response, psalms, and hymn which, with the Magnificat, make up the *Vespers.* In the broad sense, these works are types of motets, and they are certainly in motet style. The pieces that make up the *Vespers* are printed in *Tutte*

le Opere, xiv. See also Denis Stevens, "Where are the Vespers of Yesteryear?" *The Musical Quarterly,* xlvii/3 (July, 1961), 315–30.
2. Giacomo Carissimi, *Messe e Mottetti,* Vol. 1, ed. Lino Bianchi (Rome: Istituto Italiano per la Storia della Musica, 1960), 74–91.
3. Dent, *Alessandro Scarlatti.* See especially the catalogue of works, pp. 229–31.

Italy after the Venetian style culminated in Monteverdi's works. That Antonio Caldara (1670–1736) was also among the first to use orchestra is true, but he does not have undisputed claim to the practice if we may take the published examples[4] as representative, for the volume containing eight motets shows only a *basso continuo* with the two- and three-voice pieces. These motets date from 1715. There is, however, a setting of *Stabat Mater* in the same volume, of uncertain date, that calls for an orchestra of strings and trombones to play with the chorus *a 4* and four soloists.

The course of Italian motet composition appears to exhaust itself shortly after this period. Dr. Burney's reports of performances he attended throughout his Italian travels give some evidence that attention to the motet was perfunctory and less careful than was the creation of secular music. Nevertheless, Burney's opinions cannot always be unreservedly accepted, and we must not pass too lightly over the Italian works. While it now seems that interest in secular music all but stopped the production of religious pieces that were uncontaminated by the stage, the lack of materials in modern editions, the relatively unexplored Italian scene, and the late-blooming interest of serious researchers in the religious music of composers of stature in opera and instrumental music have combined to delay a complete study of this area. The absence of evidence is not sufficient reason for us to abandon the Italians entirely. It may well be that future research will uncover important religious works that have been overshadowed by a disproportionate interest in secular music. In the meantime, however, it is in the transfer of interest in the motet to Germany that we can take note of a development that runs a longer course and provides a variety of types.

We have recognized already that German composers knew the *a cappella* practice and employed it in Passion settings and shorter pieces using psalms and biblical verses as texts. The continued use of these traditional settings in polyphonic style was sporadic and became overshadowed by works that followed the more exciting Venetian pattern so convincingly employed by Heinrich Schütz. At no point, however, did the restrained imitative style for voices alone disappear completely from the musical scene. A group of motets that appeared in 1610 from the pen of Christoph Demantius (*CW* 39) solidly

4. *DTÖ*, xxvi.

proclaims the German mastery of polyphony. The few examples that
are now available of his pieces show no corresponding striving for
new methods or the use of other styles.

On the other hand, Michael Praetorius (1571–1621) moved in a
new direction without abandoning old methods. His *Musae Sioniae*,
published between 1605 and 1610, contains nearly 1250 different settings of chorales.[5] There are many duplications of tune and text—
there are, for example, fourteen settings of *Allein Gott in der Höh sei
Ehr (To God on high alone be praise)*—done in a number of styles: note
against note, involved counterpoint, with and without *cantus firmus*,
and in *concertato* interplay of voices. Praetorius recognized a number
of motet styles, not simply one. In the last book of this set, he specified
the methods he was using in these chorale settings.[6] Among them was
one he referred to as "simple motet fashion." By this he meant those
pieces in which the chorale melody was the basis of imitative contrapuntal writing, thereby appearing in all voices after the fashion of
the Latin motet of Josquin, where points of imitation were established
and exhausted. The pieces in "madrigal fashion" often begin in the
same way, the chorale phrase given imitatively by one chorus, then by
a second chorus in similar fashion, after which fragments of the chorale tune are tossed back and forth between the two groups, this practice resulting in cells or sections that deal with each segment of text
in similar fashion. Praetorius meant still one other thing when he
said motet. His *Musarum Sioniarum Motectae et Psalmi Latini* (1607)[7]
contains Latin motets for four to sixteen voices, for one to four choruses. There are clearly identified solo passages, and other sections
that contrast with them are equally specific in demanding voices and
instruments together *(chorus vocibus instrumentis et organo)*. These
tutti passages range from hammering block-chords to graceful contrapuntal sections.

Combinations of old and new ideas were also conveniently put
together by Johann Hermann Schein. The year 1623 saw the publication of his *Fontana d'Israel*, a collection of pieces with biblical text for
five or six voices in the Italian madrigal manner (*CW* 12). Whether
these are madrigals with religious text or motets in madrigal style is
less the point than the fact that pieces which had, up to that time,
usually not been associated with madrigal style were now showing a

5. Michael Praetorius, *Gesamtausgabe der musikalischen Werke von Michael Praetor-ius*, ed. Friedrich Blume (Wolfenbüttel: Georg Kallmeyer Verlag, 1928–1941), i–ix.
6. *Ibid.*, ix, ix.
7. *Ibid.*, x.

direct interrelationship. In addition, the use of a figured bass and the optional use of an accompanying instrument bring to the motets another dimension, that of more than a single method of performance. While imitative counterpoint is not discarded, it is often interrupted or replaced by homophonic sections that alternate between high and low voices. Schein is also represented among a group of composers who wrote chromatic motets (*CW* 14). The chromatic element is melodic rather than chordal, and it is used principally to intensify text. In *Die mit Tränen säen (They that sow in tears)* which was also part of the 1623 *Fontana d'Israel,* the chromaticism is restricted almost entirely to the presentation of the first four words, becoming far less evident with subsequent text portions *(Ex. 87).*

There is little need to dwell here on the contributions of Heinrich Schütz to German music generally or to the motet specifically, for much of what was said of him in connection with the development of oratorio applies here. The transfer of Italian style, the liberal application of text-painting, and the *concertato* interplay are all evident in the *Cantiones sacrae* of 1625.[8] These settings *a 4* of Latin texts were published with a figured *basso seguente* that was not originally the composer's idea. It can then be dispensed with in any consideration of the pieces. There was a place in the Lutheran observance for motets with Latin text. These texts represent a wide range of ideas, perhaps indicating a close connection with the Propers for various occasions. An outstanding example of the *concertato* treatment in this four-voiced texture is the setting of Psalm 149, *Cantate Domino canticum novum (Sing unto the Lord a new song).* The German motets of *Die*

Ex. 87 Chromatic subject from motet, *Die mit Tränen säen, Schein, CW*, XIV, 24f

From Blume, *Das Chorwerk*, 14. Used by permission.

8. Heinrich Schütz, *Neue Ausgabe Sämtliche Werke,* VIII–IX; *Sämtlicher Werke,* IV.

Psalmen Davids (1619)[9] are for multiple choruses with instruments, demonstrating with German text and lavish use of performers the transfer of the many-voiced *concertato* into new surroundings. The distinction between *favoriti* (selected voices from the chorus) and the full choral ensemble is clearly made by Schütz, a distinction that continues in some of the works of Andreas Hammerschmidt.

In the second volume of Hammerschmidt's *Musicalische Andachten* (1641) are pieces that use *favoriti* and full chorus as equal-textured alternating groups. The fourth volume (1646) contains *concertato* alternation between unequal textures, *cappella a 5* and *favoriti a 4* in a setting of *Vater unser*, and between a *cappella a 5* and a *favorito* TTB group in the motet *Ehre sei Gott in der Höhe (Praised be God in the highest)*. The *basso continuo* is, as the title page states, simply a *gedoppelten General Bass*.[10] While Hammerschmidt distinguished between motets, concertos, and pieces in the madrigal manner, his distinction had to do with the way in which the voice parts were treated in reference to imitation and alternation, and did not mean that the pieces were not all motets from the standpoint of their function as religious choral music.

The typically German process of using chorale stanzas is found in the works of two early members of the Bach clan. The motet *Unser Leben ist ein Schatten (Our life is but a shadow)* by Johann Bach (1604–1673)[11] employs two unequal groups of voices, one *a 6* singing the principal music of the motet, another "hidden chorus" *a 3* interrupting with chorale verses. Another chorale motet by Johann Michael Bach (1648–1694) is *Herr, ich warte auf dein Heil (Lord, I wait upon Thy call)*[12] for two equal four-part choruses. The second chorus sings biblical text and the first chorus breaks into the piece with phrases of a chorale.

The use of chorale melodies and their texts was a common feature of the German motet in the first half of the eighteenth century, as may be seen in numerous examples by relatively unknown Thuringian composers of that period.[13] While double-chorus writing is not entirely lacking, there is a variety of other methods of incorporating chorales. The New Year's motet *Das ist meine Freude (That is my delight)*, by a composer identified only as Liebholdt, uses a chorale

---

9. *Heinrich Schütz's Sämtliche Werke*, ed. Philipp Spitta *et al.*, (Leipzig: Breitkopf & Härtel, [1885–1927]), Vol. xvii. Not yet published in *Neue Ausgabe*.
10. The pieces are printed in *DdT*, xl.
11. Geiringer, *Music of the Bach Family* (Cambridge: Harvard University Press, 1955), 6–10. Only part of the motet is printed here.
12. *Ibid.*, 59–66.
13. *DdT*, xlix/l.

melody in *cantus firmus* fashion in the upper voice while the other three parts engage in elaborate figurations. In a number of such motets the chorale material is framed by choral settings of biblical text upon which the chorale can comment. There are motets of various lengths. Some are basically strophic, with the first phrases set as note-against-note harmonizations, and the remainder of the piece in imitative style. Others may be extended works, such as *Preise, Jerusalem, den Herren (Praise the Lord, Jerusalem)*, by G. T. Reineccius, which expands three verses of Psalm 147 to over two hundred and sixty measures of music for double chorus, using antiphonal sections in chordal style as contrasts for imitative passages, and breaking the piece into distinct sections at these changes by sharp contrasts of tempo as well. Another method of varying a long piece, even though only a single scriptural verse makes up its choral text,[14] is found in the anonymous motet *a 4, Herr, hebe an zu segnen (Lord, begin to bless)*. The scriptural text is divided into two sections, each in imitative polyphony and each followed by an "aria" for soprano and bass on a text of undetermined origin. After the second aria there is a choral Amen in imitative style, balancing the two settings of the verse in length and outdoing them in complexity, including a hocket section immediately before the final cadence.

The question arises: why was there a continuing interest in the German motet at a time when the Latin motet seemed to be declining? The answer lies in the structure of the Lutheran service, where the optional use of figural music, both in the form of motet and cantata (to use the modern term), provided ample opportunity for composers to continue production of new music until the same forces that ended the reign of the cantata at mid-eighteenth century brought motet composition to its close. There were two opportunities to use motets at the morning service, one at the beginning of the *Hauptgottesdienst* (see Table x, p. 233) and the other in connection with the Lord's Supper. The other opportunity for motet performance was in connection with Vespers. One could also speculate that the motet, especially as an unaccompanied composition, may have been used as the principal *Kirchenmusik* in such churches as had insufficient instrumental forces, but that could muster up a capable choral group. Such speculation cannot, of course, be supported by firm evidence. Without debate, however, we must accept the fact that the need for German motets dimin-

14. 1 Chron. 17:27 *DdT*, xlix/l, xxiv, erroneously lists the text as 1 Chron. 18:27.

ished, as did the need for larger forms of *Kirchenmusik*, when the simplification of musical portions of the service became common, the choirs and orchestras virtually disbanding, and the composer-director being displaced by the organist. This disintegration of a complex musical service took time, and remnants of the once voluminous cantata and motet literature may be found after the period had passed its height.

The position of Johann Sebastian Bach as the summarizing figure for Baroque music in Germany needs no defense. If anything, his penchant for adapting various methods of procedure is strongly evident again in the settings of his six extant motets.[15] They do not have many features in common except that they seem to have been written for use at Vespers and that most of them were specifically composed as funeral music. Four of the motets are for double chorus. In all of Bach's works, this is the point at which he gave greatest attention to the possibilities of pitting two four-part choruses against each other.[16] The results show that Bach saw more than one solution to writing for this combination of singers. The middle section of *Singet dem Herrn ein neues Lied (Sing ye to the Lord a new song)* is a chorale fantasia. Chorus II introduces each phrase of the chorale *Nun lob', mein' Seel', den Herren (Now praise the Lord, my soul)* and Chorus I responds with phrases of a prayer *(Ex. 88)*, the setting of which becomes increasingly complex as the dialogue proceeds.

For *Der Geist hilft unsrer Schwachheit auf (The Spirit also helpeth us)* Bach wrote a first section in which the two choruses function as distinct separate groups, followed by another section that is *a 4*; i.e., the two choruses still sing, but share the same material. The closing chorale maintains this simpler arrangement of voices. This is the only one of the motets that has full instrumental accompaniment and this differs from cantata accompaniments in that it is entirely *colla parte*. String instruments double the voices of Chorus I; wind instruments duplicate the vocal lines of Chorus II.

Another manner of treatment is found in *Fürchte dich nicht, ich bin bei dir (Be not afraid, I am with thee)*. During the first half of the motet, the two choruses are treated antiphonally, but in the second half they combine. In this *a 4* section, while the three lower voices participate

15. *BG*, xxxix. The entire set is published in a new practical edition (New York: C. F. Peters Corporation, 1958).
16. The other works using double chorus are *the Osanna* of the *Mass in B minor*, the *St. Matthew Passion*, and cantata number 50, *Nun ist das Heil und die Kraft (HMS, v, 54)*.

Ex. 88 Opening measures of middle section, motet, *Singet dem Herrn ein neues Lied*, Bach

in a fugue, the subject of which is a descending chromatic figure, the sopranos intone a verse of the chorale *Warum sollt' ich mich denn grämen (Why should I then grieve)* in discontinuous sections. The chorale tune is never adopted as part of the fugal texture, and the two elements—one strongly diatonic, the other richly chromatic—stand out in clear contrast to each other.

The remaining motet for double chorus, *Komm, Jesu, komm, mein Leib ist müde (Come, Jesus, come, for I am weary)* develops each line of a hymn stanza with a different musical idea, an extension of the old principle of points of imitation. Each line carries a distinctive musical idea, and the music of the last line is developed to considerably greater length than the others. Echoes, varied repetitions, and the use of complete choirs in canon with each other are among the *concertato* devices used. The second stanza of the hymn, set as an "aria" *a 4*, concludes the motet.

The four-voice motet *Lobet den Herrn, alle Heiden (Praise the Lord, all ye nations)* is unique in this group because it has a *basso continuo*, it is not a setting of text that is suitable to a funeral service, and it does not contain a chorale. It is possible that the piece originally was the opening chorus of a cantata that has not come to light. While such a connection is completely speculative, it cannot be lightly dismissed, especially since the cantata choruses were invariably *a 4*, a voice arrangement that appears only in this one of the six motets.

In *Jesu, meine Freude (Jesus, dearest pleasure)* one finds chorale verses inserted between sections of free text that paraphrase biblical verses. The chorale from which the motet gets its name opens the work, and its verses, as well as sometimes its music, are the basis of alternate sections of the piece thereafter. The resulting form is an arch with a fugue as its keystone, and sides consisting of trios, chorale verses, and choruses. The choruses balance the work by employing the same music for their opening sections. There is also considerable alternation of voice combinations, with SATB, SSATB, SSA, ATB, and SSAT used.

The generation after Bach produced no great names in the field of German motet writing. This fact may reflect the declining interest in compositions for the church, and the relative lack of a market for religious pieces in the concert hall, unless they were accompanied by instruments. The accompanied motet, as we have seen, failed to make a place for itself in Germany. Texts for motets of the late eighteenth century were either chosen entirely from biblical verses, coupled with chorale verses, or based on religious poems. The works were mostly for four or five voices, sometimes with figured bass, but usually without any form of instrumental support. A representative group of motets, far more modestly conceived than those of Bach, by Johann Ludwig Krebs (1713–1780), Johann Philipp Kirnberger (1721–1783), and

Gottfried August Homilius (1714–1785) has recently been published (*CW* 89). A degree of stylistic variety is present, including fugue sections, homophony with figurated melody, block-chord harmonizations, and short chorale fantasia movements. Perhaps the simplest arrangement of all is found in the four-voice motets of Karl Heinrich Graun. Typical of these is *Herr, ich habe lieb die Städe deines Hauses*,[17] a fugue in binary form. A small amount of text is used over and over as is, of course, the material of the fugue subject for the principal musical material.

The motets of J. J. Fux (graduals, offertories, communions, introits, and tracts)[18] are mostly *a cappella* works for four voices, although there are also instances when a group of instruments are designated to play *colla parte*. There are a few pieces also for five voices. All is accomplished with the greatest restraint. There is no trace of elaborate writing or of secular influence; the motets are entirely restricted to imitative style in points of imitation. Each time a new point is first introduced, the first voice to present the material enters after a rest. Coming out of a momentary silence, the new melodic fragment is therefore clearly free of any confusing relationship with the preceding thematic material. No new developments in motet composition are in evidence here. There is, rather, a return to an idealized Palestrina idiom, more restrained than its prototype, imbued with academic caution that was never evident in the works upon which they were patterned. The texts come from the Propers and, lacking any unnecessary repetition or extended florid passages in the music, they generally result in brief musical settings. In only a few cases are there contrasts of tempo, although changes of meter are common in all but the shortest pieces.

In the volume devoted to church pieces by Michael Haydn,[19] only one piece for solo quartet, SATB chorus, orchestra, and organ is designated as a motet. The other compositions are an antiphon, an offertorium, and a number of graduals (*HMS*, vii, 33f). They, too, qualify as motets in the broadest meaning of the term, and they show a wide variety of treatments. One is for double chorus *a cappella;* some are for chorus and trio sonata; others substitute or add various wind instruments. Significantly, in the works of this last great Catholic church composer there is found a mingling of old and new styles, unaccom-

17. English version under the title, *Lord, I Love the Habitation of Thy House* (Lubbock, Texas: Gamut Company, 1963).   18. *DTÖ*, iii.

19. *DTÖ*, lxii.

panied and orchestra-supported, simple settings with instruments doubling the voices, and complex works in which the instruments play elaborate introductions and interludes between the solo and choral sections. No firm line of tradition existed any longer; the motet not only lost its purpose, but, except for a few efforts by composers who were demonstrating their skill in older styles, it also disappeared from the scene.

The relative absence of motets from the works of the elder Haydn and Mozart can be explained by their preoccupation with secular music. Only when convenience or interest stirred them did they compose large-scale church works. Mozart's *Ave verum* stands alone as a widely known example of the motet.

The most significant contribution to German motet literature after Bach comes from the pen of Johannes Brahms (1833–1897). His seven motets,[20] opp. 29, 74, and 110—if the more festive works that make up op. 109 are also considered as motets the total is increased to ten— display a variety of styles that bespeak an affection for, and mastery of, the unaccompanied vocal style. Brahms's indebtedness is to the German church tradition in his choice of texts and in his musical styles. The entire group cannot be examined in detail here, but their immense variety and their position at the end of a long tradition demands at least a rapid inventory.

The two five-voice motets of op. 29 differ from each other in many respects. *Es ist das Heil uns kommen her (Salvation is come unto us)* is in two sections: first, a chorale setting of a single verse of text; second, a series of fugal expositions that use the chorale phrases as their subjects, and that repeat the same verse of text. The upper of two bass parts is withheld from the fugal sections as a normal participant. Instead it carries the melody in augmentation at the close of each exposition. The second motet, *Aus dem 51. Psalm*, the text beginning *Schaffe in mir, Gott, ein rein Herz* ("Create in me a clean heart, O God"), is in three movements. The first is a homophonic setting *a 5;* the second is a fugue *a 4.* The final movement is in two contrasting parts: it opens with an antiphonal section that pits an SAA group against a TBB combination. A five-voice fugue closes the motet.

There are also two motets in op. 74. *Warum ist das Licht gegeben dem Mühseligen (Why is the light given unto the weary)* is divided into four movements: two settings for six voices enclosed by two for SATB. The

20. *Johanne Brahms Sämtliche Werke,* xxi.

final movement is a verse of the chorale *Mit Fried und Freud ich fahr dahin (With peace and joy I journey thither).* A five-stanza poem is set for four voices in *O Heiland, reiss die Himmel auf (O Savior, rend the heavens).* Each stanza shows a different treatment of imitative counterpoint. A single melody *(Ex. 89)* forms the soprano line of the first, second, and fifth stanzas, the tenor melody of the third stanza, and the bass of the fourth. Its broad lyricism is typical of many of Brahms's vocal melodies. One of the op. 110 motets is for SATB chorus, a simple setting in *Bar* form of three short stanzas of text. The other two are for double chorus. Along with the three double-choir *Fest- und Gedenksprüche* of op. 109, they display Brahms's considerable skill and variety in writing polychoral music. These last pieces, not intended as service music and therefore not properly motets, have been said to show traces of Handelian influence. The absence of similar characteristics from pieces by Handel, plus Brahms's knowledge of German traditions, seems to relate them more closely with Bach and Schütz.

German motet activity came to a virtual halt with Brahms. There were a few composers of ambition, but of lesser ability, who produced works of this kind, but they contributed nothing to the literature. In the twentieth century a German interest in pure choral music was kindled by a number of composers who closely associated themselves with music for the church.[21] Settings of Gospel texts, psalms, Graduals, and Epistles are among the examples that find their way into this new activity for the service. These pieces are generally for three to eight voices unaccompanied, with imitative counterpoint. Fragments of text are extended over relatively long sections of music. Hugo Distler (1908–1942) used thirty-three measures to give out the first phrase of his five-voice motet, *Wachet auf, ruft uns die Stimme (Wake, awake, a*

Ex. 89 Melody of Brahms's motet, *O Heiland, reiss die Himmel auf*

21. These composers and their works are considered in greater detail in Chapter XI. The cantatas and oratorios mentioned there show substantially the same treatment as is found in the motets, but on a larger scale.

voice is calling), employing the chorale melody of the same name. Most of the section consists of the words *wachet auf* repeatedly tossed about among the voices in figures that feature rising thirds and fourths, figures that are then inverted and finally used in opposition to each other. The chorale melody, subtly disguised by melodic and rhythmic alteration, appears at various points during the first of the three movements in the motet. The other two movements present the chorale in imitative fashion, the second with the addition of two soprano soloists.

Siegfried Reda (1916–) has written many motet settings of Graduals, psalms, and Epistles. These works again link the music closely to the Proper texts of the service, as in the settings by composers of the Baroque period. The pieces are generally of modest length and method; although there are some for double chorus, most of them are for the usual mixed chorus *a 4.* His motet for the Tenth Sunday after Trinity may be taken as an example. The Epistle for that Sunday is 1 Cor. 12:1–11. Reda has taken only the second half of the third verse, *Niemand kann Jesus einen Herrn nennen ausser: durch den heiligen Geist*[22] ("No man can say that Jesus is the Lord, but by the Holy Ghost"). The upper voices are paired in opposition to the lower until the final segment of text is taken up (after considerable repetition of the first six words), at which point all voices enter in successive imitation, but the tenor repeats a descending pattern of three diatonic notes in increasing diminution, from dotted half to half notes to quarter notes. In this piece, as in others, Reda selects the heart of the Epistle text and presents it in compact form.

Returning to the Baroque period in France, we find an interest in the motet among several composers, most of whom use the form as a vehicle of varied, exciting musical ideas with chorus, solo voices, and orchestra in several movements. Such large works are known as grand motets, and have as their opposite number the petit motet for one or more solo voices and orchestra or *continuo.* The relationship between these grand motets and the *a cappella* motet that developed in Italy and Germany is negligible. Far closer is the connection between them and the German church cantata or the English verse anthem, a connection in outward appearances, relationship of separate sections, and generally elaborate performing forces. It is not suggested that the grand motet was directly influenced by either the German or English parallel forms, but that it grew, as they did, out of the taste of a period that

22. Slightly modified from Luther's translation.

demanded jubilant and grandiose expressions of text in certain situations, both secular and religious. The French court did not distinguish clearly between the world and the church; ceremonial pomp that originated in the court was carried into religious observances, especially on those occasions when Louis xiv or Louis xv happened to be present. The reigns of these two monarchs encompassed the period in which the grand motet rose to prominence and again dropped from the musical picture. It is to musicians who came under their influence, inasmuch as the bestowal of favor was a major factor in French musical patterns of that period, that we turn for examples of this form of the motet.

Jean-Baptiste Lully (1632–1687) is credited with the composition of at least twenty-three motets, eleven of them grand motets; twelve, petit motets. Six grand motets were published during the last years of his life, four of which were printed in the so-called complete edition of Lully's works.[23] One of these will be sufficient to illustrate the way Lully dealt with large religious pieces of this type. His *Miserere mei, Deus (Have mercy upon me, O God)*, a setting of Psalm L (51), was first heard at Tenebrae in 1666. It was used again six years later in connection with a funeral service, where it was widely acclaimed. The double chorus arrangement is different from those we have seen in most other pieces. The two choirs are unequal in two ways: Chorus i is made up of soloists and a small group of performers on each part for the full sections; Chorus ii consists of a larger body of singers without any solo voices. This is not Lully's own development. The use of differentiated choruses is already found in motets by Nicolas Formé (1567–1638) and was adopted by several other composers, including Henry Dumont (1610–1684), from whom Lully most probably learned the style during their long association. Lully and the other composers of grand motets who followed him were composing their pieces for performance at the *Chapelle Royale* (established 1663) where elaborate music with orchestral accompaniment was the rule. The textural balance between Lully's two groups is also a matter of contrast. Chorus i tends to produce a lighter sound than Chorus ii: the former is SSATB; the latter, SATBB. When the first chorus sings alone, it is supported by *continuo* only. The string ochestra plays only with the second chorus. Even when both choruses sing at the same time, the orchestra is confined to material that belongs to the large group. The two bassoons are divided

23. *Oeuvres complètes de J.-B. Lully, pub-liées sous la Direction de Henry Prunières* (Paris: Editions de la Revue Musicale, 1930–1939), *Les Motets*, Tomes i & ii.

according to function: the first bassoon is coupled with the bass line of Chorus I; the second, with the bass of the orchestra. The motet is a continuous piece of about half an hour's duration, divided into differentiated sections at new verse segments not by strong cadences and pauses, but by changes of tempo, shift of emphasis from one body of performers to another, and by the insertion of a few short instrumental interludes. The second chorus often reinforces and accompanies, but it is by no means without interesting or even difficult musical materials. Imitative patterns are present in both groups, and the isolation of some solo voices in the first chorus is simply a matter of convenience rather than one of setting apart a highly skilled group of performers for music of greater difficulty. Lully's later motets generally abandoned polyphony and took on theatrical characteristics of simplicity and declamation, features that found the king's favor and so became the norm.

The French grand motet has received little attention until the last two decades. Leichtentritt dismissed it, insofar as he was familiar with it at all, as something entirely outside the classification, although he recognized the fact that the term "motet" was being used in a general rather than a specific sense in many parts of Europe by the time of the Baroque period.[24] There is no reason to quarrel with his conviction that the grand motet lies nearer the cantata than to the *a cappella* choral motet. Nevertheless, the French use of the term, the choice of text, and the function of these works indicate that they should be considered here rather than as types of the cantata.

It does not appear that Marc-Antoine Charpentier played any important part in changing the course of motet development in France, but he produced such works, including some for double and triple chorus with, of course, the usual complement of instrumentalists. Although he composed ninety of these large compositions,[25] his principal importance still seems to lie in the stream of oratorio development. The next figure of importance was Michel Richard de Lalande (1657–1726) who became the most influential person in French religious music.[26] He rose to prominence early, sharing the post of *surin-*

24. Hugo Leichtentritt, *Geschichte der Motette* (Leipzig: Breitkopf & Härtel, 1908). Chapter XII deals with the French motet, most of the attention being directed to the traditional, unaccompanied works of the Renaissance and early Baroque.
25. Seven of the grand motets are studied in detail in James P. Dunn, "The *Grands*

Motets of Marc-Antoine Charpentier (1634–1704)" (unpublished Ph.D. dissertation, State University of Iowa, 1962).
26. James E. Richards, "Structural Principles in the Grand Motets of Michel-Richard de Lalande (1657–1726)," *Journal of the American Musicological Society,* XI/2–3 (Summer-Fall, 1958), 119–27.

tendant de la Chapelle Royale with three other men from 1683 to 1704, when he was given sole charge of the *Chapelle*. His forty-two motets, published after his death, go beyond the confines of the Lullian pattern by the skillful reinstatement of polyphony into the essentially harmonic framework. His lyricism and overall attention to fine detail make his works especially appealing.

By 1722 the duties at the *Chapelle Royale* were more than Lalande could comfortably handle by himself, especially as he was burdened with several other responsibilities.[27] He therefore asked that the work be divided among four musicians, one to each quarter of the year, as it had been done in earlier years. The other men who now shared the position with Lalande were Nicolas Bernier (1664–1734), Charles Hubert Gervais (1671–1744), and, most important of the group, André Campra (1660–1744). Campra, after twenty years of work as a church musician (1680–1700), had been released from his church obligations, had taken up a profitable career as an opera composer and, in accepting the position at the *Chapelle* in his sixth decade, was returning to a kind of composition for which he was suited both by experience and temperament.

There are thirty-one of Campra's grand motets in complete form and a lesser number that have certain parts lacking. He maintained the distinction between small chorus and larger chorus, with an additional element of differentiation: his small chorus is often thinned down to an SSA combination, especially in dialogue choruses. His treatment of the orchestra undergoes a certain amount of change also. His earliest grand motet, published in 1703, used the orchestra after the fashion of Lully, i.e., divided into five parts; in his later motets "the basic five-part orchestra is reduced to four parts, the abandoned instrument being the lower viola or viol."[28] *Obbligato* instruments, especially violin, flute, and oboe, singly and in combination, are called for in connection with solo and ensemble sections as well as in choral movements. Lalande also specified such instrumental participation, especially in dialogue sections. Campra's use of the orchestra before, during, and after vocal sections exceeds that of Lully to a considerable extent, but these purely instrumental sections are still relatively brief and do not compare in any way with the more elaborate pieces found in large German choral works of the same period. Im-

27. Much of the information concerning the music and personalities discussed in this section is based on Conan Jennings Castle, "The Grand Motets of André Campra" (unpublished Ph. D. dissertation, University of Michigan, 1962).
28. *Ibid.*, I, 92.

portant to the grand motet was the *récit,* an aria-like solo accompanied
by orchestra. The grand motet *Lauda Jerusalem* (1727) contains them in
the following order: *récit, choeur, récit, récit, récit, dialogue, choeur.*
Benedictus Dominus (1728) disposes of the sections in an entirely different fashion, giving greater emphasis to the chorus and substituting
a duo for one of the solo pieces: *choeur, récit, duo, récit, choeur, récit,*
choeur.[29]

After the death of Campra, his position at the *Chapelle Royale* was
filled by Jean-Joseph Cassanéa de Mondonville (1711–1772). Before he
became part of the court chapel's musical staff, some of Mondonville's
grand motets had already been performed at the *Concert Spirituel*
where, incidentally, those of Lalande had also been well received.
Mondonville simplified the form of the grand motet by writing for
only one chorus *a 5*, SATBB, at least in the works that appear in modern editions.[30] The orchestra is similar to that of Campra, rather·than
to that of earlier periods; that is, the distribution of material is among
four parts rather than five. Mondonville's *Jubilate* divides Psalm xcix
(100) into seven sections as follows: (1) *Récit* (tenor) *et choeur;* (2) *duo*
(soprano and bass); (3) *récit* (soprano); (4) *récit et choeur* (soprano solo
and soprano chorus); (5) *récit* (soprano); (6) *choeur;* and (7) *choeur.*
Polyphony is absent, even in the choruses, but as several of the five
voices sometimes carry different rhythms at the same time, there is
considerable contrast to the basic pattern of simple note-against-note
part-writing.

In the complete works of Jean-Philippe Rameau (1683–1764),[31]
there are five motets, four of which are grand motets for chorus, soloists, organ, and orchestra. The other is a short, single movement on
the text *Laboravi clamans (I cried aloud in my travail)* for SSATB and
continuo or organ. It first served as an example in Rameau's *Traité de*
l'harmonie (1722).

The grand motets have a number of features in common: they are
all for a single chorus; they distinguish between *récits* and *airs;* they
are all based on psalm texts. Their differences are numerous and are
best considered singly.

29. Both of these motets are transcribed
in their entirety by Castle, *op. cit.*, ii, 1–
188.
30. Two motets, *Jubilate* and *Cantate Dom-*
ino, have been edited by Edith Borroff and

published by the University of Pittsburgh
Press.
31. Jean-Philippe Rameau, *Oeuvres com-*
plètes publiées sous la Direction de C. Saint-
Saëns, 18 vols. (Paris: A Durand et Fils,
1895–1913).

In convertendo (When the Lord turned again) (Psalm cxxv [126]) calls for SATBB chorus, first attached to a *récit* for contralto, again after a *récit* for soprano and, finally, as a closing chorus. The choral writing is largely chordal and supported by an orchestra of flutes, oboes, bassoons, and strings. There are a duo for soprano and bass and an air for bass, both with orchestral support. The SAB trio that precedes the final chorus is supported by violins and *continuo*. The violins are not divided as in a trio sonata, but all play a single part.

Psalm LXXXIII (84), *Quam dilecta tabernacula (How amiable are thy tabernacles)*, opens with an *air* for soprano. Whereas an earlier generation of composers had employed the term *récit* indiscriminately for solo pieces, Rameau made a distinction between *récit* and *récitatif* as solos with attached choral sections, and *air* as a form of greater lyrical content. (In his setting of Psalm XVII, see below, he put the terms together as an indication of contrast in a *récitatif et air* for contralto.) Following the first *air* of Psalm LXXXIII, Rameau wrote a five-voice fugue, the only fugal piece among the motets printed in the complete works. An *air* for contralto is followed by a trio for SSB and *continuo*. A *récitatif et choeur* (tenor followed by SSATBB), an *air* for bass, and a final chorus *a 6* complete the work.

Rameau's Psalm XLV (46), *Deus noster refugium (God is our refuge and strength)*, and Psalm XVII (18), *Diligam Te, Domino (I will love thee, O Lord)*, continue the tendency toward variety, their most apparent common feature being the SATB chorus. In addition, however, there are a trio and an *air* accompanied by trio sonata, an *ariette da capo* (unusual in French motets), *airs* accompanied by florid *obbligato* solos for violin or flute, and solo ensembles for unusual groupings of voices as, for instance, ATTB.

The Rameau motets are not formula pieces; each is an individually conceived work of carefully planned materials and combinations of voices and instruments. Such variety is indicative of a freedom from formulas, a lack of conformity to taste imposed upon the composer by outside forces. In that age, the varied creations of Bach, of Handel, as well as these examples by Rameau, are the kinds of musical works that signify a facile expression that marks the end of a period. After each of these men, no one appeared on the scene to challenge their positions by imitation. His country's prevalent taste was synthesized by each. In Rameau's case, the grand motet had reached the end of a long trail that had been trod by Lully, Charpentier, Lalande, Campra, and Mondonville. The next steps were toward simplicity, for with the diminishing influence of the *Chapelle Royale* and the end of the *Concert Spirituel* (1791) religious music was again directed toward regular church activities and consequently lost much of its theatrical character. After this time a motet composed in the grand manner had, as its first purpose, the entertainment of a secular audience, no matter how serious (or pompous) the import of the piece. Conversely, motets for church were usually simple and avoided lavish use of instruments and complex vocal structures. Only in exceptional cases did the orchestra figure in a church composition in France after the Revolution. The continuation of the large-scale composition not classified as oratorio was sporadic. Charles Gounod's (1818–1893) *Gallia,* composed for the opening of the International Exhibition in London (May, 1871), is representative. It is not intended as a work for the church, yet it is constructed on a series of scriptural Latin texts that do not offend church needs; indeed, the closing section of the piece has had considerable popularity in the English translation, *Jerusalem, O turn thee to the Lord thy God.*

More to the pattern of that time is César Franck's (1822–1890) Offertory, *Dextera Domini,* for STB chorus, soloists, organ, and double bass, written in 1871, the same year that saw the first performance of Gounod's *Gallia.* Franck's general eschewal of alto parts for church pieces probably reflected nothing more than a shortage of boys in his own choir. It was certainly not a deliberate mannerism. When Franck wrote works of greater pretensions, like his oratorios or the Psalm CL (1888) for chorus, orchestra, and organ, the alto parts were present and completely functional. What is significant in this connection is the subordinate position given to soloists and ensembles. The traces of the multisectional grand motet are gone. In their place are cohesiveness and continuity, a no-nonsense presentation of a piece that has a variety of thematic material depending as much upon earnestness and simplicity as it does upon visible skill and talent.

The motets of Camille Saint-Saëns (1835–1921) are of various kinds. In the published group of twenty,[32] there are seven for solo voice and organ, five for two voices and organ, three for trio, one for treble quartet, and only four for chorus and organ. This distribution of vocal combinations points to a revival of functional music for the church service, music that can be performed under various circumstances by whatever singers may be available, barring restrictions of

32. *Vingt Motets par Camille Saint-Saëns* (Paris: A. Durand & Fils [between 1891– 1909]). The firm was known as A. Durand & Fils only between the dates given here.

inappropriate texts. Such a view is supported by the simplicity of most of the pieces.

Let us consider the four motets for chorus. *Ave verum* and *Tollite hostias (Take the offerings)* are for mixed voices. The former has a *colla parte* organ accompaniment, the latter a piano accompaniment of the same type. The voice parts are almost entirely homophonic. His eight-part *Tantum ergo (Bow we then)* uses the organ as an independent accompanying instrument. Chords bridge over breathing spaces of unaccompanied parts, and the organ has slow broken chord patterns against sustained vocal lines. Saint-Saëns did not use two equal choruses in opposition here; he simply wrote for four-part male chorus at the beginning, four-part treble chorus later, and finally for all of the voices together. The remaining motet is a setting of the hymn *Veni, creator* for four-part male chorus. The organ part is unessential; it doubles the voices throughout. The piece is a fairly long contrapuntal one and is the best of the group, not simply because it returns to polyphonic principles, but because the melodies are long-breathed, flowing lines that contain none of the square phrase-chunks that debilitate the rest of these motets.

Because of the subordinate, and even suppressed, position of the Catholic Church in England at the end of the eighteenth century, we can discern no tradition in motet composition there. Some few motets were written by Samuel Webbe (1740–1816) and a greater number by Samuel Wesley (1766–1837), the most esteemed being his *In exitu Israel (When Israel went out of Egypt)*, an outstanding work for double chorus. But the strength of the English lay in the composition of the anthem which, although at its nadir after Handel's day, was destined to rise again to a place of importance beginning with the Wesleys.[33]

33. The development of the anthem from this point to its numerous present-day types is too complex for discussion in detail here. The material that follows must be considered simply as a brief survey that touches on only a few of the leading figures and their contributions in the nineteenth century. There is no single volume that approaches the development of short English language pieces for the Protestant service. I am undertaking such a book in collaboration with Dr. Robert H. Young, which will deal with anthems from mid-eighteenth century to the present. The following studies will be helpful, although their authors did not intend them to serve as historical studies of this entire period: Dwight Steere, *Music for the Protestant Church Choir* (Richmond: John Knox Press, 1955); *The Church Anthem Book*, ed. Walford Davies and Henry G. Ley (London: Oxford University Press, 1933); Charles L. Etherington, *Protestant Worship Music* (New York: Holt, Rinehart & Winston, 1962); Myles Birket Foster, *Anthems and Anthem Composers* (London: Novello and Company, 1901).

What had befallen the elaborate *Kirchenmusik* of the Lutherans and the French music of the *Chapelle Royale* also befell the complex anthems of the English Royal Chapel. Changing tastes and the transformation of customs uprooted these intricate works from their favored positions. There came a time when such pieces were simply no longer needed; the kind of situation for which they had once been written had ceased to exist. Simplicity was the new watchword, acceptance of the piece by the congregation was an important criterion. Indifferent craftsmanship and facile emptiness threatened, on every front, to replace art. The problems were the lack of experience and low level of taste in the new audience for music, and the lack of skill among composers. In England the glorious days of the Chapel Royal were ended, even though the choir continued to exist, as indeed did the choirs of cathedrals in other parts of England. But more and more, attention was turned to the parish churches, large and small, where choirs were harder to establish, train, and maintain, and where music was neither complex nor elaborate. The need for a practical kind of choral fare was evident, and its widespread adoption is attested by the compilation of collections such as the *Ten Full Anthems Collected from the works of several Eminent Composers, Published principally for the Use of Country Churches,* issued about 1760 by J. Johnson. Works of this type—and the one mentioned is by no means unique—made available to smaller churches a variety of moderately easy pieces.[34] Still, since they were anthems that had not been written for inexperienced singers, they probably were too great a challenge to many choirs. Perhaps as a result of the continuing gap between ambition and execution, new pieces of smaller dimensions and pretensions began to appear as separate compositions: some of them following the patterns laid down by the verse anthem and the full anthem, but on a lesser scale; others, breaking away from established English practice, beginning to branch out in new directions.

The wide distribution of one work in the style of past generations has led to a certain amount of confusion about the prevalent style after Handel's death. Edmund Ayrton (1734–1808) wrote a verse anthem, *Begin unto my God with timbrels,* SSATB, with an orchestra of trumpets, timpani, oboes, bassoons, strings, and *continuo,* as the exercise submitted for a Doctor of Music degree at Cambridge in 1784. The work was again performed on July 29 of the same year at St. Paul's

---

34. A modern edition of one of these anthems is William Child's *Praised Be the*   *Lord* (Lubbock, Texas: Gamut Company, 1963).

Cathedral, London, and was published in 1788. The large list of subscribers and the number of surviving copies of that edition attest to its wide dispersion. It is not, however, truly representative of church music of that time. The large verse anthem was no longer employed as a regular tool of worship; Ayrton's decision to present this type of composition was probably based on academic requirements rather than religious practices. It requires an instrumental group of considerable facility, even though the choral parts call for little more fluency than do the formulas that were by then well established in oratorio. The final chorus, for instance, is a "Hallelujah, Amen" piece that faithfully treads the Handelian path, solid, appropriate, and pedestrian. In the opening chorus, a gesture toward fugal writing is defeated either by Ayrton's lack of interest or his inability to continue the voices after they have made statements of the subject. One by one they enter, and they drop out in like manner *(Ex. 90),* leaving the scene with the same thin sound that was present when they entered, and taking refuge in homophonic solidity after the disaster.

The true picture is more fairly represented by the *Eight Anthems in Score, for the use of Cathedrals and Country Choirs* by Samuel Webbe. This collection of anthems may have been published as early as 1788[35] and contains eight verse anthems—one that is called a full anthem

Ex. 90 Fugal statement from Ayrton's *Begin unto my God with timbrels* (1784)

35. The Baylor University copy is inscribed as a gift by Webbe, and is dated 1788. The *British Union Catalogue* suggests that the first edition appeared later, but evidence is lacking. The New York Public Library catalogue also dates the work as 1788.

contains a substantial solo section—that put considerable interest on
the solo voices, although the choruses are well written. There is no
provision for accompaniment other than that indicated by the usual
continuo. Webbe's note that "most of the principal Treble parts may
be sung by a Tenor, as may also the Tenor parts by a Treble" indicates
that the choirs were not always blessed with enough singers. Webbe

was active in producing music for both the Catholic and Anglican communions. As organist for Catholic services which, being banned at that time, were held on the "foreign soil" of the Sardinian and Portuguese embassies, he wrote motets and Masses. In other places, he found it equally practical to write anthems, and in them he adopted the idea of giving titles other than opening lines of text to some of his work. His texts are not simply continuous passages of Scripture, but, as he wrote in his *Eight Anthems in Score:*

> instead of being taken in the Order in which they stand in any One Psalm, have been arranged from different Ones, or other parts of the holy Scriptures, with a View to obtain by such Means, if not a greater Connection of Sentiment, at least Words adapted to a richer, and more varied musical Expression of that particular Affection which the Titles placed at the head of each Anthem shew it was the Intention and wish of the Author to excite in the Minds of those who either perform them or hear them performed.

His anthem based on Psalm 16 begins with the text, "Save us, O God," but bears the title, *Confidence in God.* It is typical of his verse anthems. The chorus is employed at both the beginning and end of the anthem with a framing two-sectional piece composed of nine slow measures in quadruple meter followed by nine of slightly faster triple meter. Between the choruses are a bass solo, a duo for soprano and alto, a tenor recitative, an alto-tenor duo, and a soprano solo. The entire anthem is less than a hundred and fifty measures long. It makes no great demand upon the singers, but it is not dull. Interest is sustained through changes of tempo, meter, key, and mode.

A collection that shows a later development is William Crotch's (1775–1847) *Ten Anthems,*[36] of which six are full anthems. The term is not used without some qualification, however, for several of those full anthems contain solo sections. The distinction between full and verse seems to lie in the way the solos appear. In the verse anthems, the solos and ensembles are set off as separate sections with change of meter, tempo, or thematic material, while in the full anthem the solo voices simply take up phrases of continuous material, and that only

---

36. While no date of publication appears on the printed copies, it is possible to approximate the year it appeared by consulting the list of subscribers. For example, a "Mr. Pratt, Organist, Cambridge," appears on the list. John Pratt (1772–1855) was appointed organist at King's College in 1799, and to the University in the following year. The publication of the volume, then, dates from after the turn of the century. How much later could be ascertained by tracing other names on the list.

briefly. The full anthems are generally shorter than the verse anthems, since conveying text was not so time-consuming as displaying a variety of singers in addition to the chorus. In a few places, Crotch went to the trouble to write out the entire organ part, but generally the accompaniment was left to be realized from a *continuo* part.

The organ parts of all eight of the anthems in *Attwood's Cathedral Music* are written out, but not by Thomas Attwood (1765–1838), the composer. The pieces were not published until about fifteen years after Attwood died, at which time they were edited, and the organ accompaniments "arranged" by Thomas Attwood Walmisley (1814–1856), godson of the composer. While it is interesting to notice the presence of written accompaniments by mid-nineteenth century, even when they are simply *colla parte*, it is still the substance of Attwood's anthems that concerns us here, inasmuch as the organ parts are not his own. The anthems make no concession to the country choir or parish church as did those of Webbe, but continue to follow the cathedral tradition. Attwood was active at both St. Paul's and the Chapel Royal, and his pieces must be viewed as representative of the performance of those centers rather than of that found at lesser centers of worship. Five of the anthems in the volume are full; three are verse. The verse anthems are somewhat longer than the full, but all are of considerable length. Attwood's full anthem, *Grant, we beseech thee,* composed in 1814, is a setting of the Collect for the Twenty-first Sunday after Trinity, and employs much repetition of text. Syllabic treatment was not the norm in cathedral settings, but Attwood's piece shows more than usual of the repetition of the first six words of the Collect because the piece is written as a fugue, using a subject that in expanded form was later to become famous at the hands of Schubert *(Ex. 91)*. Schubert's *C major Symphony* was composed in 1828, so there is no question of Attwood having borrowed from his more illustrious contemporary. The reverse is not necessarily true, but the exact parallel of the two themes is remarkable.

Of the same generation as T. A. Walmisley are Sir John Goss (1800–1880) and Samuel Sebastian Wesley (1810–1876). These men made massive strides toward a new type of anthem, simple, forthright, uncomplicated for the choir, and difficult only in solo passages.

Ex. 91 Fugue subject of Attwood's *Grant, we beseech thee* (1814)

While it would be gratifying to attribute these features to genius and foresight, necessity played a large part in the new shape of choral pieces for the religious service. In a pamphlet by Wesley,[37] first printed in 1849, we can read a stinging indictment of the clergy and of Parliament concerning their lack of understanding and interest in maintaining the quality of cathedral music and the manpower to present it properly. He complains of lack of funds, lack of interest, lack of support, and, most damaging, lack of singers. In the face of this situation, Wesley, Goss, and a number of the lesser figures of the same period, turned their attention to anthems that still have a place as emergency material in many churches today. Such works as Goss's *O Saviour of the World* and Wesley's *O Lord, my God* show many of the traits that made them practical then and now: they are syllabic, they are firmly based on the traditional harmonic foundation of the middle nineteenth century, they rarely employ elaborate solo material, their principal melody is clear in the top voice of the choir and accompaniment, and they have a dignity that remains even when changing harmonic tastes have threatened them with obsolescence. Wesley and Goss set a pattern for simplicity and directness that, while it may have been the child of necessity, was the parent of a new style vital enough to revive a failing mode of expression. To the style of the anthem they gave stability for a time; to the church musicians they gave an opportunity to regroup their forces before it became necessary to deal with religious texts in chromatic and emotional fashion, with the vocabulary of Romanticism. From that time onward, the anthem was pulled in several directions by the experimentalists and the traditionalists.

The most prolific composer of anthems in this period was Sir Frederick Arthur Gore Ouseley (1825–1889), from whose pen flowed at least seventy anthems. Eighteen of them are included in a volume of his works, published about the middle of the century.[38] All are true full anthems without solos, and all are printed with *colla parte* accompaniments. Three are for eight voices, one is for six, and the rest are for four. The eight-voice pieces lean heavily on the alternation of the full *decani* and *cantoris* complements, repeating sections of text *alternatim*, and sometimes making literal repetitions of the musical material as well. *I will give thanks* (Psalm 138:1–2) concludes with a

37. Samuel Sebastian Wesley, *A Few Words on Cathedral Music and the Musical System of the Church, with a Plan of Reform* (London: F. & J. Rivington, *et al.*, 1849)

reprinted, Hinrichsen Edition, 1961.
38. The Revd. Sir Frederick A. G. Ouseley, Bart., *Cathedral Music, Services & Anthems* (London: J. Alfred Novello, [1850?]).

double fugue that begins on the *decani* side *(Ex. 92)* and eventually involves all eight voices in quite skillful fashion. The six-voice anthem on the beginning of Psalm 117, *O praise the Lord, all ye heathen*, is SSAATB and, when it does not move in full six-voice texture, alternates the combinations SSA and ATB. It is in the four-voice pieces that Ouseley shows himself as a practical composer working along traditional lines. The anthems are all short settings of a few psalm verses, short scriptural passages, or the Collects, this last assigning them to specific occasions as did the Gospel text with German cantatas. There is not much repetition of text unless the piece contains a polyphonic section, in which case fugal writing is common.

To this generation of composers a new source of text became available, the hymn, but its adoption was neither immediate nor widespread. The first type of hymn-anthem was built upon the verses with entirely original musical settings. There is still no evidence of the second type, employing both the hymn text and the tune in variation or fantasia form. When that second type appeared, it served both American and English composers well. In its earlier form, the hymn-anthem drew quite naturally upon the prominent authors of that period; Henry Francis Lyte's *Abide with me* became text for an anthem by William Sterndale Bennett, Charles Wesley's hymn, *Thou Judge of quick and dead,* was set as an anthem by Samuel Sebastian Wesley, and T. A. Walmisley drew upon Isaac Watts's hymn *From all that dwell below the skies* for one of his.

Still during the nineteenth century, when the hymn-anthem finally began to employ both the text and tune of the hymn, or even when it was built upon the familiar melody with new text, it presented itself as a counterpart to the German chorale, which has been the basis of

Ex. 92 Subjects of double fugue from anthem, *I will give thanks*, Ouseley

so many pieces. The hymn-anthem was one of the few things that members of the Anglican Church could hold in common without its being liturgical and, consequently, limited in its flexibility. Familiar hymns thus provided familiar music, familiar text, and opportunity for the composer to exercise his skill in manipulating existing material. Sir Arthur Sullivan used a hymn tune in his anthem, *The Son of God goes forth to war*, which is based on the *St. Anne's tune*. The practice of using associated texts and music that had achieved popularity, or at least familiarity, in congregational use became widespread and was the basis of much American and English choral material from that time onward.

Composers who were well grounded in composition were slow to adopt the hymn-anthem. It was to reach its greatest popularity with composers in the twentieth century who, lacking skill or imagination to continue creation of entirely original material (or did they have a practical eye on the size of royalty checks?) made increasingly greater use of familiar words and tunes. Certainly the hymn-anthem received no unusual attention from Sir John Stainer (1840–1901), Sir Charles Villiers Stanford (1852–1924), or Charles Wood (1866–1926), although we may see in some of their anthems a growing recognition of the usefulness of such familiar materials.

The fate of American music is usually that it undergoes perfunctory treatment at the end of a chapter devoted to other material. Unfortunately, this is the case again, not because it lacks importance, but because most of its contributions lie in the present century, which, in the case of anthems, is not part of our discussion.[39] During the eighteenth century there were three lines of religious music developed for choral participation. One begins with William Billings (1746–1800), a Bostonian primitive whose works are now treasured more for their healthy vigor and rugged denial of European artistic practices than for sophistication or polish. While the line has no direct successors, its aim is continued in other individual approaches to the problems of providing music for the American singing group, some of the practices confining themselves to the problem of the hymn, but another, as we shall see, approaching group singing as well. A second tradition that generated no artistic offspring is an imported one with a high quality

39. Also omitted because of our limits here is consideration of the Russian music that has made its way into American choral literature. The wide acceptance and appropriateness of the Russian liturgical music with English text has broadened the possibilities of American choral groups considerably. Our volume on anthems will deal with this material, as well as with those other areas that do not appear here.

of musical practice and composition, centered in Bethlehem, Pennsylvania, and Winston-Salem, North Carolina, among the Moravian settlers. The third and most important, because it is the one that survived, is that of the American composers who were trained in or influenced by European practices. A brief examination of each will show their relative importance.

The first American collection containing original choral music was James Lyon's *Urania or a choice Collection of Psalm-Tunes, Anthems and Hymns* . . ., published in Philadelphia in 1761. The volume contains anthems and settings of psalms, both by Lyon and other composers. Lyon was closely followed by William Billings who, in 1770, published the first of a steady stream of books directed toward a public of those who enjoyed singing in parts. While the pieces of Lyon have found no place in modern choral literature, Billings's vigorous fuguing tunes and varied anthems continue to enjoy popularity. His ingenuous *When Jesus Wept* and his moving setting of *David's Lamentation* are typical of the simpler, but by no means least expressive, of the forty-five anthems he composed according to his own system. Billings and Lyon had followed the old method of setting the melody in the tenor part. Andrew Law (1748–1821) was not only concerned about the quality of church music in his time, but he introduced two changes that were to speed its practical use in America. The first would inevitably have happened somehow, and Law's connection with it is more fortuitous than far-seeing, for it involved simply the European practice of writing the melody in the soprano instead of the tenor. The second was the introduction of shape-notes. These were not invented by Law, but his method of writing them without staff lines was different from the other systems that were to achieve greater popularity. Among the other leading figures in the homegrown group was Oliver Holden (1765–1844) who, with Samuel Holyoke (1762–1820), opposed the exciting style that was found in Billings's fuguing tunes. Composers of church music generally lined up for or against the style of Billings,[40] but neither side came to be the developer of a lasting tradition. The stream of anthem writing, when it finally began to flow strongly, fed upon the springs of European tradition and training. These springs were to be tapped by a small group of composers who then passed on the responsibility to their students.

40. The development of these opposing camps is investigated in Gilbert Chase, *America's Music* (New York: McGraw-Hill Book Company, 1955), chapter VII.

Some composers who appeared too late to line up on the side of either Billings or Law employed the style of gospel songs. A curious volume,[41] compiled by two men who had already produced popular collections with such appealing titles as *The Garner* and *The Wells of Salvation,* contains numerous pieces that drew upon the devices of gospel songs *(Ex. 93),* such as patter repetitions and simple parallel

Ex. 93 Gospel song formulas in pieces from Sweney and Kirkpatrick, *Anthems and Voluntaries for the Church Choir*

41. John R. Sweney and Wm. J. Kirkpatrick, *Anthems and Voluntaries for the* *Church Choir* (Philadelphia: John J. Hood, 1881).

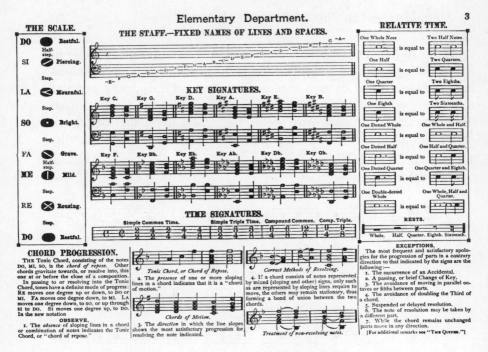

PLATE 7a.   *Hood's Notation, as illustrated and explained in Sweney and Kirkpatrick's* Anthems and Voluntaries . . ., *1881.*

melodic lines. J. R. Sweney (1837–1899) and W. J. Kirkpatrick (1838–1921) were popular composers of gospel hymns, and were certainly not the worst of their group. It is not surprising that they turned their abilities to anthem publication. Strongly rhythmic choral accompaniment of predictable melodic material may be found in many volumes of this type, but the other two distinctive features of their volume are not part of the general musical usage of that period. The first of these is a new kind of character notes, not the shape-notes of Law or any other more commonly employed system. The publisher of this volume apparently developed the characters himself, for the system is called "Hood's Notation" and he cautions the reader that both it and the music in the volume are protected by copyright. The notes are not "shaped." Instead, they are differentiated by marks that appear on the note-heads (*see Plate* VII). The system is well thought out; probably, its late arrival, coupled with lack of interest in its perpetuation, kept it from wider use, since Hood's copyright stood in the way of other printers' deriving any advantage from it. Another unusual feature of the book is the way the parts are printed (*cf. Plate* VII).

Let the People Praise Thee.

PLATE 7b.   *Hood's Notation as applied to a piece by Sweney.*

The tenor is printed on the top staff by itself, the soprano and alto share the middle staff, and the bass is printed in a separate staff at the bottom of each system. The melody is in the soprano part, so there is no reason why the tenor should have been set apart because of its special qualities.

The more than 140 pieces in the volume are not all the works of the two compilers. There is also a selection of pieces by European composers, the English examples printed as they were composed, the others with appropriate texts substituted. Among the familiar composers are to be found Abt, Bellini, Sterndale Bennett, Tallis, Attwood, Farrant, and Rossini.

The second line of development in music for religious observances was not grown from the native soil, but was imported from Bohemia by a group of Pietists we now know as the American Moravians. It was part of a self-sustaining musical community that had its principal centers in Bethlehem, Pennsylvania, and Salem (now Winston-Salem), North Carolina. The wealth of material these composers left is not completely known, for the archives of the brotherhood are still being studied. Modern editions of a number of these pieces have appeared, and significant anthems for chorus and orchestra, in the style of German cantata compositions, have been printed from manuscripts by John Frederik Peter, David Moritz Michael, and Johannes Herbst, among others. Significant as the anthems of the Moravians may be, and they do represent the finest music that any American churches of the eighteenth and early nineteenth century knew, they left no musical progeny. The tradition was ingrown and died out without causing a stir among native-born composers.

The first generation of music book compilers had been concerned with the establishment of a home-grown musical idea. The next generation came, in one way or another, under the influence of Europe. Lowell Mason (1792–1872) was given instruction by F. L. Abel, one of the first of the large number of immigrants who would help America form its musical culture. Mason also made two trips to Europe, during which he heard and observed the best music on its home ground. The fruit of his travels is found in his adoption of much music by important Europeans, to which he set English words. Mason's many publications were intended to serve several levels of musical life, both in the home and the church. The anthems he composed and compiled were not of the English pattern. Often the only feature they had in common with the English anthem was their name. Still, they came to be known as anthems, and the name has stuck. It is now commonly used for any religious part-song that is more extended than a hymn.

The first native-born composer to have a strong impact on choral music was Dudley Buck (1839–1909). His influence was immediate through his numerous and widely distributed compositions, and it was spread through the works of his pupils, among them Harry Rowe Shelley and William H. Neidlinger, who continued to dominate one level of America's religious choral music until recently. Buck's name may be linked firmly to American music, but his musical education was received in a four-year sojourn abroad, and it was there his taste and style were formed. His music is no longer in vogue. It is, indeed, *de rigueur* to downgrade everything he did.[42] Nevertheless, his music was the best that the churches could find from an American

42. One of the few sources to credit him with positive contributions is Leonard Ellinwood, *The History of American Church*   *Music* (New York: Morehouse-Gorham Company, 1953), 114f.

musician, and even when we discern convenient formulas, they are descended from the international stream of choral practice and were not weakened by being self-consciously American or educational.

In one way, Buck was far ahead of his contemporaries in this country. He had not set out to learn how to write church music; he had studied musical performance and composition, and circumstance had caused him to specialize in religious composition. He composed operas and symphonic works — we are concerned here with his capabilities, not the quality of his secular pieces — and his regular employment as a church organist led him to compose cantatas and shorter choral works for religious services. He brought considerable technical skill to the task and, while it is unfortunate that he compromised in matters of taste and quality, he was faced with the dilemma of doing so or finding no market for his anthems. The years of Buck's productivity were also the years of the convenient, but inappropriate, quartet choir which, as often as not, was simply a paid quartet.[43] The wide dispersal of such groups is evident from the advertising on many anthems printed during Buck's life. They are listed as anthems for mixed quartet or for solos and mixed quartet, but not as anthems for mixed chorus. The quartet of "capable" singers brought with it another of the evils that were visited upon American church music, the great stretches of solo singing with organ accompaniment that were included in these anthems, for each member of the quartet was presumed to be capable of solo performance. The taste that was there developed has not yet been completely eradicated, especially among the older generation of parishioners and choir singers.

When a composer was not forced to depend upon church positions for his livelihood, the pressures of public taste weighed less heavily upon his compositions. Horatio Parker was fortunate in that respect for, although his inclinations did not cause him to avoid church music, he was able to depend upon the salary from his professorship and to turn more attention to large works that have won for him a stronger place in musical history. Parker's anthems show less reliance on the display of solo voices than did Buck's, and there is more variety in his treatment of the chorus. He wrote few anthems in comparison to Buck, but those few are works that do not compromise with musicianship.

43. For more about quartet choirs, see *ibid.,* 72–75.

It is perhaps fortunate that this chapter pursues the anthem no farther. On the American scene especially, but to some extent on the English as well, craftsmanship displaced art after the twentieth century got well under way. Church music has not attracted the best composers; the possibilities for good performances are not numerous except outside the church, and we shall examine the larger works of our century in a later chapter.

3

THE BREAKDOWN OF

DENOMINATIONAL

DISTINCTIONS

THE SOCIAL FORCES that removed much religious music from the churches provided a convenient refuge for that same music in new surroundings, away from the devotional practices that had supported the development of the music through many generations. Although much music ceased to be written for the church or to be performed in the church, it was still related to the church in many of its ideas. A new danger was opened to this music and its composers, for when it was removed from the religious service it lost one of its strongest defenses. Inside the church, criticism of music could be construed as a criticism of dogma, of religious procedures, of morality itself; outside, the music had to stand on its own intrinsic quality. It was either good or bad music, not simply church music. Another side of the coin became visible, too. When music is performed for the approbation of the public, and when it no longer needs to edify the spirit, a new relationship exists between musicians and audiences. The public is pitted against the musician, the trite composition often wins greatest favor, and the composer who provides the superficial expression becomes the toast of audiences as well as the object of his fellow composers' scorn.

The rising tide of secularism drove music away from the churches; the diminishing needs of the churches for large choral pieces also forced the musicians to take their wares to the concert hall. There the demands of denominationalism were no longer felt. On an equal basis in the audiences were Gentiles and Jews, Catholics and Protestants, music lovers and untutored spectators.

When music moved outside the church a major change in performing personnel became possible and even necessary. The choral forces were no longer simply those of the church establishment, but were a collection of willing amateurs and talented professionals. By the year 1773, in a performance of Thomas Arne's *Judith* at Covent Garden Theater, women were a part of the chorus, and they had for some time been heard in solo roles both in England and on the Continent. This radical change in performance practice was to affect the writing of choral parts, and it was also important in freeing the orchestra from the responsibility of supporting the vocal lines.

Those pieces that had earlier been confined to the church were, as we have observed time and again, at the mercy of the instrumental forces that could be gathered for a forthcoming performance. The repeated use of the trio-sonata group as instrumental support gives evidence of the low reserve of performers that could be found in some church situations. The development of the opera orchestra and the symphony orchestra of the late eighteenth century fortuitously went hand in hand with the growing popularity of choral music outside the church. Inasmuch as the theater was the natural habitat of those orchestras that were not captives of princely courts, the movement of choral music to the theaters wedded these vocal and instrumental forces into a new, dynamic body for musical expression. Even when a composer felt that the church still had a place for his large religious choral work, the possibilities for his having it performed well and received with critical attention lay in the theater and concert hall.

The most severe test that faced these composers was not that they were bringing religious ideas into the marketplace, but that their product now had to be judged on the same basis as secular compositions on which the best composers lavished their attention and upon the standards of which taste was becoming established. No longer was it possible to produce works in styles of past generations simply because they were to be part of a religious service that was tied to custom and tradition. The new choral works had to compete with their modern, secular counterparts. They sometimes succeeded, but a large share of pieces were little more than brash, sentimental, contrived, rowdy, or even mismated fragments of the older church compositions and the new theatrical showpieces. Lost was the literal use of scriptural passages as they had appeared in cantatas and oratorios. Poetic license was freer; the affinity to the theater sometimes seemed even greater than it actually was.

Chapter XI

Oratorio and Cantata After 1800

AS THE use of large-scale compositions within the church decreased, the reasons for maintaining clear distinctions between the various kinds of religious music were less compelling. No longer was it necessary to consider that the principal music for a Sunday service need be known as a cantata in contrast to a specialized composition of roughly the same length and structure that might be known as an oratorio. Nor was the use of these terms now the sole—or even principal—right and property of the religious composers. Oratorios and cantatas might be on any subject, secular or religious, and might be performed on the slightest pretext, especially in England and Germany where amateur choral singing had grown and flourished. Is it not possible that the proliferation of compositions so much like each other in their facile tedium spurred the amateur singers on to their repeated efforts? When they found that they could sing, and that the formulas of choral writing were not beyond their skills, nothing seemed to stop them. While the names given these pieces could rarely be depended upon to describe them accurately, it may be said that the vague use of the term "oratorio" ceased at the beginning of the nineteenth century, "for with the spread of public music unconnected with either church or stage other more adequate titles came into use, and the modern definite idea of oratorio as a non-liturgical work of religious character became firmly established."[1]

Choral music was no longer identified solely with the church, but there was an even stronger impetus for developing it in the concert hall—a growing taste on the part of a paying public. It had been generated by the immense popularity of oratorio with the English public from Handel's time. His successors had tried to follow in his

---

1. *Grove's*, VI, 257.

steps, and failing that, had at least continued to meet the demand for quantities of choral music with their uninspired fare. Great composers who were able to contribute to the literature did not appear until the very end of the eighteenth century, when Joseph Haydn, who was soundly impressed by the Handelian idiom, produced two oratorios that again aroused new activity in other composers on the Continent.

Haydn's first attempt at oratorio was a lengthy work, Il ritorno di Tobia,[2] first performed at Vienna's Kärntnertortheater in April, 1775. Written in the commonly accepted and easily understood Neapolitan tradition, the work contains little that is distinctively Haydn, although it is a skillful composition of its kind. More widely known, and certainly of greater significance as a religious composition, is his setting of The Seven Last Words, Die Sieben letzten Worte unseres Erlösers am Kreuze.[3] The original set of sonatas that was commissioned for the Cathedral at Cadiz contained no text. Its seven sections were to be played during the periods of silent meditation that followed the reading of each of the Words. The oratorio version (1796) — to use the term loosely — is an arrangement for chorus, solo voices, and orchestra. Each Word is preceded by introductory material; the fifth one by an introduction for wind instruments, the others by a simply-harmonized a cappella intonation of the Word itself. The style of the music is almost entirely homophonic (Ex. 94), supported by the full symphony orchestra. Each section — excepting the final earthquake, a presto setting for chorus and orchestra — is a slow movement. Still, a great amount of variety is achieved in the course of the work through careful attention to dynamic changes, especially in the orchestra, and to the division of material between soloists and chorus.

The best of Haydn's oratorios is Die Schöpfung (The Creation) (1798).[4] Haydn again called upon all available orchestral resources and showed his debt to Handel and England by writing numerous fine choruses in the piece. Although the oratorio has five characters represented by solo voices, three people are sufficient to sing the parts. Gabriel (soprano), Uriel (tenor), and Raphael (bass) appear in the first two sections. In the third, the soprano is assigned the part of Eve and the bass takes that of Adam. This third section, incidentally, is an

2. Joseph Haydn Werke (München: G. Henle Verlag, 1958–), xxviii (1).
3. Ibid., xxviii (2).
4. Available in a number of editions. Still most common in this country is the G.

Schirmer edition arranged by Vincent Novello. The Eulenburg miniature score provides a better picture of the relationship between voices and orchestra.

Ex. 94 Fourth intonation and beginning of fourth "Word" from *Die Sieben Letzten Worte*, Haydn

Printed by special permission of G. Henle Verlag, München, Germany. The volume from which it is taken bears the title, *Die Sieben Letzten Worte unseres Erlösers am Kreuze*, Vokalfassung (Reihe XXVIII, Band 2, Joseph Haydn-Gesamtausgabe). G. Henle, München 55, Schongauer Strasse 24.

unnecessary appendage, a pastoral cantata that is too pale to follow the mighty process of creating heaven and earth. The compositional techniques of *Il ritorno di Tobia* were remnants of a dying era, full of formalized patterns that drew upon the fully developed Neapolitan style; *Die Schöpfung* is the first great work that calls upon the resources of the symphonic orchestra in connection with the Handelian choral idiom. The older style used the orchestral players in small, differentiated groups at the various sections of the piece, strings for the recitatives with accompaniment, and instruments appropriate to the affection—or in later days, the mood—of the aria or chorus. The new style used the orchestra in another fashion: the woodwinds and strings were in constant demand as full groups; the brasses were added or omitted according to the vigorous or lyrical character of the sections. It was not even a matter of thinning the texture by splitting the pairs of wind instruments, for most of them performed in the same way that one expected to find them in the symphony orchestra of that time. Added to the usual pairs was a full complement of trombones and the contrabassoon.

Much has been said of the orchestral and vocal depictions of events in *Die Schöpfung;* the first brilliant entry of the full orchestra (after the initial representation of Chaos) at the text *und es ward Licht* ("and there was light") *(Ex. 95),* and the tone-painting at the references to the animals in Raphael's recitative and aria near the end of the second part. It is notable that the task of pictorial representation had been removed from the singer in these cases and the others, and given to the orchestra. It matters not at all whether the performance is given in the German text to which Haydn wrote his work or in the English to which we have become accustomed. The descriptive passages usually come after the sections of text and are entirely instrumental and therefore equally successful in either language.

Beethoven's only oratorio, *Christus am Oelberge (Christ on the Mount of Olives),* op. 85, was completed in 1803. Following closely on the heels of *Die Schöpfung,* it, nevertheless, should not be judged by the same standards. Beethoven never achieved a comfortable familiarity with large vocal materials, he lacked the insight into the possibilities of oratorio that Haydn had gained through his English experience, and, generally, he could not restrain himself suitably for

Ex. 95 Haydn, *Die Schöpfung*

his subject, the tragic undertones of which escaped the poet F. X. Huber as well. The Beethoven recitatives often contain imperious demands shaped into short phrases that are thunderously punctuated by orchestral chords, and the vocal solo lines dissolve into meaningless flourishes and florid *passagi*. Even so, it is an over-simplification to dismiss Beethoven as a composer who was unsympathetic to the human voice. While he treated it more as an instrument of declamation than of lyric sensitivity, there are undeniably great moments in his oratorio. They happen, unfortunately, at rather widely separated intervals.

Composition for the remainder of the nineteenth century was by men who were most at home in the new fields of instrumental expression, especially in those of the orchestra or piano. No longer did composers exist whose principal skill lay in the creation of choral music with the instrumental forces acting as a desirable supplementary sound—nowhere, that is, except in England and America. Among those instrumentally oriented composers was Louis Spohr (1784–1859), a violin virtuoso and composer in all of the major forms of music. He belonged to an age that saw little need for contrapuntal skill, but that felt impelled to recognize it when writing large choral works. Only a small portion of any composer's effort was directed toward large vocal works during that century, and it is not to be expected that Spohr would have developed skills that were to be used only rarely, inasmuch as counterpoint found small use in instrumental works unless they were making a token bow to the church. The extent to which polyphony was equated with religion is demonstrated in the choruses of Spohr's *Der Fall Babylons*, his last work in this genre, dating from 1842. The choruses of Jews make the appropriate polyphonic gesture toward religious propriety by containing at least one fugal exposition; the choruses of the Persian warriors, the courtiers, priests of Baal, and other groups that do not belong to the Old Testament religious elect are not dignified with counterpoint. The popularity of Spohr's oratorios may, in part, be attributed to the ease with which the amateur singer might embrace their technical demands, but they contained also corresponding weakness in imagination and, above all, inappropriate fugal subjects *(Ex. 96)*.

Often linked with Spohr in a subordinate position is Friedrich Schneider (1786–1853), a composer of fifteen oratorios between 1810 and 1838. His popularity in both Germany and England was considerable, and it would appear that his claim to attention was as well de-

Ex. 96 Fugue subjects from Spohr's *Der Fall Babylons*

O hör' die Bit - ten der Dein-en, die in frem-den Land

Der Lö - we ist vom La-ger ge - sprung - en

Herr, wir flehn in tie - fen Leid - en dei - ne

ew' ge All - macht an!

Er wird die Vol - ker un - ter uns zwin - gen, er er -

wählt uns zum Erb - theil die Herr-lich-keit Ja - cobs,

served as that of Spohr. Had the quality of large choral works not deteriorated to such a marked extent, Schneider might have been recognized by his contemporaries as greater than Spohr, for his command of the choral idiom was superior. Unfortunately for him, though, there was no continuing tradition. Neither had awareness of Germany's musical heritage come upon the music-loving public until near the end of Schneider's series of oratorios—Mendelssohn's revealing performance of Bach's *St. Matthew Passion* did not take place until 1829, too late also to affect an established composer like Spohr. If any thread of understanding of the old choral style existed, Schneider was in a position to grasp it, as he was, among his many occupations, a church organist, and among his posts was Leipzig's Thomaskirche. His understanding of counterpoint may have been gained from his church connections and his skill as an organist, and his use of the chorale may be attributed to the same cause.

Schneider was attracted, as were others of his time, to texts of cataclysmic dimensions. Among his oratorios are *Das Weltgericht*

(The Last Judgment) (1819), and *Die Sündfluth* (1823). The latter was performed in England in 1833 in an English translation by Edward Taylor (1784–1863) under the title, *The Deluge*. Taylor, a bass singer of considerable importance, also made English translations and adaptations of the three oratorios of Spohr's mature years and was thereby directly involved in keeping a vision of German style before the English public. This German style, as it was seen through these works of Spohr and Schneider, included a lavish use of choruses and the employment of no more than half a dozen soloists. The narrator had been dropped from oratorio by this time; his function had been taken by the soloists and the chorus. While Spohr continued to make use of the recitative as a preface to the aria or chorus, Schneider presented the same kind of material as lyric dialogue, solo exposition, or choral narrative. His few uses of recitative style are extremely brief. They are not intended to deliver expository text, but simply to introduce lyric set pieces. Both Spohr and Schneider made liberal use of the solo ensemble. They wrote for quartet alone and as one of the groups in multiple choir pieces. One of Schneider's triple choruses in *Die Sündfluth* calls for three choruses of angels, one of which presents continuous text while the other two accompany with overlapping ejaculations of praise *(Ex. 97)*. Spohr's lack of contrapuntal skill was evident both in his weak fugue subjects and in the absence of complete fugues; Schneider's fugues abound and they are fully developed, not simply expositions interrupted by homophonic choruses. His fugue subjects are vigorous, easy to sing, and suited to their texts. Chorales do not play an important part in the oratorios of this period, although Schneider made an interesting use of one by framing a double chorus in *Das Weltgericht* with two verses of a chorale.

It is not, then, as if Felix Mendelssohn Bartholdy (1809–1847) appeared suddenly upon the oratorio scene with new ways of producing this favorite choral music for the concert hall. He had no formula that made the oratorio better than it had been, but his greater interest in the past, his numerous experiences in England, and his greater facility in music placed him above his older contemporaries. Nor can we say that a single pattern was present in his completed works. They differ from each other in several ways. *Paulus (Saint Paul)* appeared in 1836, shortly before the final work by Schneider and only six years before Spohr's final contribution to oratorio literature. It differs from any composition of its generation in taking its text entirely from the Bible, except for the four chorale verses that appear in the

Ex. 97 Last measures of triple chorus from Schneider's *Die Sündfluth*

course of the work. From the standpoint of text alone, *Saint Paul* returns to an earlier pattern wherein the Scriptures furnished all of the
words. Mendelssohn's audience knew from the first notes that this
work probed deeply into Lutheran tradition. The Overture is based

upon the chorale, *Wachet auf, ruft uns die Stimme (Wake, awake, a voice is calling)*, which appears again in the course of the work. The narrative text is not assigned to one singer as recitative. Mendelssohn divided the duties of the narrator among three of his soloists; soprano, alto, and tenor. The bass, having the characterization of Paul, is assigned text that Paul speaks in the Scriptures. The composition abounds in choral sections, usually fugal in character, and it is devoid of any overtly secular ideas that might be traced to the operatic stage, even though it was intended for performance in the concert hall, as was common with such works by that time.

On the other hand, *Elias (Elijah)*, coming a full decade after *Saint Paul*, exhibits an understanding and mastery of the dramatic oratorio, a form in which a series of scenes is presented. If *Saint Paul* reflects the influence of Lutheranism and of Bach, *Elijah* is Mendelssohn's acceptance of the later and, by then, stronger, tradition following the pattern of Handelian oratorio. It would be futile to speculate on the probable pattern of other Mendelssohnian efforts, had he lived to complete them; there is no doubt of where the public taste led. It was away from the church-directed pattern of denominationalism as found in Bach and reflected in *Saint Paul*, and toward the nondenominational concert oratorio. *Saint Paul* generated renewed interest in the oratorio, if such were possible; *Elijah* represented the end of the line for a style of composition. It must be emphasized that Mendelssohn wrote his music to German words. Our common use of the English version leads us to lose sight of that fact. The translation of *Elias* was assigned to William Bartholomew (1793–1867) who worked in such close collaboration with Mendelssohn on both the original and revised versions, and with such immense success, that much of the world still thinks that the work was originally set to English text.[5]

Another indication of the interest that was generally felt in oratorio throughout Germany is the fact that Richard Wagner (1813–1883) tried his hand at such a work. *Das Liebesmahl der Apostel (The love-feast of the apostles)* (1843) was not simply a youthful enthusiasm or the work of a composer undecided in his career, for he had already had successful performances of *Rienzi* and *Der fliegende Holländer* by that time, and in that same year was appointed to several important positions in Dresden, among them a place on the musical committee of the Dresden *Liedertafel* (glee club) for which he wrote this biblical scene. To call it an oratorio seems overly generous; its *raison d'être* was that it was to be performed at a festival that brought together all the male choral groups in Saxony. Wagner's description of the work he composed for the twelve hundred singers is this:

> The task had been assigned to me of writing an important piece for male voices only, which, if possible, should occupy half an hour. I reflected that the tiresome monotony of male singing, which even the orchestra could only enliven to a slight extent, can only be endured by the introduction of dramatic themes. I therefore designed a great choral scene, selecting the apostolic Pentecost with the outpouring of the Holy Ghost as its subject. I completely avoided any real solos, but worked out the whole in such a way that it should be executed by detached choral masses according to requirement.[6]

He set the major portion of the work for *a cappella* performance and added an elaborate orchestral accompaniment for the remainder. The composition neither sets a pattern for subsequent composers nor follows a previous example. That it inspired no imitations is fortunate, for even Wagner recognized its relative unimportance when he

5. The collaboration is chronicled in F. G. Edwards, *The History of Mendelssohn's Oratorio "Elijah"* (London: Novello, Ewer and Co., 1896), especially Chapters III and v.

6. Richard Wagner, *My Life* (New York: Dodd, Mead and Company, 1927), 311.

said, "I do not mind including this in the list of my uninspired compositions."[7]

The crowning achievement of German oratorio came from Johannes Brahms (1833–1897) who, although he did not call his work an oratorio, made for himself a place of great importance with the appearance of *Ein deutsches Requiem*. Brahms did not intend national identification in the title of his composition. His adjective should be considered a designation of Protestant usage rather than linguistic. The composition made its way into the repertoire through both the concert hall and the church. An 1867 performance of the first three movements in Vienna was poorly received, but when Brahms conducted the six movements then completed (the fifth movement was added later) at Bremen Cathedral on Good Friday of the following year its complete success was assured.

All of the text is taken from the Bible, although it does not combine to make a liturgical unit. In its final form, the text sections stand in admirable balance one to another. At the extremes are two concepts of blessedness, the first related to the mourners, the second to the dead. The second and sixth sections deal with the brevity of man's stay on earth. Between the first and last movements there is yet another connection. The melodic figure that appears first in the voices (*Ex. 98a*) is transferred to the instruments as well, where it appears

Ex. 98 Thematic relationships in Brahms's *Ein deutsches Requiem*

7. *Ibid.*

in connection with another vocal theme derived from the inversion of the first melody *(Ex. 98b)*. The final movement opens with a modified version of the inverted theme *(Ex. 98c)* and the composition closes with references to the opening three-note pattern.

Each segment of text is related to a distinct musical idea, but these ideas flow so naturally into one another that the movements appear to be a continuous web of melody. One must return to the Renaissance motet to find an equivalent situation in choral literature, although such thematic development may be seen in Brahms's instrumental works. Attempts to relate one or more of the themes in the *Requiem* to well-known chorale tunes are futile. The opening vocal theme of the second movement can be traced to an earlier instrumental piece while the third movement sharply recalls the spirit of Schütz's *Musicalische Exequien* rather than a chorale melody.

Brahms was an excellent contrapuntist but, even more important, he was also sufficiently steeped in the traditions of an earlier time to concern himself with the most careful relationships between words and music. Nowhere in the *Requiem* do voices or instruments undertake passages that are not entirely conceived as subsidiary to the text. The restriction of solo material to two voices, both of which express text that is in the first person singular, shows further his preoccupation with the music rather than the musicians. Several instances of textual emphasis through musical means also point backward toward Baroque practices. Twice he uses the device of sounding a theme in augmentation with itself: once in the second movement where he emphasizes *Freude und Wonne* (joy and gladness), and again in the fifth movement where he stresses the texts *Ich will euch wieder sehen* ("I will see you again") and *Ich will euch trösten* ("I will comfort you") *(Ex. 99)*. His selection of words upon which to write fugues is similarly a matter of care. At the end of the third movement he chose a verse from the Apocrypha:[8] *Der Gerechten Seelen sind in Gottes Hand und keine Qual rühret sie an* ("But the souls of the righteous are in the hand of God, and there shall no torment touch them") (Wisdom of Solomon 3:1). Likewise at the end of the sixth movement, the text beginning *Herr, du bist würdig zu nehmen Preis und Ehre und Kraft* ("Thou art worthy, O Lord, to receive glory and honour and power") (Rev. 4:11) is given as a fugue. The reason that Brahms selected these particular portions of text for polyphonic treatment can again be

8. The Apocrypha are included in the German Bible. Brahms was not going beyond established practice in quoting from this source.

Ex. 99 *Ibid.*

Soprano: Freu - de und Won - ne wer-den sie er - grei - fen,

Tenor: Freu - de und Won - - - ne

Solo Soprano: Ich will euch wie-der se - hen und eu - er Herz soll sich freu - en

Tenors: Ich will euch trö - sten,

sought in the practices of earlier generations, wherein direct references to the Deity were clothed in musical symbolism or dignified
by musical complexities.

No direct successor to Brahms appeared on the German scene.
The Germans had already made their mark in England, previously
fertile ground for the oratorio, but in their home country the contemporaries and successors of Brahms continued on other paths. For
some years their attention was centered on the concert hall and the
opera house. Only in the twentieth century has there been a renewed
interest in church music composition, some of it by composers who
have been recognized principally in secular music circles, but a considerable amount coming from a newly emerging group who have
returned to performing and composing for the church, bringing
dignity back into the calling of church musician. A feature common
to many works of this group is the application of Renaissance treatment to traditional Lutheran materials, using the German Mass, the
German Passion, or large and small forms suitable to the liturgical
year. It is quite surprising that this music has not gained greater
attention outside Germany, even though its function is closely tied to
Lutheran practice, for it has a vigor and directness that is lacking in
many other kinds of religious music. It is, with few exceptions, music
for the church, and it is intended to be performed in connection with
the religious service or as a religious concert on the church premises.
Most of these pieces are written for unaccompanied chorus or for cho-

rus and small instrumental groups. Their texts range from sets of chorale verses to complete presentations of the Passion and Christmas stories, from biblical texts and settings of *de tempore* Gospels to different
treatments of an eleventh-century poem. Naturally such a variety of
text sources in the hands of several dozen composers makes for a
number of stylistic differences. The composers are not satisfied only
to duplicate the techniques of the past and, even when surface appearances point to a close connection with the cantatas and motets of other
centuries, the works are distinctively different from their Renaissance
and Baroque progenitors. There are too many for thorough examination here, but a few may be mentioned as representative.

The two leading figures of this Lutheran renascence are Hugo
Distler (1908–1942) and Ernst Pepping (1901–). Two works by Distler
appeared in 1933, his *Choral-Passion* and *Die Weihnachtsgeschichte*
(The Christmas story). In both of them, Distler showed a spiritual
affinity to the Baroque era in general and to Heinrich Schütz in
particular. The *Choral-Passion*, SSATB unaccompanied, and drawn
from all four Gospels, is a direct descendant of the Schütz Passions,
probably influenced also by the *Motet Passion* (1927) of Kurt Thomas
(1904–). The principal characters, the Evangelist and Jesus, are the
traditional tenor and bass who sing their extensive material in unaccompanied solo form, as do the lesser characters. The *turba* sections
are polyphonic, with the exception of a few brief moments that derive
their strength from the unanimous shouts of the unruly crowd of
onlookers that the chorus represents at that point. Distler, and others
after him, brought back into German church music another feature of
Baroque practice, the use of the familiar chorale as a unifying feature,
or as the basis for a set of variations. In the *Choral-Passion*, the chorale
serves both of these purposes. The Passion story is broken into seven
sections, and each section is framed by verses of the Passion chorale,
*Jesu, deine Passion will ich jetzt bedenken (Jesus, on thy Passion will I
ponder)*. That is, eight verses of the chorale enclose the seven sections
of the Passion story, each of those sections consisting of dramatic
portions of the Gospels in plainsong style, and of one or more reflective motets.

The procedure in *Die Weihnachtsgeschichte (The Christmas Story)*
is the same. Composed for four-part chorus and a quartet of solo
voices, it, too, dispenses with instrumental accompaniment. The
solo voices stand out in their unadorned declamation of the Christmas
message. The chorus sings a set of nine variations on the melody,

Es ist ein Ros' entsprungen (Lo, how a rose e'er blooming). The pentatonic scale is in evidence, especially in the solo passages, while the choral sections are cast in rich modal style.

Ernst Pepping is better known among organists than among choral singers in America, where his pieces are now played regularly in connection with religious services. His skill in composing large works involving chorus and orchestra was demonstrated in his *Tedeum* (1956), but his principal importance in the field of choral music lies in his works for unaccompanied chorus. He has written numerous pieces in that genre; settings of psalms, Gospels, and large works for the major observances of the church. It is significant that his two most elaborate religious compositions are, as were Distler's, a Passion and a setting of the Christmas story. Their greater length and complexity indicate that Pepping was at an advantage in having excellent prototypes from the hand of Distler and in having the good fortune to have these works represent the expression of his mature years. Distler's two works date from his twenty-fifth year; Pepping's Passion was written when he was nearly fifty, and his Christmas story, a decade later.

The *Passionbericht des Matthäus (Passion according to St. Matthew)* (1949–1950) for chorus *a 4* to *a 10* is a motet Passion and naturally has no soloists. An extensive work that calls relentlessly upon an *a cappella* group to sing without pauses or changes to solo texture is certainly a major challenge to the composer and performers alike. Some of Pepping's skill in approaching this problem is seen in his distribution of text. Despite its title, the piece does not restrict itself to the Passion story as told in the St. Matthew Gospel. The text is divided between two choruses. The St. Matthew story is given to the first chorus, except for the conventional *Exordium* and a *Conclusio* from another portion of Scripture. The second chorus is assigned related texts from both Old and New Testament sources or, as in the Golgotha section, material from the Latin liturgy. The composition exists on two separate planes; one with the first chorus conveying the Gospel version of the Passion story, the other with the second chorus commenting, intensifying the text of the first chorus, or sometimes supporting that text in expanded texture or doubling the text in rhythmic speech of no specified pitch against the singing of the first chorus.

At the midpoint of Pepping's Passion stands an *Intermedium*, in which the text of Luke 24:29, *Herr, bleibe bei uns, denn es will Abend werden und der Tag hat sich geneigt* ("Abide with us; for it is toward evening, and the day is far spent") and Matthew 8:25, *Hilf uns, wir verderben!* ("Lord, save us: we perish") are combined for the second chorus. The reassuring words of Matthew 28:20, *Siehe, ich bin bei euch alle Tage bis an der Welt Ende* ("Lo, I am with you alway, even unto the end of the world") are given in answer by the first chorus *(Ex. 100).* None of this text belongs to the Passion story, but it is not an unsuitable intrusion. The resulting motet separates the work into two major segments: that preceding the motet closes with Christ's betrayal; that following it continues with His appearance before Caiaphas, the high priest. The choirs maintain their separate identities for most of the composition. Their different functions are never more pronounced than in the final portion of the work when the first choir relates the episode of the Crucifixion in choral recitative against the second chorus's fugue on the text *crucifixus etiam pro nobis.*

In *Die Weihnachtsgeschichte des Lukas* (1959), Pepping followed a similar plan, writing an unaccompanied work for four to seven voices entirely in motet style. The Christmas story is related in five sections which are framed by introductory and closing motets, the first based on 1 Timothy 3:16, *Und kündlich gross ist das gottselige Geheimnis: Gott ist offenbaret im Fleisch, . . .* ("And without controversy great is the mystery of godliness: God was made manifest in the flesh, . . ."");

Ex. 100 From *Intermedium* of *Passionsbericht des Matthäus*, Pepping

Ernst Pepping, *Passionsbericht des Matthäus*. Printed with permission of Bärenreiter-Verlag, Kassel, Basel, London, New York.

the second on a poem by Paul Gerhardt, (1607–1676). The practice of writing exposition and commentary, either simultaneously or in alternation, that was used in the Passion is also in evidence here. The section entitled *Die Geburt (The Birth)* carries the story through Luke

2:6, *und als sie daselbst waren, kam die Zeit, dass sie gebären sollte* ("And so it was, that, while they were there, the days were accomplished that she should be delivered"), at which point a trope on the text is inserted, taken from the apocryphal Wisdom of Solomon 18:14, *Da alles still war und ruhte und eben recht Mitternacht war, fuhr dein allmächtiges Wort herab vom Himmel aus königlichem Thron* ("For while all things were in quiet silence, and that night was in the midst of her swift course, thine Almighty word leaped down from heaven out of thy royal throne"). At the conclusion of the trope, the text again takes up the St. Luke story with an omission of six words, those being the portion for which the trope serves as substitute. Borrowings also come from the Roman liturgy. A short setting of *Virga Jesse floruit* closes the story of the Birth. Two other Latin texts are used as direct parallels to the German of the St. Luke Gospel; *Hodie Christus natus est* is set for a second chorus, SAT, while the first chorus sings *denn euch ist heute der Heiland geboren*, and *Gloria in excelsis Deo* is sung as parallel text to *Ehre sei Gott in der Höhe*. No familiar tunes appear in their entirety, but the first section of the piece closes with a motet that borrows strongly from the first phrase of *Es ist ein Ros' entsprungen*.

A more modest Passion setting than those of Distler and Pepping is *Die Passion Jesu Christi*, a motet Passion by Hans Friedrich Micheelsen (1902 –). His treatment of the St. Matthew story calls for a chorus that uses many combinations of voices from *a 2* to *a 7*. Neither the rhythmic complexities nor the harmonic richness of the other works we have seen are to be found here. In their stead Micheelsen writes strong melodic lines that pervade all the parts of the chorus. He does not hesitate to write voices in unison or to emphasize short sections by employing simple organum. The Passion story is enclosed by a motet setting of the chorale, *Christe, du Lamm Gottes*, to be sung both before and after the main portion of the work. Micheelsen has also written Passions on the Gospels of St. John and St. Mark. His *Lutherchoralkantate*, SATB, with string orchestra and timpani, is likewise a work that strongly emphasizes melody, both in voices and instruments. Its four familiar chorales are set in varied style, each as a separate movement consisting of a set of variations. There are sections with all voices in unison against strong syncopated accompaniment, some in which the instruments engage in imitative dialogue against choral statements of the chorale melody in a manner that is even more strongly reminiscent of Baroque *concertato* style.

The list of cantatas by contemporary German composers is formidable. Most of them draw upon the rich heritage of the chorale for their material, dealing with them as a set of variations. Distler's *Nun danket all und bringet Ehr (Now bring thanks and glorify)*, SATB with strings and organ, is of this type, as are *Christ lag in Todesbanden*, for three-part chorus and five-part wind ensemble, by Johannes H. E. Koch (1918–), *Nun freut euch lieben Christen gmein (Rejoice, beloved Christians)*, for chorus of one to four parts with instruments of whatever suitable and convenient combination may be available, by Gerhard Schwarz (1902–), and *Such, wer da will, ein ander Ziel (Let him who chooses seek another goal)*, for unison congregational singing, SATB chorus, and winds, by Friedrich Zipp (1914–).

Common to these cantatas is a degree of flexibility and general adaptability that makes them practical in many situations. The prevalence of music for fewer than four parts, even though each cantata contains at least one chorus *a 4*, is an indication that composers are hoping to provide something for churches without large choirs of skilled singers. The flexibility of instrumentation and, in some cases, the possibility of substituting organ for the instruments, makes possible the performance of the works with whatever performers may be available, instead of necessitating a search for a specific group of players. Of greatest importance is the return to scriptural texts in the large works, and to the inclusion of chorales as supporting material or, as in the cantatas, as the entire substance of which the piece is formed.

Although Johann Nepomuk David (1895–) is the oldest of the group under consideration here, some features of his work are the most advanced in style. The composer of a number of motets to both German and Latin texts, he completed his oratorio, *Ezzolied*, in 1957. Ezzo was an eleventh-century priest of Bamberg whose poem relates such varied happenings as the Creation, the major episodes of the Old Testament, and the life of Christ. David's setting is an hour-long continuous piece for three soloists, two sopranos and a bass, SATB chorus, orchestra, and organ. It is built on the grand scale of the stage oratorio and calls for the highest proficiency in its performers, certainly not a feature that will lead to numerous hearings. While David employs such an obviously Brahmsian device as a fast-moving melody that appears in canon between the violins while the basses play the same tune in greatly augmented values, he introduces later methods of organizing his materials as well, notably the use of serial technique. The twelve-tone row is not consistently employed, but it sometimes serves as a method of intensifying portions of text. The row is horizontal rather than vertical; its use is occasional rather than consistent. The treatment of such rows in the vocal parts is not one of regular unrelenting adherence to rule, but is free and flexible. The row is used in augmentation against itself and as strict canon between the original and transposed pitches as some of its forms.

Willy Burkhard (1900–1955), one of the leading Swiss composers of this century, had been led to the same poem early in his life. His setting of *Das Ezzolied* (1927) is written for unaccompanied chorus using variable voice combinations *a 4* to *a 8*. The musical style has a debt to the Renaissance in its wealth of flowing imitative counterpoint, but there are equally prominent sections of reiterated chords, ranging from simple triads to eleventh-chords with all factors present, which deliver short sections of text with great force. Burkhard's works are little known in this country. His oratorio *Das Gesicht Jesajas (The vision of Isaiah)* (1936) is slightly known by reputation and his smaller choral works are finding their way into libraries, even though they are still absent from the repertories of performing groups. The style of works composed in his last years indicates that a considerable degree of change has taken place since *Das Ezzolied*. Written during the years 1954–1955, *Die Sintflut (The Deluge)* shows a virtual abandonment of the older polyphonic procedures. In their place there is an increased interest in rhythmic complexity, an angular approach to melodic writing and, where earlier had been found reiterated chords without change of harmony, an interest in the movement of phrases from relaxation to tension and back to relaxation by moving from unisons to rich sonorities and returning to the unison again *(Ex. 101)*.

Ex. 101 Closing measures of Part III, *Die Sintflut*, Burkhard

Willy Burkhard, *Die Sintflut*. Printed with permission of Bärenreiter-Verlag, Kassel, Basel, London, New York.

The other fertile field for oratorio in the nineteenth and twentieth centuries was England. Before tracing its progress there, we shall digress to examine its lesser development on the Continent.

It is not generally recognized that Franz Liszt (1811–1886) had much interest in religious choral music. Nevertheless, he composed more than sixty such works. Among them are two oratorios: *Die Legende von der heiligen Elisabeth (Saint Elizabeth)*, which was completed in 1862, and *Christus*, composed as several separate sections over the years 1855–1867. *St. Elizabeth* is, for all its apparent religiousness, a throwback to the earlier type of Catholic oratorio that was based on a religious fable rather than on a biblical story. It is not suitable for performance in a church. *Christus*, on the other hand, is a Latin work that derives directly from the Bible and from Catholic liturgical texts.[9] If a criticism were to be levelled at its externals, it would be on the basis of its size and seeming lack of focus. Liszt created a massive dramatic work in three segments. The first of these bears the name "Christmas Oratorio" and is divided into five parts; the second deals with the post-Epiphany period and is also in five sections; the last is a series of four reflections on the Passion and Resurrection with appropriate texts such as the entire Sequence, *Stabat mater dolorosa*.[10] One way that Liszt attempted to infuse religious music with dramatic vitality was by the use of these traditional musical materials in a manner that recalls the liturgical drama; another was the employment of the orchestra for long sections of programmatic music intended to sustain a mood or create a graphic representation. The extensive orchestral passages seem to indicate that he saw the instruments as equals to the voices. This is further borne out by his failure to go beyond the use of a single chorus and a rather modest number of soloists. Contrasts of color and emphasis are left to the orchestra. *Christus* is scored for five soloists, SATBarB, chorus, orchestra, and organ.

After French composers failed to pursue the composition of oratorio in the fashion of Marc-Antoine Charpentier, nothing in that genre appeared on the scene. The composers who wrote large works that had religious texts or that dealt with biblical subjects chose the operatic stage. Opera was adopted by leading Frenchmen from Rameau to Meyerbeer. It was only with Hector Berlioz (1803–1869) that a large choral piece came to the concert hall, and its appearance there

9. John Julian, *A Dictionary of Hymnology* (2nd rev. ed., London: John Murray, 1907; Dover Edition reprint, 1957), II, 1084, says that the *Stabat mater speciosa*, which Liszt used in the Christmas section, never came into liturgical use.
10. *LU*, 1634ᵛ–1637ʳ.

was as the outgrowth of a good-natured hoax perpetrated by Berlioz who, in 1850, began a short piece that was the seed of what four years later was presented to the Parisian public, and which became the most popular French work of its kind. *L'Adieu des Bergers à la Sainte Famille,* which he ascribed to an imaginary seventeenth-century composer, Pierre Ducré, was widely acclaimed from its very first performances. It is not easy to see why so much interest should have attended the appearance of a chorus in three short stanzas, but it was even hailed by some hearers as the kind of music that Berlioz was incapable of writing. After the lapse of four years and the addition of much more material for soloists, chorus, and orchestra, Berlioz brought out his dramatic trilogy, *L'Enfance du Christ,* of which the original chorus stood as the central piece. While much may be said of the composition as an unusual demonstration of Berlioz's restraint and an expression of his religious sentiments, it must also be recognized that the dramatic impulse surges as mightily through its pages as it does in his stage works. Not only did Berlioz preface each scene with stage directions, and provide lengthy descriptive interludes for the orchestra, but he took care that his text indicated specific characters that were heavily underscored by appropriate music. Not all of the dramatic devices are forced on the ear by the lengthy unfolding of scenic ideas as are the steady, rhythmic pacing of the Roman patrol in the *Marche nocturne* or the seven-beat measures to which the soothsayers conjure up spirits. More effective than these contrived devices is the simple door-knocking motive given to timpani ♫♪|♪,♪|♩ ♪|as Joseph goes from house to house in the town of Saïs, seeking help and shelter for the Mother and Child.

Effective as these devices are, they do not show this oratorio as a religious work. The impulse — and it was sheer impulse and ennui that caused Berlioz to write the chorus from which the work developed — that generated Berlioz's interest, first in the middle section of the trilogy and, a few years later, in the other parts, developed into an expression of Catholic faith and into the expansion of a few biblical fragments to dramatic proportions suited to concert hall or stage, but never to the church. Berlioz made severe concessions in style when he undertook the composition. His orchestra is limited to classical dimensions; still, he could not forego the haunting color of the English horn, and his characteristic melodic and harmonic trademarks are usually present even though he was almost painfully careful to use modal patterns in a few places. There are not many choral sections, for the pieces belong mostly to the dramatic soloists.

Those who are unfamiliar with the work can easily be misled by the title. Berlioz did not deal with Christ's childhood, but with the flight of two frightened adults with an infant who, according to the text, is still unweaned. Only in the Epilogue is there a single reference to the passage of the first ten years of Christ's life, and this is compressed into one sentence. It is for good reason that the English translation, *The Infancy of Christ,* has been suggested to replace the literal, but inexact, rendering, *The Childhood of Christ.*

César Franck (1822–1890) worked assiduously in the cause of church music. He produced much of what was performed at Sainte-Clotilde, the Paris church where he was choirmaster and organist. It was Franck's misfortune that he worked where tastes were not demanding and where examples of the finest quality were not to be heard. Even the staunchest of his defenders are unable to explain away the painfully pedestrian choral writing of *Les Béatitudes,* upon which he worked from 1869 to 1879. This was no mere potboiler, but a work for which Franck felt true concern and upon which he lavished careful attention. He assigned dramatic identities to most of the soloists, and characterized the two choruses as well, calling one "celestial," the other "terrestrial." But there are few points at which the choral writing is not dull and ill-suited to the text, made up of the Beatitudes and dramatic scenes intended to develop their meaning. That the solos often fare no better than the choruses is evident in the lack of characterization, perhaps displayed most tellingly in the Seventh and Eighth Beatitudes, where Satan (bass) and The Voice of Christ (baritone) are presented in unconvincing dialogue. Franck was probably limited by his personal musical style that offered little of dramatic impact, whatever else could be found among its qualities.

More serious was the charge levelled against Charles Gounod (1818–1893), that he lacked even religious motivation for his oratorios. In *La Rédemption* (1881) he set about to produce a trilogy on a text of his own, an apparent attempt to duplicate the pattern and success of Berlioz's *L'Enfance du Christ.* His insertion of several sections in the vein of the Lutheran chorale may be viewed as an effort to capture one of the features associated with Mendelssohn's successful oratorios. The variety of choral writing is not notably better than Franck's, and the level of musical taste has generally been judged even worse. Charity and good manners — *nil nisi bonum* — cause most writers to pass quietly over these works, but honesty demands recognition that they and some of their English counterparts spawned hundreds of others that are no better than trash, their immense popularity notwithstanding.

The relatively uneventful course of French oratorio found another supporter in Camille Saint-Saëns (1835–1921) whose Latin oratorio for Christmas did little to disturb the musical scene. His choral writing, nevertheless, is superior to that of his immediate predecessors as it often breaks away from the deadly block-chords that marked the choruses of Franck and Gounod. Amateur choral groups find the piece a convenient, if not satisfying, work to present in church.

Gabriel Fauré[11] (1845–1924) was the only French composer to produce an outstanding piece of religious choral music in the second half of the nineteenth century. His *Messe de Requiem* (1887) calls for soprano and baritone solos, chorus, orchestra, and organ. In seven movements, each of which has an orchestral beginning—sometimes only a sustained chord, sometimes a few measures—the composition recaptures the calm that was a feature of Renaissance music. Fauré's dynamics run the entire range of possibilities, but in no other way does he deviate from a reflective and simple presentation. The melodic contours are often reminiscent of plainsong, and the choral sections have an interesting amount of variety. From the note-against-note style of the "Introït et Kyrie" to the fluid diatonic lines of the Sanctus, where sopranos and men alternate and overlap the long phrases—the altos do not sing until the closing chord of this movement—the style remains consistently one of refinement and cultivated taste. Fauré's restrained expression may not suit some listeners, but it is difficult to find fault with a piece that is limited only by the composer's self-imposed concept, and not by any lack of musical skill.

The last important works in the line of French dramatic choral composition are those of Arthur Honegger (1892–1955). *Le Roi David (King David)* (1918) embodies the dramatic impulse that had motivated most Frenchmen since Charpentier. Whether it should be considered as a religious piece or as a dramatic work for the stage depends upon how far we see the oratorio legitimately invading the theater. *King David* may qualify as an oratorio because of its development of a biblical story, but it is never removed from its original milieu, the stage. Honegger wrote it as incidental music to a play, and its original performances were in that connection, with the orchestra considerably smaller than that used for performances now. The sub-

11. Not the composer of *Les Rameaux (The Palms)*, a perennially popular piece that has been arranged for almost every combination of voices. It is the work of a famous baritone, who is not known for any major compositions, Jean-Baptiste Faure (1830–1914).

sequent removal of the piece to the concert hall, because the music was more successful than the play, has not changed its episodic character. The twenty-seven sections do not present a connected series of texts; there is a feeling that something has been omitted from the dramatic unfolding of ideas, something that is not sufficiently provided by the narration that was added when the piece was revised.

The theatricality of *King David* tends to overshadow any religious ideas that Honegger may have meant to convey, but his periodic absorption with such subjects continued throughout his life, becoming most evident in his last work, *Une Cantate de Noël (A Christmas Cantata)*, completed, performed, and published in 1953. It is a considerably shorter work than *King David*, lasting about twenty-five minutes. It is conceived as a unit, the parts of which interlock tightly and sometimes overlap to a point where the ear is taxed to accept them all at once. In roughly five hundred measures of music, Honegger brought into play no fewer than seven familiar tunes and a fragment of liturgical text for which he provided original music. While such a wealth of material cannot entirely escape sounding like a medley of Christmas tunes, the dramatic organization of the parts makes the work something more than a monstrous *quodlibet*. A somber section for organ and orchestra opens the piece, and the chorus joins in a wordless vocalization that leads to a statement of the first verse and a half of *De profundis,* Psalm cxxix (130). This grows in intensity through an accumulation of voices, and then returns to more vocalization leading to a setting of the text, "O come, O come Emmanuel," to Honegger's music rather than the traditional melody. Whether it is in the quotation of text only, or in the statement of text and melody together as he later undertakes it, Honegger usually states only the opening phrases of his borrowed material rather than complete carols or plainsong. In this fashion he announces the birth of the Christ Child with French, English, and German carols at one time and, by indicating that each carol is to be sung in the original language, tries to insure the understanding of all segments of his audience. The choice of carols is heavily weighted toward the familiar German ones. *Es ist ein Ros' entsprungen, O du fröhliche,* and *Stille Nacht* are given prominent attention. Strangely, though, the tune and text that is usually sung with English words, *Susanni, Susanni,* is of German origin also. The strong ties of the composition with Catholic tradition are apparent in its reversion to Latin text exclusively for the final section. The solo baritone — the only extensive solo part in the piece — sings *Gloria in excelsis Deo* and a single voice from the children's chorus states the first hemistich of Psalm cxvi (117), *Laudate Dominum omnes gentes*,[12] which becomes the basis for the rest of the cantata against a vigorous, almost percussive accompaniment. The entire work is summed up by an orchestral postlude that restates the head motifs of all the tunes in the cantata.

English oratorio had little of quality to offer the nineteenth century until its domination by Mendelssohn and Spohr, and the less successful assaults of a few Frenchmen, had become things of the past. The memory of Handel's greatness, and the reiterated evidence of his genius in the form of a near cult of *Messiah* perpetuation, continued to set up a model of quality that native composers could not match.

Palestine,[13] composed in 1812 by William Crotch, is generally accepted as one of the best English oratorios to come from this bleak period. References to it are usually brief and general, providing so little information that it is profitable to examine it in some detail here. The text, by the Reverend Reginald Heber, is bombastic and laden with arcane references to biblical history, cast in words that may have seemed clear to its author, but which are always oblique and aimed at the theological insider rather than the world in general. Granting that prose was more florid in that day, it is still hard to see why the work should have received wide acceptance. The story attempts the impossible—a presentation of Judaic history from the Diaspora to the Book of Revelation, with only brief references to the Nativity and the Crucifixion—and it lacks both continuity and dramatic drive. As an example of the high-flown text, the following passage is quoted verbatim, with punctuation added for the sake of clarity. It follows a chorus, the burden of which is "Peace on Earth."

RECITATIVE, BASS

Thou palsied earth with noonday night o'erspread,
Thou sick'ning sun, so dark, so deep, so red,
Ye hov'ring hosts that throng the starless air,
Why shakes the Earth? Why fades the light?
Declare!

12. *LU*, 168. (Also printed as Example 14). Honegger uses Tone v, probably because the ascending triadic figure that opens it makes possible a more vigorous treatment than do the other plainsong formulas. The correspondence between the first hemistich and the first phrase of the chorale *Wachet auf, ruft uns die Stimme* is well known.

13. William Crotch, *Palestine* (London: Cramer, Addison & Beale, [1812?]).

AIR

Are these his limbs with ruthless scourges torn,
His brows all bleeding with the twisted thorn,
His the pale form, the meek forgiving eye,
Raised from the cross in patient agony?

CHORUS

Be dark, thou sun.
Thou noonday night, arise,
And hide, O hide
The dreadful Sacrifice.

There is no narrator, nor is the chorus required to narrate, for there is nothing more specific to communicate than the sample given here. The distinction between the text of recitative, air, or chorus is not always clearly marked. Crotch did his best to differentiate between the styles of singing, however. His recitatives are made up of series of short, jerky segments that are academically proper, but consistently dull. His airs have some breadth, but they are stifled by turgid text. The choruses are generally either polyphonically conceived on weak fugue subjects, or homophonic with relatively slow harmonic rhythm. Crotch's recognition of English taste and traditions probably helped him to decide that the closing *"Hallelujah, Amen"* chorus was both necessary and appropriate.

The next generation was represented by William Sterndale Bennett (1816–1875), a student of Crotch and disciple of Mendelssohn. His one oratorio, *The Woman of Samaria* (1867), reflects his indebtedness to Mendelssohn. The work opens with an instrumental introduction that includes a chorale for sopranos, the words and melody from *Nun freut euch, lieben Christen g'mein*. The text is taken from John 4:5–42 with additional material from other portions of Scripture, especially from the Psalms. The usual quartet of soloists is called upon individually, and their unaccompanied quartet, *God is a Spirit*, near the middle of the cantata has been a standard work for quartets and choirs until recent years. In fact, the entire cantata was popular with choral groups until long after its composer's death, sharing the limelight with works by Parry, Stanford, Sullivan, Stainer, and Mackenzie. The position held by these men was sufficiently strong that all five were knighted in recognition of their musical contributions. The necessity for them to seek teachers with prestige drove all of them except Stainer to Germany for some of their musical study. Their musical importance has not outlasted their lives in most cases, but, as the best composers that England produced in the Victorian era, they were widely acclaimed and imitated in Britain and in the United States. A few representative examples will show why most of their compositions have not continued to command the attention of musical directors in either the concert hall or the church.

Sir Arthur Sullivan (1842 – 1900) recognized the difficulties of finding suitable religious texts from the pens of his contemporaries, for he trusted none of them to provide words for *The Prodigal Son* (1869). Instead, he extracted them from the Bible. Unfortunately, the subject he chose lacks both substance and breadth, and Sullivan saw the necessity for expanding it with related text:

> The only drawback is the shortness of the narrative, and the consequent necessity for filling it out with material drawn from elsewhere.
> In the present case this has been done as sparingly as possible, and entirely from the Scriptures.[14]

Sullivan used only the first half of the story as it appears in the Bible (Luke 15:11 – 24), and he set these sections as recitative, aria, or duet; the material he chose from other portions of Scripture appears as solos, choruses, and ensemble of solo voices. His debt to *Elijah* is obvious in the dramatic placement of an unaccompanied quartet immediately before the closing chorus, a convenient way to display the soloists one last time before the show closes, whether it be in opera, operetta, or oratorio. The recitatives are straightforward, if dull. All of the other sections virtually exhaust each phrase of text before another is introduced. Text repetition in polyphonic music is to be expected, and it is usually effective, but in homophonic writing, with which *The Prodigal Son* abounds, it is a mechanical and tiring process. Musically, it results in the presence of numerous ternary forms caused by two statements of text, a line of different text, and the repetition of the first line. The pattern can be expanded by increasing the number of repetitions. Sullivan did this several times in *The Prodigal Son*. The following example, from the first solo for tenor, is typical:

> For I know that there is no good but for a man to rejoice,
> and also that ev'ry man should eat and drink, and enjoy the good
> of his labour. *(repeated)*

14. Arthur S. Sullivan, *The Prodigal Son* (New York: G. Schirmer, n.d.), [iii].

Father, give me this day the portion of goods that falleth
to me.

For I know that there is no good but for a man to rejoice,
and also that ev'ry man should eat and drink, and enjoy the good
of his labour.

For I know that there is no good but for a man to rejoice,
for I know that there is no good but for a man to rejoice.

The popularity of *The Crucifixion* (1887) by Sir John Stainer (1840–
1901) was for many years unchallenged, and it still receives many
performances each Easter season. The eager acceptance of Stainer's
piece was not entirely due to the quality of the music, although it
made a strong visceral appeal to audiences, its delights ranging from
chromatic sweetness to pompous tunes with exciting upward leaps
in the melodies. What has been overlooked is even more significant.
Stainer appropriated some of the ingredients of the Passion and the
German church cantata, supplied English equivalents for them and, in
so doing, captured the interest and enthusiasm of the church-going
musical audience. His contemporaries were more or less slavishly
imitating the concert-hall successes they heard on the Continent, but
Stainer brought to the public a work that was suitable for church, was
based on a biblical story that had significance annually, and made an
appeal to the musical sensibilities in a way no other English composer's pieces were doing. With a single exception, each quotation
from Scripture is sung in recitative and the poetic insertions are solo
arias, ensembles, or choruses. The exception is the unaccompanied
quartet, *God so loved the world* (John 3:16–17), strategically placed near
the middle of the composition. A final point of comparison with the
German cantata lies in the presence of the five hymns—of twenty sections in the entire composition—that are given a function similar to
that of the chorale. Stainer did not hold to a single stanza, but spread
himself over as many as ten. It is indicated that the hymns should be
sung by choir and congregation. In view of their unfamiliarity, this
seems to be more of a gesture than a real hope.

Despite the fact that Stainer had no contact with German teachers,
he came closer to restoring a vital stream of church music than his contemporaries who had studied in Germany. Their exposure was to the
concert hall, while Stainer, as a scholar, employed his critical knowledge of the past to the reconstruction of an appealing, yet religious
work. Sullivan had gone back to Scripture, but had chosen a weak
story; Stainer found the vital ingredient. Had his successors, with

their greater skill, followed his lead rather than returning to the Handelian pattern, English church music might have been restored to a position of world prominence.

The two best known oratorios of Sir Hubert Parry (1848–1918) are musically superior to others of the Victorian period, but they suffer from the prevailing problems of text. It must have been a huge task for composers to search out ideas that were not already shopworn for the oratorio-hungry choral societies, and *Judith* (1888) and *Job* (1892) come off better than many others. Parry's skill in setting words with scrupulous attention to accentuation made even the weaker sections of his texts more vital than had been the efforts of other men of his era. *Judith* especially contains some fine, vigorous choral writing.

It is perhaps significant that Sir Edward Elgar (1857–1934), who alone of this group broke through the tedium of England's choral music, did not study in Germany, was largely taught at home by his father, was exposed to Catholic music from his youth, and thereby escaped much of the wearisome round of current anthems and Services, and was capable and interested in the instrumental idiom. This last qualification was found among Continental composers almost as a matter of course; among the English, who were lacking in wide experience, it was in most cases a missing ingredient of major importance.

Most of Elgar's oratorio effort was devoted to the first half of his productive years, but not to the exclusion of his other interests in composition. He was busy with minor works as well as some large pieces until the production of his last finished oratorio. His earliest religious oratorio, *The Light of Life*, first performed in 1896, is relatively short. It follows a traditional pattern in setting a text of biblical materials and commentary upon them in an orderly procession of solos, ensembles, and choruses. A vitality that had been absent from English music is at once apparent in both the vocal and instrumental writing. Elgar did not burst the bonds of tradition, but only because he had never been in their confines. His home-grown, non-Anglican, instrumental orientation permitted him to develop along lines that may have been considered vulgar by those who accepted a tradition of blandness, but that had to be recognized as permeated with a new intensity.

The widest recognition of Elgar's position in English oratorio came with his setting of Cardinal Newman's poem, *The Dream of Gerontius*. It was not the English who saw its qualities first, however; until the first performance in Germany where Elgar was hailed as a true prophet in the island desert, the English found little of value in an idiom that was foreign to the audience and, almost disastrously at the first performance, to the singers. The work had its first hearing in 1900, and Elgar had spent about a year at composing it, although he had studied the poem and considered its musical possibilities during the decade preceding. His setting of the poem was much more than just another one of the academically correct pieces that mark the end of the Victorian period. Epic proportions and concept are perhaps lacking, but the scope of this work exceeds that of all contemporaneous efforts. Skillful counterpoint, expressive melody, and sensitive treatment of text are mingled with leitmotivic concepts and the use of adventurous harmonizations that take full advantage of the new ideas on the Continent, but that were quite foreign to English audiences and musicians. It is only necessary to recall that the Victorian era saw the death of Wagner and the rise to prominence of Richard Strauss in order to see the gulf that existed between the style of German composers and their English counterparts and, to a lesser extent, between Elgar and his own countrymen.

Not only did Elgar exhibit a taste for the newer harmonic idiom, but he provided a quality of mysticism that was not expressed in music of composers who developed under Anglican-German influence. Gerontius becomes a symbol of Catholic humanity and, for those who can see through the denominational aura, a symbol of Christian humanity. The first part of the work deals with the body of the dying Gerontius, his relation to the church and to the world projected through both Latin and English text. The second, longer part of the oratorio follows Gerontius' soul as it is conducted toward its judgment by an angel guide. Dramatic characterization is attempted by the assignment of identities (Priest, Chorus of Assistants, Angel, Chorus of Demons, Choir of Angelicals, Chorus of Souls in Purgatory) at all points of the oratorio.

It has been suggested that English composers turned to dramatic (but undramatized) choral works because they were untrained in the theatrical tradition and had not sufficient opportunities awaiting them even if they attempted to invade the field of opera.[15] Untrained they were, but their greatest weakness lay in their failure to keep up with the times. Those who studied in Germany were inoculated with

15. *Grove's*, II, 910.

the traditions of Spohr and Mendelssohn. When these traditions were
brought at third hand to the English concert hall, they were at once
both vitiated and anachronistic. Elgar broke the mold that had held
English choral music enslaved to outmoded tradition and to the limits
of cathedral taste. In two generations after his own, England would
be able to accept as a matter of course a resurgence of imaginative
choral composition.

It was Elgar's plan after *The Dream of Gerontius* to complete a trilogy
upon texts selected from Scripture. *The Apostles* (published 1903)
and *The Kingdom* (published 1906) were to be the first two parts. He
became involved in symphonic works after their completion and
never returned seriously to the third part. A few sketches are all
that were completed.

Mysticism continued to dominate the English scene in choral
music in a pair of works by Gustav Holst (1872–1934) and Ralph
Vaughan Williams (1872–1958). Holst was next on the scene after
Elgar with a major work of this genre, and it may well be due to the
solid acceptance of *The Dream of Gerontius* that his *Hymn of Jesus*
(1917) was greeted with acclaim instead of dismay. The words are
translated from the *Acts of Saint John,* one of the heretical books of
pseudepigrapha not ordinarily thought of as part of the Apocrypha.
The Hymn of Jesus is in two parts: first, a short prelude; second, the
hymn itself. The prelude sets forth the tunes of two Gregorian hymns
in the orchestra and then repeats them with text, using only a few of
the singers.[16] Much of the text of the main portion falls into sentences
with balanced halves. Holst divided such places between two SATB
choirs, sometimes in simple alternation, at other times in different
rhythms and meters *(Ex. 102).* Among the features that stirred the
imagination of Holst's contemporaries were a "dry canon" in which
spoken text was introduced in rhythmic imitation over orchestral
accompaniment, the juxtaposition of chords unrelated by key,

 and and of course the

alternation of irregular and regular meters. There is also a return of

16. One stanza of *Vexilla Regis prodeunt,*
LU, 575, is sung by the treble (i.e., soprano)
voices of the semichorus against an accompaniment that is rhythmically independent of the chant. The orchestral
chords use only the tones of a pentatonic
scale (c, d, e, g, a); the chant uses the entire
diatonic series of tones. Only the first
half of the text comes from *LU. Pange*
lingua gloriosi uses text from *LU,* 709, and
the tune of *LU,* 950. It is sung by a few
male voices and is supported by a sustained orchestral chord using another
pentatonic scale (b^b, c, e^b, f, g). *The Hymn*
of Jesus is published by Stainer & Bell.

Ex. 102 Alternation of text segments in Holst's *Hymn of Jesus*

Used with permission of Stainer & Bell Ltd.

the *Vexilla Regis prodeunt* melody near the end of the piece, vocalized wordlessly by the sopranos of the two full choirs and the semichorus. There are no solos in the composition.

Vaughan Williams drew on a number of sources for the text of *Sancta Civitas (The Holy City)* (1925), but the main portion of it comes from The Revelation of Saint John the Divine. The composition calls for a full chorus, a semichorus of about twenty singers who sit behind the full chorus, and a distant choir, SSAA, preferably of boys' voices. The reassignment of voices from these choruses into other combinations—for instance, the tenors and basses of the onstage choirs combine as a male chorus—makes for a great degree of flexibility in the treatment of vocal colors. There are extensive solo passages for baritone, and a few measures for solo tenor. The apocalyptic and mystical qualities of the text are intensified by Vaughan Williams's distinctive musical setting which ranges from quiet wonder to glorious tumult. At his hands, parallel motion became respectable in England, not with the mannered gentility of Debussy or Delius, but with a vigor that lay in its unpredictability. His idiom is not easily classifiable, for he moves from passages involving consecutive fifths to others rich in chords of superimposed fourths, to series of parallel triads in root position or second inversion, and to sections of chords colored by added seconds and sixths. One consistent feature of his harmony is the raising of the fourth degree of the scale, and the occasional alteration of the third and sixth degrees as well. The choirs sing as separate groups, in alternation with each other, and in combination. The selection of smaller groups to sing brief passages between or against other sections of text assigned to the full chorus is common. One passage *(Ex. 103)* calls for a small choir to sing a lament that is then commented upon by the full chorus. *Sancta Civitas* contains passages that are forbidding to choir singers; the sopranos and tenors of both choruses are required to sing at the top of their ranges several times, but with excellent effect.

Elaborate organization of choral forces is again evident in *Belshazzar's Feast* (1931) by Sir William Walton (1902–). Two semi-choruses and two full choruses are required for performance of the work, although the semichoruses are paper choirs only. Since they never sing at the same time as the full choruses, they may be made up of selected voices from each of those groups, and they need not exist as independent choirs. The baritone soloist has some fine moments, both lyrical and declamatory. Much of the excellent quality of the choral sections may be attributed directly to Walton's skill in the vertical distribution of his chordal elements. While this is an impor-

Ex. 103 Passage from *Sancta Civitas*, Vaughan Williams

Used with permission of J. Curwen & Sons Limited. 29 Maiden Lane, London, W.C.2

tant factor in any kind of writing, it becomes a prime factor when chords become increasingly dense and complex. Certainly such intervals as diminished octaves and chords that contain the ninth in the lowest part require the most dexterous handling in order to serve their purposes.

In addition to full orchestra, the score calls for two brass bands, one to be situated at each side of the choir and orchestra. The score is so arranged that the bands, organ, and a few other instruments may be omitted if necessary. The orchestra and bands come in for some exciting moments, especially in the section where praises are sung to the gods of gold, silver, and other precious substances. The instrumental interludes that separate these invocations are studded with opportunities for the percussion instruments, whose use tends to modify the dissonant character of the music, a character that was forbidding three decades ago, but that has since become comfortable, if not commonplace.

Since *Belshazzar's Feast,* there has been a continuing interest in choral works among English composers. Among the considerable number of active and promising composers, Benjamin Britten (1913–) has made the greatest impact. As early as 1933 he became recognized through a set of six variations on a theme for unaccompanied voices,[17] *A Boy Was Born.* No two successive variations employ the same combination of voices. Among the groups that are called upon are a unison chorus of boys, a chorus of women's voices, and another of men's. These appear in various combinations and, in the finale, as an ensemble *a 9.* The theme upon which the entire piece is constructed is a simple four-note pattern that appears at many pitch levels and in numerous rhythmic alterations throughout the work. In itself this dependence upon a single figure as a basis for the entire composition is not significant, but it marks clearly Britten's intense interest in structure from the early years of his career, an interest that finds full expression in his mature works. Also of significance is his selection of texts from several sources, in this case mostly fifteenth- and sixteenth-century carols.

His popularity became firmly established through *A Ceremony of Carols* (1942), a set of eleven carols for treble voices and harp, and a short cantata, *Rejoice in the Lamb* (1943). More significant in pointing toward his later style, however, is his *Festival Te Deum* (1945) for choir

17. A revision (1955) published in 1958 includes an organ accompaniment.

and organ. Pentachords and tetrachords are used as basic melodic structures, in their original form and in inversion, in some sections of the voice parts (and in the organ near the end of the composition). A rhythmic flexibility that equates measure length with syllable distribution becomes more prominent, resulting in melodic patterns and metrical arrangements that are dictated by the text rather than by traditional musical principles of regularity and balance.

In December 1961, Britten completed the score of his *War Requiem*, commissioned for the consecration of St. Michael's Cathedral, Coventry. In creating a work that was to mark the formal re-emergence of a house of worship destroyed by war, Britten gave vent to his own strong feelings. His composition is at once painful and moving, accusing and forgiving. Much may be made of the association of words. The liturgical text of the *Missa pro defunctis* is intersected by poems of Wilfred Owen, anti-war poems that are as bitter as some of the liturgical words are hopeful. The early performances and the recorded version of the *War Requiem* were reviewed in glowing terms.[18] No one seems to escape emotional involvement in discussion of the piece, for it brings into sharp focus a number of sensitive matters: a criticism of war; the conjunction of liturgical and secular (and sometimes anti-clerical) texts; and the casting of a major musical work in an up-to-date musical idiom. The masterful fashion in which Britten has brought his materials together cannot be discussed successfully. He has produced such a tightly-knit work that only a careful study of the score and repeated hearings of the recording can begin to unravel the various threads that bind the work together. For the *War Requiem* is as full of unifying devices as ever was a Mass that took advantage of isorhythms or *cantus firmi*. The first and most apparent of these devices is a recurrent use of the tritone. It appears as a harmonic interval between voice parts and in the orchestra, as a melodic leap, as a distinctive interval that emerges from diatonic lines, and as the pivotal points upon which successive phrases begin or end *(Ex. 104)*. The piece begins with the recurrent and overpowering repetition of the tritone and closes with its resolution. A nearly identical passage, removed from any distractions of orchestral accompaniment, closes the first, second, and last sections of the Requiem *(Ex. 105)*. Each appearance has different text as required by the liturgical meaning of the section to which it belongs: the first movement closes with a brief statement

18. The most complete discussion at this writing is the analytical essay by Peter   Evans, "Britten's 'War Requiem'," *Tempo* (Spring & Summer, 1962), 20–39.

Ex. 104 *War Requiem*, Britten

Ex. 105 Closing measures of Britten's *War Requiem* (soprano and alto as written; tenor and bass an octave lower)

of the Kyrie; the second, with the text *Pie Jesu Domine, dona eis requiem. Amen.*

There are three distinct planes of communication in the *War Requiem.* The first employs the boys' choir and organ. In the first movement, violins are added to emphasize the tritone. Except for the closing formulas given to the unaccompanied full chorus, the sections for boys are the purest utterance of liturgical text; associated almost entirely with the organ, they provide the closest link to an acceptable piece of service music that is found in the composition. Even so, their fearful cry of *Domine Jesu* at the opening of the Offertorium becomes, in retrospect, the cry of Isaac upon the sacrificial altar in Owen's poem that follows. The second plane of communication is occupied by the chorus, the main orchestra, and the soprano soloist. This group deals only with Latin text, but it is less liturgical in its impact because it alternates with Owen's English text that occupies the third plane, given to the tenor and baritone soloists and the chamber orchestra that accompanies them. While the second plane may be representative of all mankind, the third represents the victims of war and their cries against its futility.

The musical treatment is too complex to examine in detail here, but several outstanding features must be mentioned. In a general climate of tonal, but chromatically enriched, material, there are occasional encroachments of serial technique. These are not in the form of slavish adherence to twelve-tone regulations, but have certain freedoms of convenience; viz., the use of fewer than twelve tones or the use of each of the twelve tones as a root of a group of chords. Both of these methods can be found in Example 105. Here and in certain of the solo passages the use of serial construction seems to be no more important than the simultaneous outlining of the tritone at the two ends of the phrase. The serial concept for its own sake does not seem important, but as a means of underlining another structural complication it takes on significance. The opening of the Sanctus is a case in point. The solo soprano establishes the tritone (which is reinforced by the orchestra) in a pair of twelve-tone phrases that are interrupted by nonserial statements. The chorus then begins a pyramidal accumulation of sound that eventually encompasses all twelve tones. The selection of tones for the pyramid is such that the tritone is effectively resolved, but a new kind of tension replaces it. Instead of singing the text in exactly notated rhythm, the chorus is directed to chant *Pleni sunt coeli et terra gloria tua* in free rhythm through a gradual crescendo that seems truly to fill all heaven and earth with vibrant praise.

Britten did not return church music to the church with this composition, even though its first performance was given in a cathedral, but he did attract wide attention to a work based upon a liturgical text that has significance outside its own faith. Interest has again turned to a composition of religious connotations and, whatever its eventual place in musical literature, Britten has established for the time being England's pre-eminence in the writing of large choral works.

The first large choral pieces by American composers did not impress anyone except other Americans or Europeans who felt that no good could come out of the cultural wilderness. America had no musical traditions upon which to build in the nineteenth century. Young men who wished to become composers did just as those who were born in England at that time—they went to Germany to study.[19] Three leading figures of the century were John Knowles Paine (1839–1906), George W. Chadwick (1854–1931), and Horatio W. Parker (1863–1919). Both Paine and Chadwick tried their hands at oratorio, but Parker's *Hora Novissima* (1893) stands as the first significant oratorio from an American, although nothing distinctly American can be discerned in it. In setting a relatively lengthy Latin poem by the twelfth-century Bernard of Cluny—thirty-five stanzas of six lines each —that has an unvarying pattern, Parker chose to deal with an insistent rhythmic idea that is saved from tediousness only through his alterations of it in many of the eleven sections of the piece. Although the poetic line is the same length in each verse, he created a varied motive that still retains some vestige of its original shape *(Ex. 106)*. Harmonically, there is nothing extraordinary about the work. It provides sturdy chord progressions enlivened with chromaticism. The usual four soloists are given an opportunity to appear in solo sections; there is a double chorus, an *a cappella* chorus, a quartet, and each section closes with a quartet and chorus in which all forces combine. It is not unusual that Parker did not adopt biblical text for his work. The English composers of his time who made gestures in that direction had come up with unexciting portions of Scripture, and he must have been familiar with their efforts. *Hora Novissima* broke away from a series of texts that were already beginning to pall upon the British taste, and, in so doing, gained a place of distinction in both American and English repertories. Nor should it be expected that Parker would have miraculously pulled away from the concert hall tradition and brought

19. One exception is George Bristow (1825–1898), who was born and trained in this country. His teachers, however, came from Germany and England. His oratorios, *Praise to God* and *Daniel*, remain unpublished.

Ex.106   Related motives in *Hora Novissima*, Parker

music back into the church. The tradition of church choirs was weaker in America than in Europe since there was no long history of liturgical singing in this country. *The Legend of St. Christopher* (1898) is a more dramatic work than *Hora Novissima*, assigning solos to identifiable characters in operatic fashion, but its story removes it even farther from the realm of religious music than most works of its type. It bears the same tenuous relationship to religious music as does Liszt's *Saint Elizabeth*.

The course of American oratorio was not plain for another generation. For works of merit and substance, capable of matching the European product and providing a contribution to American music, it is necessary to await the maturity of the composers who were born during the years of Parker's best works. As one example of the interim product, we may examine briefly *The Prodigal Son* (1901) by Henry B. Vincent (1872–1941). His setting of the story is complete, going in this respect beyond that of Sullivan. However, in order to fill out the work, Vincent gave other portions of biblical texts to soloists and chorus in the same way that Sullivan had done. The similarity between the two works does not end at that point, for Vincent felt no qualms about text repetition. The restatement of phrases to slightly varied music was a common feature in anthems and longer works of the period, and blame should not be laid entirely on either Vincent or Sullivan for a widespread failing. Vincent and many other Americans of that generation, however, can be criticized for uninspired musical material and a prosody that produced music ranging from dull to inept.

The slow development of American church music for large choral forces may be attributed to a number of things, but three are most significant. Foremost in the minds of composers from the middle to the end of the nineteenth century was the need to match the European standard, to prove some degree of equality. To accomplish this, they went, in most cases, to Germany to study with the academicians who were also training the British composers of the period. Inasmuch as most of the group that went to Germany came from a limited area of our country—the New England states—a regional hegemony was established that was then reflected in the students of these same German-trained composers, many of whom took important teaching posts in the same part of America from which they had come. Progress was thus delayed by a disinclination on the part of the best composers to leave the East, and even now art that springs from other parts of the country is viewed with suspicion. A second barrier was the absence of a choral tradition in American churches. It is true that some isolated large choruses existed, but for the most part the development of large choral groups did not take place until the present century, when college groups were formed in great numbers. Unfortunately, even now those groups do not generally foster American works of large scope; their conductors prefer established masterpieces of Europe, usually those of past generations.

American composers, then, did not have the ready-made audiences and performing groups that existed for their European counterparts. They tended to compose in smaller forms, or, as exercises to prove their facility, to limit themselves to one work in the large vocal forms. A third deterrent may also be seen in the constant stream of renowned European composers who took up residence in this country. The stream was at flood level during the fourth and fifth decades of this century. While their appearance stimulated American musical activity considerably, it served at the same time as a brake upon the efforts of native-born composers. When faced with a choice between the products of a Stravinsky, a Milhaud, a Hindemith, and that of an unknown but creditable local talent, the publishers, conductors, and audiences generally chose the proven product, and the American composer remained unsung or, at best, poorly sung. Many young Americans, when faced with such competition, turned to producing cantatas that would serve the amateur church choir, works that are generally tuneful, relatively easy, and that appeal to the congregation rather than to the musician. Works of this type are not necessarily bad, but many of them fall into the lowest level of banal taste and require few musical skills from the performers. There is such a wide variety of these works that it is impossible to deal with them here. It may be mentioned that many of the same composers under discussion were mentioned in the previous chapter as composers of anthems and other easy service music. Such names as J. H. Maunder and Harry Rowe Shelley are representative of this type of cantata that generally called for SATB choir, soloists, and organ. Works for Christmas and Easter outnumber all others, and American amateur choirs of nonliturgical faiths have tended to place their principal attention on works appropriate to these seasons.

Among the present generation of composers, there are few who have undertaken the composition of large religious choral works as a regular practice, but a number of them have provided examples numerous enough to illustrate the changes that have come about in American choral music. It is symptomatic of the number and quality of choral groups in our universities and colleges that composers have set a major number of their works to secular texts. This has not resulted in a dearth of religious pieces, for these too find performance in such organizations, but it has made a drastic reduction in the number we can use to illustrate the development of American religious choral music.

A free treatment of the Passion story taken principally from St. Matthew is the basis of *The Passion* (1944) by Bernard Rogers (1893 –). Two soloists are required, a baritone as The Voice of Jesus, and a tenor as Pilate. The incidental solos assigned to male and female voices may be sung by members of the chorus. Although the story is continuous, it is not bound together by recitatives of a single narrator. A remnant of the older practice is found, however, in the assignment of *turba* passages to the chorus.

A set of eight unaccompanied choruses by Randall Thompson (1899 –) is *The Peaceable Kingdom* (1936). The texts, all taken from Isaiah, do not make a continuous narrative. A variety of styles appear

Ex. 107 *a)* Section of chorus VI, *The Peaceable Kingdom*, Randall Thompson (dominant pedal point in soprano and tenor solos omitted)

b) Chorus V, *Ibid.*

in the several sections, and the composer makes use of double chorus for the fourth, sixth, and last choruses. One of these (*Howl ye*) is a sharply rhythmical antiphonal setting for two SATB groups; another (*But these are they that forsake the Lord*) uses the same voices in less vigorous fashion, and near its conclusion, divides continuous quarter notes into overlapping patterns (*Ex. 107a*); and the final piece pits the female voices against the male in brilliant fashion. The four-voice writing is no less arresting, the absence of contrapuntal sections not-withstanding. Several sections of the works are strongly modal, and added vigor is provided by the spacing of the voices, especially by the placement of the tenor part above the alto *(Ex. 107b)*. Totally different is *The Nativity according to Saint Luke* (1961), subtitled *a musical drama in seven scenes*. Intended for performance in a church—the work was composed for the bicentennial of the dedication of Christ Church, Cambridge—it has elaborate stage directions and calls for small orchestra, organ, and optional hand bells. The text includes, of course, a setting of the Magnificat given entirely to a soprano soloist. The piece has no end of variety, including a fugue and a scene in which the shepherds first dance and then sing a charming *Nowel,* endlessly repeating that single word as its text. The composition requires a dozen solo singers and choir. This, as well as the need for dramatic presentation in church, will probably prevent its wide performance.

A Canticle of Christmas (1959) by Vittorio Giannini (1903–) uses the St. Luke story of the Nativity in the fashion of a German church cantata. For baritone narrator, chorus, and orchestra, the composition uses fragments of familiar material, portions of the carol *Angels we have heard on high* and all of *O come all ye faithful* along with humming backgrounds, chords built of successive fourths, and generally dramatic treatment of the story. From the beginning of the piece, the opening notes of *O come all ye faithful* are brought into use, and the entire carol is sung, with optional audience participation, against the closing fugue which uses both carols as ingredients.

Two cantatas by Normand Lockwood (1906–) are aimed directly at the amateur choir, but are still vigorous and challenging music. *Jesus, the King* (1959), for soprano and tenor solos, chorus, and piano, sets the texts that may be used during the Lenten and Easter seasons. Hymn tunes, some of which are familiar, are used along with original material that is interesting, but well within the grasp of amateur church singers. The greatest complexities lie in the solo parts, and the choir has the satisfaction of a closing chorus (with soloists added) that moves from a whisper to a mighty shout. For the Christmas season, Lockwood has written a similar setting of the St. Luke Gospel, *The Holy Birth* (1959), this time using soprano and baritone soloists, but dealing with the material in the same fashion as in the other work.

Two works by Alan Hovhaness (1911–), both published in 1958, are specific in their demands upon instrumental groups not found in our churches. His cantata, *Glory to God,* and his *Magnificat* adapt themselves poorly to keyboard reductions, either because his instrumental idiom is lost at the console or because the percussion parts cannot be duplicated in another medium. The cantata uses solo soprano and alto, mixed chorus, and an orchestra of brass, percussion, and organ with a saxophone prominently placed in the introduction. The *Magnificat* calls for a quartet of soloists, chorus, and an orchestra that omits the weaker and dark-textured wind instruments. To attempt to describe the style of so prolific a composer in few words smacks of flippancy, but two characteristics of the *Magnificat* will have to suffice as illustration here. Doubling each vocal line at the octave produces a broad sound that is further characterized by the absence of a stable foundation where second-inversion chords are the predominant structure *(Ex. 108a)*. Also throughout the compo-

Ex. 108 *a) Magnificat,* Hovhaness (women's voices are doubled an octave below by men's)

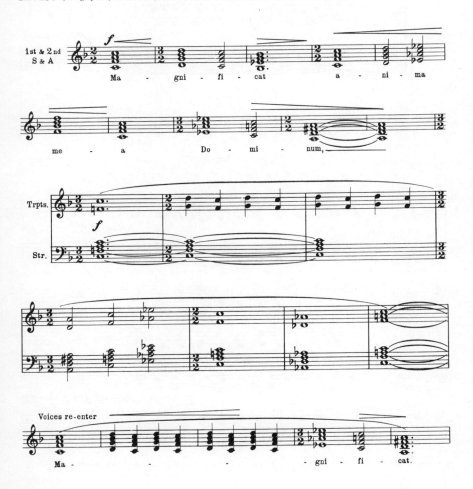

sition are passages *senza misura* for both instruments and voices
(Ex. 108b) in which a mystic hubbub is created by the repetition
of different lines that revolve around a central pitch, subject to flexibility of duration at the discretion of the conductor. By mingling

Ex. 108 *b) Ibid.*

exotic influences and some latter-day Impressionistic vocabulary, Hovhaness has introduced to the settings of religious text a totally new kind of music. Still, this is not his only approach to religious music. In an *Easter Cantata* (1958) that is part of a four-part composition entitled *Triptych,* he uses ostinato patterns, sections of *falsobordone* and second-inversion chords, and a fugal chorus. While the score calls for a chamber orchestra that could not be assembled easily in most church situations, the accompaniment could be played at the keyboard, although much of the flavor would thereby be lost.

A deliberate imitation of Renaissance practice is found in *A Psalm of David* (1951) by Norman Dello Joio (1913–). The text of Psalm L (51) is set for chorus and an orchestra of brass, strings, and percussion. The musical phrase upon which it is based *(Ex. 109)* is taken directly from the setting of the same psalm by Josquin des Prez. While the phrase, as a *cantus firmus*, was used with authority on successive scale degrees throughout the entire octave, Dello Joio's efforts in the same direction are less successful, probably because counterpoint is a more gracious host to such treatment than is chordal harmony. Some of the variety in the choral parts is achieved through sheer force, and the borrowed theme, lacking the subtle variety that can be implanted in imitative writing, soon becomes uncomfortably insistent.

The two-hundred-fiftieth anniversary of Charles Wesley's birth was celebrated in 1957. For the occasion, a libretto based on Wesley documents, hymns, sermons, and on biblical passages was assembled by Tom Driver, the whole set to music by Cecil Effinger (1914–).[20] For a quartet of soloists, chorus, and full orchestra, the work contains fine declamatory singing for the soloists as well as some lyrical passages. The choral writing is not complex, possibly because its first performance was to be by a large student choir at the National Methodist Student Conference of 1957. The choruses, nevertheless, are forthright and convincing. Aimed directly at the church choir is Effinger's *St. Luke Christmas Story* (1954). For SATB chorus, soloists, organ, and optional added instruments, the piece can be negotiated by any willing choir. The choruses are generously filled with unison passages, and the ranges are comfortable. The solos are also carefully planned so that they may be sung by soprano, tenor, or baritone in any combina-

Ex. 109 *Cantus firmus* of Josquin's setting of Psalm L (51), used in Dello Joio's *Psalm of David*

Mi - se - re - re me - i, De - us

20. The Invisible Fire (New York: H. W. Gray Co.).

tion. The solo range lies entirely within the treble staff except for a few notes, for which the composer has provided optional readings.

One of a number of American works for the Lutheran service in which the return to liturgical considerations may be found is an Easter cantata *Christ Jesus Lay in Death's Strong Bands* by Richard Wienhorst (1920–). Not only is the text made up of the Propers for Easter, with the Introit, Epistle, Gradual, and Gospel given in plain-song so they may be intoned, but the choruses are chorale variations on five stanzas of the familiar chorale. Convenience and practicality are foremost considerations. The accompaniment is for organ or trio sonata, and shortened versions of performance are suggested in the foreword.

The dramatic setting of religious text for nonliturgical Protestant observances has had to be acceptable to the tastes of fundamentalist congregations. The restriction of materials and methods has placed a challenge squarely before the church composer. The cheap solution of creating cantatas that are simply a collection of maudlin tunes with dance-band harmonies has been extremely profitable to a few com-posers, but it has done nothing toward providing music that is really suitable in church. One thing that has affected the quality of multi-movement pieces in those faiths is the lack of a suitable place in the service for such a piece. Since it must be performed outside the wor-ship service, it is too easily viewed as a form of entertainment. The search for a dignified form of expression that does not imply a lack of perception or taste on the part of the congregation has caused com-posers to give these pieces an appearance of worship in a form and time other than that encountered in morning or evening worship. Involvement of the minister, who recites text from scriptural sources between solo and choral settings—as a substitute for recitative—has, in a small way, maintained a sense of dignity in special musical programs. Most such compositions may be equally well presented if the text is read by a capable member of the choir. A Christmas cantata that carries this line of development even farther is *The Word Was Made Flesh* (1963) by T. W. Dean (1915–). Choral narration that permits antiphonal treatment of text with control of both volume and tempo is a departure from standard treatments *(Ex. 110)*. These narrative sections do not entirely replace recitative, for they are used in addition to choral recitative, and both of these methods for presenting dramatic text are followed by hymns, a canticle, and a short anthem, all easily within the grasp of the volunteer choir and the perception of the congregation.

Ex. 110

CHORAL NARRATION: John 1:1–3, 14

<pre>
             mf
WOMEN: In the beginning was the Word, and the Word was with God,
MEN: In the beginning was the Word,   and the
             mf
</pre>

<pre>
                     f
                 The same was in the beginning with God.
Word was God. The same was in the beginning with God. All things
                 f   p
</pre>

<pre>
                 pp
                 All things,
were made by Him;   and without Him was not anything
                             mp
</pre>

<pre>
        p   mf
        All things were made by Him,   and without Him was not
made.   and without Him was not
                                     mf
</pre>

<pre>
                     f
anything made that was made.   And the Word was made flesh,
anything made that was made.   The
                                                           f
</pre>

<pre>
                 made flesh,   and dwelt among us,   and we
Word was made flesh,   made flesh,   and dwelt among us,
</pre>

<pre>
beheld His glory,   the only begotten
            the glory as of the only begotten,   the only begotten
</pre>

<pre>
                                     rit.
of the Father,   full of grace and truth.
of the Father,   full of grace,   full of grace and truth.
                     rit.
</pre>

*This arrangement of the text is only a suggestion. Other original arrangements may be used either by narrators or a large speech choir.
Reprinted by permission of Gamut Company.

An *Easter Cantata* (1962) by Daniel Pinkham (1923–) illustrates still one more way of dealing with religious text. The words are taken from the Gospels of John and Matthew, and from the Psalms. The cantata is for mixed chorus without solos. The instrumental parts are scored for brass, percussion, and celesta. Structural considerations rank high in Pinkham's method; the instrumental prelude makes much of a four-measure theme that, in its fourfold repetition, takes up more than half of the movement. The second movement is enclosed between two statements of a wordless unison evocation *(Ex. 111a)* and the body of the movement is built entirely on the material of the trombone duo from the beginning of the movement, sometimes in exact repetition in the voices, and sometimes using new melodic material resulting from the redistribution of pitches between the parts *(Ex. 111b)*. In other portions of the cantata Pinkham employs canon as accompaniment for chordal singing and as the total structure of an *a cappella* section. The voices alternate effectively between unison, coupled two-part, and four-part declamatory singing.

The American composers who have been considered here do not exhaust the list of either the active or qualified workers. It must be remembered that many more composers are working, a number of them by choice or economic pressures producing pieces that are

Ex. 111 *a) Easter Cantata*, Daniel Pinkham

Ex. 111 *b) Ibid.,* voice parts derived from instrumental parts

musically less exciting, but that are more acceptable and satisfying to their public, the church choir, and the congregation. When they are examined outside their functional area, some of them are guilty of compromise or outright weakness. References to them should not be considered as recommendations, but simply a part of the sampling of the current materials.

Chapter XII

From the Romantic Period
to the Present

IT WAS DURING the nineteenth century that church support was finally withdrawn from elaborate musical works, and they began to appear regularly in the concert hall. Their transfer was already under way in the eighteenth century, for only in a few situations where large establishments were under the direct influence of high officials were there impressive musical programs in connection with the church. The rise of the concert hall, the need for wooing audiences, and the presence of the finest performers in the more rewarding world of secular music all sped the migration of large religious works to the marketplace. Those few composers who clung to the old way of church composition were induced to do so by true piety or by their inability to compete in the musical affairs of the world. Sheer necessity often compelled them to write for small choirs with few or no accompanying instruments. There was already sufficient liturgical choral music available for Roman Catholic use by the beginning of the nineteenth century, and many of the pieces that appeared during the previous two centuries had been written expressly for commemorative or dedicatory occasions. Lutheran service music also existed in sufficient quantity that, whenever need arose, it could be brought into use again. The emergence of a twentieth-century school of unaccompanied church music indicates not the failure of the past, but the changing needs and tastes of the present. The Church of England, similarly, had a large storehouse of Services upon which choirmasters could draw. Those men who worked principally as church composers and organists, and who felt that additional works bearing their names would somehow be of benefit, have left their own additions to the mountain of material from earlier years. Thus we may find Services, Magnificats, Te Deums, and other settings by many of the same composers who were active in developing the anthem to the point where we left off its study. The small religious works of the past two centuries still await a complete study. Only after the results of such a study are known can we see their true place in the church service. Church music of this shorter kind, however, regardless of the faith for which it is written, tends to be modest and without a sense of participation in the musical developments of its own generation. For a view of the extent to which religious music continued to claim public attention, we must turn to the concert hall (or, in some instances, to the church itself in the guise of a concert hall).

Many composers who lived well into the Romantic period do not come to mind when we mention religious music. One reason is their prominence in other musical fields; we think of composer X as a symphonist and of composer Y as an opera specialist. Large numbers of these same people paid their spiritual debt to the church through their art, with more or less success, depending on how completely they could leave their secular habits behind or adapt them to a religious expression. It will not be necessary to emphasize the fact that some of those who achieved the greatest acclaim did so with works that were similar to their pieces for the stage or concert hall. We must remember also that some composers, after making a career with secular music, turned almost entirely to church music in their later years. We have encountered one such composer in Campra; another is Luigi Cherubini (1760–1842). After displaying early promise in church music—he had produced several Masses, an oratorio, and a number of lesser works after he had been composing only a few years—he undertook a highly successful career as opera composer. Even though two operas date from the last part of Cherubini's life, it is apparent that after 1816, when he was appointed to share the position of superintendent of the *Chapelle Royale*, his interest and attention were devoted to church music once more. There are two sides to Cherubini's religious music: on the one hand, he was a master of counterpoint in an age when interest in the polyphonic craft was viewed as archaic; on the other, he was a successful Romantic who carried into many of his religious works the devices of his secular successes. His Requiem in C minor (1817) is usually mentioned as his finest work, but it is certainly not typical of all his Masses. Some of them include solo voices, but the F major Mass of 1816 and the *Coronation Mass* of 1824 are for STB chorus and orchestra. The Requiem, SATB and orchestra without solo voices, may be widely known and admired only because it has seen wider publication than the other of his religious choral works.[1] The superficial resemblance of its *Dies irae* to that of Mozart is not sufficient to mark Cherubini's work as derivative. Its setting makes clear enough use of the Romantic vocabulary to escape criticism on that count. Each of its seven sections stands as a unit, independent of the others, two of them utilizing the nearby keys of A-flat major and F minor. Romantic traits abound in the over-emphasis on forte-piano treatment of entire phrases of block-chords in the *Lacrimosa*, the sentimental *Pie Jesu*, and in the way the closing phrases of text overlap from one section of the chorus to another in the final measures of the piece, all on a single pitch, all in hushed, mysterious tones. The section at *Quam olim Abrahae promisisti* is written (perhaps symbolically) as a triple fugue that moves along with great vigor.

We cannot look to Cherubini for a new tradition in church music. The demands of the *Chapelle Royale* were not those of the usual church establishment, and ample funds and a strong tradition guaranteed the continuation of a fashionable musical style. We may safely say that tradition is neither the aim nor the result of nineteenth-century musical production. The pieces that stand out are often those that are highly individualistic.

Neither is there anything unusual in the Masses of Spohr, Weber, or Schubert, but that is no cause for ignoring some creditable settings of liturgical text. If nothing new is to be found in these works, they stand as examples of their composers' skill, at the very least. The Masses of Franz Schubert (1797–1828) are not only representative of the period, but have the decided advantage of outnumbering the works of the other two composers mentioned, and, since they are divided into a distinct early and late style, demonstrate some development. His first four Masses date from 1813–1816 and cannot be compared to the output of his mature period. The last two, while skillful, are not generally given much attention because they follow entirely predictable paths in form and technique. The Schubertian alternation of major and minor sections is often observed, the writing is largely homophonic and perfunctory, and only a few sections of the liturgical text seem to have moved the composer to put forth more than a minimum of effort. Had Schubert lived at a time when artistic ideas altered more slowly, he might have continued to demand more attention for

1. Erich Valentin, *Handbuch der Chormusik* (Regensburg: Gustav Bosse Verlag, [1953?]), I, 363, lists only five published Masses by Cherubini, the Requiem in two different editions and from several publishers. The *Messa di Requiem*, TTB and orchestra, is also listed, I, 440.

these works. It was his misfortune to compose them in an age when the old was looked upon with disdain and his own best attempts produced neither the excitement of experimentation nor the dangerous violations of practice and good taste that were indulged in by his longer-lived contemporaries.

The occasional excursions of operatic composers into the paths of religious music are nowhere more interesting than in the nineteenth century, when several such late arrivals appeared on the scene in church music. Gioacchino Rossini (1792–1868) undertook no religious composition in his most fruitful years. More than three decades passed between the widely acclaimed production of *Guillaume Tell*, his final operatic venture in 1829, and the composition of his *Petite Messe solennelle*. The Mass is for four-part chorus with the usual four solo voices and, in its first version, was accompanied by piano and harmonium, the latter intended chiefly to sustain the voice parts, the former providing rhythm, ornamented accompaniment patterns, and sometimes the entire background for the voices. There are also a few places in which the chorus sings without accompaniment of any kind. It may not have been a sense of suitability that moved Rossini to limit the accompanying part to two keyboard instruments, but the fact that he wrote the Mass for performance in the Paris mansion of Count Pillet-Will, where it was given a first hearing on April 24, 1865. It was later in that same year that Rossini orchestrated the piece, in which new form it was performed at the Théâtre-Italien four years later, on February 28, 1869.[2] The Mass is essentially a lyric work. Rossini had given up operatic composition many years earlier, but he had neither a background of earlier church music experience (the few religious works of his youth were apparently unsatisfactory, and only the second version of his *Stabat Mater* stands out) nor clear ideas about stylistic distinctions between music for the church and music for the thea-

2. The date of the first performance is open to question. *Grove's*, VII, 252, says the piece was first heard on March 14, 1864; however, the score from which the present information is taken, published by G. Brandus and S. Dufour sometime before July 25, 1872 — it was then that the firm changed its name — indicates that the Mass was performed *pour le première fois, le 24 avril 1865, dans l'hôtel du comte Pillet-Will. Grove's* states further that the accompaniment was for two pianos and harmonium; the score, on the other hand, specifies one of each and indicates that if the harmonium is not available, the accompaniment may be played with only one piano inasmuch as the function of the harmonium is simply that of supporting the vocal lines. The misleading *petite* does not appear on the title page of the printed score. Information about the several changes in the name of the publishing firm may be found in Cecil Hopkinson, *A Dictionary of Parisian Music Publishers, 1700–1950* (London: The author, 1954), 17.

ter. It is true that the Mass was written as a concert work, as was the case with most large-scale religious music of that century, and what can be excused as typical of the period is still open to assessment on the basis of propriety. Rossini did not exceed these bounds, at least not to the point of outright vulgarity, but his lack of a clear distinction between the two styles is symptomatic of the ills of an entire group of composers, many of whom happened to be principally operatic experts. Lest it appear that Rossini is being singled out as an example of the worst in nineteenth-century music, it should be emphasized that only three features of the Mass are open to judgment on the score of taste and appropriateness: (1) the use of piano accompaniment figures that tend to perpetuate formulas of doubtful taste; (2) the adoption of solo lines that in no way enhance the text, but actually deprive it of its meaning *(Ex. 112)*; and (3) the insertion of sections for *a cappella* choir, employing imitative counterpoint simply because it is the "approved" style for religious music. The counterpoint is not very good and, further, produces an offensive anachronism in the midst of the concert hall idiom *(Ex. 113)*. Rossini pointed up his use of the archaic section visually by the use of a meter signature and note values no longer common in his own time.

Rossini's Mass, and most of the other pieces that are the subject of this chapter, pandered to the taste for concert music in lavish style. Inasmuch as our aim here is to consider music for the church, any extensive evaluation of choral music for the concert hall is out of place. That the works are mentioned at all merely underlines the strong shift of emphasis by the composer and his audience, and the contrast between the few works of truly devotional character and those that represent music for public approval.

Despite our repeated disavowal of interest in pieces for concert, we are again and again driven to consider them at greater length than we may wish simply because they preponderate in the age of box-office considerations. When the occasional work that was written expressly for the church appears, it is somewhat a surprising phenomenon, a duckling among peacocks. What we had taken for granted in the fifteenth, sixteenth, and seventeenth centuries developed into a sometime thing with the eighteenth, and into quite a rare one in the nineteenth. It is possible to resurrect much music from the last century written expressly for the religious service, but it would, in many cases, simply provide embarrassing examples of inept craftsmanship or convenient re-composition. Our attention must remain centered

Ex. 112 Soprano line from duetto, *Messa solennelle*, Rossini
(harmonium part omitted)

upon the better known composers who were recognized in several
fields of composition or, if their works were not of great interest, who
were at least outside the periphery of church activity. One of the men
who turned to setting religious text to more or less suitable music was

Ex. 113 *Ibid.*

Vincenzo Bellini (1801–1835). Among his teachers was one of the most facile and productive composers of all time, Nicola Zingarelli (1752–1837). Some of the teacher's easy way with music must have been communicated to the student and, keeping in mind that facility is not a qualitative term, it is probably evident in much of Bellini's religious composition. It is certainly present in the two-movement Mass for four solo voices, SATB chorus, and orchestra,[3] which may be examined for its accessibility rather than its outstanding quality. Only the Kyrie and Gloria exist in the surviving manuscript, but it seems to be a complete work. The assumption is that the remaining movements were intended to be rendered in plainsong. The choral parts are the essence of simplicity, except for the closing "Amen" section. That alone is composed as counterpoint; a double fugue at that point emphasizes the reliance of the composer upon the soloists who can now assist the chorus with the only difficult group singing of the composition. Where the solo voices are called for specifically, they are much

3. Vincenzo Bellini, *Mass* (New York: Mills Music, 1959).

more elaborate than the usual choral material, ranging from lyrical to florid. The orchestra plays a dual role: it supports the soloists by duplicating their parts or playing formula accompaniment figures; when the chorus sings by itself, the orchestra carries the principal interest by stealing attention from the voices by its greater rhythmic activity and melodic contrivance. The work is not suitable to religious worship, but it is not offensive outside the church; it is simply inappropriate.

Whether a piece is inappropriate, or vulgar, or simply in bad taste is difficult to determine. When a piece is open to such pejorative consideration, it does not automatically become guilty of shortcomings, but it is immediately set apart from similar works that never find themselves under such fire. Features that were acceptable in an age of ostentation are increasingly less desirable in this generation. The number of people who are surprised and even appalled at the pomposity of some nineteenth-century compositions still increases; the search for values in the music of that period is giving less importance to pieces that were once highly touted simply because of their immense size or startling means of expression. It is entirely possible that Berlioz's *Grande Messe des Morts* (1837) and his *Te Deum* (1849) will one day be viewed as interesting examples of human frailty, of the misapplication of skills to the setting of religious text. Liszt's *Missa solennis zur Einweihung der Basilika in Gran* may become simply another example of its composer's use of thematic materials in an age when interest in the *leitmotif,* thematic transformation, and *idée fixe* occupied the attention of composers. Other oversized works exist as well, foremost among them the *Requiem* of Giuseppe Verdi (1813–1901). None of these works was performed in its own time without some adverse criticism; none receives performance in our own without inviting debate in matters of taste. Whatever decision results after another generation or two of listeners adds further opinion, the works do not fall under the present discussion because they are in the idiom of the concert hall. They should not be considered as church music; neither should they be presented as such.

If criticism may be levelled at the large concert works, the smaller compositions intended for church use are not exempt from harsh judgment. For public performance the composers were able to let their imaginations run riot; in church they were confined by the limitation of singers who were too few and too ill-prepared to undertake anything extraordinary. Added to these restrictions was the necessity for eschewing counterpoint. Gounod fell victim to these compound ills a number of times, but never more than in his early *Messe Bréve et Salut,* a setting for male voices of the Kyrie, Sanctus, and Agnus Dei, in company with three motets for unaccompanied male chorus. Much of the composition has a plodding, note-against-note movement that is unrelieved by either melodic interest or harmonic variety. Even the best moments in the work *(Ex. 114)* have little to lift them above average level. The piece is by no means Gounod's earliest, even though it was printed as his Opus 1. It dates from about 1846, before which date its composer had already been awarded a number of prizes for composition and had also undertaken a study of the works of Palestrina. There is no indication that he was in any way influenced by Renaissance counterpoint.

It is not simply by accident that Brahms and Anton Bruckner (1824 – 1896) stand out as leading figures in religious music of the nineteenth century. They had a number of common attributes, among them the absence of theatricalism in their attitudes, in their mode of life, and in their musical productivity. Neither showed any affinity with music for the stage; neither of them was forced to disown personal stylistic methods in order to write religious music. In some works of each, the symphonic element rises strongly, but each of these men dealt with the orchestra in methods less flamboyant than did some of their more outgoing contemporaries. Bruckner wrote a considerable amount of music for the church. Three Masses, their first versions dating from the 1860s, are the pinnacle of his efforts in this genre. Two clearly different means of dealing with the material are found there. The first (D minor) and third (F minor) are symphonic; some writers have referred to them as vocal symphonies. The second

Ex.114 *Messe Breve et Salut,* Gounod

(E minor) is a polyphonic work with wind accompaniment. The styles are sufficiently different to warrant comparison of the second and third Masses here.

Bruckner wrote his three great Masses at a time when the purists of the Catholic Church were especially vocal. There had been recurrent evidences of puristic tendencies in the past; Fux and Michael Haydn were among the many composers whose work was touched by such attitudes. Now, in the nineteenth century, the pressure of reactionary thought, of adherence to the polyphonic ideal that had been recognized, although not widely practiced, since the Council of Trent, blossomed forth in the form of the Cecilian movement.[4] Bruckner was not directly involved in the Cecilian upsurge, but he was unable to remain aloof from it. Parts of the E minor Mass fall clearly into the style advocated by the Cecilian proponents of conservatism, although the work as a whole belongs to the nineteenth century. Even though it comes between the two great symphonic Masses, it conforms to principles of the past in a number of respects. It offers no music for solo voices, the parts for its double chorus are largely contrapuntal, and the accompanying instruments are all of the wind families. Its close relationship to the liturgical function of the Mass is apparent in the absence of the opening phrases of both the Credo and Gloria, where the officiant or soloist is expected to open the section with the appropriate fragment of plainsong. The writing for expanded chorus does not constantly follow the lines of antiphonal singing. The Kyrie begins with a four-part homophonic setting for sopranos and altos, later taken up by tenors and basses. This is followed by a contrapuntally conceived Christe involving all eight voices, and the final Kyrie returns to homophonic style for the massed voices. Of the remaining movements, only the Sanctus and the Agnus Dei are built on such grand lines; the other movements alternate between modest sections *a 4* and episodes in which the parts are expanded to eight, but in which the exciting alternation of complete groups or the full sound of all the singers are not used to beguile the interest. Bruckner's use of the accompanying group is similarly modest. The wind instruments have no introductory sections, and only occasionally do they play short,

4. Detailed information in English is not to be found. The Cecilian movement was German from the outset. Among the accessible sources are *MGG*, II, 621–28, and Ernst Tittel, *Österreichische Kirchenmusik (Schriftenreihe des Allgemeinen Cäcilien-Verbandes für die Länder der deutschen Sprache*, II) (Wien: Herder & Co., 1961). A general discussion in English may be found in Karl Gustav Fellerer, *The History of Catholic Church Music*, trans. Francis A. Brunner (Baltimore: Helicon Press, 1961), 173–98.

transitional material between text phrases. They are restricted to arpeggiated emphasis of the chord structure or to flowing melodic patterns that also appear briefly as portions of the vocal material. Never does the accompaniment intrude upon the choral material or remove the listener's attention from the text and the music that carries it.

The pronouncements of the Cecilian movement, the dicta of which are suitably framed in Bruckner's E minor Mass, were not official in any sense. When such matters finally appeared as authoritative announcements from high Church authority, Bruckner had been dead for some years. It was in the *Motu proprio* of 1903 that the world received the papal pronouncement of the principles that were already part of a widespread reaction in Catholic church music during the latter half of the nineteenth century.[5] The document of Pope Pius x was not directed against any single composition, against the secularized quasi-religious concert pieces of any school of composers — although an accusing finger was pointed at the nineteenth-century theatrical style of Italy — or against the effects of the emotional music of the preceding century. The abuses that led to its appearance had been present in earlier years; the issuance of the edict at the beginning of the twentieth century simply indicated that once again the Church felt compelled to state its position, one that was really little more than a modification of what had been considered appropriate for a long time. The *Motu proprio* stated, in official terms, substantially the line of thought of the Cecilian movement.

Bruckner's two other great Masses were not written in any spirit of conformity with the Cecilian attitude; they are symphonic Masses in which the orchestra is the central object, the soloists and chorus, by the good fortune of being able to provide exact text, are not entirely removed from the area of musical interest, but they have relinquished the center of attention to the instruments. The orchestra is the full symphonic organization, its medium is the symphonic form, into which liturgical text has been thrust as a necessary ingredient. In the F minor Mass, for example, the orchestra is not subordinated to the vocal lines. Its central position is emphasized by the fact that it has both the first and last opportunity to be heard, that it serves as a vital link between the sections for chorus and the solo passages. Be-

5. The complete text of the *Motu proprio* is printed in English by Paul Hume, *Catholic Church Music* (New York: Dodd, Mead & Company, 1956), 180–93, and Erwin Esser Nemmers, *Twenty Centuries of Catholic Church Music* (Milwaukee: Bruce Publishing Co., 1949), 197–206. A discussion of its contents appears in H. T. Henry, "Music Reform in the Catholic Church," *The Musical Quarterly*, 1/1 (January, 1915), 102–17.

cause its material is not derived from the vocal substance, but is a series of organic units that benefit from their relationship to the voices, it does not require text in order to achieve completeness. The self-limiting skills of Bruckner that saved him from an outright violation of acceptable religious expression are found in his avoidance of theatrical solo sections, for his voices are most often found as an ensemble of soloists participating in a style of singing that is not out of balance with that given to the chorus.

In Bruckner's Masses, the two styles of which are not so remote from each other as, say, those of Gounod and Berlioz, the long tradition of large Mass composition reached a point of near exhaustion. The fascination that composers felt for transplanting the words of liturgical functions into the concert hall continued with the settings by such skillful men as Antonin Dvořák (1841–1904), and it continues even today, although it is now less frequent in a world that has begun to deal with religious words in a fashion that can be solemn without being pompous, jubilant without being vulgar, intense without being dramatic.

The generation that rose to prominence in the twentieth century set out along new paths of composition. Ralph Vaughan Williams (1872–1958) was English, Anglican, and, fortunately, dissatisfied with the musical training he had received from his English and German teachers. He can be identified with English folk music, the growing awareness of nationalism, and with many of the finer features of *The English Hymnal*. But it is not any of these things that are evident in his finest piece of religious music, the *Mass in G minor*. One would least expect that an unaccompanied work for double chorus, recalling the style of sixteenth-century counterpoint, with Latin text, would come from a man with his background. What he wrote was not a slavish imitation of Palestrina counterpoint; this is evident from the harmonic sections of the work, and especially from those that contain parallel movement of voices forbidden in more styles than that of the Renaissance. His was a vital polyphonic setting of the Ordinary that derives some of its stylistic features from the sixteenth century, although it is not confined by the limitations of that period. The Mass is only superficially in Renaissance style, for a closer examination reveals that the melodic patterns are not limited by the common practice of that period. Not only is there a melodic freedom that is not native to sixteenth-century counterpoint; there is a vitality that stems from the mixture of unaccompanied practices in both the contrapuntal and homophonic styles.

The Mass calls for double chorus and four solo voices, combinations of which are found in almost every possible variation. The Kyries, two similar sections for the two choirs combined, frame a contrasting Christe that is written for the solo voices. The Gloria opens with both choirs in quiet, widely spaced block-chords, followed by a brilliant antiphonal section and a litany-like responsive choral utterance of *miserere nobis* against the laudatory passages for soloists. The Credo develops alternating choirs with both at the same dynamic level, so that one chorus often seems to continue a musical line that has been established by the other. Since most of the Credo is in triple meter, it provides an excellent opportunity for the use of *hemiola* patterns, rhythmic alterations that Vaughan Williams used in their usual fashion as well as in altered form. In Example 115 the *hemiola* in Chorus I is perfectly straightforward; its parallel section in Chorus II has been expanded so that it covers three measures instead of two, but the contrast between triple and duple patterns is not lost unless the chords of the weak half of each measure are given undue stress in performance. The remaining movements display the degree of control and variety of voice combinations that the composer had at his command.

Vaughan Williams could not establish a strong tradition in the writing of Latin Masses, nor does such music find its way suitably into the Anglican tradition. An English version of the *Mass in G minor* does exist for use in the Anglican church, but a number of unaccompanied Latin Masses also have appeared despite the secondary position of Catholic activity in England. Among these pieces are a *Missa in Honorem Sancti Dominici* by Edmund Rubbra (1901–) and a *Missa Liturgica* by Julius Harrison (1885–). Rubbra has also written *The Service of the Holy Communion (Missa Cantuariensis)*, a work in which *decani* and *cantoris* groups have plenty of opportunity to carry on double-chorus singing in the practice that is unique to the Anglican tradition, and that shows no trace of the Venetian polychoral style (*HMS*, x, 58–60).

It is indeed fortunate that the anti-Catholic feeling that was afoot in England in the eighteenth and nineteenth centuries subsided. The favor with which Latin Masses could be received probably had more to do with their reappearance in England than did the mild challenge of writing music that would not violate the stipulations of the *Motu proprio* of Pope Pius x. Britten's *Missa Brevis in D* (1959) is one of the latest liturgical pieces that has come out of this new interest in appropriate music for the Catholic service. It is a *Missa brevis* in

Ex. 115 Contrasting hemiola patterns in Credo, *Mass in G minor*, Vaughan Williams

By permission of J. Curwen & Sons Ltd., 29 Maiden Lane, London, W.C.2

two respects: first, it has the simplicity and directness that the term implies, for there is little text repetition and the work is scored for small forces—boys' voices *a* 3 and organ; second, the Mass is lacking a Credo, the absence of which shortens it considerably.

There has been substantial interest outside England in a continuing tradition of setting the Mass. This is natural, inasmuch as many other countries are directly in a line of Catholic tradition while England is not. The quality and incidence of these settings is not so much greater as one would anticipate, however. Some of the countries — for example, Italy — devoted such interest to secular music that suitable church music is difficult to find; others failed to develop sufficient interest in liturgical music before being swept away before the onrush of Romanticism which diverted the interest of composers from the less exciting settings in the approved style. Among the works that fail to measure up to the requirements for church use is the *Mass in G* by Francis Poulenc (1899–1963) which does not qualify on several counts of theatricality and because the celebrant's intonations have been set polyphonically.[6] The *Missa Brevis* (1950) by Zoltán Kodály (1882–) is also unacceptable in the light of the papal pronouncement of 1903, inasmuch as it employs full orchestra and has independent orchestral sections both prior to and following the settings of liturgical text. The earlier version of this same Mass is free of some of these difficulties since it was originally for chorus and organ. These discrepancies should not be permitted to loom large in the assessment of the compositions as successful settings of the text, nor should the limitations imposed by Pope Pius x be made retroactive upon Beethoven, Bach, Gabrieli, or Bruckner. In our own time, the composer either writes for a specific occasion upon which certain of the limitations are suspended or he intends only that his work be for the concert hall and he is guided rather than dominated by the rules of strict procedure. The Catholic composer must, in every case, come to terms with his own intentions; he must decide without quibbling whether the work he composes is for the box-office public or for ecclesiastical use.

The *Mass* for mixed chorus and double wind quintet by Igor Stravinsky (1882–) hesitates between the two points of practice. While an intonation appears for the celebrant (or professional singer) at the beginning of the Credo, the opening of the Gloria is given to an alto soloist in melismatic accompanied style. On the other hand, the text is projected with a clarity that no contrapuntal setting is able to achieve. Whether the work is truly suitable for church use, then, depends, except for the matter of the Gloria intonation, upon the interpretation

6. Elise Cambon, "Sacred Music by Francis Poulenc," *American Guild of Organists Quarterly*, viii (October, 1963), 127.

and observance of that section of the *Motu proprio* which specifies that "only in special cases with the consent of the Ordinary will it be permissible to admit wind instruments, limited in number, judiciously used, and proportioned to the size of the place—provided the composition and accompaniment be written in grave and suitable style, and conform in all respects to that proper to the organ."[7] The point at issue is not the difference between any composer and the critics of musical taste; it is whether a composition is intended for the church as an act of worship or for some other place as a musical concert. The lines are more clearly drawn than they are for any branch of Protestantism, and if the composer crosses those lines his music does not suffer as a result, but it does lose its right to be classed as sacred music *for the church*. The rules have been set down by the highest authorities of the Roman Catholic Church and are violated only in defiance of that authority.[8] The composer is not barred from setting liturgical texts by any such documents; the words are available to all. He is simply required to choose the place in which he wishes his music to be performed. Stravinsky's religious works have generally been pointed toward the concert hall. His *Symphonie de Psaumes* does not lack religious depth simply because it violates the intentions of papal pronouncements—to which Stravinsky was not fully obligated at the time anyway, since he was still a member of the Russian Orthodox Church—but it gains strength through its masterful use of instruments and voices in a manner never achieved by the overpowering, and often bombastic, nineteenth century. Not one of Stravinsky's other large religious works, *Canticum Sacrum*, *Threni*, or *A Sermon, a Narrative and a Prayer*, was intended to have a liturgical function and, inasmuch as our examination of pieces is restricted to music for the church at this point, information on their substance must be sought elsewhere.[9]

Liturgical texts will probably continue to fascinate composers, and we may look forward to works that fall anywhere between the extremes of complete acceptability to church requirements and utter disregard of them in favor of a more lavish expression for concert.

7. *Motu proprio*, vi, 20.
8. All matters of permissible practice, as contained in the statements set forth by papal decrees and encyclicals, are given clearly in *Sacred Music and Liturgy*, trans. J. B. O'Connell (Westminster, Maryland: The Newman Press, 1959).
9. A detailed discussion of the *Canticum Sacrum* is given by Dika Newlin, "Four Revolutionaries," *Choral Music*, ed. Arthur Jacobs, 311–14. Of special interest are Stravinsky's continuation of the arch-form principle and his use of twelve-note rows.

There is, for instance, a *Proprium Missae (in festo Ss. Innocentium Martyram)* by Ernst Krenek (1900–) that sets the Propers for December 28.[10] The composition is for four voices *a cappella*, employs counterpoint throughout, including such esoteric devices as infinite double canon by inversion in the Gradual and double canon by inversion and retrogression in the Tract. Although it is written for women's voices, it is suitable for use in church because of the relaxation of practice following the reform of Pope Pius x. On the other hand, the *Missa Pro Defunctis* (1960) by Virgil Thomson (1896–) is not acceptable for church use because of its orchestral setting. There is no question of its having been intended for church at all. The work was commissioned by an educational institution and its dimensions and instrumentation were most probably influenced by the wishes of that body. Inasmuch as the Catholic Church does not have a place for such large works[11]—concerts, as such, are forbidden in churches and, when circumstances require that they be given there, specific steps must be followed in order to render the place and performance appropriate— it is fortunate that there exist so many excellent performing groups in colleges and universities. It is there that the performances of new, and many of the older, large religious compositions must be undertaken. The expense and time involved for professional performance generally prohibits the production of anything other than the established box-office favorites by professional groups.

Finally, some of the Germans who are now writing cantatas, motets, and Passions have composed Masses as well, some of them in Latin and others in German, some for voices alone and others with orchestra. While there is less interest in Masses—and the interest is almost certainly related to the degree of suitability and the amount of functional need—it is interesting to note the relatively large number of examples in print and the variety they represent. Most of these Masses are uncomplicated, practical, unaccompanied, short works for few voices.

10. The work exists in manuscript bearing a copyright notice for 1940. The published version (Los Angeles: Affiliated Musicians, Inc., 1953) does not identify the Propers.
11. The encyclical, *Musicae sacrae disciplina*, issued by Pope Pius xii, Christmas, 1955, provided for greater latitude than before in the use of string and wind instruments in the church, but it did not grant license for the opening of churches to concert performances. The encyclical is discussed briefly in Fellerer, *op. cit.*, 199 *et passim*, and forms part of the material presented in *Sacred Music and Liturgy*. It is printed in full in Hume, *op. cit.*, 157–80. See also Fidelis Smith, C. F. M., "*Musicae Sacrae Disciplina:* Pius xii's Encyclical on Sacred Music," *The Musical Quarterly*, xliii/4 (October, 1957), 461–79.

Not only brevity in the setting of each movement, but a selectivity of movements is seen in the two short Masses by Ernst Pepping. His *Kleine Messe* (1929; published 1948) for SAB contains only the Kyrie, Gloria, and Sanctus. The *Missa brevis* (1948; published 1950), also SAB, sets the Kyrie and Gloria only, after the traditional German usage of the term. The earlier work is entirely polyphonic and the three voices are often confined to the austerity of strict canonic writing. The *Missa brevis* is mostly homophonic and its three-voice texture is maintained throughout the Kyrie. The writing for soprano and alto in that movement is almost entirely in perfect fourths. The bass part moves vigorously against these upper voices and joins in a brief unison passage with the alto. After the middle of the Kyrie nothing new can be found; that is, nothing has been added as fresh material from the analytical viewpoint. Yet, the ear finds nothing familiar because the central point of the movement is a moment of repose upon which all three voices pivot and then proceed in retrograde statement of all that has been heard up to that point. The Gloria expands the three-voice texture by dividing each of the parts into two. Pepping never calls for all six parts at once, however. His most common grouping is SSABB. He has also written some complete Mass cycles for four to eight parts sometimes using German text, sometimes Latin.

The names of Heinrich Kaminski, Karl Marx, Willy Burkhard, and Johannes Driessler are among the twentieth-century composers of Masses. The one that recalls most sharply the practices of the past is the *Deutsche Messe a 5* by Hans Friedrich Micheelsen. Most of the German words come from sixteenth-century sources, and old melodic material is also used. The Gloria uses the seventeen couplets of the old substitute verse *All Ehr und Lob soll Gottes sein (All glory and honor shall be unto God)*. Micheelsen found it necessary to warn performers in the foreword and at the beginning of the Gloria that no *fermate* should be placed at the end of each couplet, but that one should follow another *a tempo*. The distribution of voices varies from one part of the Mass to another; sometimes there are as few as two or three voices, but most often, four or five. The absence of accompanying instruments and the use of strict canon give the piece an appearance of simplicity that is belied by sections in parallel fourths, fifths, and triads. A small amount of thematic material serves well for entire movements because it is essentially melodic and survives the manipulation of polyphony without loss of its identity.

Chapter XIII

The Shape of the Future

IT HAS BEEN apparent during our examination of the development of religious choral music that the attention of musicians has several times been wooed from the purpose of such music, the worship of God. We have observed, for instance, that only the strongly liturgical branches of Christianity have provided sufficient place and material for the establishment of a choral tradition. But we have found also that this same liturgical basis restricted the free demonstration of the musicians' emotive powers. A strong tradition that is controlled by formal practices encourages the development of the kind of music that has been our concern, but its rules often repel the composer who is not motivated to write in its vein because of personal religious convictions.

At the beginning of this book certain qualities were listed as desirable and even necessary to suitable church music. Their presence in music was expected to cause it to (1) induce reflection; (2) stimulate imaginative comprehension; (3) heighten awareness; and (4) nurture objective ideals. These qualities may appear to be arbitrarily chosen, but their selection is not the result of mere caprice. They are common to all organized types of Christian worship that have a foundation of dignity and sensitive understanding. It is not possible to evaluate all church music, or even all music with religious text, in its relation to these qualities. Still, various styles of music have reflected these qualities to differing degrees, sometimes one of them dominating the musical expression and sometimes another. An immense variety is possible within the boundaries of these seeming restrictions. Since they do not force all religious music into reactionary molds, it is not beyond the limits of good sense to employ them once more as a measure of some of our newer means of musical expression.

One of the natural results of a static situation in choral singing — and the situation in many choirs has become just that — has been a levelling of taste and of the demands made upon performers. Church music is not usually written and submitted to the publisher because it is best suited to the needs of a single denomination; the composer often is interested in producing a piece that is suited to all Protestant beliefs, or at least without objectionable features to most.[1] On the supposition that there are few fine choral groups in churches, much music for the "average" choir has appeared, and there is also a selection for the choir that lacks traditions, trained voices, and sufficient singers. We have learned to compartmentalize church music. It is now classified as easy, medium, or difficult; it is accompanied or unaccompanied; it is specifically for the few church festivals that are shared by all Christian beliefs, or it falls into that incredibly large classification called "general." Our ideal has become the SATB choir, and we have lost sight of the variety that can be achieved with fewer voice parts as well as with more. It is too often assumed that a piece for two or three parts is inferior to one for four parts simply because it is less complex in texture than the common type. By the same token, a piece for double chorus may be impressive not because of its musical qualities, but because it requires more voices. With such a set of false standards before us, we should not wonder at our inability to cope with problems arising from new musical styles. We are faced with myriad possibilities, but we find it necessary to reject most of them on grounds of impracticality or unsuitability. Foremost among the candidates are the serial techniques and the jazz or folk elements.

The employment of tone rows is not the hallmark of all contemporary styles, but it represents many of the same problems as do modern techniques generally. One problem is the relative difficulty of music that employs devices beyond those of the common-practice period. Compositions in which the solid tonal relationship provided by a key center is weakened are not easy to learn or to perform; compositions that are in a style owing no allegiance to a tonal center are almost impossible for all but a few of the most highly trained and dedicated of choir singers. The skills demanded by such pieces are greater than church musicians possess; the demands upon the attention and

---

1. A number of publishers can still be identified with single denominations: Concordia Publishing House is Lutheran; J. Fischer and Bro., and McLaughlin and Reilly are Catholic; Abingdon Press is Methodist, and so on, but most houses have found it necessary to seek out a mass market by supplying larger catalogues of varied music, much of which is of a general nature.

understanding of the congregation are even greater, for they are being required to submit to something they may neither want nor comprehend.

Must we then exclude from church music any style simply because it is difficult or because it is foreign to the congregation? There is no historical precedent for exclusion on the grounds of difficulty. From the time when organum first appeared as a new element in a world dominated by plainsong, every new style in church music contained elements that were strange and difficult. Up until the encroachment of operatic style, however, most of the new ideas had developed within the church and still had a suitability to liturgical usage and traditional methods of vocal production. At the point when styles were introduced into the church from outside — from stage or concert hall — elements appeared that were sometimes instrumental rather than vocal, dramatic or virtuosic rather than worshipful, and intended for professional performers rather than simply for willing participants of limited skills. The styles that have appeared within our own generation contain elements of strangeness that do not fall into the musical experience of church singers or congregations. In the case of serial techniques, the church musician is left without a precedent in his performing experience. Some highly literate and curious members of church groups may have read descriptions of such music and may even have heard examples in concert or on recordings. But such limited contact is of no help when the singer is asked to negotiate atonal materials in rehearsal. Composers have wisely avoided this kind of expression for church. Whether they feel it is too far removed from the bland post-Romantic style of today's church music, or whether church composers have not yet caught up with an important principle in composition, tone rows are not a part of that expression. The few instances in which we have seen serial techniques used have been those that presupposed performers of superior training, skill, and experience, and that assumed further a performance before a musically sophisticated audience. Such performance preparation is generally foreign to church choirs in our time, and the performances themselves are not welcomed by most congregations.

During the past few years a number of experiments have been made using folk music or jazz as a basis for church works. The most common reasons for using these materials are the concern for new means of communication between the secular world and the church; the desire to replace old traditions that now lack meaning with modern equivalents; and the development of a musical means for winning converts to Christianity. The aims are probably above criticism—it is, after all, improper to hold pejorative views about female virtue, the flag, or the value of religious activity—but their solutions are beset by flaws that are destined to prevent their continuing success.

If the addition of folk or jazz materials is intended to provide a new means of communication, it is doomed to small success because most of the musical material that is being added has an appeal to only a limited part of our society. The presentation of religious ideas in rhythms or instrumental combinations that are not a common part of the worship experience does not speak to a large segment of any religious group. It must be emphasized that the current popularity of the hootenanny offshoot of folk music represents no more than one of the fads that beset commercial popular music. Likewise, jazz enthusiasts knowledgeable enough to be moved by that expression are a decided minority who will continue to seek good jazz in its natural habitats. The best performances of either folk music or jazz are to be found somewhere other than the church. Religious music in those idioms is destined to be inferior or, if of suitable quality, localized, infrequent, and imported. Any substitution of obviously foreign elements into the service destroys the historical continuity in a procedure that depends, in its present forms, entirely upon the perpetuation of a historical tradition. The substitution of an instrumental concert of hymns by a jazz group, known as Singleton Palmer and his Dixieland Six, for the sermon at Christ Church Cathedral (Episcopal) in St. Louis in 1961 led to the following mismating of religious and secular materials: "dirge-like openings" and "belting closings" in the eight hymns and spirituals (only two of which are not totally foreign to the Protestant Episcopal tradition and hymnal); an unexpectedly large congregation that behaved like an audience, for "many could be seen with feet tapping and heads swaying to the rhythm of the music" while the presiding priest "clapped his hands softly from time to time as the band played."[2] Such a concert does not take on any religious qualities simply because it is done in church and employs hymn tunes. The language of jazz is esoteric and communicates only to the few who have learned its ways. Its specialized techniques are not familiar to church musicians and it will remain an intruder into

2. *St. Louis Post-Dispatch*, Monday, February 13, 1961.

established forms of worship. It does not bring into focus the four desirable qualities of church music.

We may sympathize with the attempt to replace old traditions with new practices, but the forms of religious worship have not often been changed by shifts of local custom. Importation of a new type of music into an otherwise fixed form of worship, especially in isolated cases, will have no effect on the mainstream of worship. New forms and customs in religion have developed slowly and naturally; the appearance of modern elements in any age has been due to the great similarity between religious and secular practices, not to their differences.

If the reason for the new musical expression is extending the kingdom and winning new souls, the reliance on music is wrongly placed. The secular world supplies greater skill, excitement, and polished performance than the choir loft. The people who are sought as converts are not to be wooed by jazz, which is regularly heard in expert performance in night clubs. Folk music, as well, has proved itself alien to the formal church situation, being more at home in coffee-houses and store-front churches. The ill-considered substitution of these styles for the "good old music" that any congregation has become accustomed to is not likely to be hailed as a successful venture. While some people will endure an experiment, they tend to take offense if the new becomes commonplace, or if their sense of historical continuity is threatened.

Whether these random attempts to change religious music are successful or not, the fact remains that an increasing number of people are voicing doubts that the church is adequately served by a dependence on historical materials, by complete reliance on styles that are no longer viable. A more interesting and fruitful development may be seen in the multisectional pieces that have appeared. They are not consistently high in quality, but their organization into longer forms at least removes them from the suspect area of gimmick concerts that may be done for publicity or notoriety. It will be noticed in the four works that are discussed below that the quality and method varies considerably, but a common feature is the reliance on some familiar form, either in the text or the music. Each work appeals to at least one large denominational group, and in some cases universal acceptance is hoped for. It is dangerous to predict the course of the arts, but one might hazard a guess that any general acceptance of modern idioms must have the stamp of approval of a large established group. It is not sufficient for a new idea to appeal to a minority, whether that minority be suppressed or in a position of command. Converts may not be won by music, but they may be driven away by it.

One of the multisectional works that have appeared recently is a *Twentieth Century Folk Mass* by Geoffrey Beaumont (1904 –). In an attempt to create an English setting of the Mass that uses an idiom close to the people, Beaumont chose to expand the general meaning of the term "folk music." He draws upon the musical materials of the slick commercial entertainment world, the rhythms and melodic-harmonic elements of musical spectacles native to the motion picture theater and the television show. These are not folk elements by any semantic rationale. While they may be elements that assault every ear that comes within range of a loudspeaker, they are not the idiom of the people, and that is what a folk utterance must be.

Liturgical Jazz: A Musical Setting for an Order of Morning Prayer (1959) by Edgar Summerlin is an attempt to set a Methodist liturgy (as recognized by John Wesley, but not necessarily by American Methodists of today) to some truly idiomatic jazz patterns. All of the melodic material except for two hymn settings is completely original. The entire composition is held together by thematic repetition, not in the fashion of a cantata held together by a familiar chorale, but as a work that states and restates a few basic ingredients in various forms.

Both Beaumont's and Summerlin's pieces make unusual demands on performers. The former calls for a large professional orchestra, skilled in the ways and style of the stage band; the latter is written for a smaller group of jazz players who must be skilled in that idiom. Such groups must be artificially introduced into the church and their rare appearances in the sanctuary does not presage a general practice.

An *American Jazz Mass* (published 1960) by Frank P. Tirro must be mentioned here not for its virtues, but for its deficiencies. Its choral writing is largely without interest, relying too much on unison passages, parallel motion of triads, and seventh chords in conductus style. The instrumental group (trumpet, two saxophones, string bass, and traps) lends small interest. A walking bass line in nearly constant quarter notes is supported by an equally insistent iteration of drumsticks and brushes. The wind instruments move in similar rhythms and unison patterns too often to justify their presence. It does not appear to be good jazz, and it is certainly not good church music.

Among these three compositions, Summerlin's work stands out as the effort of a skilled musician who has achieved considerable control of his expressive medium; Tirro's Mass is weak because it does not deal authoritatively with either the vocal or instrumental idiom; and Beaumont's Mass is a slick piece that required a professional arranger to complete the composer's best efforts, which were limited apparently to the outlines of the music. Regardless of the craftsmanship displayed in any of them, each fails to produce a musical aid to worship that can be used by existing church groups. Neither the pit band of musical comedy nor the jazz combo is available in our religious establishments, nor is either likely to be.

The step beyond an occasional foray into modern idioms was taken by a German, Heinz Werner Zimmermann (1930–), who attempts to make the jazz idiom available to church performers by calling for only a few instruments and by writing choral parts that are not beyond the skills of "any chorus that merits that name."[3] Zimmermann has a preference for works *a 5* with string bass and, in some cases, vibraphone, and piano. The use of pizzicato bass alone, or of bass and vibraphone, is identifiable with the jazz idiom as much as any simple instrumental combination can be, but this is not the only means that Zimmermann uses to relate his work to a current style. The singers employ jazz materials also. Why can this kind of piece be considered acceptable for church music when most of the others that use jazz elements fail? An answer can be found in the most complex of these works that Zimmermann has produced to this time, the *Psalmkonzert* composed in 1957.[4] His simpler works call for five-part chorus and bass, but this one, in five movements, requires a baritone soloist, a boys' unison choir, his usual five-part chorus, three trumpets, vibraphone, and bass. The one part that may be omitted in performance is the vibraphone. Recognizing that the instrument may be harder to find than to play—he confines his part for it to single melodic lines—Zimmermann provides an organ part that may be used in its absence. This organ part is not a substitute for the rest of the instruments; the bass and trumpets are still necessary for the performance. But the organ is not simply given the vibraphone melody with added harmony; its part creates a completely different harmonic framework, so different that an attempt to play both parts at once

3. Heinz Werner Zimmermann, *Psalmkonzert* (Berlin: Verlag Merseburger, 1958), [2].
4. Other works by Zimmermann are discussed in Erik Routley, *Twentieth Century Church Music* (Vol. I of *Studies in Church Music*) (New York: Oxford University Press, 1964), 92f. Routley also devotes considerable space to Beaumont's place in English "pop" church music.

would result in a disaster. The only problem arising from the need for instruments is finding the people to play them. Their parts are not difficult in any respect, and players do not have to be of high professional caliber to perform the *Psalmkonzert*, although the church should not be forced to accept lesser quality. The piece deserves the finest performers available.

Zimmermann does not expect his music to serve as an entire liturgical setting. Its function is that of its ancestral types, the Baroque motet and cantata, special music that heightens the religious service but that does not displace it. The *Psalmkonzert* sets psalm texts that deal with praise and thanksgiving. It is suitable to any occasion that can use a joyful piece of cantata length. The work is framed by nearly identical movements setting the opening verses of Psalm 96. In the first movement, chorus and instruments are treated in a *concertato* style that features mild syncopations and short contrasting sections of homophonic and contrapuntal material; the fifth movement is exactly the same as the first, but the boys' choir is added to the material of the opening movement, singing the third verse of *Nun danket alle Gott* as a whole-note *cantus firmus*. The second movement sets the opening of Psalm 40 for solo baritone and instruments in slower, but still rhythmically vital, style. In the middle movement, the chorus, accompanied only by string bass, sings a lyrical fugue to the words of Psalm 103:7 – 11 *(Ex. 116)*. Fugues with lovely melodies are rare enough, but one that achieves grace and breadth without sacrificing the characteristic rhythms of the other movements is without question a gem of great price. In this movement especially, Zimmermann has successfully combined Baroque discipline with current materials. The *concertato* style of the fourth movement differs from that of the first. At the beginning and end of the piece the opposing groups are the chorus and orchestra, but in this movement, to the joyful text of Psalm 107, the soloist and chorus are brought together in the style of a solo concerto. Instruments are withheld, except for a few brief moments, until a final tutti in which they combine with voices.

The *Psalmkonzert* succeeds where the other works fail because the jazz elements are not used at the expense of the piece, but as an ingredient of it. Not every rhythm, not every melodic pattern, not every harmonic combination that Zimmermann knows from jazz style is brought into use. A few characteristic patterns supported by an equally restrained use of instrumental styles are made the basis of the entire composition. Jazz is not brought into the picture as the most

Ex. 116 Beginning of fugue *a 5* from Zimmermann's *Psalmkonzert*

By permission of Verlag Merseburger, Berlin. Copyright, 1958.

important part of the piece, but certain idiomatic features are selected to become the prime substance of a work that is no less religious for their employment. The *Psalmkonzert* proves that jazz is not out of character with religious expression, but that it must be used with the same careful judgment, skill, and integrity as any other musical materials. It cannot be an end in itself, nor a shocking gimmick; it must take its place simply as another vehicle for the presentation of musical ideas.

What of the future? Now that we have emerged from the period when it was thought necessary for the church to match the concert hall in grandeur and size, now that modest works of high quality may again be found, what new things can we expect for the choir loft? The Lutheran movement in Germany has shown one way, but all Christianity cannot espouse the materials and methods of that single source. Catholic practices, for all the liberal attitudes that have been displayed within the present decade, are not going to change because of Protestant experiments. The Fundamentalists, even though they are generally beginning to see a need for a better quality of choral music in their services to replace a literature based earlier on gospel hymns, will not knowingly accept practices that are closely identified with liturgical observances. Each separate religious group will continue to proceed on its own independent path in years to come. The disparate practices of the various Protestant sects tend to keep them separate, and the lack of a common observance in the use of *de tempore* texts brings into existence a large body of music that is intended to serve any of a number of occasions. In some churches the dictum is simple: any text, so long as it is scriptural; in others, the only requirement is that the text be religious in its intention. Common ground is seen in a general observance of the principal seasons of the church year, but not all faiths approach these with equal emphasis. Lent receives varying degrees of attention, Palm Sunday is all but ignored in some churches, Pentecost may be of great importance in one belief and hardly mentioned in another, and some churches deliberately make little of Easter because they emphasize the Crucifixion every Sunday. In the face of these and many other differences, it cannot be expected that a common effort toward the development of a contemporary musical language will be seen in the churches.

Another deterrent to a common body of material for Protestantism is the increasing prevalence of several translations of the Bible. Most of us have accustomed ourselves to the comfortably archaic flow of the King James Version, and musicians for generations have turned to that familiar source for anthem texts as well as for settings of cantatas for principal religious holidays. Now, however, the sensitive worshipper questions the unity of a service in which the spoken portions come from the Revised Standard Version or the New English Bible, but the musical sections provide only the King James texts. Music cannot be expected to keep pace with every change in worship, but there appears to be an unwarranted delay in attempts to fall into line.

It is not to be expected that the King James Version will lapse into complete disuse. Still, the appearance of a substantial body of service music using the new texts would seem to be sufficiently welcome to stir interest among composers, publishers, and buyers.

For the Roman Catholics, the present decade has seen the greatest change in centuries. Not simply as a papal pronouncement, but as the result of a Vatican Council session has come the permission to make greater use of living languages in the celebration of the Mass. First convened by Pope John XXIII, Vatican II was continued after his death under the guidance of Pope Paul VI who, in December, 1963, promulgated a constitution that authorizes the celebration of certain parts of the Mass and the sacraments in the vernacular. Much of what has been freed of Latin — at the discretion of local celebrants — belongs to the Propers. It will have little immediate effect upon music. It seems, in fact, that musical alterations will be slow in any case because what is required is not only the production of entire new pieces for chorus, but even the simpler plainsong that exists only in Latin versions. It is obvious that English cannot be substituted for Latin in chanting when the relationship between that text and the very structure of plainsong is so close. All we can do is watch with interest the changes that will take place, some of them inevitably too slowly to become evident in our lifetime.

Never before has there been such awareness of what happens in religious faiths other than one's own. Modern transportation facilities have made it possible to see and hear things that were denied to all but the wealthy a generation ago; broadcasts and telecasts of church services have brought rituals and practices of many beliefs into our homes; printed music is abundant; phonograph records have also put performances of religious masterpieces (unfortunately separated from their functions in the religious service) into a form available to anyone. Still, the possibilities for hearing good church music performed well, in connection with actual services of worship, are all too few. Only in a few centers of unusual church activity or in large cities are people able to find carefully prepared performances of suitable music.

It would be most valuable if representatives of various faiths could mingle and discuss musical matters freely without denominational prejudice. Communication is freer than it has been before, but too few people take advantage of opportunities to exchange ideas, and too many are convinced that denominational identification and musical excellence go hand in hand. Sectarianism will ever stand in the way of a single line of development in church music, even more than does the variety of existing musical styles. Inasmuch as sectarianism will not disappear from the scene, and stylistic unity is both improbable and undesirable, the thing to be hoped for is an increasing interest in the continued development of a high quality of church music.

APPENDIX

APPENDIX

ORDINARY OF THE MASS

The sections given here are those that are sung polyphonically.

Kyrie

Kyrie eleison.	Lord, have mercy.
Christe eleison.	Christ, have mercy.
Kyrie eleison.	Lord, have mercy.

Gloria

Gloria in excelsis Deo. Et in terra pax hominibus bonae voluntatis. Laudamus te. Benedicimus te. Adoramus te. Glorificamus te. Gratias agimus tibi propter magnam gloriam tuam. Domine Deus, Rex caelestis, Deus Pater omnipotens. Domine Fili unigenite Jesu Christe. Domine Deus, Agnus Dei, Filius Patris. Qui tollis peccata mundi, miserere nobis. Qui tollis peccata mundi, suscipe deprecationem nostram. Qui sedes ad dexteram Patris, miserere nobis. Quoniam tu solus sanctus. Tu solus Dominus. Tu solus altissimus, Jesu Christe. Cum Sancto Spiritu, in gloria Dei Patris. Amen.

Glory be to God on high, and on earth peace to men of good will. We praise Thee, we bless Thee, we worship Thee, we glorify Thee. We give thanks to Thee for Thy great glory, O Lord God, heavenly King, God the Father Almighty. O Lord, the only-begotten Son, Jesus Christ; O Lord God, Lamb of God, Son of the Father, that takest away the sins of the world, have mercy upon us. Thou that takest away the sins of the world, receive our prayer. Thou that sittest at the right hand of the Father, have mercy on us. For Thou only art holy; Thou only art the Lord; Thou only, O Jesus Christ, with the Holy Ghost, art most high in the glory of God the Father. Amen.

Credo

Credo in unum Deum, Patrem omnipotentem, factorem caeli et terrae, visibilium omnium et invisibilium. Et in unum Dominum Jesum Christum, Filium Dei unigenitum. Et ex Patre natum ante omnia saecula. Deum de Deo, lumen de lumine, Deum verum de Deo vero. Genitum, non factum, consubstantialem Patri: per quem omnia facta sunt. Qui propter nos homines, et propter nostram salutem descendit de caelis. Et incarnatus est de Spiritu Sancto ex Maria Virgine: ET HOMO FACTUS EST. Crucifixus etiam pro nobis sub Pontio Pilato: passus, et sepultus est. Et resurrexit tertia die, secundum Scripturas. Et ascendit in caelum: sedet ad dexteram Patris. Et iterum venturus est cum gloria judicare vivos et mortuos: cujus regni non erit finis. Et in Spiritum Sanctum Dominum, et vivificantem: qui ex Patre, Filioque procedit. Qui cum Patre, et Filio simul adoratur, et conglorificatur: qui locutus est per Prophetas. Et unam, sanctam, catholicam et apostolicam Ecclesiam. Confiteor unum baptisma in remissionem peccatorum. Et exspecto resurrectionem mortuorum. Et vitam venturi saeculi. Amen.

I believe in one God, the Father Almighty, Maker of heaven and earth, and of all things visible and invisible. And in one Lord Jesus Christ, the only-begotten Son of God, born of the Father before all ages. God of God, light of light, true God of true God, begotten not made, consubstantial with the Father, by whom all things were made. Who for us men, and for our salvation, came down from heaven and was incarnate by the Holy Ghost of the Virgin Mary, AND WAS MADE MAN. He was crucified also for us, suffered under Pontius Pilate, and was buried. And the third day He rose again according to the Scriptures, and ascended into heaven. He sitteth at the right hand of the Father, and He shall come again with glory to judge the living and the dead, of whose kingdom there shall be no end. And I believe in the Holy Ghost, the Lord and giver of life, who proceedeth from the Father and the Son, who together with the Father and Son is adored and glorified, who spoke by the Prophets. And in one holy Catholic and Apostolic Church. I confess one baptism for the remission of sins, and I look for the resurrection of the dead, and the life of the world to come. Amen.

Sanctus-Benedictus

Sanctus, Sanctus, Sanctus Dominus Deus Sabaoth. Pleni sunt caeli et terra gloria tua. Hosanna in excelsis. Benedictus qui venit in nomine Domini. Hosanna in excelsis.

Holy, holy, holy, Lord God of Hosts. Heaven and earth are full of Thy glory. Hosanna in the highest. Blessed is he that cometh in the name of the Lord. Hosanna in the highest.

Agnus Dei

Agnus Dei, qui tollis peccata mundi: miserere nobis.
Agnus Dei, qui tollis peccata mundi: miserere nobis.
Agnus Dei, qui tollis peccata mundi: dona nobis pacem.

Lamb of God, that takest away the sins of the world, have mercy on us.
Lamb of God, that takest away the sins of the world, have mercy on us.
Lamb of God, that takest away the sins of the world, grant us peace.

REQUIEM
(Missa pro defunctis)

Introit

*Requiem aeternam dona eis
Domine: et lux perpetua luceat
eis. Te decet hymnus Deus in
Sion, et tibi reddetur votum in
Jerusalem: exaudi orationem meam,
ad te omnis caro veniet. Requiem.*

Rest eternal grant unto them,
O Lord: and let light eternal
shine upon them. Thou, O God,
art praised in Zion; and unto
Thee shall the vow be performed
in Jerusalem; Thou who hearest
the prayer, unto Thee shall all
flesh come. Rest.

Kyrie

*Kyrie eleison.
Christe eleison.
Kyrie eleison.*

Lord, have mercy.
Christ, have mercy.
Lord, have mercy.

Sequence

*Dies irae, dies illa,
Solvet saeclum in favilla:
Teste David cum Sibylla.*

Day of wrath and doom
impending,
Heaven and earth in ashes
ending!
David's word with Sibyl's
blending!

Quantus tremor est futurus,

Quando judex est venturus,

Cuncta stricte discussurus!

Oh, what fear man's bosom
rendeth,
When from heaven the Judge
descendeth,
On whose sentence all
dependeth!

Tuba mirum spargens sonum

Wondrous sound the trumpet
flingeth,

447

Per sepulcra regionum,	Through earth's sepulchres it ringeth,
Coget omnes ante thronum.	All before the throne it bringeth.
Mors stupebit et natura,	Death is struck and nature quaking,
Cum resurget creatura,	All creation is awaking,
Judicanti responsura.	To its Judge an answer making.
Liber scriptus proferetur,	Lo! the book exactly worded,
In quo totum continetur,	Wherein all hath been recorded;
Unde mundus judicetur.	Thence shall judgment be awarded.
Judex ergo cum sedebit,	When the Judge His seat attaineth,
Quidquid latet apparebit:	And each hidden deed arraigneth,
Nil inultum remanebit.	Nothing unavenged remaineth.
Quid sum miser tunc dicturus?	What shall I, frail man, be pleading?
Quem patronum rogaturus?	Who for me be interceding,
Cum vix justus sit securus.	When the just are mercy needing?
Rex tremendae majestatis,	King of majesty tremendous,
Qui salvandos salvas gratis,	Who dost free salvation send us,
Salva me, fons pietatis.	Fount of pity, then befriend us.
Recordare Jesu pie,	Think, kind Jesus, my salvation
Quod sum causa tuae viae:	Caused Thy wondrous Incarnation;
Ne me perdas illa die.	Leave me not to reprobation.
Quaerens me, sedisti lassus:	Faint and weary Thou hast sought me,
Redemisti crucem passus:	On the Cross of suffering bought me,
Tantus labor non sit cassus.	Shall such grace be vainly brought me?

Juste judex ultionis,	Righteous Judge, for sin's pollution,
Donum fac remissionis,	Grant Thy gift of absolution,
Ante diem rationis.	Ere that day of retribution.
Ingemisco, tamquam reus:	Guilty now I pour my moaning,
Culpa rubet vultus meus:	All my shame with anguish owning;
Supplicanti parce Deus.	Spare, O God, Thy suppliant groaning.
Qui Mariam absolvisti,	Through the sinful woman shriven,
Et latronem exaudisti,	Through the dying thief forgiven,
Mihi quoque spem dedisti.	Thou to me a hope hast given.
Preces meae non sunt dignae:	Worthless are my prayers and sighing,
Sed tu bonus fac benigne,	Yet, good Lord, in grace complying,
Ne perenni cremer igne.	Rescue me from fires undying.
Inter oves locum praesta,	With Thy sheep a place provide me,
Et ab haedis me sequestra,	From the goats afar divide me.
Statuens in parte dextra.	To Thy right hand do Thou guide me.
Confutatis maledictis,	When the wicked are confounded,
Flammis acribus addictis,	Doomed to flames of woe unbounded,
Voca me cum benedictis.	Call me, with Thy saints surrounded.
Oro supplex et acclinis,	Low I kneel, with heart-submission,
Cor contritum quasi cinis:	See, like ashes my contrition.
Gere curam mei finis.	Help me in my last condition!
Lacrimosa dies illa,	Ah! that day of tears and mourning!

Qua resurget ex favilla   From the dust of earth returning,
Judicandus homo reus: Man for judgment must prepare
                                         him.

Huic ergo parce Deus.   Spare, O God, in mercy spare
                                         him!
Pie Jesu Domine,   Lord, all pitying, Jesus blest,
dona eis requiem.   Grant them all eternal rest.
Amen.   Amen.

Offertory
Domine Jesu Christe, Rex gloriae,   O Lord Jesus Christ, King of
libera animas omnium fidelium de-   Glory, deliver the souls of all the
functorum de poenis inferni, et   faithful departed from the pains
de profundo lacu: libera eas de ore   of hell and from the depths of
leonis, ne absorbeat eas tartarus,   the pit. Deliver them from the
ne cadant in obscurum: sed signifer   lion's mouth, that hell devour
sanctus Michael repraesentet eas   them not, that they fall not into
in lucem sanctam: Quam olim   darkness. But let the standard-
Abrahae promisisti, et semini ejus.   bearer Saint Michael bring them
                                         into the holy light which, of old,
                                         Thou didst promise unto
                                         Abraham and his seed.

Hostias et preces tibi Domine   We offer unto Thee, O Lord,
laudis offerimus: tu suscipe pro   sacrifices of prayer and praise: do
animabus illis, quarum hodie   Thou receive them for the souls
memoriam facimus: fac eas,   of those whose memory we this
Domine, de morte transire ad   day recall: make them, O Lord,
vitam. Quam olim Abrahae prom-   to pass from death unto life,
isisti et semini ejus.   which, of old, Thou didst
                                         promise to Abraham and his
                                         seed.

Sanctus-Benedictus
Sanctus, Sanctus, Sanctus Dominus   Holy, holy, holy, Lord God of
Deus Sabaoth. Pleni sunt caeli et   Hosts. Heaven and earth are full
terra gloria tua. Hosanna in excel-   of Thy glory. Hosanna in the
sis. Benedictus qui venit in nomine   highest. Blessed is he that
Domini. Hosanna in excelsis.   cometh in the name of the Lord.
                                         Hosanna in the highest.

Agnus Dei

Agnus Dei, qui tollis peccata mundi: dona eis requiem.

Lamb of God, that takest away the sins of the world, grant them rest.

Agnus Dei, qui tollis peccata mundi: dona eis requiem.

Lamb of God, that takest away the sins of the world, grant them rest.

Agnus Dei, qui tollis peccata mundi: dona eis requiem sempiternam.

Lamb of God, that takest away the sins of the world, grant them eternal rest.

Communion

Lux aeterna luceat eis, Domine: Cum sanctis tuis in aeternum, quia pius es. Requiem aeternam dona eis Domine, et lux perpetua luceat eis.

May eternal light shine upon them, O Lord, with Thy saints forever, because Thou art merciful. Eternal rest give to them, O Lord, and let perpetual light shine upon them.

The Responsory, *Libera me,* is not part of the Requiem Mass, but follows it on solemn occasions. Some composers have included it in their choral settings.

Responsory

Libera me, Domine, de morte aeterna, in die illa tremenda: Quando caeli movendi sunt et terra: Dum veneris judicare saeculum per ignem. Tremens factus sum ego, et timeo, dum discussio venerit, atque ventura ira. Quando caeli movendi sunt et terra. Dies illa, dies irae, calamitatis et miseriae, dies magna et amara valde. Dum veneris judicare saeculum per ignem. Requiem aeternam dona eis Domine: et lux perpetua luceat eis.

Deliver me, O Lord, from eternal death on that dreadful day when the heavens and the earth shall quake, when Thou shalt come to judge the world by fire. I am in fear and trembling for the coming wrath and judgment. O that day, that day of wrath, calamity, and misery, that great and bitter day, when Thou shalt come to judge the world by fire. Eternal rest give to them, O Lord, and let perpetual light shine upon them.

MAGNIFICAT

1. *Magnificat anima mea Dominum.*

My soul doth magnify the Lord,

2. *Et exsultavit spiritus meus in Deo salutari meo.*

And my spirit hath rejoiced in God my Saviour.

3. *Quia respexit humilitatem ancillae suae: ecce enim ex hoc beatam me dicent omnes generationes.*

For he hath regarded the low estate of his handmaiden: for, behold, from henceforth all generations shall call me blessed.

4. *Quia fecit mihi magna qui potens est: et sanctum nomen ejus.*

For he that is mighty hath done to me great things; and holy is his name.

5. *Et misericordia ejus a progenie in progenies timentibus eum.*

And his mercy is on them that fear him from generation to generation.

6. *Fecit potentiam in brachio suo: dispersit superbos mente cordis sui.*

He hath showed strength with his arm; he hath scattered the proud in the imagination of their hearts.

7. *Deposuit potentes de sede, et exaltavit humiles.*

He hath put down the mighty from their seats, and exalted them of low degree.

8. *Esurientes implevit bonis: et divites dimisit inanes.*

He hath filled the hungry with good things; and the rich he hath sent empty away.

9. *Suscepit Israel puerum suum, recordatus misericordiae suae.*

He hath holpen his servant Israel, in remembrance of his mercy;

452

10. *Sicut locutus est ad patres nostros, Abraham et semini ejus in saecula.*

11. *Gloria Patri, et Filio, et Spiritui Sancto.*

12. *Sicut erat in principio, et nunc, et semper, et in saecula saeculorum. Amen.*

As he spake to our fathers, to Abraham, and to his seed for ever.

Glory be to the Father and to the Son, and to the Holy Ghost;

As it was in the beginning, is now and ever shall be, world without end. Amen.

BULL OF POPE JOHN XXII

ISSUED IN THE YEAR 1324-1325

AT AVIGNON *

Nonnulli novellae scholae discipuli, dum temporibus mensurandis invigilant, novis notis intendunt, fingere suas quam antiquas cantare malunt; in semibreves et minimas ecclesiastica cantantur, notulis percutiuntur. Nam melodias hoquetis intersecant, discantibus lubricant, triplis et motetis vulgaribus nonnumquam inculcant; adeo ut interdum antiphonarii et gradualis fundamenta despiciant, ignorent super quo aedificant; tonos nesciant quos non discernunt, imo confundunt cum ex earum multitudine notarum, ascensiones pudicae descensionesque temperatae plani cantus, quibus toni ipsi cernuntur adinuicem, obfuscentur. Currunt enim et non quiescunt,

Certain disciples of the new school, much occupying themselves with the measured dividing of the *tempora*, display their prolation in notes which are new to us, preferring to devise methods of their own rather than to continue singing in the old way; the music therefore of the divine offices is now performed with semibreves and minims, and with these notes of small value every composition is pestered. Moreover, they truncate the melodies with hoquets, they deprave them with discants, sometimes even they stuff them with upper parts (*triplis et motetis*) made out of secular songs. So that often they must be

*Latin and English translation from Oxford History of Music, Vol. I (London: Oxford University Press, 1929), pp. 294–96.Reprinted by permission.

aures inebriant et non medentur,
gestis simulant quod depromunt;
quibus devotio quaerenda con-
temnitur, vitanda lascivia
propagatur.

losing sight of the fundamental
sources of our melodies in the
the Antiphoner and Gradual, and
may thus forget what that is
upon which their superstructure
is raised. They may become
entirely ignorant concerning the
ecclesiastical Tones, which they
already no longer distinguish,
and the limits of which they
even confound, since, in the
multitude of their notes, the
modest risings and temperate
descents of the plainsong, by
which the scales themselves are
to be known one from another,
must be entirely obscured. Their
voices are incessantly running to
and fro, intoxicating the ear, not
soothing it, while the men themselves endeavor to convey by
their gestures the sentiment of
the music which they utter. As a
consequence of all this, devotion,
the true end of worship, is little
thought of, and wantonness,
which ought to be eschewed,
increases.

Hoc ideo dudum, nos et fratres
nostri correctionis indigere per-
cepimus; hoc relegare, imo potius
abiicere, et ab eadem ecclesia Dei
profligare efficacius properamus.
Quocirca de ipsorum fratrum con-
silio districte praecepimus, ut
nullus deinceps talia, vel his
similia, in dictis officiis, praesertim
horis canonicis, vel cum missarum
solemnia celebrantur, attentare

This state of things, hitherto
the common one, we and our
brethren have regarded as standing in need of correction; and we
now hasten therefore to banish
those methods, nay rather to cast
them entirely away, and to put
them to flight more effectually
than heretofore, far from the
house of God. Wherefore, having
taken counsel with our brethren,

praesumat. Si quis vero contra-
fecerit, per Ordinarios locorum ubi
ista commissa fuerint, vel depu-
tandos ab eis, in non exemptis, in
exemptis vero per Praepositos vel
Praelatos suos, ad quos alios
correctio et punitio culparum, et
excessuum huiusmodi vel similium,
pertinere dignoscitur, vel deput-
andos ab eisdem, per suspensionem
ab officio per octo dies auctoritate
huius canonis puniatur.

we straitly command that no one
henceforward shall think himself
at liberty to attempt those
methods, or methods like them,
in the aforesaid Offices, and
especially in the canonical Hours,
or in the solemn celebrations of
the Mass.

And if any be disobedient, let
him, on the authority of this
Canon, be punished by a suspension from office of eight days;
either by the Ordinary of the
diocese in which the forbidden
things are done or by his
deputies in places not exempt
from episcopal authority, or, in
places which are exempt, by such
of their offices as are usually
considered responsible for the
correction of irregularities and
excesses, and such like matters.

Per hoc autem non intendimus
prohibere, quin interdum, diebus
festis praecipue, sive solemnibus in
missis, et praefatis divinis officiis,
aliquae consonantiae quae melo-
diam sapiunt, puta octavae,
quintae, quartae, et huiusmodi
supra cantum ecclesiasticum
simplicem proferantur. Sic tamen ut
ipsius cantus integritas illibata
permaneat, et nihil ex hoc de bene
morata musica immutetur. Maxime
cum huiusmodi consonantiae
auditum demulceant, devotionem
provocent, et psallentium Deo

Yet, for all this, it is not our
intention to forbid, occasionally —
and especially upon feast days or
in the solemn celebrations of the
Mass and in the aforesaid divine
offices — the use of some consonances, for example the eighth,
fifth, and fourth, which heighten
the beauty of the melody; such
intervals therefore may be sung
above the plain *cantus ecclesi-*
asticus, yet so that the integrity of
the *cantus* itself may remain
intact, and that nothing in the
authoritative music be changed.

animos torpere non sinant.

Used in such sort the consonances would much more than by any other method both soothe the hearer and arouse his devotion, and also would not destroy religious feeling in the minds of the singers.

LETTER OF ARCHBISHOP

CRANMER

TO KING HENRY VIII

IT MAY PLEASE your majesty to be advertised, that according to your highness' commandment, sent unto me by your grace's secretary, Mr Pagett, I have translated into the English tongue, so well as I could in so short time, certain processions, to be used upon festival days, if after due correction and amendment of the same your highness shall think it so convenient. In which translation, forasmuch as many of the processions, in the Latin, were but barren, as meseemed, and little fruitful, I was constrained to use more than the liberty of a translator: for in some processions I have altered divers words; in some I have added part; in some taken part away; some I have left out whole, either for by cause the matter appeared to me to be little to purpose, or by cause the days be not with us festival-days; and some processions I have added whole, because I thought I had better matter for the purpose, than was the procession in Latin: the judgment whereof I refer wholly unto your majesty; and after your highness hath corrected it, if your grace command some devout and solemn note to be made thereunto, (as is to the procession which your majesty hath already set forth in English,) I trust it will much excitate and stir the hearts of all men unto devotion and godliness: but in mine opinion, the song that shall be made thereunto would not be full of notes, but, as near as may be, for every syllable a note; so that it may be sung distinctly and devoutly, as be in the Matins and Evensong, *Venite*, the Hymns, *Te Deum*, *Benedictus*, *Magnificat*, *Nunc dimittis*, and all the Psalms and Versicles; and in the mass *Gloria in Excelsis*, *Gloria Patri*, the Creed, the Preface, the *Pater noster*, and some of the *Sanctus* and *Agnus*. As concerning the *Salve festa dies*, the Latin

458

note, as I think, is sober and distinct enough; wherefore I have travailed to make the verses in English, and have put the Latin note unto the same. Nevertheless they that be cunning in singing can make a much more solemn note thereto. I made them only for a proof, to see how English would do in song. But by cause mine English verses lack the grace and facility that I would wish they had, your majesty may cause some other to make them again, that can do the same in more pleasant English and phrase. As for the sentence, I suppose will serve well enough. Thus Almighty God preserve your majesty in long and prosperous health and felicity! From Bekisbourne, the 7th of October. [1544]

> Your grace's most bounden
> chaplain
> and beadsman,
> T. CANTUARIEN.

To the king's most excellent majesty.

Acknowledgments

I am grateful to the following publishers for permission to print extracts from copyrighted works. Their property is identified at the points in the book where it is quoted: Akademische Druck- u. Verlagsanstalt, Graz / G. Alsbach & Co., Amsterdam / Bärenreiter-Verlag, Kassel-Wilhelmshöhe / Boosey and Hawkes Inc., New York / Breitkopf & Härtel, Wiesbaden / The Carnegie United Kingdom Trust, Dumferline, Fife / Concordia Publishing House, St. Louis / J. Curwen & Sons Ltd., London / Editions Salabert, Paris / Gamut Company, Lubbock / Haydn Society Inc., Wien / G. Henle Verlag, München / Istituto Italiano per la Storia della Musica, Roma / The Mediaeval Academy of America, Cambridge / Verlag Merseburger, Berlin / Möseler Verlag, Wolfenbüttel / C. F. Peters Corporation, New York / E. C. Schirmer Music Company, Boston / Stainer & Bell Ltd., London/Oxford University Press, London.

Most of the material printed on pp. 21–23 first appeared in a magazine article I wrote some time ago, copyright 1960, Christian *Century*. Also, I thank Dr. Armen Carapetyan, Director of the American Institute of Musicology, Rome, for permission to quote freely from the volumes of *Corpus Mensurabilis Musicae*.

461

BIBLIOGRAPHY

SELECTED PERIODICALS

Many music periodicals take notice of church music in articles, book reviews, and reviews of new music. Comprehensive listings may be found in *Grove's,* VI, 637–72, and X, 344–47, as well as in *The Music Index Annual Cumulation* for any year. The titles listed here are especially useful to the student of religious choral music.

American Choral Review. New York, 1959–.

  Articles, reviews, lists of new music and books.

American Guild of Organists Quarterly. New York, 1956–.

  The articles and reviews are of interest to choirmasters as well as to organists.

The American Organist. New York, 1918–.

  The reviews in this periodical are its most valuable feature.

Caecilia. Omaha, 1874–.

  Informative articles on Catholic church music. Reviews of new music, references to composers and performance practice.

The Catholic Choirmaster. Glen Rock, N. J., 1914–.

  Articles and editorials. A practical magazine for Catholic church musicians.

Choral and Organ Guide. Mount Vernon, N. Y., 1948–.

  Music lists, service suggestions, articles on performance. Directed to organists and choirmasters.

The Diapason. Chicago, 1909–.

  The official journal of the American Guild of Organists. Reviews of music, notices of performance, occasional articles on performance practice and historical research.

English Church Music. Croydon, Surrey, England, 1920–.

  Articles of interest to students of religious music.

Journal of the American Musicological Society. Richmond, 1948–.

  Scholarly studies and penetrating reviews. Of little interest to the director seeking material for service use.

The Journal of Church Music. Philadelphia, 1960–.

Articles on church music, choral and instrumental; the place of music in worship; the history of church music.

Der Kirchenchor. Kassel-Wilhelmshöhe, 1940 – .
Confines its attention to the church choir and church music.

Music and Letters. London, 1920 – .
A general music periodical, but with some articles and reviews in the field of church music.

Music Library Association NOTES (Second Series). Washington, 1943 – .
Valuable lists and reviews of new books and music. The most comprehensive bibliography of new materials generally available.

The Music Review. Cambridge (England), 1939 – .
Articles of general musical interest, some pertaining to religious music. Book and music reviews.

The Musical Quarterly. New York, 1915 – .
Articles for the scholar and the well-informed musician. Excellent reviews of books, music, and records.

The Musical Times. London, 1844 – .
Generally of greatest interest to organists, but contains articles and reviews of general value to church musicians as well.

Response. St. Paul, 1959 – .
Articles and reviews directed to a Lutheran audience.

RECORDINGS

Because of the rapid changes in record lists, a discography may easily be out of date before it appears in print. Therefore, rather than supplying a list of specific records, this section mentions only a few sources of information and names some important sets of religious choral music. For up-to-date information on new issues, both monaural and stereo, reviews in music magazines as well as in such other sources as *The Saturday Review* and Sunday issues of *The New York Times* are recommended. A complete list of current long playing records is available in the monthly *Schwann Long Playing Record Catalog.* For evaluations of various pressings of a single title, comparative ratings appear in each issue of *Music Library Association NOTES.* The volumes listed below are helpful in checking on recordings of earlier years.

Clough, Francis F. and Cuming, G. J. *The World's Encyclopaedia of Recorded Music.* London: Sidgwick & Jackson, 1952. (*First Supplement* is bound with above title. *Second Supplement*, 1953; *Third Supplement*, 1957).

Miller, Philip L. *The Guide to Long-Playing Records: Vocal Music.* New York: Alfred A. Knopf, 1955.

Record Ratings. Kurtz Myers, compiler; Richard S. Hill, editor. New York: Crown Publishers, 1956.

The sets and labels mentioned below are only a few of those that contain works closely related to this study. The large domestic companies are not mentioned, as it is assumed that their listings are adequately reported in the Schwann catalog.

Storia della Musica Italiana. A four-volume RCA Victor set (ML 40000 – 40003) of which three volumes have appeared. This is a sumptuous edition, complete with illustrated booklets. The performances, however, are of uneven quality.

L'Anthologie Sonore. Examples from

Gregorian Chant through the Classical Period. Originally a set of sixteen volumes, each containing ten 78 r.p.m. records dating from about 1935. Reissued on LP by The Haydn Society.

2000 Years of Music. A historical survey edited by Curt Sachs. Now available on Folkways LP.

HMS }
MM } See List of Abbreviations,
TEM } pp. xi–xii.

Recordings of New York Pro Musica, conducted by Noah Greenberg, Decca. Excellent performances with scrupulous attention given to authentic performance practice.

Bärenreiter-Musicaphon. A relatively new series of fine quality. Not generally available from retail outlets in U.S. Send to Bärenreiter agent in New York or directly to Kassel for catalogue.

Deutsche Grammophon Gesellschaft. A series featuring large works.

Archive Production (History of Music Division of the Deutsche Grammophon Gesellschaft). The most complete historical set available. With few exceptions, the performances are of finest caliber. The record liner notes and the enclosed data cards are carefully written. The project is only partially completed. New titles appear regularly. Catalogues are available from MGM Records, Classical Division.

NOTE: Most record companies have catalogues available and will send them to educational institutions on request. Some companies also honor requests from individuals without institutional affiliation.

MUSIC EDITIONS, BOOKS, AND ARTICLES

Abraham, Gerald, editor. *Handel: A Symposium.* London: Oxford University Press, 1954.

———, editor. *The History of Music in Sound.* 10 vols. New York: Oxford University Press, 1953–1959.

Apel, Willi. *Gregorian Chant.* Bloomington: Indiana University Press, 1958.

———. *Harvard Dictionary of Music.* Cambridge: Harvard University Press, 1947.

———. *The Notation of Polyphonic Music: 900–1600.* Cambridge: The Mediaeval Academy of America, 1949.

Arnold, Samuel. *Cathedral Music.* 4 vols. London: For the editor, 1790.

Ashton, Joseph N. *Music in Worship.* Boston: The Pilgrim Press, 1943.

Aubry, Pierre. *Cent Motets du XIIIe siècle.* Paris: A. Rouart, Lerolle & Co., 1908.

Bach, Carl Philipp Emanuel. *Die Israeliten in der Wüste.* Edited by Fritz Steffin. Berlin: Bote & Bock, 1955.

Bach, Johann Sebastian. *Johann Sebastian Bachs Werke.* Herausgegeben von der Bach-Gesellschaft. Leipzig: Breitkopf & Härtel, 1851–1926. Reprint, Ann Arbor: J. W. Edwards, 1947. 61 vols. in 47. (Vol. 47 not reprinted).

———. *Neue Bach Ausgabe.* Kassel und Basel: Bärenreiter-Verlag, 1954–.

Baillie, Hugh. "A London Church in Early Tudor Times," *Music and Letters,* XXVI/1 (January, 1955), 55–64.

Bainton, Roland H. *The Reformation of the Sixteenth Century.* Boston: The Beacon Press, 1952.

Baker's Biographical Dictionary of Musicians. Edited by Nicolas Slonimsky. 5th ed. New York: G. Schirmer, 1958.

His Life and Works. London: Edward Arnold, 1905; reprint, 1960.

Des Prez, Josquin. *Werken van Josquin des Prez.* Edited by A. Smijers. Amsterdam: G. Alsbach & Co., 1925–. 51 vols. to 1964.

Donington, Robert. *The Interpretation of Early Music.* London: Faber and Faber, 1963.

Dorez, Léon. *La Cour du Pape Paul III d'après les Registres de la Trésorerie Secrète.* 2 vols. Paris: Librairie Ernest Leroux, 1932.

Douglas, Winfred. *Church Music in History and Practice.* New York: Charles Scribner's Sons, 1937. Revised edition with additional material by Leonard Ellinwood, 1962.

Drinker, Sophie. *Music and Women.* New York: Coward-McCann, Inc., 1948.

Dufay, Guglielmi. *Opera Omnia. (Corpus Mensurabilis Musicae,* I*).* Tomus II. Edited by Heinricus Besseler. Rome: American Institute of Musicology in Rome. 1960.

———. *Opera Omnia. (Corpus Mensurabilis Musicae,* I*).* Edited by Guillaume de Van. Rome: American Institute of Musicology in Rome, 1948.

Dunn, James P. "The *Grands Motets* of Marc-Antoine Charpentier (1634–1704." 2 vols. Unpublished Ph.D. dissertation, State University of Iowa, 1962.

Dunstable, John. *Complete Works.* Vol. VIII of *Musica Britannica.* Edited by Manfred F. Bukofzer. London: Stainer and Bell, 1953.

Edwards, F. G. *The History of Mendelssohn's Oratorio 'Elijah.'* London: Novello, Ewer and Co., 1896.

Eitner, Robert. *Chronologische Verzeichniss der gedruckten Werke von H. L. von Hassler und O. de Lassus.* Berlin: Bahn, 1874.

Ellinwood, Leonard. *The History of American Church Music.* New York: Morehouse-Gorham Co., 1953.

Etherington, Charles L. *Protestant Worship Music.* New York: Holt, Rinehart and Winston, 1962.

Evans, Peter. "Britten's 'War Requiem,'" *Tempo,* (Spring & Summer, 1962), 20–39.

Eversole, Finley, editor. *Christian Faith and the Contemporary Arts.* New York: Abingdon Press, 1962.

Fellerer, Karl Gustav. "Church Music and the Council of Trent," *The Musical Quarterly,* XXXIX/4 (October, 1943), 576–94.

———. *The History of Catholic Church Music.* Translated by Francis A. Brunner. Baltimore: Helicon Press, 1961.

Fellowes, Edmund H., editor. *The Collected Works of William Byrd.* 20 vols. London; Stainer & Bell, 1937–1950.

———. *English Cathedral Music.* London: Methuen & Co., 1948.

Ferris, John R. "Cantate Domino Canticum Novum," *American Guild of Organists Quarterly,* VII/2 (April, 1962), 51 *et seq.*

Foster, Myles Birket. *Anthems and Anthem Composers.* London: Novello and Company, 1901.

Fox, Charles Warren. "The Polyphonic Requiem before about 1615," *Bulletin of the American Musicological Society,* No. 7 (October, 1943), 6–7.

Gabrieli, Giovanni. *Opera Omnia. (Corpus Mensurabilis Musicae,* 12*).* Rome: American Institute of Musicology, 1959.

Geiringer, Karl. *The Bach Family.* London: George Allen & Unwin, 1954.

———. *Music of the Bach Family.* Cambridge: Harvard University Press, 1955.

———. "The Small Sacred Works by Haydn in the Esterhazy Archives at Eisenstadt," *The Musical Quarterly,* XLV/4 (October, 1959), 460–72.

Gleason, Harold, editor. *Examples of Music before 1400.* New York: Appleton-Century-Crofts, Inc., 1942.

Gombert, Nicolai. *Opera Omnia. (Corpus Mensurabilis Musicae, XI).* Edited by Joseph Schmidt-Görg. Rome: American Institute of Musicology, 1959.

Gombosi, Otto. "Machaut's *Messe Notre-Dame,*" *The Musical Quarterly,* XXXVI/2 (April, 1959), 204 – 24.

Graduale Romanum. Tournai: Desclée & Co., 1924.

Graun, Karl Heinrich. *Lord, I Love the Habitation of Thy House.* Lubbock, Texas: Gamut Company, 1963.

——. *Oratorium in Festum Nativitatis Chr. Mache dich auf, werde Licht, in Musik gebracht vom Herrn Cappelmeister Graun.* MS in Library of Congress.

——. *To Us A Child is Given.* Edited by Elwyn A. Wienandt. New York: Carl Fischer, 1965.

Grew, Eva Mary. "Martin Luther and Music," *Music and Letters,* XIX/1 (January, 1938), 67 – 78.

Grout, Donald Jay. *A History of Western Music.* New York: W. W. Norton and Co., 1960.

Grove's Dictionary of Music and Musicians. Edited by Eric Blom. 5th edition. 9 vols. New York: St. Martin's Press, 1955. Vol. 10, 1961.

Hammerschmidt, Andreas. *How Then Shall We Find Bread?* Edited by Harold Mueller. St. Louis: Concordia Publishing House, 1960.

Handel, G. F. *Georg Friedrich Händels Werke.* Edited by F. Chrysander. 96 vols. and 6 supplements. Leipzig: Breitkopf & Härtel, 1858 – 1894, 1902.

Harrison, Frank Llewellyn. "An English 'Caput,'" *Music and Letters,* XXXIII/3 (July, 1952), 203 – 14.

——. *Music in Medieval Britain.* London: Routledge and Kegan Paul, 1958.

Hawkins, Sir John. *A General History of the Science and Practice of Music.* 2 vols. New York: Dover Publications, Inc., 1963.

Haydn, Joseph. *Joseph Haydn Kritische Gesamtausgabe.* Edited by Jens Peter Larsen. Boston: Haydn Society, 1951.

——. *Joseph Haydns Werke.* Edited by H. C. Robbins-Landon, *et al.* München: G. Henle Verlag, 1958 – .

Henry, H. T. "Music Reform in the Catholic Church," *The Musical Quarterly,* I/1 (January, 1915), 102 – 17.

Hewitt, Helen, compiler. *Doctoral Dissertations in Musicology.* 3rd edition. Philadelphia: American Musicological Society, 1961.

Heyer, Anna Harriet. *Historical Sets, Collected Editions, and Monuments of Music.* Chicago: American Library Association, 1957.

Hibberd, Lloyd. "*Musica Ficta* and Instrumental Music *c.* 1250 – *c.* 1350," *The Musical Quarterly,* XXVIII/2 (April, 1942), 216 – 26.

Hiller, J. A., editor. *Vierstimmige Motetten und Arien in Partitur . . .* Leipzig: Dyckischen Buchhandlung, 1776, 1779, 1780.

Hispaniae schola musica sacra. Edited by Felipe Pedrell. 8 vols. Barcelona: Juan Batista Pujol, 1894 – 1898.

Hitchcock, H. Wiley. "The Latin Oratorios of Marc-Antoine Charpentier," *The Musical Quarterly,* XLI/1 (January, 1955), 41 – 65.

Hoelty-Nickel, Theodore, editor. *The Musical Heritage of the Lutheran Church.* St. Louis: Concordia Publishing House, Vol. V, 1959; Vol. VI, 1963. The first four volumes are out of print.

Hopkinson, Cecil. *A Dictionary of*

Parisian Music Publishers, 1700– 1950. London: The author, 1954.

Hume, Paul. *Catholic Church Music.* New York: Dodd, Mead & Co., 1956.

Husmann, Heinrich. "The Origin and Destination of the *Magnus liber organi,*" *The Musical Quarterly,* xlix/3 (July, 1963), 311–30.

Jackman, James L. "Liturgical Aspects of Byrd's *Gradualia,*" *The Musical Quarterly,* xlix/1 (January, 1963), 17–37.

Jacobs, Arthur, editor. *Choral Music,* Baltimore: Penguin Books, 1963.

Julian, John. *A Dictionary of Hymnology.* 2nd revised edition. 2 vols. London: John Murray, 1907. Dover Edition reprint, 1957.

Kamienski, Lucian. *Die Oratorien von Johann Adolf Hasse.* Leipzig: Breitkopf & Härtel, 1912.

Keuchenthal, Johannes. *Kirchen-Gesenge Latinisch und Deudsch, sampt allen Evangelien, Episteln, und Collecten, auff die Sontage und Feste, nach Ordnung der zeit, durchs gantze Jhar, . . . Witteberg,* M.D.LXXIII.

Lang, Paul Henry. *Music in Western Civilization.* New York: W. W. Norton and Co., 1941.

Larsen, Jens Peter. *Handel's Messiah: Origins, Composition, Sources.* New York: W. W. Norton & Co., 1957.

Leichentritt, Hugo. *Geschichte der Motette.* Leipzig: Breitkopf & Härtel, 1908.

———. "The Reform of Trent and its Effect on Music," *The Musical Quarterly,* xxx/3 (July, 1944), 319–28.

Leo, Leonardo. *Miserere.* Edited by H. Wiley Hitchcock. St. Louis: Concordia Publishing House, 1961.

Lerner, Edward R. "The Polyphonic Magnificat in 15th-Century Italy," *The Musical Quarterly,* l/1 (January, 1964), 44–58.

Levy, Kenneth Jay. "New Material on the Early Motet in England: A Report on Princeton Ms. Garrett 119," *Journal of the American Musicological Society,* iv/3 (Fall, 1951), 220–39.

The Liber Usualis. Tournai: Desclée & Co., 1950.

Lockwood, Lewis H. "Vincenzo Ruffo and Musical Reform after the Council of Trent," *The Musical Quarterly,* xliii/3 (July, 1957), 342–71.

Lully, Jean-Baptiste. *Oeuvres complètes de J.-B. Lully, publiées sous la Direction de Henry Prunières.* Paris: Editions de la Revue Musicale, 1930–1939.

The Lutheran Hymnal. St. Louis: Concordia Publishing House, 1941.

Machabey, Armand. *La Messe de Tournai.* Paris: La Revue Musicale, 1958.

Machaut, Guillaume de. *La Messe de Nostre Dame.* (*Corpus Mensurabilis Musicae,* ii). Edited by G. de Van. Rome: American Institute of Musicology in Rome, 1949.

———. *Messe de Nostre Dame.* Herausgegeben von Friedrich Gennrich. (*Summa Musicae Medii Aevi,* i). Darmstadt, 1957.

———. *Messe Notre Dame.* Edited by Armand Machabey Liège: Editions Dynamo, 1948.

———. *Musikalische Werke.* Edited by Friedrich Ludwig. 3 vols. Leipzig: Breitkopf & Härtel, 1929. Reprint, 1954. Vol. iv edited by Heinrich Besseler, 1943. Reprint, 4 vols., 1954.

Mansfield, Orlando A. "What is Sacred Music?" *The Musical Quarterly,* xiii/3 (July, 1927), 451–75.

Marrocco, W. Thomas and Harold Gleason. *Music in America: An Anthology from the Landing of the Pilgrims to the Close of the Civil War.*

1620–1865. New York: W. W. Norton & Co., 1964.

Marshall, Robert L. "The Paraphrase Technique of Palestrina in His Masses Based on Hymns," *Journal of the American Musicological Society,* xvi/3 (Fall, 1963), 347–72.

Mees, Arthur. *Choirs and Choral Music.* New York: Charles Scribner's Sons, 1924.

Mendel, Hermann, editor. *Musikalisches Conversations-Lexicon.* Berlin: R. Oppenheim, 1873.

Miles, Russell H. *Johann Sebastian Bach: An Introduction to His Life and Works.* Englewood Cliffs: Prentice-Hall, 1962.

Mondonville, Jean-Joseph Cassanéa de. *Cantate Domino.* Edited by Edith Borroff. Pittsburgh: University of Pittsburgh Press, 1961.

———. *Jubilate.* Edited by Edith Borroff. Pittsburgh: University of Pittsburgh Press, 1961.

Monte, Philippe de. *Opera.* Edited by C. van den Borren and J. van Nuffel. Düsseldorf: Sumptibus L. Schwann, 1927–1935.

Monteverdi, Claudio. *Tutte le Opere di Claudio Monteverdi.* Edited by G. Francesco Malipiero. Asolo: G. Francesco Malipiero, 1926–1942; also Vienna: Universal-Edition.

———. *Vespers.* Edited by Denis Stevens. London: Novello, 1961.

Morales, Cristóbal de. *Opera omnia.* Edited by Higinio Anglés. Barcelona: Consejo Superior de Investigaciones Cientificas, 1954.

Moser, Hans Joachim. *Heinrich Schütz: His Life and Work:* Translated by Carl F. Pfatteicher. St. Louis: Concordia Publishing House, 1959.

Music of Gabrieli and His Time. Ossining, N. Y.: William Salloch, 1960. (Reprinted from Carl von Winterfeld, *Johannes Gabrieli und sein Zeitalter.* Berlin: 1834).

Myers, Rollo M. *Handel's Messiah: A Touchstone of Taste.* New York: Macmillan Co., 1948.

Nathan, Hans. "The Function of Text in French 13th-Century Motets," *The Musical Quarterly,* xxviii/4 (October, 1942), 445–62.

Naumann, Emil. *The History of Music.* Translated by F. Praeger. Edited by Rev. Sir F. A. Gore Ouseley. 2 vols. London: Cassell and Company, 1886.

Nemmers, Erwin Esser. *Twenty Centuries of Catholic Church Music.* Milwaukee: Bruce Publishing Co., 1949.

The New Oxford History of Music. [Various editors]. London: Oxford University Press, 1954–. 3 vols. to 1964.

Nicholson, Sydney H. *Church Music: A Practical Handbook.* London: The Faith Press, 1927.

Obrecht, Jacobus. *Opera Omnia.* Edited by A. Smijers. Amsterdam: G. Alsbach & Co., 1958.

Ockeghem, Johannes. *Collected Works.* Edited by Dragan Plamenac. New York: American Musicological Society, 1947.

O'Connell, J. B., trans. *Sacred Music and Liturgy.* Westminster, Maryland: The Newman Press, 1959.

O'Connell, Laurence J. *The Book of Ceremonies.* Revised edition. Milwaukee: Bruce Publishing Co., 1956.

Officium majoris hebdomadae et octavae Paschae. Dessain edition, 1932.

Ouseley, The Revd. Sir Frederick A. G., Bart. *Cathedral Music, Services & Anthems.* London: J. Alfred Novello, [1850?].

Page, John. *Harmonia Sacra.* 3 vols. London, 1800.

Palestrina, Giovanni Pierluigi da. *Giovanni Pierluigi da Palestrina: Werke.* Edited by F. Espagne, *et al.* Leipzig: Breitkopf & Härtel, 1862–1907.

————. *Le Opere Complete di Giovanni Pierluigi da Palestrina.* Edited by Raffaele Casimiri. Rome: Edizione Fratelli Scalera, 1939–.

Palmer, William. "Gibbons's Verse Anthems," *Music and Letters,* xxxv/2 (April, 1954), 107–13.

Parrish, Carl, editor. *A Treasury of Early Music.* New York: W. W. Norton and Co., 1958.

———— and John F. Ohl, editors. *Masterpieces of Music Before 1750.* New York: W. W. Norton and Co., 1951.

Pauly, Reinhard G. "Some Recently Discovered Michael Haydn Manuscripts," *Journal of the American Musicological Society,* x/2 (Spring, 1957), 97–103.

————. "The Reforms of Church Music under Joseph II," *The Musical Quarterly,* xliii/3 (July, 1957), 372–82.

Pergolesi, Giovanni Battista. *Opera Omnia.* Edited by Francesco Caffarelli. Rome: Gli Amici della musica da Camera, 1939–1942.

Phillips, C. Henry. *The Singing Church.* London: Faber and Faber, Ltd., 1945.

Pirro, André. *J. S. Bach.* Translated by Mervyn Savill. New York: The Orion Press, 1957.

Praetorius, Michael. *Gesamtausgabe der musikalischen Werke von Michael Praetorius.* Edited by Friedrich Blume. 21 vols. Wolfenbüttel: Georg Kallmeyer Verlag, 1928–1960.

Proske, Carl *et al.,* editors. *Musica Divina.* 10 vols. Ratisbon: F. Pustet, 1853–1875.

Purcell, Henry. *The Works of Henry Purcell.* 29 vols. London: Novello and Co., 1878–1928.

Rameau, Jean Philippe. *Oeuvres complètes publiées sous la Direction de C. Saint-Saëns.* 18 vols. Paris: A. Durand et Fils, 1895–1913.

Ramsbotham, Alexander, editor. *The Old Hall Manuscript.* Nashdom Abbey: The Plainsong & Mediaeval Music Society, 1935.

Reed, Luther D. *The Lutheran Liturgy.* Revised edition. Philadelphia: Muhlenberg Press, 1960.

Reese, Gustave. *Music in the Middle Ages.* New York: W. W. Norton and Co., 1940.

————. *Music in the Renaissance.* Revised edition. New York: W. W. Norton and Co., 1959.

————. "The Polyphonic Magnificat of the Renaissance as a Design in Tonal Centers," *Journal of the American Musicological Society,* xiii/1–3 (1960), 68–78.

Rhea, Claude H., Jr. "The Sacred Oratorios of Georg Philipp Telemann (1681–1767)." Unpublished Ph.D. dissertation, Florida State University, 1958.

Rice, William C. *A Concise History of Church Music.* Nashville: Abingdon Press, 1964.

Richards, James E. "Structural Principles in the Grand Motets of Michel-Richard de Lalande (1657–1726)," *Journal of the American Musicological Society,* xi/2–3 (Summer-Fall, 1958), 119–27.

Robertson, Alec. *Christian Music.* New York: Hawthorn Books, 1961.

Routley, Erik. *Church Music and Theology.* (*Studies in Ministry and Worship,* No. 11). London: SCM Press, Ltd., 1959.

————. *Twentieth Century Church Music.* Vol. i of *Studies in Church Music.* New York: Oxford University Press, 1964.

Saint-Saëns, Camille. *Vingt Motets*

par Camille Saint-Saëns. Paris: A. Durand & Fils, [between 1891 and 1909].

Scarlatti, Alessandro. *Messa d. S. Cecilia.* Berlin-Wiesbaden: Bote & Bock, 1957.

Schering, Arnold, editor. *Geschichte der Musik in Beispielen.* Leipzig: Breitkopf & Härtel, 1931. Reprint, New York: Broude Brothers, 1950.

Schmieder, Wolfgang. *Thematisch-systematisches Verzeichnis der musikalischer Werke Johann Sebastian Bach.* Leipzig: Breitkopf & Härtel, 1950.

Scholes, Percy A., editor. *Dr. Burney's Musical Tours in Europe.* 2 vols. London: Oxford University Press, 1959.

Schrade, Leo, editor. *Polyphonic Music of the Fourteenth Century: Commentary to Volume I.* Monaco: Editions de l'Oiseau-Lyre, 1956.

Schütz, Heinrich. *The Christmas Story.* Edited by Arthur Mendel. New York: G. Schirmer, 1949.

——. *Heinrich Schütz's Sämtliche Werke.* Edited by Philipp Spitta *et al.* 18 vols. Leipzig: Breitkopf & Härtel, 1885–1927.

——. *Neue Ausgabe sämtlicher Werke.* Kassel: Bärenreiter-Verlag, 1955–. 10 vols. to 1964.

——. *The Seven Words of Christ on the Cross.* Edited by Richard T. Gore. St. Louis: Concordia Publishing House, 1951.

Schweitzer, Albert. *J. S. Bach.* Translated by Ernest Newman. 2 vols. New York: Macmillan, 1950.

Seay, Albert. "The 15th-Century Cappella at Santa Maria del Fiore in Florence," *Journal of the American Musicological Society,* XI/1 (Spring, 1958), 45–55.

Shaw, Harold Watkins. "John Blow's Anthems," *Music and Letters,* XIX/4 (October, 1938), 429–42.

Smend, Friedrich. "Die Johannes-Passion von Bach," *Bach-Jahrbuch,* 1926, 105–28.

Smend, Julius. *Die Evangelischen deutschen Messen bis zu Luthers Deutscher Messe.* Göttingen: Vandenhoeck & Ruprecht, 1896.

Smith, Fidelis, O. F. M. "*Musicae Sacrae Disciplina:* Pius XII's Encyclical on Sacred Music," *The Musical Quarterly,* XLII/4 (October, 1957), 461–79.

Söhngen, Oskar. "Church Music and Sacred Music: Allies or Competitors," *The Diapason,* LII/12 (November, 1961), 34ff.

Sparks, Edgar H. *Cantus Firmus in Mass and Motet (1420–1520).* Berkeley & Los Angeles: University of California Press, 1963.

Spitta, Philipp. *Johann Sebastian Bach.* Translated by Clara Bell and J. A. Fuller-Maitland. 3 vols. London: Novello, 1884–1885. Reprint, New York: Dover Publications, 1951.

Squire, Russel N. *Church Music: Musical and Hymnological Developments in Western Christianity.* St. Louis: The Bethany Press, 1962.

Starr, William J. and George F. Devine. *Music Scores Omnibus.* 2 vols. Englewood Cliffs: Prentice-Hall, 1964.

Steere, Dwight. *Music for the Protestant Church Choir.* Richmond: John Knox Press, 1955.

——. *Music in Protestant Worship.* Richmond: John Knox Press, 1960.

Stevens, Denis. *Tudor Church Music.* London: Faber and Faber, 1961.

——. "Where are the Vespers of Yesteryear?" *The Musical Quarterly,* XLVII/3 (July, 1961), 315–30.

Stevens, R. J. S., editor. *Sacred Music for one, two, three & four Voices . . .* 3 vols. London: Charterhouse, *c.* 1798–1802.

Stevenson, Robert M. *Patterns of Protestant Church Music*. Durham: Duke University Press, 1953.

——. *Spanish Cathedral Music in the Golden Age*. Berkeley and Los Angeles: University of California Press, 1961.

Sullivan, Arthur S. *The Prodigal Son*. New York: G. Schirmer, [n.d.].

Sweney, John R. and Wm. J. Kirkpatrick, *Anthems and Voluntaries for the Church Choir*. Philadelphia: John J. Hood, 1881.

Terry, Charles Sanford. *Bach: The Cantatas and Oratorios*. (*Musical Pilgrim Series*). 2 vols. London: Oxford University Press, 1926.

Thompson, Oscar, editor. *The International Cyclopedia of Music and Musicians*. 7th Edition. Revised by Nicolas Slonimsky. New York: Dodd, Mead & Co., 1956.

Tischler, Hans. "English Traits in the Early 13th-Century Motet," *The Musical Quarterly*, xxx/4 (October, 1944., 458–76.

Tittel, Ernst. *Österreichische Kirchenmusik (Schriftenreihe des Allgemeinen Cäcilien-Verbandes für die Länder der deutschen Sprache, II)*. Wien: Herder & Co., 1961.

Tudway, Thomas. "A Collection of the Most Celebrated Services and Anthems . . ." British Museum MSS Harley 7337–7342.

Ulrich, Homer; Paul A. Pisk. *A History of Music and Musical Style*. New York: Harcourt, Brace & World, 1963.

Vail, James Harold. "The Choral Eucharist in the Anglican Church from the English Reformation to the Oxford Movement." Unpublished D.M.A. dissertation, University of Southern California, 1961.

Valentin, Erich. *Handbuch der Chormusik*. 2 vols. Regensburg: Gustav Bosse Verlag, [1953?].

Van den Borren, Charles, editor. *Missa Tornacensis*. (*Corpus Mensurabilis Musicae*, 13). Rome: American Institute of Musicology, 1957.

Von Rauchhaupt, Ursula. *Die vokale Kirchenmusik Hugo Distlers*. Gütersloh: Gütersloher Verlagshaus Gerd Mohn, 1963.

Wagner, Richard. *My Life*. New York: Dodd, Mead and Company, 1927.

Werner, Eric. *Mendelssohn: A New Image of the Composer and His Age*. New York: The Free Press of Glencoe, 1963.

Werner, T. W. "Die Magnificat-Kompositionen Adam Rener's," *Archiv für Musikwissenschaft*, ii (1919), 195–265.

Wesley, Samuel Sebastian. *A Few Words on Cathedral Music and the Musical System of the Church, with a Plan of Reform*. London: F. & J. Rivington, *et al.*, 1849.

Whittaker, W. Gillies. "Byrd's Great Service," *The Musical Quarterly*, xxvii/4 (October, 1941), 474–90.

——. *The Cantatas of Johann Sebastian Bach*. 2 vols. London: Oxford University Press, 1959.

——. "The Choral Writing in the Missa Solennis," *Music and Letters*, vii/3 (July, 1927), 295–305.

Wienandt, Elwyn A. "Baroque Arrangements." *The Instrumentalist*, xiv/5 (January, 1960), 36 *et seq.*

——. "*Das Licht scheinet . . .*, Two Settings by K. H. Graun," *The Music Review*, xxi/2 (May, 1960), 85–93.

——. "Jazz at the Altar?" *The Christian Century*, lxxvii/12 (March 23, 1960), 346–48.

Wolf, Johannes. *Music of Earlier Times*. New York: Broude Bros., 194? Reprinted from *Sing- und Spielmusik aus älterer Zeit*. Leipzig: Quelle & Meyer, 1926.

Young, Percy M. *The Choral Tradition.* New York: W. W. Norton & Company, 1962.

Zimmerman, Franklin B. "Purcell's 'Service Anthem' *O God, Thou Art My God* and the B-flat Major Service," *The Musical Quarterly,* L/2 (April, 1964), 207–14.

Zimmermann, Heinz Werner. *Psalmkonzert.* Berlin: Verlag Merseburger, 1958.

INDEX